Links in the Chain

SHAPERS OF THE JEWISH TRADITION

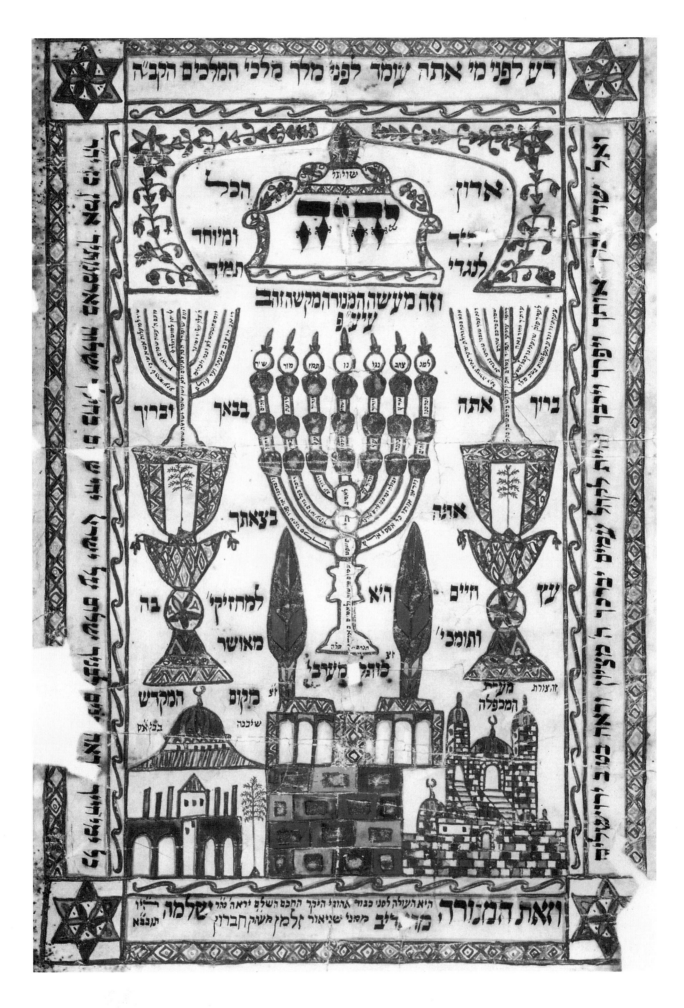

Links in the Chain

SHAPERS OF THE JEWISH TRADITION

NAOMI PASACHOFF

OXFORD UNIVERSITY PRESS

NEW YORK · OXFORD

To my husband, Jay

Oxford University Press
Oxford   New York
Athens   Auckland   Bangkok   Bogotá
Bombay   Buenos Aires   Calcutta   Cape Town
Dar es Salaam   Delhi   Florence   Hong Kong
Istanbul   Karachi   Kuala Lumpur   Madras   Madrid
Melbourne   Mexico City   Nairobi   Paris
Singapore   Taipei   Tokyo   Toronto   Warsaw
and associated companies in
Berlin   Ibadan

Published by Oxford University Press, Inc.,
198 Madison Avenue, New York, New York 10016

Oxford is a registered trademark of Oxford University Press, Inc.

Library of Congress Cataloging-in-Publication Data

Pasachoff, Naomi E.
Links in the chain : shapers of the Jewish tradition / Naomi Pasachoff.
p.   cm.   —   (Oxford profiles)
Includes bibliographical references and index.

ISBN 0-19-509939-7
1. Jews—Biography—Juvenile literature. 2. Jewish scholars—Biography—Juvenile literature.
3. Jewish philosophers—Biography—Juvenile literature. 4. Zionists—Biography—Juvenile literature.
[1. Jews—Biography.] I. Title. II. Series.
DS115.P37   1997
320.5'4'0956940922—dc20   96-28469
                                  CIP
                                  AC

1 3 5 7 9 8 6 4 2

Printed in the United States of America
on acid-free paper

On the cover: (clockwise from top left) Maimonides, Isaac
Mayer Wise, Golda Meir, and David Ben-Gurion
Frontispiece: A *Shivviti*, or synagogue plaque, from the late
19th century.

Design: Sandy Kaufman
Layout: Valerie Sauers
Picture research: Patricia Burns

Contents

Preface

In assessing what their Jewish identities mean to them, Jews today sometimes describe themselves as links in a chain of tradition that stretches back to biblical times. Jewish books and songs also make use of the image of a lengthy chain that connects Jews across time and space. Many Jews feel a deep responsibility to maintain the continuity of the chain of tradition. They try in different ways to pass it on to the next generation, in the hope that its members will form their own links with it.

Every Jew who maintains a connection with Judaism becomes a link in the chain of Jewish tradition. But in the following pages you will meet more than 40 men and women whose outstanding contributions to the development of Judaism single them out as shapers of the Jewish tradition.

This volume is divided into three sections: Laying the Foundation, Shapers of Modern Judaism, and Shapers of the Jewish State. Each section profiles, in chronological order, men and women who influenced the development of Judaism in a variety of ways, ranging from scholarship to philanthropy to spiritual or political leadership.

Many other individuals, of course, contributed to the shaping of Jewish tradition. Suggestions for Further Reading, which you will find beginning on page 234, will help you track down information about other important Jewish figures and about Jewish history, religion, and culture in general.

Reading about the people whose lives and thought contributed to the development of the chain of Jewish tradition sheds light on much more than a single religious tradition. Judaism, the oldest religion professing a belief in a single God, is at the base of Christianity and Islam. In addition, an appreciation of the historical circumstances in response to which Jewish tradition developed can deepen an understanding of contemporary issues. The more one knows about Jewish history, for example, the more insight one has not only into antagonisms in the Middle East but also into racial persecution and religious strife in various parts of the world. Further, the lives of the people profiled in this volume suggest how commitment to an ideal can be expressed in a multiplicity of ways.

Naomi Pasachoff
Williamstown, Massachusetts

This illustration from a 14th-century German Pentateuch (a collection of the first five books of Jewish scriptures) shows Moses receiving the Torah from God.

1 Laying the Foundation

 Jewish tradition began to take form thousands of years before the birth of the first shaper of Jewish tradition profiled in this book. The religion of Judaism began in the days described in the Hebrew Bible. According to the Bible, God sought out Abraham, the forefather of the Jewish people, and entered into a covenant, or pact, with him. God promised Abraham that his descendants would form a significant people. Abraham's descendants—called the children of Israel, the Hebrews, and later the Jews—entered into a new relationship with God when they followed their leader Moses out of slavery in Egypt and received the Torah at Mount Sinai. The word *Torah*, often translated as "guidance" or "instruction," has many different meanings. It refers not only to the Ten Commandments, which the Bible tells us Moses brought down from the mountain to the waiting Hebrews, and not only to the Hebrew scriptures that Jews read from a scroll during synagogue services. Torah also includes all the Jewish beliefs, practices, and writings handed down through the centuries.

Having accepted God's Torah, the children of Israel lived under various forms of leadership during biblical times. Moses and Joshua led the people in the conquest of the land of Israel, which God had promised to Abraham's descendants. This era, defined by the leadership of individuals, was followed by a period during which the people were ruled by judges; later the people demanded a king. Under the kings, the children of Israel fully emerged as a nation based in their own land. When King Solomon built a magnificent temple in Jerusalem, the people's worship of God became centralized. There, at what became known later as the First Temple, they marked different seasons and the significant events in their lives by sacrificing animals to God.

Though the nation was ruled by kings in this period, it was also guided by prophets, who acted as the conscience of the entire people. The prophets rebuked both the people and their kings when they failed to live according to God's will. They foresaw that the misdeeds of the Jewish people would lead to a national disaster. Catastrophe indeed befell the nation in the year 586 B.C.E. (Before the Common Era; that is, before the year 1 of the current calendar). In that year the Babylonians conquered the Jews, destroyed the First Temple, and drove them out of the land of Israel. While in exile in Babylonia, deprived of the temple as a central place of worship and sacrifice, the Jews began to worship in synagogues, community meeting places for prayer and study, where the observance of the Sabbath became their focus. The synagogue and Sabbath observance became defining elements of Jewish tradition.

Jewish history did not end with the destruction of the temple. Soon the Jews' Babylonian conquerors were themselves conquered by the Persians, who in 538 B.C.E. permitted the Jews to return to the land of Israel. There, around 515 B.C.E., they reestablished the temple, which became known as the Second Temple. Some Jews chose to remain in Babylonia, however. From that time on, Jewish tradition developed not only in the land of Israel but also in other countries where Jews lived in large numbers. The term *Diaspora* refers to the establishment of these scattered Jewish communities outside of Israel.

Although the Jews emerged as a people, received the Torah, and began to develop their relationship with God in the days of the Bible, it was not until the 1st century of the Common Era that modern Judaism began. Most scholars consider Hillel, whose profile is the first in this book, to be the forerunner of today's Judaism. Information about the life and teachings of Hillel and of the next four individuals profiled—Johanan ben Zakkai, Akiba, Beruriah, and Judah Hanasi—is contained in the Talmud.

If the Torah is the first text of Judaism, the Talmud, which means both "learning" and "teaching," became equally important. In fact, according to Jewish tradition, at Mount Sinai God gave the Jewish people not only the written but also the oral Torah—that is, the teachings of the rabbis, or wise men, that are recorded in the Talmud. Although the Talmud is considered the oral Torah, because its contents were originally handed down by the spoken word, those teachings were eventually written down to keep them from being forgotten. The Talmud is, in effect, a type of encyclopedia that touches on all aspects of Jewish life. It contains not only the laws of Judaism but also many interesting stories about the lives and times of the teachers whose words are recorded in its pages. Though the Bible can easily be bound in a single volume of a normal size, the Talmud is usually bound in 12 to 40 large volumes.

Three historical events played an important role in the development of early Jewish tradition, of which this section provides an overview. The first event was the Romans' destruction of the Second Temple in the year 70 C.E. Just as the destruction of the First Temple led to the development of synagogues and a focus on Sabbath observance, the destruction of the Second Temple led to a major shift in Jewish tradition.

Now that they had no temple in which to perform animal sacrifices, the rabbis of the Talmudic period had to shift the emphasis of observance away from that time-honored ritual. And instead of centralizing the practice of their religion in a single location, the rabbis taught that every aspect of life could be made holy. For example, they transformed Jewish dietary habits. Eating was no longer to be considered simply a means of sustaining life; it was now seen as an opportunity for holiness. Washing one's hands before eating, blessing the food before eating, and saying an extended blessing after meals symbolized the holy nature of eating. The rabbis taught that every Jewish home was a miniature temple, where Jews could indicate their awe of God and respect for the holiness of all life by carrying on everyday functions in an attitude of reverence. The rabbis also taught that Torah study, prayer, and pious deeds were worthy replacements for animal sacrifice and worship at the temple.

The second major historical event in the development of early Jewish tradition was the rise of the religion of Islam, which originated in Arabia during the 7th century and quickly spread through the Middle East, North Africa, and parts of Europe. Islam's spectacular success led to a centuries-long struggle with Christian monarchs determined to drive Islam out of Europe and the Christian holy places of the Middle East. Against this background, Jewish thought began to take shape. Jewish philosophers such as Saadia Gaon (882–942) and Maimonides (1135–1204) were deeply influenced by Muslim philosophy. They developed a tradition within Jewish thought based on the claim that Judaism is a religion of reason. A second strand of Jewish thought was developed by Judah Halevi (around 1075–1141), who developed a philosophy based not on reason but on the Jew's personal experience of a relationship with God.

The development of early Jewish tradition was also deeply affected by the expulsion of the Jews from Spain in 1492. For more than a thousand years before this expulsion, the Jews had lived in Spain, where they had not only produced a great culture of their own but had also contributed much to the economic, intellectual, and overall cultural life of the region. The attempt to make sense of this upheaval led to the development of another influential strain of Jewish thought. In the decades following the expulsion of the Jews from Spain, the mystical thinker Isaac Luria developed a view of the world that put Jewish suffering in a new, more positive light. The expulsion also led to the development of two different branches of Jewish tradition. Henceforward, the traditions of the Sephardic Jews, whose roots were in Spain and Portugal, differed in significant ways from those of the Ashkenazic Jews, whose origins were in central and eastern Europe.

The 1,600 years covered in this section witnessed the emergence of the Talmud and the shaping of Jewish tradition in response to major historical events. But Jewish tradition was also shaped by the writing of important commentaries on the Bible and the Talmud by the French grape grower and winemaker Solomon ben Isaac, known as Rashi (around 1040–1105). Rashi's work made it possible for any Jew to understand the basic texts of Judaism. The *Shulhan Arukh* (The Prepared Table), which remains the basic guide to traditional Jewish observance to this day, was also written during this period, by the scholar and mystic Joseph Caro (1488–1575). And the period witnessed three responses to Jewish life in exile that became models for later Jews: Nahmanides' defense of Judaism against attacks by the church, Samuel Hanagid's balancing of Jewish and secular roles as he held prominent positions in both the Jewish and the wider community, and Doña Gracia's efforts to rescue other Jews in need (in her case, Jews fleeing the Inquisition, an institution of the Catholic Church that sought and punished those who did not conform to official church doctrines).

Hillel

"DO NOT SEPARATE YOURSELF FROM THE COMMUNITY"

There are few hard facts about the life of Hillel, whom later generations have honored as the founder of classical Judaism. Legends abound concerning this wise man. Many sayings attributed to him have echoed across the generations, giving shape and substance to the many forms of Judaism that have developed since his day.

Although the biographical details about Hillel himself are scanty, historians know a great deal about the conditions of the Jewish community in the land of Israel, where Hillel lived and worked from around 50 B.C.E. to approximately 30 C.E. In 63 B.C.E., some years before Hillel's birth, two Jewish brothers, each claiming to be the rightful ruler of the land of Israel, took their dispute to the Romans, the possessors of a growing empire. The Romans quickly took advantage of the Jews' disunity by conquering their nation and imposing heavy taxes. A succession of natural disasters, including an earthquake and crop failures, worsened the situation of the Jews.

Rather than joining together to resolve this crisis, the Jews of Israel splintered into several groups. The wealthier members of the community, as well as the priests who controlled the rituals in the temple in Jerusalem, tended to belong to the Sadducee party. The middle and lower classes belonged to the Pharisee party. The Pharisees believed that the Torah that God had given Moses on Mount Sinai consisted not only of the five books of Moses but also of an oral tradition that explained the Torah's written statements more fully. For example, when the Torah describes how to observe Yom Kippur, the Day of Atonement, it simply says, "You shall afflict your souls." According to the Pharisees, the oral Torah gives a detailed explanation of exactly what laws the Jews should follow in order to observe Yom Kippur properly. The Sadducees, who believed only in the written Torah, rejected the Pharisees' claim.

Still other Jews wanted nothing to do with either the Sadducees or the Pharisees, believing that both groups were corrupt. These disaffected Jews, who included the Essene and Dead Sea sects, saw in the calamities that had befallen the community a sign that the end of the world was near. They left their cities and towns to gather together in small groups in the desert, where they shared their material goods, studied the Torah, and tried to live lives of strict purity.

Hillel was thus born into a world of discord. Attracted to the Pharisees by their social class and educational philosophy, he became their spiritual leader. A modest man who was not at all power-hungry, he was nonetheless so effective in promoting his party's beliefs that modern

A potential convert to Judaism challenged Hillel to teach him the entire Torah while he stood balanced on one foot. Hillel won the man over with his reply: "What you find hateful, do not do to your neighbor. This is the whole Torah. All the rest is commentary. Go and study it."

Hillel

BORN

Around 50 B.C.E.
Babylonia

DIED

Around 30 C.E.
Israel

EDUCATION

Early and secondary studies in Babylonia, advanced studies in Jerusalem at the academy of Shemaya and Avtalyon

ACCOMPLISHMENTS

Established the basic values of Judaism; taught that Judaism can be made stronger only by acting within the community, not by removing oneself from it; systematically applied logical rules of textual interpretation to Torah study and Jewish law; was the first of a dynasty of official Jewish leaders that flourished in the land of Israel until the 5th century

Judaism traces its roots back to the Pharisees rather than the Sadducees or other groups. Although Hillel may have shared the Essenes' disgust with the world around him, he believed that withdrawal was not the proper response. "Do not separate yourself from the community" is one of the best-known sayings attributed to Hillel. When the world seems riddled with problems, he taught, one should not abandon it but rather strive to improve it.

A number of legends tell of Hillel's humble beginnings as an immigrant in the land of Israel and of the display of

"Love your fellow creatures and draw them near to the Torah."

—Hillel, quoted in *Ethics of the Fathers* (compiled not later than the end of the 2nd century)

scholarship that led to his recognition as a sage. According to these traditions, Hillel came from Babylonia, an ancient empire in what is now southeastern Iraq. Babylonia had been an important center of Jewish life since 586 B.C.E., when the Babylonian king, Nebuchadnezzar, destroyed the First Temple in Jerusalem and exiled many Jews. Hillel was thus able to receive a basic Jewish education in his home country of Babylonia. But he had heard of an academy in Jerusalem led by two scholarly Pharisees, Shemaya and Avtalyon, and he wanted to study with them.

He turned down an opportunity to go into business with his wealthy brother, because he was afraid that the demands of a career in business would leave him little time to study. Instead he became a woodcutter, making just enough to support himself and his family after paying the entrance fee to the academy run by Shemaya and Avtalyon.

On one particular wintry Friday, Hillel found no work. Unable, as a result, to pay the fee to attend class, he could not convince the superintendent of the academy to let him enter. He was so eager to learn, however, that he climbed to the roof of the school and listened through a skylight as his teachers discussed the Torah. Hillel became so absorbed in what he was hearing that he did not budge from his spot even when it began to snow. Only the next morning, when Shemaya and Avtalyon noticed that less light than usual was coming through the skylight, was Hillel's presence on the roof detected. Although normally no work was permitted on the Sabbath, the teachers quickly climbed up to the roof, removed the snow, and discovered the unconscious Hillel, then brought him indoors and revived him in front of a fire. "For a man like this," they said, "the Sabbath must be violated."

As a result of this event, Hillel was able to complete his education with

Shemaya and Avtalyon free of charge. Then, some years after the death of his teachers, he himself became their successor, in a dramatic fashion. As the story goes, the religious leaders of the day could not answer a particular question about religious observance. The festival of Passover that year was scheduled to begin on the Sabbath, but no one could remember whether sacrificing the paschal lamb was considered a violation of the Sabbath or not. Although the religious leaders of Israel were reluctant to call upon a Babylonian immigrant for advice, Hillel was so highly recommended that they appealed to him.

He decreed that the Passover sacrifice should be carried out even on a Sabbath, just as many other sacrifices were offered on the Sabbath. To validate his decision he pointed to several passages in the Torah. He showed how similar words are used to describe the Passover sacrifice and another sacrifice that is routinely carried out on the Sabbath. Then he compared the nature of the two sacrifices: both were offered by the community. And he made another logical argument by comparing the punishments described by the Torah for failure to carry out the two sacrifices.

When the religious leaders refused to accept any of his arguments, Hillel finally announced that his teachers Shemaya and Avtalyon had taught him the tradition that permits the Passover sacrifice to be held on the Sabbath. The leaders had so much reverence for the tradition represented by the two eminent teachers that they immediately accepted Hillel's ruling and even asked him to take their place and become the religious leader of the community.

According to legend, then, it was not Hillel's analysis of the Torah but rather his claim to being in the mainstream of Jewish tradition that led to his rise. In his role as leader Hillel nonetheless made wide use of rules of biblical interpretation based on comparison, contrast, and other logical techniques. Although he was not the first to follow these guidelines, he left his mark on Judaism by using them in a particular way. He studied texts to uncover what he considered the original intent of the law in the Torah. If conditions had changed so much that observing the law would make people's lives worse rather than better, Hillel found a way to change the law.

Hillel's most famous use of biblical interpretation to better society involved the practice of lending money to those in need. According to a law in the Torah (Deuteronomy 15:2), all loans and debts are to be automatically annulled every seventh year. Hillel understood that the Torah intended this law to protect needy people from becoming too debt-ridden. But by Hillel's time the law was actually working against the needy. As every seventh year approached, the well-to-do refrained from making loans out of concern that they would not be repaid.

In order to solve this problem, Hillel went back to the text in the Torah that states, "Whatever of yours that is with your brother your hands should release." Hillel focused on the word *yours* and *your*, which, according to him, prove that only *individuals* have to give up their claim to money they have loaned. But the Torah does not impose the same requirement on a Jewish *court*. So Hillel ruled that a lender could file a document, called a *prozbul*, with the court, entrusting the court with the collection of the debt. The *prozbul* benefited both the wealthy, by securing their loans, and the poor, by enabling them to borrow. Thus Hillel's insightful reading preserved the Torah's original intent, even though it seemingly stood the prevailing law on its head.

In time, Hillel came to share the leadership of the religious community

This illustration from a 14th-century German manuscript shows a teacher brandishing a whip as he encourages his pupil to learn Hillel's famous summary of the Torah's contents.

with another scholarly Pharisee named Shammai. Like Hillel, Shammai led an academy, known in this case as Bet Shammai, or the House of Shammai. Hillel's academy was called Bet Hillel, or the House of Hillel. The two academies often differed on legal matters. Many of their differences involved sacrifices and other ritualistic concerns that are now obsolete. But Jews everywhere who commemorate the miracle of Hanukkah are familiar today with at least one law that follows Bet Hillel.

The first Hanukkah was celebrated in 165 B.C.E., when Judah Maccabee and his followers defeated the Syrian armies of King Antiochus. The

Maccabees found that the Syrians, in their attempt to desecrate the temple in Jerusalem, had contaminated nearly all the holy oil used to light the temple menorah, or candelabrum. But the Maccabees discovered a single jar of unpolluted oil, which the Syrians had mistakenly overlooked. Although the jar's contents were sufficient to burn for a single day only, the oil miraculously burned for eight days—long enough for a new supply of oil to be prepared. Relighting the temple menorah was the first step in rededicating the temple after it had been defiled and used for worship of Greek gods. The miracle of the jar of oil became a symbol of the heroic struggle for religious freedom.

Bet Shammai believed that on the first night of Hanukkah eight candles should be lit, and that as the holiday progressed one fewer candle should be lit each night. Bet Hillel argued, however, that only one candle should be lit the first night and an additional candle lit every successive night. Bet Shammai based its argument on an analogy to the number of bullocks sacrificed on the holiday of Sukkot, when one fewer animal is sacrificed each day as the holiday progresses. The logic underlying Bet Hillel's argument is summarized in the Talmud's teaching that "we promote in matters of sanctity but do not reduce."

According to Jewish tradition, the scholars of the two academies debated a single point of the law for three years. Each side claimed that its interpretation was correct. Then a mysterious voice was heard, announcing that "both sides speak the words of the living God, but the law follows the rulings of Bet Hillel." The scholars at first wondered why the law favored Bet Hillel, given that the words of both schools were divinely inspired. They concluded that Bet Hillel deserved this honor because of the modesty of its members, who honored their opponents' views by mentioning them first.

The modesty that characterized Bet Hillel as a group was also a trait associated with its founder. Many stories not only describe Hillel as the most modest of men but also contrast his patient, even-tempered nature with Shammai's rather fiery one. Probably the most famous story about these early sages concerns a non-Jew who approached Shammai with the following challenge: "I will convert to Judaism if you can teach me the entire Torah while I stand on one foot." Shammai, insulted by the request, pushed the man away. The challenger then approached Hillel with the same demand. Instead of rejecting the man, Hillel won him over as a convert with the following statement: "What you find hateful, do not do to your neighbor. This is the whole Torah. All the rest is commentary. Go and study it."

Other sayings attributed to Hillel, passed down from generation to generation, have contributed to the way Jews have defined their religion and sought to lead their lives. For example, the Jewish emphasis on study finds expression in Hillel's words "Do not say, 'I will study when I have time,' for it is possible that you will never find the time."

Hillel also taught that the misbehavior of those around us should not serve as an excuse for our own misbehavior: "Where there is no other human being, strive to be one." Among Hillel's other teachings perhaps the most famous consists of three consecutive questions: "If I am not for myself, who will be for me? But if I am for myself only, what am I? And if not now, when?"

By refining the approach of the Pharisees to the Torah and to the problems of contemporary life, Hillel became the foremost member of his party. He thus helped lay the foundation for all later forms of Judaism. For the Judaism of today did not develop directly from biblical Judaism but rather from the Judaism that arose in Hillel's time.

In a time of community upheaval, Hillel taught that society can be improved only by working from within. To do so, he used tools of logic to make the Torah responsive to the needs of the day. He thus established the idea that even though the Torah was given by God, Jews of every generation can interpret it to find solutions to the issues confronting them. Hillel stressed that study is important not only as a source of facts but also as a bridge between human beings and God, and that by perform-ing acts of kindness to one another people model themselves on God. It was not the Jewish officials appointed by Rome but rather Hillel's descendants, such as Rabbi Judah Hanasi, whom the Jews considered their true leaders over the next several centuries.

FURTHER READING

Glatzer, Nahum N. *Hillel the Elder: The Emergence of Classical Judaism*. New York: B'nai B'rith, 1956.

Neusner, Jacob. *First Century Judaism in Crisis*. New York: Ktav, 1982.

———. *Judaism in the Beginning of Christianity*. Philadelphia: Fortress, 1984.

Neusner, Jacob, and William Scott Green, eds. *Origins of Judaism: Religion, History, and Literature in Late Antiquity*. New York: Garland, 1990.

Johanan ben Zakkai

OVERCOMING
CATASTROPHE

J ohanan ben Zakkai played the decisive role in
rescuing Judaism and the Jewish people from a
catastrophe that might have destroyed both: the
total defeat of the Jews in their war against Rome.

Jewish hatred of Roman oppression had been
building since the Roman conquest in 63 B.C.E.
The Romans had imposed heavy taxes on all the inhabitants of the land of Israel, and economic hardship was
widespread. Only the merchant classes were thriving under
Roman rule, which had opened up new markets for them
throughout the empire.

Even worse than the economic oppression, however,
was what the Romans had done to the high priesthood. The

A detail from a menorah that stands in Israel's parliament
building, the Knesset, shows Johanan ben Zakkai weeping and
tearing his clothes upon learning of the destruction of the
Temple in Jerusalem.

high priest of the temple should have been the most respected figure in Jewish religious life. Instead, the Romans had turned the high priest into a puppet of the emperor, even to the point of taking custody of the garments the high priest wore during holy rituals. As a result, no self-respecting or tradition-honoring priest wanted such a position. To the horror of the sages, the high priests who did come forward to fill the position often required basic instruction before Yom Kippur, the holiest day of the Jewish year, to enable them to carry out the sacred rituals of that day. Such untrained lackeys, eager to line their own pockets, took advantage not only of the Jewish masses but also of other priests who were not as well connected politically.

Not surprisingly, a number of Jewish political groups were eager to throw off Roman rule. One such group, the Zealots, arose among the Pharisees. Like other Pharisees, the Zealots believed that Moses had received from God not only the written Torah but also the oral law, which explained the details of laws that were only vaguely described in the biblical text. But unlike other Pharisees, who believed in the supreme value of peace, the Zealots sought an independent Jewish state through military means. They also refused to pay the taxes demanded by Rome, on the grounds that God alone was the ruler of the Jews.

The immediate cause of the Jewish revolt against Rome in 66 C.E. was the offensive behavior of an imperial official who first seized some money from the temple's treasury and then instructed his soldiers to insult the Jewish citizenry. A group of priests led the rebellion. They ousted the high priest, whom they reviled as an instrument of Rome, and refused to offer the required temple sacrifice in honor of the emperor. Unfortunately, the rebellion soon split the Jewish community, as some groups joined the rebels

and others advocated making peace with the Romans. The most radical of the rebel groups, the Sicarii—named for the *sica* (dagger) carried by each member—even used terrorist tactics against Jews they regarded as collaborators with Rome.

Although the rebels achieved some victories, they could not hope to defeat the mighty Roman legions. The failure of the rebellion had devastating consequences for the Jews of the land of Israel. Large numbers were killed in battle during the rebellion or executed afterward. Others, both soldiers and civilians, were sold into slavery. The Sicarii, surrounded by Roman soldiers at the citadel of Masada overlooking the Dead Sea Valley in 73 C.E., chose to commit mass suicide rather than surrender. The Romans also confiscated large amounts of Jewish property. The victors boasted to the world of their humiliation of the Jews. They erected an arch in Rome depicting scenes of the Jewish degradation and minted coins commemorating their utter rout of the rebels.

The most overwhelming blow of all, however, was the destruction of the Second Temple and Jerusalem, around which the Jewish religion had been centered for hundreds of years. The temple was more than a symbol of unity for Jews everywhere; in religious terms, temple sacrifices were also the main way for Jews to express their connection to God. Compounding the loss, the Romans forbade the Jews to rebuild the temple, declared Jerusalem off-limits as a place for Jews to live, and demanded that the half-shekel each Jew used to pay for temple maintenance now be paid to Rome for the upkeep of pagan shrines.

Judaism and the Jews had survived another such devastating loss once before. In 586 B.C.E., the Babylonian king had destroyed the First Temple, built by King Solomon, and had driven many Jews into exile in Babylonia. At

that time the prophet Jeremiah had refused to despair in the face of loss. As a sign of his belief in the future of the Jewish people in their own country, he bought a plot of land in Israel. Within 70 years, another temple was erected. Now, nearly 600 years later, would Judaism be able to survive such a defeat again? Who would be Jeremiah to this generation?

The family background of Johanan ben Zakkai (literally, "Johanan, son of Zakkai"), the man who was to bring Judaism out of catastrophe, is unknown. However, *zakkai* means "righteous" in Aramaic, the language of everyday speech in the land of Israel and neighboring countries for nearly 1,000 years. It is also known that a large family named Zakkai figured prominently among the first Jews who returned to their ancestral land from the Babylonian exile.

According to tradition, Johanan—like Moses and Hillel before him—lived 120 years, devoting himself to business until the age of 40 and then dividing his remaining years equally between study and teaching. Historians do not take this legendary life span at face value. They see it instead as a form of homage by later generations comparing Johanan both to Moses, the leader who received God's Torah, and to Hillel, the founder of Judaism as we know it.

Tradition also claims that Johanan ben Zakkai was the youngest of Hillel's 80 pupils. One source states that Hillel, on his deathbed, predicted that Johanan would grow up to be "a father in wisdom and a father for future generations." Whether or not the two had an actual student–teacher relationship, this mandate to Johanan ben Zakkai ensured that Hillel's belief in the oral law would survive the war against Rome.

A few probable details about ben Zakkai's activities before the rebellion can be gleaned from various sources.

A fireworks display to commemorate the 40th anniversary of Israel's independence in 1988 lights up the sky over the ancient fortress of Masada, where in 73 C.E., extreme Jewish nationalists, surrounded by Roman soldiers, committed suicide rather than yield to Roman rule. Johanan ben Zakkai rejected such extreme measures and saved Judaism by persuading the Romans to grant him a school for the teaching of Torah.

After studying the teachings of the Pharisees in Jerusalem for a number of years, ben Zakkai served for 18 years as a teacher and magistrate in Galilee, in northern Israel. These were not satisfying years for him. He had only a single student, and only two legal questions, both dealing with Sabbath laws, were brought before him.

Ben Zakkai eventually returned to Jerusalem, where he became a popular teacher. Believing that Torah study was a Jew's primary role in life, he taught, "If you have learned much Torah, do not pride yourself on that achievement, since it was to that end that you were created." At his school he used Hillel's interpretive methods.

The result of ben Zakkai's probing of Torah texts was often an insightful idea that went far beyond the passage under consideration.

For example, ben Zakkai examined the biblical law requiring the piercing of the ear of a Jewish servant who refuses to go free (Exodus 21:2–6). According to him, the ear is so marked because all Jews heard with their ears God's statement at Mount Sinai that the children of Israel are God's servants. A Jew who nonetheless chooses a human master therefore deserves to have his ear perforated.

From his school in Jerusalem, ben Zakkai represented the views of the Pharisees in public disputes with the

Sadducees. But he was not in agreement with all factions of the Pharisee party. For example, he strongly opposed the Zealot policy that insisted on waging war with the Romans. He taught the importance of peace "between nation and nation, between government and government, between family and family," and urged the Jews not to destroy Roman property. Such behavior, he cautioned, would result in Roman decrees ordering the Jews to rebuild with their own hands whatever they had damaged. Ben Zakkai's opposition to war did not mean that he admired the Romans. It arose instead from his conviction that Torah study was the purpose of life and that

> *"I ask of you only Jabneh, where I might go and teach my discipline and there establish a prayer house and perform all the commandments."*
>
> —ben Zakkai, quoted in *Fathers According to Rabbi Nathan* (date uncertain, probably 1st–2nd century)

this purpose could be better achieved in peacetime than wartime.

As the rebellion against Rome escalated, ben Zakkai began to worry that the future of the Torah itself was in danger. When the Roman general Vespasian gave the Jews of Jerusalem an opportunity to save their city and temple by surrendering, ben Zakkai repeatedly urged the Zealot leaders to do so, but they rejected his advice. Although he understood the Zealots' unwillingness to yield to the Romans, ben Zakkai was convinced that their strategy would result in defeat. He believed that other tactics were needed to save Judaism from destruction. Ben Zakkai developed a daring ruse to outwit the Zealots that became the crucial point in the long-term survival of Judaism.

Understanding that many of Jerusalem's inhabitants would prefer surrender to military action, the Zealot leadership refused to let anyone out of the city. Ben Zakkai, however, worked out an escape plan with the assistance of his two best students. First the students spread the rumor that their teacher was on his death-bed. Then they wrapped his body in a cloth and carried him to the gates—because of the holiness of the city, dead bodies were not allowed to remain within it even overnight. Worried that the guards would fail to detect the smell of death, Johanan even thought to have a piece of decaying meat placed under the

cloth. The plan succeeded, allowing the "corpse" and its bearers to leave Jerusalem.

Following their instructions, ben Zakkai's students then carried their teacher to the Roman camp, where they requested an interview with the Roman general Vespasian himself. Because Vespasian had heard reports from his spies in Jerusalem that ben Zakkai favored surrender, the general was well disposed toward the sage and asked what favor he might do him. Ben Zakkai's response seemed modest, but it was to have long-lasting consequences. He asked the general for permission to set up a school in the town of Jabneh, to the west of Jerusalem, where he might teach the Torah to his students. Vespasian agreed without hesitation, unaware that by granting this request he was ensuring the future of the Jewish people.

In addition to setting up his school, ben Zakkai later established—this time without Roman permission—an institution that would serve as the supreme legal body for all Jews. While the temple had stood, this institution, called the Sanhedrin (from a Greek word meaning "council"), had functioned in Jerusalem. The Sanhedrin served as a sort of combined legislature and supreme court of Judaism. Ben Zakkai effectively re-created the Sanhedrin in Jabneh, where it functioned for the next 60 years.

Ben Zakkai's main achievement at Jabneh was the replacement of the

Jerusalem temple's cult of sacrifice with a thoroughgoing religious program that transformed the Jews' day-to-day lives. He had been deeply aggrieved when he learned after his escape that the Romans had destroyed the temple. According to tradition, ben Zakkai set an example for his students by tearing his clothes, as if mourning the death of a family member, and broke down in tears. But he refused to believe that the destruction of the temple was a cause for utter despair. Others responded to the catastrophe by refusing to eat meat or drink wine, since both had been used in temple sacrifices. Ben Zakkai taught instead that such self-denial was not an appropriate response, for life must go on.

But how could Judaism itself, many of whose laws revolved around the temple, its sacrifices, and its festivals, go on? Ben Zakkai found the answer one day when he discovered one of his students weeping because the Jews could no longer seek forgiveness for their sins through temple sacrifices. Ben Zakkai comforted the student by referring to the prophet Hosea, according to whom God says, "I desire kindness, and not sacrifice." And so ben Zakkai taught that the Jews could continue to seek forgiveness even in the absence of a temple by going out of their way to do kind deeds. "Do not grieve over the destruction of the temple," he taught. "We have another means to obtain forgiveness for our sins besides making sacrifices there, and that is through performing acts of loving-kindness."

To help the Jews carry out their observances, ben Zakkai ruled that some of the ceremonies that had previously been performed only in the temple could now be observed wherever there were practicing Jews. The priests could no longer perform sacrifices, but they should continue to bless the people as they had done in the temple. The Jews would forever remain a holy people, ben Zakkai believed, despite the loss of their national shrine.

At Jabneh, ben Zakkai also began the practice of ordaining rabbis. His students there were the first actually to hold the title *rabbi*, which means "my master." Now for the first time the religious leaders had both a formal title and an official role to play in Jewish life. It became their task to provide leadership to a people brought to the brink of despair. As head of the Sanhedrin at Jabneh, ben Zakkai himself held the special title *rabban*— "our master."

Rabban Johanan ben Zakkai was not a power-hungry man, however. When a descendant of Hillel became available to assume the leadership of the newly reconstituted Sanhedrin, ben Zakkai deferred to his teacher's offspring. In his old age, he moved to Beror Hayil, a village in the Judaean foothills, where he established yet another academy and court of justice. There, some 10 years after the destruction of the temple, Johanan ben Zakkai died. He was buried in Tiberias, in Galilee.

Johanan ben Zakkai had been opposed to a revolution against Rome, but what he accomplished at Jabneh was no less than a revolution in Jewish history. Jabneh will always be remembered as the site where Johanan ben Zakkai saved Judaism from extinction.

FURTHER READING

Bader, Gershom. *The Jewish Spiritual Heroes: The Lives and Works of the Rabbinical Teachers from the Beginning of the Great Synagogue to the Final Completion of the Talmud: Seven Centuries of Jewish Thought.* Vol. 1. New York: Pardes, n.d.

Bokser, ben Zion. "The National Disaster and the Emergence of the Rabbi." In *The Wisdom of the Talmud.* New York: Philosophical Library, 1951.

Glatzer, Nahum N. "Johanan ben Zakkai, the Disciple." In *Hillel the Elder: The Emergence of Classical Judaism.* New York: B'nai B'rith, 1956.

Neusner, Jacob. *First-Century Judaism in Crisis: Yohanan ben Zakkai and the Renaissance of Torah.* New York: Ktav, 1982.

———. "Judaism Beyond Catastrophe: The Destruction of the Temple and the Renaissance of the Torah." In *Judaism in the Beginning of Christianity.* Philadelphia: Fortress, 1984.

Johanan ben Zakkai

BORN

Probably 1st century C.E.
Israel

DIED

Around 80 C.E.
Beror Hayil

EDUCATION

Said to have been the youngest of Hillel's 80 students

ACCOMPLISHMENTS

Enabled Judaism to survive the catastrophic destruction of the temple by the Romans in 70 C.E. by transforming it from a religion centered on sacrifice to one focusing on study, prayer, and the performance of good deeds

Akiba ben Joseph

FROM SHEPHERD TO SCHOLAR

Nothing about the circumstances of the birth of Akiba, which took place about 40 C.E., pointed to a future that would mold him into one of the most honored Jewish scholars and spiritual leaders of all time. His father, Joseph, was a poor peasant who worked on the property of a rich neighbor. Uneducated and probably illiterate, Joseph raised his son to hold scholars in contempt. Under his father's guidance, Akiba learned to tend their rich neighbors' sheep and give no thought to learning. He later recalled, "When I was an uneducated boor, I used to say, 'Would that I had a scholar in my hands and I should bite him like an ass.'"

As in a romantic novel, Akiba's transformation from anti-intellectual shepherd to one of the outstanding shapers of Jewish tradition was brought about by the love of a woman. According to legend, Rachel, the daughter of ben Kalba Sabua, one of the richest men in Jerusalem, discerned a man of singular talents beneath the shepherd's rude exterior. Despite her father's objections, she promised to marry Akiba if he would agree to study with the scholars for whom he had thus far expressed only contempt. The bargain was struck, and the newlyweds lived in poverty for several years while Akiba labored to educate himself.

Not surprisingly, the metamorphosis from shepherd to scholar was painful. Akiba was so discouraged by his first attempts to master the Hebrew alphabet and memorize the laws of the Torah that he actually gave up for a while. But one day, a few years after the birth of his first son, an encounter with nature convinced him to try again. As Akiba sat by a stream thinking about his future, he noticed how the running water ate into the surrounding rocks. This natural process suggested to him a comparison to his own situation. If soft water could erode hard rock, surely the words of the Torah could impress themselves on his brain. Together with his son, who was now old enough to begin his own studies, Akiba sat with children and mastered the alphabet and the elementary course in Torah. Then, when the children's teacher had nothing more to teach him, Akiba applied for admission to the academy in Jabneh that trained rabbis.

Some of the scholars at Jabneh welcomed the middle-aged pupil and took him under their wing. Soon it became clear that this newcomer had natural abilities that would enable him to surpass his teachers. After Akiba had been studying under various rabbis for 13 years, his outstanding performance in one of the scholarly debates marked the end of his student life. No longer a rough, uncultured shepherd,

Rabbi Akiba's picture adorns the margin of a 14th-century Spanish *haggadah,* the prayer book used at the festive Passover meal, the seder. Some scholars say that Rabbi Akiba and four colleagues made use of the occasion of the seder in 132 C.E. to discuss the forthcoming Jewish rebellion against the Roman forces occupying the land of Israel.

he was now acknowledged to be one of the outstanding rabbinic minds of his generation. Once, when he was absent from the academy, his colleagues missed his intellectual contributions so much that they are reported to have said, "The Torah is outside."

As one of the leaders of the rabbinical academy, Akiba left a permanent mark on Jewish law and practice through his scholarly activities and rulings. Rabbi Akiba was aware of the fact that different interpretations of Jewish law had been transmitted from one generation to another by word of mouth. Concerned that these different opinions and interpretations might disappear if they were not logically organized, the rabbi began to arrange them systematically. One of his pupils described the organizational undertaking in this way: "To what may Akiba be compared? To a peddler who goes about from farm to farm. Here he obtains wheat, there barley, and in a third place, spelt [a type of grain]. When he comes home, he arranges them all in their respective bins. So Akiba went about from scholar to scholar, getting all the

traditions he could. And then he proceeded to arrange them in an orderly granary." Since his system for the organization of the laws is the basis for the Mishnah, the great compilation of Jewish law that his students would later complete, Rabbi Akiba has been called the Father of the Mishnah.

Rabbi Akiba also originated a school of Torah interpretation that continues to influence Jewish scholarship. While he was still a pupil, one of his teachers impressed upon him that because God is the source of the Torah, every word and every letter in that divine document has significance. Later, as a rabbi in his own right and leader of his own academy—which he set up in Bene Berak, a village not far from Jabneh—Rabbi Akiba continued to develop this concept into a method of interpreting the Torah.

Rabbi Akiba's emphasis on a method of interpretation that carefully considered every word was not simply a scholarly game. He was a man with a strong social conscience, and he wanted to make sure that Jewish law reflected the ideals of human equality. Some of his rabbinical colleagues came

In 130 C.E., while in Rome on an unsuccessful mission to Emperor Hadrian, Akiba might have seen this detail from the Arch of Titus. The arch had been erected to commemorate the Roman victory over the Jews and the destruction of their temple 60 years earlier.

from privileged backgrounds and had less sympathy with the downtrodden than Akiba did. He knew that to convince these fellow scholars that his ideals of social equality reflected God's intent he would have to find justification in the text of the Torah.

For Rabbi Akiba, the Torah teaches not simply that all Jews should have equal rights but that all human beings are equal. As he taught, "The fundamental principle of the Torah is the commandment, 'Love thy neighbor as thyself'" (Leviticus 14:18). His friend ben Azzai, worried that some people might interpret "thy neighbor" as applying only to other Jews, suggested a different verse that made the point more clearly. Akiba accepted ben Azzai's substitution, which taught that the Torah views all people, of any faith and of either sex, as equally valued creatures under God: "This is the book of the generations of Adam. In the day that God created man, in the likeness of God He made him, male and female created He them" (Genesis 5:1–2).

Later rabbis so admired Rabbi Akiba's skill in interpreting the Torah that they described him as having a better understanding of God's intent than Moses, the man to whom God had originally entrusted the Torah. According to these rabbis, "Matters not revealed to Moses were revealed to Akiba."

Akiba was destined to be much more than a great scholar, however. Although the Jewish community in Israel was blessed with tranquility and prosperity during Akiba's first years at Jabneh, the situation soon changed. In the year 110, the Roman emperor Trajan announced that the temple— destroyed 40 years earlier by his predecessor Vespasian—would be reconstructed, and the Jews would be permitted once more to sacrifice animals to God there. Although many Jews, including Rabbi Akiba, greeted this news with joy, others were not so enthusiastic. This group, which included some of Akiba's colleagues, doubted that the promise would ever be fulfilled and saw it as falling far short of their goal of Jewish self-government.

As it turned out, anti-Jewish Romans vigorously opposed Trajan's idea and the emperor withdrew his proposal. Jews in several parts of the

Roman Empire rioted in protest. In putting down this rebellion, the Romans mistakenly identified the rabbinical academy at Jabneh as an organized center of anti-Roman activity. They first forbade the rabbis from meeting, then permitted them to do so but only in a different location, Lod (where Israel's Ben-Gurion Airport is now located). The Romans also curtailed the powers of the rabbis to decide questions of Jewish law.

Things took a sharp turn for the worse in 125, under the new emperor, Hadrian. That year he issued a decree forbidding the Jews to circumcise their newborn sons, thus denying them the right to observe a religious ritual that dates back to biblical times. He also forbade other Jewish observances that seemed likely to spark rebellion. For example, Jews were no longer permitted to recite in public the *Shema*, the biblical phrases that summarize the Jewish belief in one God.

The rabbis now met at Lod to decide on Jewish policy. Should Jews accept these new restrictions, or should they be willing to die rather than submit? Rabbi Akiba was convinced that Judaism was primarily a system of knowledge rather than a checklist of rituals to be observed. As long as the Romans permitted Jews to study the Torah, he felt, the Jewish community could accept the other restrictions on its practice. At his urging the rabbis reached two conclusions. First, they decreed that study rather than observance is the most basic Jewish activity. "Study is important," they said, "for it alone can lead to observance." Second, they defined three categories of sin— idol worship, murder, and incest—that Jews should refuse to commit, even if refusal led to martyrdom.

Another political upheaval oc-curred in 130, when Hadrian visited the Jewish province. Surveying the pile of rubble that had once been Jerusalem, the emperor announced that the city would be rebuilt and a temple once again erected. However, the temple he envisioned would be dedicated not to the Jews' God but to the emperor. Horrified, the Jews sent Rabbi Akiba, now in his 90th year, to plead with Hadrian on their behalf. The emperor, however, was unmoved by Akiba's arguments. As a result, the aged rabbi, who had always believed that if the Jews peacefully adapted to Roman rules they would be treated fairly, now experienced a change of heart.

When a rebellion broke out in full force, Rabbi Akiba did not try to calm the rebels. In fact, after the leader of the rebellion, Simeon ben Koziba, led his peasant army to several victories against the heavily armed Romans, Akiba was prepared to endorse Simeon's nickname, bar Kochba, "Son of the Star." Akiba applied to the warrior a biblical verse, "The star hath trodden forth out of Jacob" (Numbers 24:17), and identified him as the Messiah, the redeemer who Jews believed would come at the end of days to usher in an age of peace.

Despite bar Kochba's initial successes, however, the Romans suppressed the rebellion over a three-year period. The consequences for the Jews were dreadful: many were killed, others were sold into slavery, and all observance of Jewish practice was forbidden. A statue of the emperor was the outstanding feature of the new temple. Even Jerusalem's name was changed, to Aelia Capitolina, referring to the *capitolium*, or temple, in honor of the emperor, whose full name was Publius Aelius Hadrianus. Only non-Jews were permitted to live in or even approach the city. The name of the entire Jewish province was changed as well. No longer Judaea, it now became known as Palestine.

Not satisfied with these attempts to undermine the Jews' identity, in 134 Hadrian delivered the final blow: he forbade the study of Torah, on pain of

Akiba ben Joseph

BORN

Around 40 C.E.
Judaea

DIED

Around 135 C.E.
Caesarea

EDUCATION

Illiterate until adulthood, learned to read with his son, then studied with scholars at the rabbinical academy at Jabneh

ACCOMPLISHMENTS

Systematically organized Jewish laws that had been passed down orally from generation to generation, thus laying the foundation for the Mishnah; developed a method of biblical interpretation based on the significance of every letter and word in the Torah; transformed the *Shema* into the Jew's deathbed affirmation of faith

"Beloved are Israel, for to them was given a precious instrument [the Torah]."

—Akiba, quoted in *Ethics of the Fathers* (compiled not later than the end of the 2nd century)

death. Akiba, for whom study was the essence of Judaism, continued to teach the Torah openly. When he was asked if he valued his life so little as to flagrantly disobey the Roman decree, Akiba answered indirectly with the following fable: A hungry fox sidled up to a riverbank and tried to convince the fish in the river to escape the fishermen's nets by coming out onto dry land. But the fish responded, "If we are in danger in the water, which is our element, imagine how much worse our situation would be on the dry land, which is not our element." Rabbi Akiba concluded, "We may be unsafe teaching the Torah, but there can be no life for us at all without the Torah, since it is the very essence of our lives."

Not surprisingly, the Romans soon imprisoned Akiba, who continued to issue legal pronouncements from his jail cell. After bringing their captive to trial, the Romans put him to death. But even in his final act the great scholar and leader helped shaped Jewish tradition. According to one version, the Roman governor of the Jewish province, who had once been on friendly terms with Akiba, had the aged rabbi tortured. Instead of crying out with pain, Akiba responded to the torture by reciting the *Shema*—the affirmation of Jewish loyalty to God—with a smile on his face. Amazed by Akiba's tolerance for pain, the officer asked his victim, "Old man, are you a magician that you can smile while being tortured?" Akiba

answered, "No, I am not a magician. But all my life when I said these words of the *Shema,* 'Thou shalt love the Lord thy God with all thy heart and soul and might,' I wondered if I should ever be able to fulfill the commandment in its entirety. I have loved God with all my heart and with all my might, or possessions, but until this moment I had not been granted the opportunity to love God with all my soul. Now I am smiling with joy at the ability to fulfill this commandment completely."

To this day, observant Jews hope that they will share the fortune of Rabbi Akiba and be able to meet their deaths with composure, with the words of the *Shema* on their lips.

FURTHER READING

Bader, Gershom. *The Jewish Spiritual Heroes: The Lives and Works of the Rabbinical Teachers from the Beginning of the Great Synagogue to the Final Completion of the Talmud: Seven Centuries of Jewish Thought.* Vol. 1. New York: Pardes, n.d.

Finkelstein, Louis. *Akiba: Scholar, Saint and Martyr.* New York: Covici, Friede, 1936.

———. "Akiba." In *Great Jewish Personalities in Ancient and Medieval Times.* Edited by Simon Noveck. Washington, D.C.: B'nai B'rith, 1959.

Beruriah

![Star of David]

AN UNLIKELY SCHOLAR

eruriah, the daughter of one famous rabbi and the wife of another, was an outstanding scholar in her own right. She was extraordinary for the depth and breadth of her learning at a time when women were routinely not educated. Her learning put her on an equal footing with the male scholars of her day. In her own era Beruriah was unique and did not shape Jewish tradition. But in modern times she has become a model for women wanting to become as accomplished in Jewish studies as their male counterparts.

After the destruction of the Second Temple, in 70 C.E., Torah study became one of the main ways for a Jew to practice Judaism. But the scholarly mode of Jewish life was virtually unavailable to women. According to the Torah itself, fathers had an obligation to teach the Torah to their sons, but it says nothing about teaching it to their

The menorah that sculptor Benno Elkan created for Israel's parliament in 1956 contains this image of Beruriah's father, Hananiah ben Teradion, being burned at the stake by the Romans, wrapped in the Torah scroll he had been holding when arrested.

A Jewish housewife blesses candles in preparation for observance of the Sabbath in this 17th-century Dutch woodcut. Most Jewish women in ancient times were expected to pursue domestic activities and leave the study of the Torah to men. Beruriah's scholarly achievements were the exception, rather than the rule, for most Jewish women.

century to create the Talmud—the encyclopedic text that has remained as central to Jewish life as the Bible itself—Beruriah's scholarly abilities were considered worthy of mention. The Talmud quotes the (doubtless exaggerated) claim of one rabbi who lived a century after Beruriah that she studied 300 laws from 300 teachers each day for three years. In addition, the Talmud and other compilations of oral Torah relate that she took part in rabbinic debates and on occasion even prevailed over scholarly opposition.

Beruriah's scholarly achievement is all the more remarkable when considered against the background of her tragic family life. Various of her family's misfortunes arose from the political situation in Palestine, the name the Romans had bestowed on the land of Israel after they put down the Jewish rebellion in 135. For the next several years, the emperor Hadrian vigorously enforced a ban on teaching the Torah and mercilessly persecuted rabbis who defied him. Akiba was the most famous of the rabbis who became a martyr during the period of the Hadrianic persecutions; Beruriah's father, Rabbi Hananiah ben Teradion, was another victim. Like Akiba, Hananiah continued to teach the Torah publicly despite the ban. To punish him, the Romans not only burned him at the stake but also executed his wife and sent Beruriah's sister to a brothel. (According to the Talmud, the young woman was able to escape with her virtue intact through the intervention of Beruriah's husband, Rabbi Meir.) But even before Hananiah's martyrdom, the family had suffered a great loss when one of Beruriah's brothers joined a band of outlaws—possibly a group that were simply robbers, but perhaps also political rebels—and was put to death by the authorities.

The most famous story about Beruriah involves another family loss,

daughters. Although they were not forbidden to teach their daughters, few did. Though there was no prohibition against women's studying the Torah, some rabbis condemned the practice. In general, they believed that women were undisciplined and easily confused and that they distracted men from their studies. Most scholars of the time believed that a woman's only duty with respect to religious education was to send her husband and sons off to the house of study. One rabbi went so far as to say that teaching a daughter Torah was equivalent to teaching her "lechery." He further claimed that a woman's wisdom is confined to her domestic activities and that he would rather see the Torah's words burned

than taught to a woman. This rabbi was perhaps more extreme and outspoken than his colleagues, but the fact that few rabbis taught their daughters is evident from the absence of female scholars in ancient times.

Beruriah, who lived in the turbulent time of bar Kochba's unsuccessful rebellion against Roman rule in the land of Israel (132–35 C.E.) and its aftermath, is the only woman scholar whose opinion was taken seriously by the rabbis. Although the details of her education are unknown, her reputation as an outstanding student was transmitted from generation to generation of men. When the rabbis' oral Torah discussions were finally collected, edited, and put into writing in the 5th unrelated to the political troubles of the day. This story is noteworthy because it demonstrates Beruriah's ability to make use of her deep knowledge of the Torah to deal with the pain of everyday life. One Sabbath afternoon, while Rabbi Meir was at the synagogue studying with his colleagues, the two sons of Meir and Beruriah both died of plague. Though grief-stricken, she merely covered the boys' bodies and considered how best to break the news to her husband. Rather than intrude on the peaceful nature of his Sabbath study, she waited for his return from the synagogue. As soon as Meir entered their home, he asked for the boys, but Beruriah did not tell him what had happened. Keeping her composure, she encouraged him to say the blessing that would signify the end of the Sabbath, and gave him some food.

Then she said she had a question to ask him: Some time ago, a man had given her a treasure to guard on his behalf, and today the man had come to ask for its return; was she obliged to return it to him? Unhesitatingly, Meir told his wife that the treasure must certainly be returned to its owner. Beruriah then took him by the hand and led him to the room where the boys' bodies lay. As she removed the cloth covering them, Meir broke down and wept. Beruriah then said to him, "Did you not say to me that one must return a deposit to its owner?" Then, quoting from the biblical Book of Job, she said, "The Lord gave, the Lord has taken away. Blessed be the name of the Lord." Beruriah's scholarship helped calm Rabbi Meir in this hour of his most intense grief. He saw that their sons had been a treasure left with them for safekeeping only until God sought the return of the deposit.

According to the Talmud, on another occasion Beruriah used her knowledge of the Torah not only to comfort her husband but also to correct him. It seems that the couple lived in a bad neighborhood, where a gang of robbers made a practice of victimizing Rabbi Meir. After having been robbed by them one time too many, Meir said in his wife's presence that he wished the gang members would drop dead. Beruriah was shocked by her husband's comment and explained to him that if he read the Torah correctly, he would understand how inappropriate his reaction was. Quoting from the Book of Psalms (104:35), she pointed out that the verse should be read "let sins [not sinners] disappear from the earth." When sin is uprooted, she continued, then the conclusion of the verse will be guaranteed: "and the wicked will be no more." She encouraged her husband to pray for the robbers to repent rather than to drop dead. According to the Talmud, Rabbi Meir then prayed for his antagonists' repentance and soon afterward the robbers saw the error of their ways and abandoned their life of crime.

Rabbi Meir was not the only man to learn from Beruriah's impressive grasp of the Torah. The Talmud describes how she once used her biblical knowledge to correct a timid scholar whom she overheard studying in a hesitant undertone. Quoting from the Book of 2 Samuel (23:5), where God's "eternal pact" with the Jewish people is described as "drawn up in full and secured," Beruriah advised the young man to "secure" his studies by "drawing up" into them all his bodily strength.

As exceptional as Beruriah's knowledge of the written Torah was for a woman of her time, her grasp of the oral Torah—the discussions of the rabbis about the Torah—was even more unusual. According to a story in the Talmud, Beruriah was once able to bring a rabbi up short by quoting a Talmudic discussion. Rabbi Jose the Galilean seems to have been uncertain

Beruriah

BORN

Before 135–38
Israel

DIED

After 135–38
Place unknown

EDUCATION

Extraordinarily for a woman of her time, she studied not only the written but also the oral Torah

ACCOMPLISHMENTS

The only woman whose views on Jewish law were taken seriously by the rabbis of the Talmud

"Rightly did Beruriah say."

—an anonymous statement in the *Tosefta* (Supplement to the Mishnah, date uncertain, possibly 4th century)

of the route he should travel to reach his destination. Meeting Beruriah along the way, he said to her in a long-winded fashion, "By which road should we travel in order to reach Lydda?" Beruriah's response may today seem a bit brusque: "Galilean fool! Did not the rabbis say, 'Talk not overmuch with women?' You should have asked: 'How to Lydda?'"

We cannot, of course, be certain of Beruriah's tone of voice in speaking to the rabbi. Was he an old friend who would take her comment as a friendly rebuke, or did Beruriah, knowing him to be one of the rabbis who felt that women should not study the Torah, want to put him in his place with a sharp gibe? Nor can we know definitely why the rabbis preserved the memory of Beruriah's scholarship. Were they eager to establish as a role model this woman who against all odds achieved parity with men in learning? Or did their grudging admiration for her contain an implicit warning suggesting that other women not try to follow her path?

A mysterious phrase in the Talmud suggests that the rabbis may indeed have harbored some such resentment against Beruriah. In evaluating why Rabbi Meir had to flee from Palestine to Babylonia, the Talmud offers two possible explanations: to escape punishment for rescuing Beruriah's sister from the brothel to which Hadrian's henchmen had sent her, or "because of the incident about Beruriah."

Although the Talmud does not shed further light on what this incident might have been, Rashi, the most famous commentator on the Talmud, does. Rashi, born in northeastern France in 1040, was himself not opposed to women's education. Unlike other scholars of his own day, he provided his three daughters with rigorous training in both the Torah and Talmud. Nonetheless, in his commentary on the Talmud's cryptic allusion to "the incident about Beruriah," Rashi relates a grim story about Beruriah's downfall. According to him, Beruriah repeatedly mocked the rabbis' belief that women are inconstant until at last her husband lost his temper. Rabbi Meir told his wife she would live to regret her insistence on the constancy of women. In order to teach her a lesson, he instructed one of his students to try to seduce her. The student did not find his assignment an easy one, but after coaxing and enticing Beruriah for an entire day, he finally succeeded. As soon as Beruriah learned that she had been the victim of a plot, she committed suicide. Because of the ensuing scandal, Rabbi Meir fled to Babylonia.

Critics today, both male and female, tend to dispute the factual nature of Rashi's story. Rabbi Meir had after all been the prize pupil of Rabbi Akiba, who identified sexual misconduct as one of three laws that no Jew should violate, on pain of death. It is simply not believable that Meir would assign one of his students to commit such a sin with his own wife. Nonetheless, Rashi's story, whatever its basis in fact, shows the antipathy with which some scholars continued to view the figure of Beruriah over the centuries.

Though Beruriah's memory has survived for nearly a millennium, only during the past several decades has the drive of Jewish women to be recognized as the scholarly and spiritual equals of their male counterparts begun to be accepted. Perhaps only in the 21st century, when it may become routine for large numbers of women to serve as rabbis and scholars, will Beruriah truly find her place as a role model for women in the Jewish community.

FURTHER READING

Adler, Rachel. "The Virgin in the Brothel and Other Anomalies: Character and Context in the Legend of Beruriah." *Tikkun*, Nov.–Dec. 1988, 28-32, 102-5.

Swidler, Leonard. "Beruria: The Exception that Proves the Rule." In *Women in Judaism: The Status of Women in Formative Judaism*. Metuchen, N.J.: Scarecrow, 1976.

Szold, Henrietta. "Beruriah." In *The Jewish Encyclopedia*. New York: Funk & Wagnalls, 1902.

Wegner, Judith Romney. "The Image and Status of Women in Classical Rabbinic Judaism." In *Jewish Women in Historical Perspective*. Edited by Judith R. Baskin. Detroit: Wayne State University Press, 1991.

Judah Hanasi

PRINCE AND HOLY ARK

Although Hanasi may seem like a family name, it is actually a Hebrew title that is still in use. Since 1948, the president of the state of Israel has been called Nasi. Rabbi Judah's title, however, is not translated as "president," but rather as "prince" or "patriarch." (*Patriarch* comes from the Latin word meaning "head of the family"; the Romans also called church leaders patriarchs.) In Rabbi Judah's day, the Nasi combined two roles. He was both the chief rabbi of the Jews of Palestine and their chief delegate to the Roman rulers, who had occupied the Jews' land for more than half a century before Rabbi Judah's birth.

Not surprisingly, it was in the role of chief rabbi that Judah Hanasi made his greatest contribution to Jewish tradition. He is remembered mainly as the editor of the Mishnah. The Mishnah is the basic text of what Jews refer to as the oral law or the oral Torah. According to the traditions of Judaism, God gave Moses not only the Torah—also called the five books of Moses, the written Law, or the written Torah—but also the oral law, which provided fuller explanations of the written laws. As Jewish scholars studied the written Torah over generations to try to uncover the oral Torah, they handed down their discussions and conclusions to their students by word of mouth. Those students in turn taught the next generation by repeating aloud the scholarly debates of the previous generations and adding their own interpretations about the oral Torah. In fact, the title of the Mishnah, Rabbi Judah Hanasi's great work, comes from the Hebrew word meaning "to repeat."

Over time, the rabbis began to worry that the laws of the oral Torah might eventually be forgotten. The amount of material was growing from one generation to the next, and the political situation of the Jews often made religious study difficult. At various times, the Romans banned the study of the Torah on pain of death. For that reason, Rabbi Akiba—who himself died as a martyr at the hands of the Romans in 135 for continuing to teach the Torah—began to organize the oral law. His student Rabbi Meir continued that work.

In the Mishnah, Rabbi Judah organized the laws that Jewish scholars had developed over the centuries, derived from their reading of the Torah. Thus, the Mishnah differs from the written Torah, where in a single passage a reader may find laws about a wide variety of topics, including family life, Sabbath observance, preparation of sacrifices in the temple, harvesting the land, and employer-employee

"The world endures only for the sake of the breath of schoolchildren."

—from the Babylonian Talmud

relations. By contrast, Rabbi Judah Hanasi divided all the laws into six main categories, each covered in a separate "order" of the Mishnah: agriculture, the Sabbath and holidays, family life, damage to property and other aspects of civil and criminal law, the temple service and dietary laws, and laws pertaining to purity. The way in which Rabbi Judah Hanasi organized the Mishnah became the basis for the further development of the oral Torah.

Rabbi Judah Hanasi's Mishnah helped shape Jewish tradition in at least two other ways. First, he wrote the entire work in a beautiful Hebrew, even though that was not the language then spoken by most Jews. The majority of them spoke Aramaic, which was also the everyday language of Syria and other non-Jewish portions of the Middle East for nearly a thousand years, from about 300 B.C.E. onward. But Rabbi Judah Hanasi was so devoted to Hebrew that even his housemaids are said to have spoken it. The use of Hebrew in daily speech did not catch on in his time; in fact, only in the late 19th century was a conscious effort made to transform the ancient tongue into a modern language. At that time, when a small number of Jews resolved to make Hebrew the language of a hoped-for Jewish homeland, they drew heavily on the pure Hebrew of Rabbi Judah Hanasi's Mishnah.

The third way in which Rabbi Judah Hanasi shaped Jewish tradition was by including in his Mishnah not only civil laws that were observed in his own time but also ones that could be observed only in the temple. In that way he helped keep alive for future generations the memory of a more glorious Jewish past and in particular a devotion to Jerusalem, the site of the former temple.

The primary contribution of Rabbi Judah Hanasi's Mishnah to Jewish tradition lies in its inspiration of scholarly debate, both in his own time and later. As soon as the rabbi had finished editing the Mishnah, rabbis and their students began to discuss and evaluate its contents. Then these discussions themselves, each dealing with a particular section of the Mishnah, were eventually organized and edited. One version, edited in Palestine, was completed in about 400 C.E.; it is called the Jerusalem, or Palestinian, Talmud. The more important edition, prepared in Babylonia, was completed in about 500 C.E.; it is called the Babylonian Talmud. The Talmud is like a massive encyclopedia of oral Torah that touches on all aspects of life. For the next 1,500 years, the Talmud— with Rabbi Judah Hanasi's Mishnah at its core—became the basic text of Judaism.

Though Jewish history honors Rabbi Judah Hanasi primarily for his work on the Mishnah, in earlier times he was also known for his associations with the Roman rulers. The Talmud tells many stories about a relationship between Rabbi Judah Hanasi and an emperor identified only as Antoninus. In fact, there were several Roman emperors by this name, who were collectively known as the Antonines. Historians are not certain which of them, if any, befriended Judah Hanasi. Whether or not the stories are strictly true, they nevertheless tell a great deal about the changed relationship between Rome and the Jews during the period of Rabbi Judah Hanasi's life.

One story bases the friendship between the rabbi and the emperor on an event that took place just days after Rabbi Judah Hanasi's birth. From biblical times on, Jewish males have been brought into the covenant, or pact, that God made with Abraham through the ritual of circumcision, performed on the eighth day after birth. According to tradition, Judah was born the very day that Rabbi Akiba died a martyr at the hands of the Romans. The emperor Hadrian had outlawed circumcision as well as the teaching of the Torah. Judah's father, Rabban Simeon ben Gamaliel, was a descendant of the great scholar Hillel and was himself the leader of the assembly of rabbis called the Sanhedrin. He was fully aware of the ban on circumcision, but even more acutely aware of the biblical commandment, so Judah was circumcised at the appropriate time.

As the story goes, news of this illegal circumcision leaked out to the Roman governor, who sent Rabban Simeon ben Gamaliel to Rome with his wife and infant son to receive punishment at the hands of the emperor himself. During their journey, the family broke their trip by stopping at an inn that happened to be run by Romans. By coincidence, the innkeepers had a son exactly the same age as Judah. With this bond between them, the two mothers struck up a friendship. When the Roman woman asked Judah's mother why she was making a trip with such a young infant, the Jewish woman explained. Once she understood the circumstances, the compassionate Roman mother expressed fear for what the emperor might do. She offered to keep Judah in her home and send instead her own infant boy, named Antoninus, with Rabban Simeon and his wife to the emperor's court.

Needless to say, when the emperor inspected the infant and saw that he was uncircumcised, he was furious at his governor in Palestine for sending the Jewish family to take up his time unnecessarily. But the emperor's advisers had their own explanation for what must have happened: Rabban Simeon ben Gamaliel, as head of the Sanhedrin, had certainly circumcised his son, but his god must have performed a miracle. The advisers coun-

seled the emperor not only to send the Jewish family back to Palestine unpunished but also to abolish the decree forbidding circumcision. Hadrian followed their advice, and Simeon ben Gamaliel and family were allowed to leave Rome in peace and safety.

When the Jewish parents returned to the inn where they had left Judah, they told Antoninus's mother what had happened and thanked her again and again for her kindness. The Roman mother then expressed a wish to her new Jewish friends: since their god had performed a miracle for their son through her son, the two boys should be friends forever. The story ends by indicating that God rewarded Antoninus for the part he played in saving Judah's life: when he grew up, Antoninus became emperor of Rome.

Other stories about Judah and Antoninus as grown men describe the development of their relationship. One story indicates that the two men remained on an equal footing despite the difference in their rank. It also contains a lesson about the nature of Jewish prayer. According to this story, Antoninus once asked Judah why Jews pray at specific times of the day rather than praying spontaneously at any time they were so inspired. Judah responded that the rabbis feared that by allowing prayer at any time they might lead worshipers to treat God with disrespect. Unconvinced, the emperor told his old friend that the rabbis' reasoning seemed unsatisfactory. Judah then devised a plan to convince Antoninus of the wisdom behind the Jewish rules for prayer.

The next day, the rabbi arrived early at the emperor's quarters and asked for an audience. When he was admitted, he praised the emperor and wished him well. Then he left the imperial chamber. Throughout the morning, he continued to seek admittance to the emperor on an hourly basis. Each time he was admitted, he

Judah Hanasi

BORN

Around 135 C.E.
Usha, Palestine

DIED

Around 217 C.E.
Sepphoris, Palestine

EDUCATION

Studied first under several of Rabbi Akiba's disciples and then under his father, Rabban Simeon ben Gamaliel

ACCOMPLISHMENTS

Edited the Mishnah, which, as the core of the Talmud, became the basic text of the oral Torah; as the Nasi he served as the prince or patriarch of the Jews and as their chief representative to the Roman government again praised the emperor and wished him well. Finally, as noon approached, Antoninus lost patience and berated the rabbi for degrading the office of emperor by his intrusions. The rabbi then explained to the emperor that if his hourly greetings seemed degrading to Antoninus, a human ruler, it followed that such praise would seem even more degrading to the king of kings. Surely now, he said, his friend the emperor must understand why the rabbis do not encourage Jews to disturb God at any hour of the day.

Not all the Talmud's stories about Rabbi Judah Hanasi paint him in such a favorable light. Among the famous sayings associated with the editor of the Mishnah is his assertion that "I have learned much from my teachers, more from my colleagues, and most of all from my pupils." The Talmud contains a number of stories that indicate how much Rabbi Judah indeed learned from his students.

One story takes the great rabbi to task for embarrassing a student unnec-essarily. One day when he entered the room where he was to lecture, he was greeted by such a strong odor of garlic that he was certain he would be unable to teach as long as the smell persisted. Turning to the students, who were already seated and waiting for the lecture to begin, he called upon the guilty party to leave the room in-stantly. Rabbi Judah's most gifted pupil, Rabbi Chiya, was horrified by his teacher's behavior. How could the great man embarrass one of the students by making him identify himself publicly? In order to protect the guilty party's identity and teach Rabbi Judah a lesson at the same time, Rabbi Chiya stood up and left the room. As he did so, all the other

students stood up in unison and quietly filed out after him. Standing alone in front of the empty classroom, Rabbi Judah understood how inappropriately he had behaved.

Rabbi Chiya was not the only one of Rabbi Judah Hanasi's students to teach him an important lesson. One year there was a poor harvest in Palestine, resulting in food shortages. Rabbi Judah Hanasi was a wealthy man, with more than enough food in his warehouses to satisfy the needs of his household. He was not stingy—he did want to help the hungry—but he was an intellectual snob, with no respect for uneducated people. So he decided to provide food only to the educated, having no intention of rewarding the ignorant.

All the rabbi's students were of course pleased to learn that they would not go hungry, but some were not pleased by his prejudice against the uneducated. One student, Rabbi Jonathan ben Amram, became deter-mined to try to open his teacher's eyes.

Rabbi Judah's practice was to interview each applicant for food to find out whether he was in fact worthy of aid. One day a young man he had not seen before showed up and asked the rabbi for something to eat. The rabbi did not know he was talking to Rabbi Jonathan in disguise. When Rabbi Judah told the applicant that he should not expect assistance unless he knew some Torah, Rabbi Jonathan claimed that he was not a learned man. But the younger rabbi went on to say that he could not understand why the great rabbi should not treat him with the same kindness he would show a hungry dog or cat.

This simple argument—especially from an uneducated person—had its

effect on Rabbi Judah Hanasi. Without another word, he had a meal prepared for the young man. He also had some food packed up for the young stranger to take home with him. Later on, however, Rabbi Judah reflected on what he had done and regretted having bent his rule of giving food only to the educated. He expressed his feelings to a group of his students. One student expressed a suspicion that the young stranger was really a fellow student aiming to teach the Nasi what he should have already known, that it is wrong to use knowledge of the Torah for personal advantage. Rabbi Judah Hanasi called for an investigation of the incident. When he learned the truth of the matter, he agreed to open his warehouse to all the hungry, without questioning them first about their level of education.

Perhaps Rabbi Judah Hanasi's willingness to learn from others contrib-uted to the reverence he was accorded. So greatly was he respected that he is often called in the Talmud either simply "Rabbi" (my master or teacher) or "our holy Rabbi." He earned the adjective *holy* not only for his brilliance but also because his conduct served as an example that taught people the ways of the Torah. As the story of his death indicates, Rabbi Judah Hanasi was compared to the Holy Ark—the cabinet in every synagogue in which the Torah scrolls are stored.

During his last days, as Rabbi Judah Hanasi lay in his bed, suffering from a terrible illness, the other rabbis urged everyone to fast and pray. The rabbis themselves surrounded the great man's house and offered prayers. Influenced by the ancient Roman belief that the bearer of bad news somehow shared the guilt for whatever deed he reported, the rabbis also decreed that whoever announced the death of Rabbi Judah Hanasi would be stabbed with a sword.

Rabbi Judah's housekeeper went up to the roof of his house and prayed: "The immortals want Rabbi to join them in Heaven, while we mortals want Rabbi to stay with us on earth. May it be God's will that we mortals may have our way." But when the housekeeper came down from the roof and went into her employer's bedroom, she saw how desperately ill he was and realized that he would not recover. She then returned to the roof and offered a different prayer: "May it be God's will that the immortals may have their way." When the housekeeper looked down from the roof, she saw that the rabbis below were still praying. She felt that their prayers would merely prolong Rabbi Judah's agony.

On the roof near her were some jars. She lifted one and threw it to the ground below. At the sound of the jar's fall, the rabbis stopped praying for a moment. It was at that very moment that Rabbi Judah Hanasi died. Now that their concentration had been broken, the rabbis sent a delegate into the house to check on the rabbi's condition. When he saw that the great rabbi was dead, as a sign of mourning he followed ancient Jewish practice and tore his coat. But remembering the rabbis' warning about the fate of the person who reported Rabbi Judah's death, he was afraid to announce the news.

The delegate therefore returned to the rabbis and spoke in this way: "The angels and the mortals were playing tug-of-war with the Holy Ark. The angels were stronger than the mortals. The Holy Ark now lies in the angels' hands."

The rabbis then asked the delegate, "Is Rabbi Judah Hanasi dead?"

"You yourselves have said so," answered the man. "I did not report the news."

Rabbi Judah Hanasi's body was buried in Bet Shearim, in northern Israel, where 20th-century archaeologists have now discovered hundreds of tombs as well as a synagogue. Like a synagogue's Holy Ark, Rabbi Judah Hanasi stored the Torah within himself. But also like the Holy Ark, which can be opened so that the words of the Torah may be made known, Rabbi Judah Hanasi brought the Torah closer to his generation and to those that followed. By editing the Mishnah, he did more than summarize the oral Torah as it had developed until his time. He also laid the foundation for the Talmud, which became as important as the Bible itself.

FURTHER READING

Bader, Gershom. *The Jewish Spiritual Heroes: The Lives and Works of the Rabbinical Teachers from the Beginning of the Great Synagogue to the Final Completion of the Talmud: Seven Centuries of Jewish Thought*. Vol. 1. New York: Pardes, n.d.

Guttmann, Alexander. "The Patriarch Judah I—His Birth and His Death: A Glimpse into the Chronology of the Talmudic Period." In *Origins of Judaism: History of the Jews in the Second Century of the Common Era*. Edited by Jacob Neusner and William Scott Green. Vol. 7. New York: Garland, 1990.

Karp, Deborah. *Heroes of Jewish Thought*. New York: Ktav, 1965.

Pasachoff, Naomi, and Robert J. Littman. "Judah the Prince and the Redaction of the Mishnah." In *Jewish History in 100 Nutshells*. Northvale, N.J.: Aronson, 1995.

Saadia Gaon

PHILOSOPHER OF REASON

From the end of the 6th century until the middle of the 11th, the spiritual leaders of world Jewry were the heads of two famous academies in Babylonia, one at Sura and the other at Pumbedita. The leader of each academy was called Gaon, meaning "excellency." Even though the office no longer exists, in modern Hebrew the word *gaon* has retained the meaning of "genius." Saadia was a gaon in both senses—a genius who was also a spiritual leader of the world's Jews.

Although little is known about Saadia's early life in Egypt, it is certain that before leaving that country at the age of 23 he had already written a Hebrew dictionary and a major work disproving the views of a breakaway Jewish sect. Judging from the wide variety of subjects in which he went on to do trailblazing work, it is safe to say that he had thorough training in both religious and secular subjects.

Saadia Gaon helped shape Jewish tradition in two main ways. First, he used his vast knowledge and deeply held convictions not only to promote scholarship but also to strengthen the world Jewish community. Second, he laid the foundation for a long line of Jewish thinkers who would argue that there is no conflict between Jewish beliefs and human reason.

Saadia's *Book of Beliefs and Opinions* was written in Arabic and translated into other languages including Hebrew.

In Saadia's day three different forces threatened to splinter the Jewish community: the attraction of Islamic culture; the attitude toward Jewish tradition of a sect, or breakaway group, called Karaism; and the rivalry between the Jewish scholars of Palestine and those of Babylonia. Saadia was born in 882, about 250 years after the death of Muhammad, the founder of the Muslim, or Islamic, religion. During that period, millions of Arabic-speaking Muslims living in the Middle East, North Africa, and Spain developed a vibrant culture based on the works of ancient Greek philosophers and scientists. Many Jews living in the midst of this thriving culture were strongly attracted to it. To them, Judaism began to seem a relic of the past, whereas all the exciting new cultural developments appeared to be products of Islam. Some abandoned Judaism altogether, but others groped for ways to strengthen their faith.

Saadia addressed the needs of his Arabic-speaking fellow Jews in several ways. He translated the Bible into Arabic and wrote an Arabic biblical commentary that helped answer some of the religious and philosophical concerns of his audience. He helped make it easier for intellectually struggling Jews to find answers about Jewish law in several books he wrote on single topics, such as the dietary laws. He also compiled an Arabic prayer book, which included the laws governing prayers as well as background information about the history and significance of individual prayers. Saadia recognized that many Jews were fascinated by modern studies of the Arabic language and its grammar and was aware that Jewish scholars had ignored those fields. Thus, in his Hebrew dictionary, which was the first, and his pioneering study of Hebrew grammar, he set out to prove that Jewish scholarship was just as capable of responding to contemporary interests as was Islamic culture.

If Arabic culture posed a threat to Judaism by hinting that it was not up-to-date, Karaism's challenge came from a different direction. Karaism, whose name derives from the Hebrew word for "Scriptures," claimed that the only authentic source of Judaism was the written Torah, the five books of Moses. Karaites, as members of this sect were called, rejected the oral Torah, including the Talmud, the basic text of traditional Judaism. They claimed that the oral Torah had been fabricated by the rabbis and in no way represented God's intent. Previously an observant Jew had had to know the laws of the Talmud in addition to the content of the Bible, but all a Karaite needed to master was the Bible. Many Jews were attracted to this new, less demanding form of Judaism. Although other sects had developed among the Jews of the Islamic world, Karaism became the most popular.

Saadia was alarmed by the Karaites' belief. He was convinced that unless Jewish scholars could reinterpret their traditions in the light of each age's new needs, Judaism would be unable to respond to modern life and would ultimately die. From his perspective, no matter what the Karaites claimed, the Talmud and the later works of the oral Torah were the very means by which Judaism could keep itself in step with new developments in the outside world. To combat the Karaite threat, Saadia wrote several works specifically aimed at disproving their views, and he included arguments against Karaism in many of his other works. (Although he was a great authority on the Talmud, in his major work he quoted directly from the Talmud only 29 times, because he wanted to use the Karaites' own weapons to destroy their arguments.)

> *"Diversity and change can take place in bodies and their accidents only, but the Creator of all bodies and accidents is above diversity and change."*
>
> —from *Book of Beliefs and Opinions* (935–37)

Saadia also used his great depth of knowledge to keep the Jewish world from splintering over a dispute within its orthodox community. The disagreement arose when a Palestinian scholar argued with the leaders of Babylonian Jewry about the date when the Passover holiday would fall in the year 921. The unity of world Jewry was threatened by the prospect of Jews in various parts of the world celebrating the holiday on different days. Saadia used his knowledge of mathematics and astronomy to uncover the flaws in the Palestinian's claims and helped avoid a potential crisis.

However much Saadia's scholarship served to unify Judaism in his own time, he remains even better known as an outstanding Jewish philosopher. His greatest work, whose title translates as *Book of Beliefs and Opinions*, created the framework for a major tradition of Jewish thought that argues that Judaism and human reason do not conflict with one another but are simply different ways of approaching the truth. Keenly aware that many Jews of his day were assailed by profound doubts, Saadia wrote this book to provide them a sort of spiritual lifeline. As he said, "I saw men who were submerged in seas of doubt and covered by the waters of confusion, and there was no diver to raise them from the depths and no swimmer to take hold of their hands and bring them ashore." Saadia assumed that responsibility, claiming that it was his "duty and obligation to help them and guide them toward the truth."

According to Saadia, it is every Jew's duty to put the basic beliefs of Judaism to the test of reason, which is just as valuable a source of truth as the Torah. In fact, he argued, wherever the Torah and reason seem to conflict, a Jew must interpret the text to figure out what its real meaning is. For example, Saadia's emphasis on reason led him to question the concept that the Jews were the "chosen people," a doctrine that would

disturb later Jewish thinkers. To Saadia it was unreasonable to believe that the God who created all human beings in the divine image would favor one group at the expense of all others. To square this belief with his understanding of the role of reason, Saadia reinterpreted the term "chosen people." In his view, the relationship between God and the Jews is no more loving than that between God and any other group of people. But Jews *feel* as if they are God's chosen ones, simply because they cherish God's goodness so intensely.

A central aspect of Saadia's philosophy was his belief in free will, the concept that human beings make their own choices in life. According to Saadia, the authority of the Torah does not rest primarily on the fact that it was transmitted by God. Even more important was the willingness of the Jewish people to accept the Torah at Mount Sinai, where they declared, "All that the Lord has spoken we shall do" (Exodus 19:8). In the same way, a Jew decides daily whether to be governed by the Torah's laws. With such arguments, Saadia's *Book of Beliefs and Opinions* doubtless helped many Jews of his day feel that practicing Judaism was something that reasonable people could do without embarrassment.

Ironically, the same man whose scholarship and principles helped preserve the unity of world Jewry also disrupted the peace of his own community for a number of years. The problem arose out of a dispute between Saadia and the man who appointed him to the office of gaon—the exilarch, or "leader of the exiled." (The Babylonian Jews were known as "the exiled," because their presence in that country dated back to their expulsion from Israel in 586 B.C.E., when the Babylonian king destroyed the First Temple in Jerusalem and took many Jews captive.) While the gaon was a spiritual leader, the exilarch was considered the highest political figure in the Babylonian

Jewish community. The Muslim king of Babylonia appointed the exilarch to maintain law and order, collect taxes, and represent the Jews in court. It was also the exilarch's responsibility to appoint the gaons of Sura and Pumbedita.

In 928, the exilarch David ben Zakkai named Saadia the gaon of the academy at Sura. (Saadia thus became the only gaon who was not a native-born Babylonian.) Because ben Zakkai had been warned that Saadia could be difficult to get along with, he made Saadia promise never to oppose him. The relationship between the two men remained peaceful for a few years until the exilarch made an official decision whose terms would benefit him financially. The decision could not be put into effect, however, until the gaons of Pumbedita and Sura signed a formal document. The gaon of Pumbedita signed without hesitation, but Saadia believed that the exilarch's behavior was inappropriate and even immoral. He therefore refused to sign the document, despite the pressure exerted on him by ben Zakkai. The situation worsened when ben Zakkai's son visited Saadia, threatened to use physical force if his father's orders were not obeyed, and Saadia threw him out of his house.

Ben Zakkai responded by appointing another scholar to replace Saadia as gaon of Sura. Not to be outdone, Saadia then claimed that ben Zakkai had lost the authority to serve as exilarch and named another man to serve in his stead. For two years the Babylonian Jewish community was in turmoil, with two contenders for the offices of exilarch and gaon of Sura, each backed by a different group of prominent Jews. Finally, ben Zakkai convinced the king to remove Saadia from office. His forced retirement turned out in the long run to be beneficial to Judaism as a whole, because it gave Saadia the opportunity to write his *Book of Beliefs and Opinions*.

In 937 a third party made peace between ben Zakkai and Saadia, who once again became the unchallenged gaon of Sura. Three years later ben Zakkai died, followed within the year by his son. Aware that the man who had once threatened him with force had now left behind an orphaned son, Saadia raised the exilarch's grandchild as if he were his own. The man who shaped Jewish tradition by stressing its foundation in reason and its openness to learning of all kinds thus set a personal example for future generations: there is no room for grudges when the future of a child is at stake.

In his *Book of Beliefs and Opinions* Saadia wrote that "the wise care tenderly for wisdom and feel for it as members of the same family are attached to one another." Saadia combined his love of wisdom with his love for the family of Israel—the Jewish people in its entirety.

FURTHER READING

Karp, Deborah. "Saadia Gaon." In *Heroes of Jewish Thought*. New York: Ktav, 1965.

Malter, Henry. *Saadia Gaon: His Life and Works*. Philadelphia: Jewish Publication Society, 1921.

Pasachoff, Naomi. "Saadia Gaon." In *Great Jewish Thinkers: Their Lives and Work*. West Orange, N.J.: Behrman House, 1992.

Weiss-Rosmarin, Trude. "Saadia Gaon." In *Great Jewish Personalities in Ancient and Medieval Times*. Edited by Simon Noveck. Washington, D.C.: B'nai B'rith, 1959.

LINKS IN THE CHAIN

Saadia Gaon

BORN
882
El Faiyum, Egypt

Died
942
Sura, Babylonia

EDUCATION
Studied both the Jewish canon and secular subjects, including mathematics, astronomy, and Greek and Arab philosophy

ACCOMPLISHMENTS
Only nonnative-born Babylonian to serve as gaon (a spiritual leader of the Babylonian Jews); wrote the *Book of Beliefs and Opinions* (935–37), which argued that Judaism is a religion based on reason; helped preserve traditional Judaism by challenging the Karaite sect; proved to Arabic-speaking Jews that Judaism was a vibrant culture

Samuel Hanagid

LIVING IN TWO WORLDS

Throughout history, military leaders have become statesmen. In recent years, some have turned to writing their memoirs following the conclusion of their military careers. But few figures have managed to combine simultaneously the roles of statesman, soldier, scholar, and poet. Samuel Hanagid was one man who did.

The word *nagid* in Hebrew means "leader," a title Samuel gained because he was not only a leader of the Jews of Spain but also the power behind the throne of the Islamic kingdom of Granada. Samuel Hanagid may be the first Jew to contribute as much to the non-Jewish world in which he lived as to the Jewish community he represented. Moreover, he became a leader in both worlds not because of family connections but because of his talents. His rise to power convinced him that education is the key to success in the world. He also believed that a person must be active

A partial view of Granada's beautiful palace and fortress, the Alhambra. Some say that Samuel Hanagid's son Joseph built the Alhambra's oldest sections.

in the pursuit of worldly success and not rely on God alone. Nevertheless, he was a practicing Jew and a rabbi of many achievements who used his powerful position in court to promote the interests of his fellow Jews.

As a Jew with connections to the crown, Hanagid was not unique in Spain. In his lifetime, that country was split up into many small principalities, each controlled by a Muslim warlord. Lacking confidence in the loyalty of their fellow Muslims, some of whom they suspected of seeking the throne themselves, these warlords often turned to talented Jews for help in running their kingdoms. Hanagid stood out as the most successful of these Jewish courtiers.

Although Hanagid rose to prominence in Granada, a city in southeastern Spain, he was born in Córdoba, in the south-central part of the country. From the 8th century onward, when the Moors—Muslims from northwest Africa—seized control of the country, Córdoba had been the capital of Muslim Spain.

Until the age of 20, Samuel lived a peaceful life in that capital. His wealthy family provided him with an excellent, well-rounded education. Not only did he master Jewish studies under the supervision of scholars, he also received training in mathematics, Greek philosophy, and astronomy. And, like other children from wealthy Jewish families, he studied several languages. In addition to these subjects, his teachers saw that he was exposed to the Koran, the sacred text of the Muslims. They also helped him master both Arabic calligraphy, or penmanship, and that language's literary style. Later in life, he would attribute his success to his training in writing. In one of his books of poetry, he advised others to "hold on to a pen, for through a pen a fortune will be gathered." He at one point even expressed gratitude to his own pen,

"because through you, my right hand became filled with fortune and honor."

Hanagid believed, however, that his success was due not only to his education but also to the hand of God. During his childhood in Córdoba, Samuel experienced a nighttime vision that convinced him that God had chosen him for a great future. As he lay in bed, the angels Michael and Gabriel appeared to him, assuring him that God would protect him. As an adult, he described this childhood vision in poetry.

In 1013, Samuel had his first encounter with serious trouble when groups of Muslim warriors from North Africa invaded Córdoba, seeking to displace the established rulers. With many others, Samuel fled the war-torn city. After wandering about for a while, he settled in the city of Málaga, which was at that time part of the Muslim kingdom of Granada. There he became a shopkeeper, selling spices. As fate would have it, his store was located near the palace of the vizier (a high official in certain Muslim countries), who served as prime minister to Habbus, king of Granada. The vizier's head servants often needed to send letters to their employer when he was on business in Granada, as the capital city was also called. Some of the vizier's servants who did business in Samuel's spice shop were so impressed with his penmanship and elegant Arabic speech that they asked him to compose their letters to the vizier. When the vizier learned who the author of the letters was, he approached Samuel and offered him the post of private secretary and adviser.

Some years later, in 1027, the vizier fell deathly ill. On his deathbed he confided in King Habbus that for some time now the kingdom of Granada had been run according to the wisdom of the Jew Samuel. When the vizier died, Habbus made Samuel his close adviser. In that same year,

Samuel Hanagid writes to his son Joseph from the battlefield. In 1066, ten years after Samuel's death, Joseph was murdered and the Jews of Granada massacred.

the Jewish community acknowledged his leadership by giving him the title Nagid.

After Habbus himself died, in 1038, Hanagid rose to even higher rank. Habbus's older son, Badis, succeeded his father on the throne and appointed Hanagid to the office of vizier. As such his responsibilities included the collection of taxes and the administration of both foreign and domestic policies. Badis also named Hanagid his military chief. Until Hanagid's death nearly 20 years later, he steered Granada through complicated political entanglements and numerous military confrontations.

Hanagid's rise to power made him a very wealthy man. According to some scholars, he and his oldest son, Joseph, were the earliest builders of Granada's magnificent Alhambra palace and lived there themselves.

But his new political influence and wealth did not blind him to what he saw as his obligations toward the Jewish community of Spain. In fact, he believed that God had selected him to protect the Jews. With this responsibility ever in mind, he accepted the moral obligation of the powerful to act with generosity. For that reason, he became a supporter of Jewish poets, scholars, and sages. Typical was his hiring of poor scribes to copy scholarly books—printing had not yet been invented—and then distributing the copies to other poor scholars and students.

Samuel Hanagid was more than a benefactor of the Jews of Spain, however. He was also an intellectual giant who made significant contributions in at least four fields: legal scholarship, biblical studies, investigations of Hebrew grammar, and Hebrew poetry.

Like other great rabbis and Jewish community leaders, Hanagid taught the Talmud, the vast oral treasury of the Torah. He also wrote an introduction to the Talmud. Unlike any other Jewish legal scholar, he combined his scholarship with a military career. When he was captured during a battle in 1049, he vowed that if he survived he would publish a book summarizing Jewish law, which he did. This work, *Sefer Hilkheta Gavrata* (the Book of Major Laws), became widely used. In it, Hanagid included decisions made by rabbis after the time of the Talmud in addition to the earlier decisions recorded in the Talmud itself.

From the time the Babylonian Talmud was compiled in the 5th century, Jews around the world had considered the leaders of the rabbinical academies in Babylonia to be the final authorities in matters of Jewish law. A striking feature of Hanagid's legal work, however, is his claim that the Spanish Jews need not look beyond their own borders for help in resolving Jewish legal problems. As he wrote, "Do not hold a man in disdain because his country is in the west, and [do not scorn] all who rush to the gates [of his academy]." Even though Hanagid believed that his own scholarly abilities equaled those of the Babylonian rabbis, in 1038 he commemorated the death of the 99-year-old leader of the Babylonian Jewish community with a respectful funeral song, or elegy. In it he noted that although the prominent Babylonian leader had died childless, he had left spiritual children "all over the lands of Islam and Christendom."

Samuel Hanagid's religious investigations also led him to write a dictionary of biblical Hebrew, of which only a few fragments remain. His biblical research aroused his interest in Hebrew grammar, thus involving him in pioneering scholarly debates about the structure of the language.

Hanagid undoubtedly made his greatest contribution to Jewish literature as a poet. He was not the first ever to write Hebrew poetry with nonreligious themes, but he was the first great Hebrew poet of the period. What is truly remarkable about his 1,750 surviving poems is the ease with which he moves between the worlds of religious piety and scholarship and those of wine, parties, song, and battle. Hanagid valued poetry highly and believed its study should be part of a liberal education. Not only did he train his sons and daughter to study poetry, but there is evidence that his daughter wrote fine Arabic poetry before dying at an early age.

In short, Samuel Hanagid believed that educated Jews should participate fully in both the Jewish world and the general society around them. In one of his poems he praised the ideal scholar as one who mastered not only "Scripture and faith / Which are set high above wisdoms all" but also "the wisdom of Greeks / And . . . Arab learning as well." In another poem he encouraged Jews to follow a schedule that many other rabbis might question:

> Do not spend the entirety of your
>   days in His service,
> Rather make time for God, and
>   periods of time for yourselves,
> Give him half the day, and the other
>   half for your own activities,
> And during your nights, give no
>   respite to wine.

Samuel Hanagid was not alone in striving to combine a life of Jewish commitment with full participation in the world at large. Many Jews who lived in Islamic Spain tried similarly to blend the best of both cultures, and the period was a highly productive era in Jewish cultural and religious life. In general, there was a tolerant atmosphere that encouraged Jewish involvement in the Muslim world. But tolerance could go only so far. Samuel Hanagid's political enemies often

Samuel Hanagid

BORN

993
Córdoba, Spain

DIED

1056
Andalusia, Spain

EDUCATION

Studied the Talmud and later Jewish law with the greatest authorities in Spain and also had a thorough general education, including training in languages, Arabic calligraphy and literary style, mathematics and astronomy, and the Koran

ACCOMPLISHMENTS

Vizier and head of the army of Granada, Spain; used his secular position to promote Jewish interests; wrote an introduction to the Talmud, a summary of Jewish law, a biblical dictionary, and studies of Hebrew grammar; was the first great Hebrew poet in medieval Spain; used his wealth to support other poets, scholars, and sages

> *"Swiftly we engraved on their flesh [the flesh of the enemies of Granada]*
> *Fine words with pens of iron*
> *With our arrows and spears*
> *Filling their bodies like quivers."*
>
> —from *Ben-Tehillim* (after 1038)

focused their attacks on him on his religion instead. For example, the first war he waged as King Badis's minister of defense was provoked by the king and vizier of Almería, a kingdom southeast of Granada. The Almeríans called on all Muslim rulers in the region to join them in a battle to oust the "foreigner," whom they called "the Jewish king of Granada." Although the army of Granada won this war under Samuel Hanagid's leadership—which he considered a victory for the Jews—the anti-Jewish attacks continued. Finally, worn out from years of fighting throughout southern Spain, Samuel Hanagid died during a campaign in 1056.

Joseph, Samuel's oldest son, succeeded his father as King Badis's vizier. The hate campaign that had swirled around Samuel intensified. In 1066, a would-be courtier whom Joseph had not favored aroused a new wave of anti-Jewish sentiment in the region. Complaining that Jews were living lives of luxury while Muslims languished in poverty, the disappointed courtier called for the murder of Joseph and his kin. The campaign bore fruit. Joseph was murdered in December 1066, and the people of Granada turned against the substantial Jewish minority who had lived among them for centuries, massacring thousands. This was the first persecution of Jews in Muslim Spain.

In spite of the fate that befell his son and the Jews of the kingdom that he had so ably served, Samuel Hanagid remains a significant figure in Jewish history. One contemporary writer stops short of calling him the first modern Jew but, because of his ability to live successfully in two worlds, refers to him as the first "post-ancient" Jew. Since the days of Samuel Hanagid, Jews have been doing their best to live simultaneously in the Jewish world and the secular one.

FURTHER READING

Dozy, Reinhart. *Spanish Islam: A History of the Moslems in Spain*, 607–653. Translated by Francis Griffin Stokes. London: Chatto & Windus, 1913.

Halkin, Hillel. "The First Post-Ancient Jew." *Commentary*, September 1993, 43-50.

Rashi (Solomon ben Isaac)

A TEACHER FOR ALL TIME

I n our modern age of instant information, it may be hard to imagine studying from the same textbook that not only your grandparents used as schoolchildren but also your remote ancestors, centuries ago and in far-flung parts of the world. But many students of the basic texts of Judaism, from primary schools to universities, still use the commentaries written by the scholar known as Rashi, a French Jew who lived in the 11th century. His word-by-word and line-by-line interpretations of the Bible and the Talmud became popular in his lifetime and are still an important part of Jewish studies throughout the world. In fact, the Bible and the Talmud—the two most important works of Jewish literature—are almost never studied seriously without a careful reading of Rashi's commentaries. Rashi shaped Jewish tradition by making it possible for Jews from all walks of life and backgrounds to study the major works of Judaism on their own.

Rashi was not the birth name of this major figure in Jewish tradition. His name comes from the initials of the words **Ra**bbi **Sh**elomo, son of **I**saac. ("Shelomo" is the Hebrew form of Solomon.) Little is known about Rashi's father, Isaac, but a colorful legend describes him as a fitting father for his illustrious son.

According to the legend, before Rashi's birth, Isaac was known for owning a certain precious jewel. The only jewel of equal value adorned the eye of an idol belonging to the emperor of the land. Somehow the emperor's jewel disappeared. Desperate to replace it, the emperor sent a messenger to Isaac, offering to pay whatever price he wanted for his jewel. Rather than being tempted by the offer, Isaac was dismayed: he felt that by surrendering the jewel to the emperor, he would be furthering the practice of idol worship.

A page from the 1475 edition of Rashi's commentary on the Bible, the first known Hebrew work to be printed. Schoolchildren and scholars alike still turn to Rashi for help in studying the Bible.

> *"Learning is hidden within the heart of the wise man, and an understanding student comes and draws it out from within him."*

> —from *Commentary to Proverbs 20:5*

While en route to the emperor's court by ship, Isaac saw a way out of the dilemma. Pretending to show off the stone to his fellow passengers, he let the jewel slip from his hand, as if by accident, into the sea. Isaac acted as if he were crushed by the loss, so that when the emperor's agent met the ship in port, the other passengers described the terrible "accident" to him. The emperor, though disappointed, did not seek to punish Isaac, who boarded the next ship home.

Upon his return, the legend relates, he was met by the prophet Elijah, who assured him that God understood Isaac's motive and would reward him by giving him an even greater jewel: within the year, Isaac's wife would give birth to a son, whose contribution to his people would exceed the value of jewels. True to the prophecy, exactly a year later Isaac's wife gave birth to Rashi, who was destined to write the most important commentaries of all time on the Bible and the Talmud.

In all likelihood, Isaac died when Rashi was still a boy. The family still saw to it that from the age of five or six Rashi received the same elementary training in Jewish studies that was customary for the Jewish boys of his time. Although he had no formal education in secular studies, Rashi's hometown, Troyes, provided a good education for any alert child. This ancient city southeast of Paris was a center of business and commerce where 100 or so Jewish families mingled on friendly terms with some 10,000 non-Jewish neighbors. From the activity that he saw around him, Rashi learned much about different types of farming and business. His own family earned its keep from vineyards they owned and worked. Rashi increased his secular knowledge when he left Troyes for several years to study at the German cities of Worms and Mainz, nearby centers of Jewish learning. In Worms, Rashi attended a Jewish academy that attracted the sons of German and French Jews involved in international trade. From his classmates Rashi learned about everything from the coining of money to shipbuilding.

Unlike most of his classmates, Rashi had no father to support him while he was at school. Since he had married at a young age and already had a family of his own by the time he left France, he knew he would not have the luxury of spending as much time studying as he would have liked. As a result, he was determined to learn quickly as much as possible. The traditional method of study in the Jewish academies of the day was to repeat over and over both the basic texts and the teachers' explanations of them. Rashi decided that taking notes would serve his needs more effectively. Other students took notes too, but theirs were often just sketchy outlines designed to help them recall what they had already committed to memory. Rashi knew that his notes would have to be much more detailed if they were to cover all the knowledge available to him in the academies.

There was one problem with this method of study. Today the paper students use for taking notes is inexpensive, but the parchment used in Rashi's day was costly for a person on a tight budget. Therefore, Rashi had to learn to summarize the teachers' detailed explanations in brief sentences in concise Hebrew, the common language of educated Jews, wherever they might live. The clear, succinct Hebrew style that Rashi developed in this way was later to contribute to the lasting popularity of his commentaries.

Although Rashi spent several years away from his young family while studying in the academies of Worms and Mainz, he returned to Troyes when possible to spend holidays with them. During one of these visits, his mother's sudden death created a family crisis. Rashi's mother had been managing the family business, but now she was gone. Rashi understood that his student days were over. He would from now on have to devote much of his time to grape growing and wine producing.

Rashi missed the intellectual excitement of the academies very keenly. The small Jewish community in Troyes earned its livelihood from business or agriculture. He found few if any local friends with whom he could share the excitement of the Bible and Talmud studies that he pursued on his own in his moments of leisure. To find an outlet for the insights his private study sessions often yielded, he wrote them down. Eventually, these notes written in solitude would find an enormous audience of readers.

On his return home from the academies, Rashi had no official position within the Jewish community of Troyes. Little by little, however, he became one of its leading figures. At first his reputation was only local, but after a number of years a group of students and other scholars began to grow up around him. Among the most outstanding of the group were Rashi's sons-in-law and, later, his grandsons. Rashi had no sons, but each of his three daughters married a scholar, and the children of those marriages became among the most important Jewish scholars of the next century. Rashi soon developed a reputation as the head of an important center of Jewish learning. Rashi was thrilled to be in the classroom once again. He found, however, that the new exchange of ideas in the classroom required him to modify his earlier notes. But even now he could not spend all his time as a teacher. The need to work in the vineyards occupied much of his time. As a result, he taught his students to use his notes as a substitute during his absences. Without intending to do so, Rashi was developing a new method of teaching and learning. Knowledge of the Talmud, which before had been transmitted only orally, could now be gained as well by reading Rashi's extensive commentaries.

During the last decade of Rashi's life, a tragic occurrence transformed his school into the most important Jewish academic center in Germany and France. In the autumn of 1095, Pope Urban II called for a crusade, or war to recapture the Holy Land from the Muslims who controlled it. The pope's call led to the First Crusade (1096–99), which culminated in the Christian recovery of Jerusalem. But on the way to the Holy Land from Europe, over-zealous crusaders massacred the Jews of Germany's Rhine Valley. In the process they also wiped out the centers of Jewish learning in Worms and Mainz, where Rashi and countless other scholars had received their training.

When the survivors found them-selves suddenly bereft of teachers, Rashi's academy in Troyes attracted many new students. Moreover, Rashi's commentar-ies found a new audience in the countless students who were now without teachers. To make home study easier for those who now had no other way to study the Talmud, Rashi once again revised his commentary to make it even clearer and more concise. This final version, which took root throughout western Europe, changed the method of Talmud study for all time. Half a century after the First Crusade, when Muslim fundamentalists destroyed the great Jewish centers of Islamic Spain, Rashi's commentary on the Talmud also enabled the Spanish-speaking students there to continue their studies effectively without teachers.

Rashi's commentary on the Talmud, like his commentary on the Bible, is not an independent book that can be picked up and read from cover to cover by itself. In fact, neither com-mentary is meant to be read on its own, without the particular text it was written to clarify. Rashi intended his comments not to substitute for the text but to help readers find their own way to its meaning.

Reading the Talmud is difficult for the beginner. Its core, the Mishnah, is written in Hebrew, but the discussions of the rabbis about the Mishnah are written in Ara-maic, without punctuation. Jews in Rashi's time had not spoken Aramaic for centu-ries. In addition, many of the technical processes, tools, and customs described in the Talmud were no longer familiar to readers. As a result, Rashi aimed to simplify the student's entry into the world of the Talmud in a number of ways.

Writing in clear Hebrew, Rashi explained every difficult term, sometimes using a French word when he could find no precise Hebrew equivalent. He drew on his secular knowledge of geography, technology, and various professions to provide the background needed to comprehend many passages. In the absence of punctuation marks, he indicated in words whether a sentence was a question or an exclamation. In general, he sensed which issues would confuse students and attempted to eliminate potential uncertainty by adding a few words. He also reassured students with comments like "this will be discussed below" or "eventually the text will raise the obvious objection." Although he rarely summarized the final decisions in a Talmudic debate, he helped the student develop the skill needed to find them in the text. In brief, Rashi's commentary made it possible for students to approach and master the Talmud with little additional assistance.

LINKS IN THE CHAIN

Rashi (Solomon ben Isaac)

BORN

Around 1040
Troyes, France

DIED

July 13, 1105
Troyes, France

EDUCATION

Introduced to Jewish studies as a child in Troyes; as a young man studied at the great German centers of Jewish learning in Worms (where he was also exposed to secular knowledge) and Mainz

ACCOMPLISHMENTS

Wrote the most influential and most enduring commentaries on both the Bible and the Talmud, the two most important texts of Judaism, making it possible for Jews over the ages to study these texts on their own without a teacher

If Rashi's commentary on the Talmud earned him the gratitude of its scholars over the ages, his interpretation of the Bible earned him the love and admiration of simpler Jews and scholars alike. In the academies in Worms and Mainz, Rashi had learned a principle that guided him in his attempts to explain the Bible. According to this philosophy, the words of the Bible convey different truths to different audiences. No word can be ignored. Each word and verse has a literal meaning, based on its grammar. The audience for the literal meaning includes the least sophisticated people. But most verses also have additional meanings that can be grasped by those with a deeper level of understanding. Rashi's Bible commentary became a masterpiece of Hebrew literature by combining these two levels of interpretation. From the interpretations of the Bible made by the rabbis of the Talmud, he selected those that seemed most appropriate for the Jews of his day but avoided those that did not fit in well with the literal interpretation. As he wrote in commenting on a verse in the book of Genesis, "As for me, I am only concerned with the literal meaning of the Scriptures and with such stories as explain the biblical passages in a manner that fits in with them."

Rashi's commentary on the Bible provided even uneducated Jews with access to the works of the great rabbis of the Talmud. For those verses of the Bible that describe the various laws, Rashi summarized the gist of each law. He also drew attention to the close connections between the practice of Jewish law and the texts on which the laws were based. For example, Jews knew that the dietary laws of Judaism prohibited them from eating, cooking, or selling meat and dairy products together. In Rashi's commentary to Exodus 23:19, those who were unfamiliar with the Talmud could learn the biblical basis for these three related laws. The verse from Genesis includes the injunction "Do not seethe a kid in its mother's milk." Rashi explains that this verse is only one of three places in the Bible where the same law appears: "Once for the purpose of prohibiting the eating of meat-food with milk-food, once to prohibit us from deriving any other benefit (besides eating) from such mixture, and once to prohibit the boiling of meat with milk." He then indicates in parentheses the Talmudic references that explain these laws in detail.

For passages of the Bible that relate Jewish history, Rashi also included for his readers meaningful selections from the rabbis of the Talmud. For example, at the very beginning of the story of Noah—whom God saved from the Flood that wiped out the rest of humankind—the Bible calls Noah a "perfectly righteous" man. Later, however, God tells Noah that he and his family are being spared because he is a "righteous" man. Rashi calls to the reader's attention the slight difference in emphasis and explains it this way: "From this we may learn that only a part of a person's good qualities should be described in his presence (since here God is speaking to Noah and calls him only 'righteous'), but that in his absence the whole of his good qualities may be told (since when the Bible speaks about him in the earlier passage it calls him 'perfectly righteous')."

Thus, by reading the Bible with Rashi's explanations a reader who had never studied the Talmud could absorb much wisdom from the ancient rabbis. But Rashi, in presenting his commentaries on the Bible, also included many things to appeal to scholars. For example, he was one of the first European Jews to study the rules of grammar, and he opened the door for scholars and beginners alike to understand the workings of the Hebrew language.

Soon it became routine for Jews to begin their Bible studies by reading Rashi's commentaries on it along with the text. Even today in Jewish schools around the world, young children use special Bibles, printed with the Hebrew text at the top of the page and Rashi's explanations at the bottom. His work was valued so highly that in 1475, when the first Hebrew book in history was printed on a mechanical press, the work chosen was neither the Bible nor the Talmud but rather Rashi's explanation of the Torah. The typeface chosen by the printer was based on the Hebrew script then used by the Jews of Spain. Since that time, this distinctive typeface has been associated with Rashi, earning it the name "Rashi script."

Jews were not, however, the only ones to profit from Rashi's commentaries. Christian Bible scholars also learned a great deal from his studies, and the first translations of the Bible into German and English were influenced by Rashi's interpretations. He also made an unintended contribution to research in linguistics. The approximately 3,000 French words Rashi used in his commentaries provide a record of the language spoken in his time and thus remain a rich source for scholars of Old French. Thus, Rashi continues to educate in ways he never anticipated as a student more than 900 years ago, when financial difficulties first forced him to take notes.

FURTHER READING

Agus, I. A. "Rashi and His School." In The World History of the Jewish People. Edited by Cecil Roth. 2nd series: Medieval Period. Vol. 2, The Dark Ages: Jews in Christian Europe, 711–1096. New Brunswick, N.J.: Rutgers University Press, 1966.

Rashi Anniversary Volume. New York: American Academy for Jewish Research, 1941.

Blumenfield, Samuel M. "Rashi." In Great Jewish Personalities in Ancient and Medieval Times. Edited by Simon Noveck. Washington, D.C.: B'nai B'rith, 1959.

Federbush, Simon, ed. Rashi: His Teachings and Personality. New York: World Jewish Congress, 1958.

Liber, Maurice. Rashi. Translated by Adele Szold. Philadelphia: Jewish Publication Society, 1906.

Judah Halevi

A HARP FOR SONGS OF ZION

Judah Halevi's contribution to Jewish tradition was truly unique: he not only helped shape Jewish thought and the Hebrew prayer book but also influenced popular Israeli music.

More than 800 years before the state of Israel was created to provide a Jewish national homeland, Judah Halevi expressed the belief that Jews could find physical security and achieve spiritual creativity only in the land of Israel. He was convinced that the restoration of the Jews to their ancient homeland was a realistic possibility, not merely a fanciful dream. He was also the first in a line of Jewish thinkers who argued that Judaism is based on something more compelling than reason. Halevi claimed that reason alone cannot explain the close relationship between God and the individual Jew. Judaism, he believed, was based on revelation, God's self-disclosure to individuals and to the Jewish people over the course of history.

Besides being a poet and a thinker, Judah Halevi was also a physician. In his day, the practice of medicine appealed to many Jews. As long as the Jews lived scattered among the nations, governed by foreign rulers who themselves might be toppled and replaced, a profession like medicine made sense. A doctor could, after all, be useful to any ruler. And if forced to leave a given country, he could establish a practice in any country of refuge.

Whether or not such political concerns guided Halevi's choice of profession, neither politics nor the problems of the Jewish people figured much in the poetry he wrote as a young man. His works were instead about

A physician prepares a cough medicine in this illustration from a 13th-century Iraqi manuscript. Judah Halevi and Moses Maimonides were two outstanding Jewish philosophers of the Middle Ages who were also physicians.

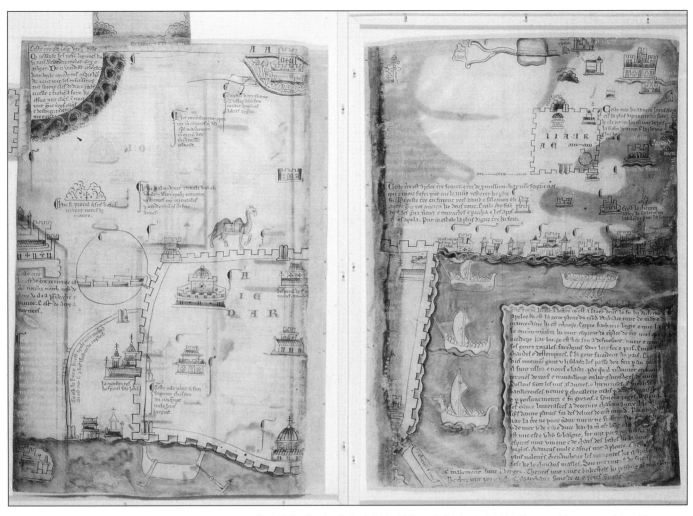

This 13th-century map of Jerusalem was drawn after Halevi's death in 1141. Although Halevi died in Egypt without reaching his goal of Zion, according to a folktale he was slain while kissing the stones of Jerusalem.

friendship, love, and wine. Outside events nevertheless transformed him from a poet celebrating life's pleasures to a man obsessed with the honor of his people.

When Muslims from North Africa conquered Spain in the early 8th century, the northernmost part of that nation remained in the hands of Christians, who established kingdoms there. Then, in the 11th and 12th centuries, these Spanish Christian kingdoms joined forces to wrest control of the country from the Muslims. In response, a new, more militant sect invaded from North Africa and established a harsh regime in southern Spain.

Although the Jews had flourished in Spain under tolerant Muslim rulers,

many Jews now became convinced that life under the Christians would be preferable to that under the new Muslim invaders. Many Jews therefore chose to fight with the Christian armies. The Christians welcomed their assistance—as long as the Christian military campaigns went well. But when the Muslims triumphed, the Christians often blamed the Jews, who were branded as traitors and attacked by Christian mobs. Among the victims of these mobs was the leader of the Jews of Castile, a Christian kingdom that had led the campaign against the Muslims. When Judah Halevi learned of the death of this Jewish leader and scholar, Solomon ibn Farissol, the news had a searing effect on him.

Judah Halevi now came to believe that Jewish life in Spain was doomed and that only by returning to the land of Israel could Jews lead meaningful lives. He expressed this new conviction in a series of poems celebrating the ancient Jewish homeland. Following a centuries-old custom, Halevi used the name of one of the hills in Jerusalem, Mount Zion, as a shorthand way of referring to the land of Israel as a whole. For that reason his 34 poems of longing for a return to Israel are called *Poems of Zion*. In these pieces he acknowledged that Jerusalem lay in ruins, but he expressed a belief that God would restore the city to its former glory.

Judah Halevi's focus on the land of Israel resulted in a new type of Hebrew poetry, and many poets after Halevi tried to mimic his treatment of the subject. His "Ode to Zion," the best known of the collection, is still read in Jewish congregations around the world on the ninth day of the Jewish month of Av, a fast day observed to commemorate the destruction of the First Temple in 586 B.C.E. and the Second Temple in 70 C.E.

In addition to his *Poems of Zion*, Judah Halevi wrote moving verses about his yearning for a closeness with God. Many of these poems became part of the prayer book of the Sephardim, as Jews of Spanish descent are called. Some also appear today in English translation in prayer books used in the United States. A major theme of Halevi's religious poems is his conviction that his close relationship with God has historical roots, dating back to the time when God gave the Hebrews the Torah at Mount Sinai. Halevi's faith is so deep that he feels as if he himself had been present there to experience God's revelation.

Judah Halevi also expressed his beliefs in a famous work of prose called *The Book of the Khazars*, named for a Turkish tribe living in present-day Ukraine. The book is often referred to as *The Kuzari*, from the Hebrew word for "Khazar." The members of this tribe converted to Judaism around the middle of the 8th century. Three centuries later, when Jews were despised by both Muslims and Christians, the mass conversion of the Khazars provided support for Halevi's argument that Judaism is superior. Indeed, the subtitle of *The Kuzari* describes the work as a "book of argument and proof in defense of the despised faith."

The Kuzari is presented in the form of a historical drama consisting of conversations between the Khazar king and representatives of Greek philosophy, Christianity, Islam, and Judaism. Each tries to prove to the king the merits of his own system of belief. But although the Khazars themselves were

an actual tribe whose defeat by the duke of Kiev in 965 is a matter of historical fact, there are no records of any such attempt to win over the Khazar king, and the arguments Halevi presents are his own.

In *The Kuzari* the representatives of Christianity and Islam both admit to the king that their religions are merely offshoots of Judaism. The book takes its greatest pains to argue against the claims of Greek philosophy, which Halevi saw as a real threat to Jewish belief. According to the Greek philosopher in the book, the use of reason does lead one to conclude that there could be no universe without a divine intelligence. He argues, however, that such a divine being cannot have any interest in human beings.

As a physician, Judah Halevi certainly believed that reason had a role to play in uncovering scientific mysteries. As a religious Jew, though, he rejected the idea that human reason could explain the laws of Judaism and the spiritual effects brought about by observing them. Thus the representative of Judaism in *The Kuzari* does not reject reason but merely expresses its limits. He tells the Khazar king, for instance, "Heaven forbid that there should be anything in the Torah to contradict that which is manifest or proved!" He nevertheless refuses to rely on reason to prove God's existence. Instead, he argues that Judaism is rooted above all in a historical event: God's revelation to the Hebrews at Mount Sinai.

Following that revelation, the prophets continued to experience God's presence. And even after the end of the period of prophecy, Jewish tradition taught—as it does to this day—that divine revelation was not a single event but one that each generation is called upon to witness. As a result, the Jewish thinker in *The Kuzari* says, "The whole of Israel . . . knew these things, first through personal experience, and afterward through an uninterrupted tradition,

Judah Halevi

BORN

Around 1075
Central or northern Spain

Died

1141
Egypt

EDUCATION

Mastered Jewish studies in various centers of Jewish learning in southern Spain and received professional training as a physician

ACCOMPLISHMENTS

Composed masterpieces of Hebrew poetry, including 34 "Poems of Zion"; author of *The Kuzari* (1130–40), a prose work in defense of Judaism

> "And Palestine has a special relation to the Land of Israel; pure life can be perfect only there."
>
> —from *The Kuzari* (1130–40)

which is equal to experience." Thus, the Jewish belief in God is not the result of logical argument but rather of personal contact, because the God of Judaism is directly involved in the lives of individuals and cares about their deeds.

In *The Kuzari*, Halevi also considers the powerlessness of the Jews in his own day. It is not a sign that God has rejected them, he asserts. Like a seed that may seem to be rotting in the earth but is actually taking root, the Jews only appear to be vanquished. The true meaning of their present suffering will someday be understood when people accept God's rule and follow his commandments.

At the end of *The Kuzari*, the Khazar king has been convinced by the arguments of the Jewish scholar and adopts Judaism on behalf of his subjects. Then, having successfully completed his mission, the Jewish scholar announces his intention to leave the Khazar kingdom and go to Jerusalem. The king tries to dissuade him, saying it is dangerous for a Jew to be in Zion now that it is in the hands of anti-Jewish Christians, and arguing that such a pilgrimage is unnecessary anyway. If one approaches God with a pure heart, he reasons, one can find God anywhere. But the Jewish scholar argues that only in the land of Israel can a Jew truly flourish. Furthermore, though the land may lie in ruins now, Jews can reverse that condition by moving to Zion: "Jerusalem can be rebuilt only when the children of Israel yearn for it to such an extent that they embrace her stones and dust."

Like his fictional Jewish scholar, Judah Halevi was also drawn toward

Zion, despite the arguments of friends and family. In 1140, assisted by a wealthy Egyptian Jew, Halevi set sail from Spain to Egypt. From there he hoped to travel overland to Jerusalem. In a number of poems he records the difficulties of the sea voyage and his conviction that a sea traveler with a belief in God, creator of the oceans, had no reason to fear. Halevi's ship eventually landed safely in Alexandria, where he was welcomed by the Jewish community. The local Jews tried to persuade him to settle there, but after some months he moved on to Cairo, where he was taken into the home of the leader of Egypt's Jews. The poems he wrote in Egypt reflect the powerful effect that this country, the site of many biblical miracles, had on him. They also make it clear, however, that his sights were still set on the land of Israel, which remained his ultimate goal. Evidently, Halevi never achieved that goal, for he died in Egypt in July 1141 and was mourned by the entire Jewish community.

In historical fact, Judah Halevi may have been prevented from fulfilling his life's dream. Legend nonetheless enabled him to do so, however tragic the outcome. In the late 19th century, the Hebrew poet Micah-Joseph Lebensohn and the German poet Heinrich Heine each published a version of the legend, rich in details. According to tradition, Halevi went to Jerusalem and followed the prescription of the Jewish scholar in *The Kuzari* for rebuilding the city: he knelt down to embrace its stones and dust. As he did so he began to recite his famous "Ode to Zion," the poem included in the synagogue service for the

ninth of Av. In the poem he compares his wails of sorrow over the destruction of Zion to the cries of jackals and his hopes for restoration to the sounds of a harp. During his recitation he was reportedly killed by an Arab horseman.

Whatever the actual circumstances of Judah Halevi's death, his literary statements about the importance of Zion have had a lasting impact on Jewish tradition. In June 1967, more than eight hundred years after Halevi's death, the state of Israel won a historic victory over its Arab enemies in the Six-Day War. During the fighting, Israeli soldiers succeeded in wresting the old city of Jerusalem from Arab control. To celebrate that event an Israeli singer, Naomi Shemer, wrote a song entitled "Jerusalem of Gold." The refrain of that popular song echoed Judah Halevi's words to Jerusalem in his "Ode to Zion": "I am a harp for your songs."

FURTHER READING

Halevi, Judah. *Selected Poems of Jehudah Halevi*. Translated by Nina Salaman and edited by Heinrich Brody. New York: Arno, 1973.

———. *The Kuzari: An Argument for the Faith of Israel*. New York: Schocken, 1987.

Kayser, Rudolf. *The Life and Times of Jehudah Halevi*. Translated by Frank Gaynor. New York: Philosophical Library, 1949.

Minkin, Jacob S. "Judah Halevi." In *Great Jewish Personalities in Ancient and Medieval Times*. Edited by Simon Noveck. Washington, D.C.: B'nai B'rith, 1959.

Pasachoff, Naomi. "Yehudah Halevi." In *Great Jewish Thinkers: Their Lives and Work*. West Orange, N.J.: Behrman House, 1992.

Maimonides (Moses ben Maimon)

INTELLECTUAL
GIANT

A ccording to legend, on the night in 1178 when the great scholar Moses Maimonides finished preparing his 14-volume summary of Jewish law, he had a dream. In it, the biblical leader Moses, who had led the ancient Hebrews out of slavery in Egypt, asked Maimonides to show him his massive manuscript. After evaluating the scholarly undertaking, Moses congratulated his namesake with a traditional blessing, "May your strength increase." It is not necessary to believe in this legend, however, to appreciate the sentiment underlying another traditional saying: "From Moses to Moses, there was no one like Moses."

Jews often refer to Moses Maimonides as the Rambam, a name that comes from the initial Hebrew letters of the words **Ra**bbi **M**oses **b**en (or son of) **M**aimon. The suffix *ides* in the name Maimonides means that he was a descendant of Maimon, his father, an important rabbi and community leader in Córdoba, Spain. The prestige and influence of Maimon's son Moses were not limited to the Jewish community of his time, but also extended through the Christian and Muslim worlds and across the centuries. The scope of Maimonides' scholarship was wide, but a common theme ran through all his work: the belief that Judaism and reason uncover identical truths.

This bust of Maimonides appears in the United States Capitol, along with those of other champions of law from around the world. The *Mishneh Torah*, Maimonides's legal code, is only one of his important works.

Maimonides's masterpiece, *The Guide for the Perplexed*, was originally written in Arabic between 1185 and 1190. The work was later translated into Latin (right) in 1520, and into Hebrew in 1551. The Hebrew edition on the left was printed in Italy in 1553.

Maimonides shaped Jewish tradition in a number of ways. He summarized all Jewish law into a code that helped Jews practice their religion. He wrote a philosophical masterpiece that helped Jews reconcile their religious studies with their secular learning. His 13-point creed, or statement of belief, found a place in the Jewish prayer book. Maimonides also exemplifies Jews whose accomplishments earn them recognition in the community but who continue to keep their place as respected Jewish leaders.

Even more remarkable than the breadth and depth of Maimonides' scholarly output is the fact that he acquired much of his learning and began the majority of his writing under the most trying conditions. While he was growing up, Córdoba was a major center of both Jewish and general learning. Instead of pursuing activities typical of childhood, young Moses spent most of his time studying the books in the family library. Then, in 1148, when Maimonides was only 13, his sheltered life came to an abrupt end when a new Muslim sect con-

quered Córdoba. This group outlawed all religions except Islam and waged a "holy war" against any ruler who did not embrace their religious views. They closed all the churches and synagogues in the city and demanded that all non-Muslims convert to Islam. Maimon and his family fled the city and for the next 10 years wandered from place to place in Spain. Despite the ordeals the refugees faced, during this time the young Maimonides was able to complete a treatise on logic and another on the Jewish calendar.

In 1160 the family left Spain and moved to Fez, Morocco, even though that city was also controlled by the same intolerant Muslim sect. The family may have chosen their new home because of a certain Jewish scholar who lived there; in any case, Maimonides, now 25 years old, studied with this man. To support his studies, Maimonides' father and younger brother went into the jewelry business. However, Maimonides' teacher was put to death for refusing to abandon Judaism, and the family fled once again.

In April 1165, under cover of night, they boarded a ship bound for the land of Israel. Their stay there was brief, however. The first two Crusades—Christian military ventures in 1096 and 1147 to wrest control of the Holy Land from its Muslim rulers—had destroyed the land and its inhabitants. There was no community of scholars with whom Maimonides could study. Nor was there opportunity in such an impoverished country for the family's jewelry business to flourish. Before the year was out the family set sail again, this time for Egypt, which would be Maimonides' home for the rest of his life. Although Egypt too was a Muslim country, its rulers permitted the large Jewish population to practice their religion openly. Within two years of his arrival in Egypt, Maimonides had become a respected leader of its Jewish community.

Shortly after the family's arrival in Egypt, Maimonides' father died. Maimonides was now dependent on his brother's management of the family business to support him in his role as scholar and community leader. Then tragedy struck. Maimonides' brother died in a shipwreck in the Indian Ocean, and the entire family fortune was lost with him. For the first time, Maimonides was faced with the responsibility of earning a living to support himself and the rest of the family. After a lengthy period of mourning, he decided to take up a profession. He had already studied medical manuscripts during his youth and the family's wanderings, so that after some additional study and practice he was able to become a skilled physician. By 1185, at the age of 50, he had become personal physician to the ruler of Egypt. Some traditions claim that King Richard the Lion-Hearted of England tried unsuccessfully to lure Maimonides from Egypt to become his own private physician.

Maimonides' life grew ever busier. As he built his medical practice, he not only continued to lead the Jewish community but also completed two major religious works, either of which could have been a lifetime's labor in its own right. The first endeavor reflected Maimonides' concern that the practice of Judaism had declined because of the difficult circumstances under which many Jews were forced to live.

To solve this problem, Maimonides set about summarizing Jewish law on a scale never attempted before or since. The result was his 14-volume *Mishneh Torah* (Repetition of the Law). In this work Maimonides subdivided and classified all Jewish laws according to their subject matter. He also listed a single ruling on each issue, without referring to disputing opinions or listing his sources.

Maimonides' method is illustrated by his treatment of the subject of charity. In the Talmud, the great collection of Jewish law and tradition edited in Palestine and Babylonia more than 700 years earlier, there is no systematic treatment of charity. Instead, comments about it and stories about charitable behavior are scattered throughout the Talmud. By reviewing all this material Maimonides concluded that there are eight levels of charity, ranging from reluctant giving, which is the least worthy method of

> *"The only form of comprehension of God we can have is to realize how futile it is to try to comprehend him."*
>
> —from *The Guide for the Perplexed* (1190)

supporting the poor, to the most laudable method—the teaching of self-reliance. According to Maimonides, the highest level of charity "is to...put [the poor person] on his feet so that he can dispense with other people's aid."

In the hope of standardizing Jewish practice throughout the world, Maimonides addressed his *Mishneh Torah* to all Jews. In contrast, his masterpiece of philosophy, *The Guide for the Perplexed,* was intended for a more exclusive readership. This work was addressed only to those who were troubled by apparent contradictions between the Torah's teachings and the knowledge they had gained from secular sources.

For example, the idea that God could have human physical or emotional attributes seemed to contradict not only reason but also the teachings of secular philosophers. The Bible, however, is filled with language suggesting that God not only has a body but also reacts in human ways. One of Maimonides' achievements in the first 47 chapters of his *Guide* is to analyze every phrase in the Bible that seems to ascribe human qualities to God. He then gives an explanation grounded in reason for every phrase. For example, the Bible states that human beings were created in God's image. Maimonides concludes that the Bible means that human beings reflect the essence of godliness—perception and intellect: "On account of the

Divine intellect with which man has been endowed, he is said to have been made in the form and likeness of the Almighty, but far from it be the notion that the Supreme Being is corporeal, having a material form."

Another section of the *Guide* analyzes the reasons behind each commandment in the Torah. Some Jews claimed that God had given a number of commandments, such as the laws forbidding certain types of food, only to test the Jews' obedience. Maimonides rejected this claim because it implied that God is inferior to human lawmakers, who try to make the laws governing society reasonable. He insisted that every law in the Torah must be reasonable and benefit human beings. In this spirit, Maimonides was the first to put forth the idea that the Jewish dietary laws were established to promote human health.

Both the *Mishneh Torah* and *The Guide for the Perplexed* were works of Maimonides' maturity. But during his early 30s, he had written another important religious work that had a lasting impact on Jewish tradition. In his *Commentary to the Mishnah*, the code of Jewish law edited by Rabbi Judah Hanasi more than 900 years earlier, Maimonides offered a statement of religious belief listing what seemed to him to be the 13 central principles of Judaism. One of those principles—"I believe in perfect faith

in the coming of the Messiah"—was the song on the lips of many Jewish victims of the Nazi Holocaust during World War II. Even as they walked to their deaths in the gas chambers, they expressed the conviction shared with Maimonides that at the end of time the Messiah will usher in an era of peace and prosperity. About a century after Maimonides' death, these 13 principles were summarized in a hymn entitled "Yigdal," after the first word of the Hebrew text. The hymn now appears in prayer books the world over.

Maimonides' *Commentary to the Mishnah* also reveals his extraordinary modesty. In an epilogue to the work, he begs his readers to let him know of mistakes or misinterpretations they find: "Whoever finds occasion to criticize me, or knows of a better interpretation of any of the laws, should call my attention to it and gracefully forgive me." Because the book was written while he was a refugee, he explains, he was often unable to consult libraries. By pointing out errors that might therefore have crept in, his critics would not be injuring his pride but would instead be performing godly work.

However impressive Maimonides' religious writings may be, he is remembered today as more than an intellectual giant. He was also a compassionate community leader, a fact demonstrated by a famous exchange of letters with a man named Obadiah, who had converted to Judaism from Islam. Obadiah wrote Maimonides to ask if it was appropriate for a convert like him to refer to God as "God of our fathers," since his ancestors had not been Jews. In reply, Maimonides pointed out that the Jews' biblical ancestor Abraham had also left his family behind in the name of his new belief in God. Maimonides thus assured Obadiah that conversion made him the equal of anyone born to a Jewish family.

Maimonides remained active as a physician, scholar, and leader until the end of his life. Not surprisingly, he died while working, in the process of dictating the last chapter of a revised edition of his medical writings. He was so widely respected that the Muslims of Egypt joined the nation's Jews in three days of public mourning. Before his death Maimonides had made it known that he wished to be buried in Tiberias, one of four holy cities in the land of Israel. His request was carried out, and to this day his tomb is visited by those wishing to honor this epochal figure.

Despite the tributes accorded Maimonides, he was a controversial figure during his lifetime and for centuries afterward. Some scholars suspected that he intended to have his legal code, the *Mishneh Torah*, take the place of the Talmud. Others believed that his emphasis on reason sapped the life out of Judaism by making God seem so different from human beings as to render him completely unapproachable. Nevertheless, modern Jews of all backgrounds, whether or not they accept all of Maimonides' legal rulings and philosophical arguments, honor him for his unparalleled achievements.

And it is not only Jews who claim a share of Maimonides' greatness. Despite the fact that he had fled Muslim persecution in Spain and Morocco, both of those countries now claim him as one of their national treasures. In 1985, on the 850th anniversary of Maimonides' birth, his native city of Córdoba hosted an international meeting of scholars who discussed the importance of his contributions. And in January 1994, Maimonides' portrait appeared on the front page of the official newspaper of Morocco in an article announcing the opening of a joint Jewish-Muslim conference on the great thinker's life and work.

FURTHER READING

Baron, Salo. "Moses Maimonides." In *Great Jewish Personalities in Ancient and Medieval Times*. Edited by Simon Noveck. Washington, D.C.: B'nai B'rith, 1959.

Goodman, Lenn E., ed. and trans. *Rambam: Readings in the Philosophy of Moses Maimonides*. New York: Viking, 1976.

Kellner, Menachem. *Maimonides on Judaism and the Jewish People*. Albany: State University of New York Press, 1991.

Pasachoff, Naomi. "Maimonides." In *Great Jewish Thinkers: Their Lives and Work*. West Orange, N.J.: Behrman House, 1992.

Seeskin, Kenneth. *Maimonides: A Guide for Today's Perplexed*. West Orange, N.J.: Behrman House, 1991.

Twersky, Isadore. *A Maimonides Reader*. New York: Behrman House, 1972.

LINKS IN THE CHAIN

Maimonides (Moses ben Maimon)

BORN

March 30, 1135
Córdoba, Spain

DIED

December 13, 1204
Cairo, Egypt

EDUCATION

Studied the books in the library of his father, Maimon, a scholar, Jewish community leader, and religious judge of the Jews of Córdoba

ACCOMPLISHMENTS

Wrote two major religious works, the *Mishneh Torah* (1178), which summarized all Jewish law and helped standardize Jewish observance, and *The Guide for the Perplexed* (1190), which helped reconcile Judaism with rational thought; also wrote a commentary on the Mishnah (1168) and influential books on the theory and practice of medicine

Nahmanides (Moses ben Nahman)

PUBLIC DEFENDER OF JUDAISM

Over the course of their long history, Jews have, like other people, engaged in serious disputes among themselves. Sometimes these disagreements have seriously threatened the unity of the Jewish people. Fortunately, a tradition has developed by which a Jew respected by both sides attempts to make peace between the disputing parties. In other instances, which have occurred all too frequently over the course of Jewish history, the principles of Judaism have been challenged by outsiders. In response to such attacks, another tradition has developed through which a Jew respected by the non-Jewish community comes to the defense of Judaism. One outstanding Jew who left his mark on both of these traditions was the 13th-century Spanish scholar who came to be known as Nahmanides.

Nahmanides' name at birth was Moses ben (son of) Nahman; the suffix *-ides* at the end of his name simply means that he was a descendant of Nahman. Once he had

The opening page from the second edition (1489) of Nahmanides' commentary on the Pentateuch. Nahmanides also wrote commentaries on the Talmud and composed poems, prayers, and sermons.

> *"In whatever you do and whenever you speak or think or, indeed, at all times, imagine yourself standing in the presence of God. For His glory fills all the earth. Let your words be in dread and fear as a slave in his master's presence."*
>
> —from a letter written by Nahmanides to his son

become a respected rabbi—first of Gerona, his native town, and then of all Catalonia, a region of the kingdom of Aragon that included both Gerona and the capital city of Barcelona—Jews often called him by a name created from his initials. Instead of **Ra**bbi **M**oses **b**en **N**ahman, they simply called him the Ramban. During his lifetime, Nahmanides was so highly regarded that the Jews of Spain often called him simply "the rabbi" or "the teacher."

Nahmanides was born in 1194, almost 60 years after the birth of the philosopher Maimonides, another great Jewish scholar who was also a native of Spain. Like Maimonides, Nahmanides practiced medicine for a living. Maimonides' great work *The Guide for the Perplexed* attempted to show that Judaism was a religion based on reason, just as Greek philosophy was. In contrast, Nahmanides did not believe that Judaism was above all a religion of reason. Whereas Maimonides had rejected all forms of mysticism—the attempt to enter into intimate communication with God—Nahmanides not only studied the works of Jewish mysticism but also contributed to them. Like some other Jews, he feared that Maimonides' writings had led some Jews to focus on secular studies instead of Jewish texts. He did not agree, however, with the mystics who went so far as to expel from their congregations any Jew who dared read Maimonides' writings.

Hoping to make peace within the Jewish community, Nahmanides wrote to the most extreme opponents of Maimonides, the rabbis of Montpellier, in southern France. He asked them to permit Jews to read the writings of Maimonides rather than risk driving them away from Judaism entirely. In defense of Maimonides, Nahmanides argued that many Jews who had been tempted by secular studies would have abandoned Judaism altogether if not for the works of Maimonides, who kept them connected to their religion. He also asserted that because the French rabbis lived in such different conditions from the Jews of Egypt, where Maimonides had written, they were not qualified to pass judgment on him. Ultimately, Nahmanides' efforts helped preserve an honored place for Maimonides' works in Jewish literature.

In the decades between Maimonides' birth in 1135 and that of Nahmanides, great changes had swept over Spain, with far-reaching consequences for the nation's Jewish inhabitants. Christians from the northernmost parts of Spain were increasingly successful in their war against the Muslims, who had occupied most of Spain since the 8th century. By the late 12th century Nahmanides' area, the northeast kingdom of Aragon, was entirely in

Christian hands. Before long, the Muslims would retain control over only the southern kingdom of Granada.

At first, the Jews of Spain fared well under their new Christian rulers. Although the Christian conquerors forced the Muslims to leave the newly captured areas, they not only allowed Jews to remain but also welcomed Jewish settlers from other regions. King James I of Aragon (who reigned from 1214 to 1276), for example, promised special protection to the Jews in his kingdom. He filled many important government positions with qualified Jews, and official documents of the kingdom were sometimes signed with Hebrew names written in Hebrew.

Soon, however, individuals within the Roman Catholic Church began a campaign to weaken the Jews' influence. Although James I ignored the pope's demands that he fire his Jewish officials, he felt compelled to take certain other steps against the Jews. In 1259, for example, he cancelled debts owed by Christians to Jews. And in 1263 his capital of Barcelona became the stage for a public debate designed to show that Judaism was obsolete and irrelevant. The debate pitted Pablo Christiani, a former Jew who had converted to Christianity, against Nahmanides, the greatest Jewish scholar in the kingdom. Nahmanides was not eager to take part, because he felt that the

This seal of Nahmanides was found near Acre, the seaport in northwest Israel where Nahmanides died in 1270.

discussion would not be fair and open. He agreed to do so only because the king promised him permission to speak his mind freely.

Pablo Christiani's intent was to use the Talmud itself—the revered Jewish text containing laws, legends, and discussions of the rabbis who lived in Palestine and Babylonia from the 1st through the 5th centuries—to prove that Judaism had no value in the modern world. In order to demonstrate that Christian beliefs had displaced those of Judaism, Christiani focused on passages in the Talmud that dealt with the Messiah, literally "the one anointed with holy oil." According to Jewish belief, the Messiah had not yet come, but Christians believed that Jesus of Nazareth was not only the Messiah or Christ (from the Greek word for "anointed"), but also the son of God and therefore a divine being.

On the first day of the formal disputation, Christiani drew the attention of the audience to a passage in the Talmud saying that the Messiah was born on the day the temple in Jerusalem was destroyed (in the year 70). This historical note appeared to confirm his argument. Nahmanides countered that just as a Christian is not bound to believe every sermon preached in church, a Jew is not required to believe every legend in the Talmud. He then declared that even if he chose to believe this particular legend, it would demonstrate that Jesus could not have been the Messiah because, according to Christian accounts, Jesus had already died decades before the destruction of the temple.

Nahmanides was even more impressive on the second day of the debate. Both Christiani and the king asked him to explain why he rejected the assertion that the Messiah, Jesus, had already come. Before responding, Nahmanides asked the king what he felt a ruler's main duties were. The king answered that waging war against his enemies and directing the courts of law were his primary concerns. Then, argued Nahmanides, "You yourself have given me the proof. The coming of the Messiah was to be followed by peace and justice. As long as Christians themselves conduct wars and as long as there is so much injustice in the world, we cannot believe that the Messiah has already come."

The king then asked Nahmanides to state clearly what he thought about the idea of Jesus as God. The scholar spoke diplomatically. For the king and other Christians, the idea that Jesus is God came naturally, since from birth representatives of the church had taught them so. "Yet that which you believe—and it is the heart of your faith—reason cannot agree to, nature opposes, and the Prophets never said such a thing. Miracle also cannot extend to this. . . . Such beliefs cannot convince either a Jew or any other human being. Thus your speeches are made in vain and emptiness, for that belief lies at the heart of our quarrel."

On the third day of the disputation, Pablo Christiani pointed to a comment in the Talmud stating that the Messiah will rank higher than the angels. Did this statement not prove, asked the convert, that the Messiah is God? At this point Nahmanides lost patience with his opponent. Did Christiani not know that Abraham, Moses, and all other righteous human beings are also said to rank higher than the angels? Was Christiani going to claim that they, too, were God?

The fourth and final session of the disputation was cut short. Rumors had circulated that Nahmanides was insulting Christianity, and a mob gathered. Only when the king promised to protect Nahmanides against attack did he agree to continue. But when he announced that he was about to question Christiani, the mob began to make menacing gestures. The king led Nahmanides to safety and the disputation was never formally concluded.

According to Christian accounts, Nahmanides' remarks had been shown to contradict each other. Having been reduced to silence, he fled Barcelona. In Nahmanides' own version, he remained in Barcelona at the king's request to witness an event unique in the history of Spain: King James himself attended the Barcelona synagogue on the Saturday following the abrupt ending of the disputation. A royal edict had been issued, ordering all the Jews of Aragon to attend the service to hear a sermon, aimed at converting them to Christianity. By attending the service himself, the king seemed to be showing that he would protect his kingdom's Jews against the mob. That evening, Nahmanides was invited to James's palace, where the king gave him a large gift of money and sent him back to his home in Gerona under the protection of royal guards.

Although Nahmanides' performance at the debate in Barcelona was in

Nahmanides (Moses ben Nahman)

BORN

Around 1194
Gerona, Aragon, Spain

DIED

1270
Acre, Palestine

EDUCATION

In addition to rigorous training in the Bible and Talmud, Nahmanides also mastered Jewish mysticism (Kabbalah), had a good background both in the sciences and in Christian theology, and trained and practiced as a physician

ACCOMPLISHMENTS

Chief rabbi of Catalonia, Spain; attempted to settle a dispute between the followers and opponents of the philosopher Maimonides in Spain; participated under summons by King James I of Aragon in a public disputation with Christians; revitalized Jewish settlement in Jerusalem; wrote a commentary on the first five books of the Bible; wrote commentaries on the Talmud, clarifications of particular Jewish laws, and criticisms of legal opinions of other Jewish authorities; composed poems, prayers, and sermons some sense both a personal triumph and a victory for Judaism, its aftermath was less positive for the Jews. Raymond Martini, one of the Christian representatives at the disputation, reacted to Nahmanides' impressive rebuttal by preparing what he considered a more effective guide for Christians to use in interpreting Jewish texts. The book that resulted, *The Dagger of Faith*, became a classic weapon for Christians seeking to attack the validity of Judaism. Despite his admiration for Nahmanides, King James bowed to pressure created by this book and ordered the Jews to erase from their copies of the Talmud any passage criticizing Jesus. If they failed to do so, they would be fined and their copies of the Talmud would be burned. The pope went even further. He ordered that, under the supervision of Pablo Christiani, all Jewish books in Aragon were to be collected and examined for offensive anti-Christian references. The pope also issued a document urging the identification and prosecution of converted Jews suspected of retaining Jewish sympathies.

Following the disputation, Nahmanides knew that his days in Spain were numbered. After returning home, he agreed to a request from Gerona's bishop to prepare an account of the debate. Soon after he had done so, charges were brought against him for allegedly slandering Jesus. King James wanted to impose only a light punishment—burning Nahmanides' account of the disputation and banishing him from Aragon for two years. But the church was not satisfied with these measures. As the church stepped up its drive to suppress Judaism, Nahmanides, now in his 70s, left Spain for Palestine, where he arrived in 1267.

Nahmanides spent the final three years of his life doing productive work in the ancient Jewish homeland. Distressed to discover fewer than 2,000 Jews in Jerusalem, he brought about a revival of Jewish life in the former capital. His presence there drew students from near and far. Despite his advanced years, he completed a commentary on the Pentateuch, the first five books of the Bible, and he is also said to have founded a synagogue in Jerusalem. Because of his efforts at renewing Jewish settlement in the city, he has been called "the father of the community." For unknown reasons, he eventually left Jerusalem for the seaport town of Acre, where he died in 1270.

When King James I rewarded Nahmanides for his role in the disputation at Barcelona, he commented, "I have never seen a man defend a wrong cause so well." Throughout the centuries, Jews have continued to revere Nahmanides for his outstanding defense of what they consider a true cause.

FURTHER READING

Maccoby, Hyam. *Judaism on Trial: Jewish-Christian Disputations in the Middle Ages*. Portland: International Specialized Book Services, 1993.

Novak, David. *The Theology of Nahmanides Systematically Presented*. Atlanta: Scholars Press, 1992.

Pasachoff, Naomi, and Robert J. Littman. "Nahmanides and the 1263 Disputation." In *Jewish History in 100 Nutshells*. Northvale, N.J.: Aronson, 1995.

Joseph Caro

"ONE LAW AND ONE TORAH"

One of the great legal scholars in Jewish history, a man whose work unified Jewish practice for centuries, was also a devoted mystic who experienced religious fantasies and hallucinations. In addition to his authoritative code of Jewish law, this 16th-century scholar, Joseph Caro, also kept a diary in which he recorded the words of what he believed was a heavenly spirit, or *maggid*, which he said had chosen to speak through him. Not only Caro's great legal achievement but also his mystical side, which seems bizarre to many Jews today, were influenced by the expulsion of the Jews from Spain. That catastrophe, which took place in 1492, numbers among the most important events in Jewish history.

By the time of Caro's birth in 1488, Jews had lived in Spain for centuries. Under Muslim and, later, Christian rule, they had developed a flourishing Jewish culture and had filled positions of importance in government. Nevertheless, in 1492

Joseph Caro compiled the most influential summary of Jewish law and also kept a mystical diary in which he recorded the words of a heavenly spirit that he said spoke through him.

"Whoever sets the Torah aside when he is rich will eventually set it aside when he is poor, but whoever keeps the Torah when he is poor will eventually keep it when he is rich."

—from *Shulhan Arukh* (1565)

King Ferdinand and Queen Isabella issued a decree ordering all Jews to convert to Christianity or leave the kingdom. These monarchs, who also financed Christopher Columbus's voyage to the New World, were influenced by the Catholic Church to impose a single religion on their subjects. And so the Jews in Spain were forced to leave behind a country that had been home to them for generations. Nearly 500 years were to pass before the decree was officially overturned in February 1990.

Among the estimated 100,000 Jewish refugees were Joseph Caro and his family. Joseph, whose father had died when he was only a boy, had been raised by his father's brother. Both his father and his uncle were scholars of the Talmud, the vast collection of Jewish laws and legends whose importance to Judaism rivals that of the Bible. It was from them that the young Joseph acquired an education.

Like many other Jews fleeing Spain, Caro's family took refuge in neighboring Portugal. But they were not to find a permanent haven there. In 1497, a similar decree in Portugal demanded that Jews in that country convert to Christianity or leave. Caro's family was again uprooted. Along with other Jewish refugees, they finally found sanctuary in the lands of the Ottoman Empire. For nearly 40 years, Caro lived in one city or another in the Balkan Peninsula, a region that now includes Bulgaria, Greece, and the European part of Turkey.

The expulsion first from Spain and then from Portugal left many Jews feeling guilty and insecure. Why had such disasters befallen them, if not for their sins? Many began to fast regularly to repent their supposed misdeeds and to encourage religious meditation and rapture. Groups of Jews anxious to understand the fate of their nation began to meet and study together. Among the works they studied was the Zohar, the sacred text of Jewish mystics, or kabbalists. Like other mystics, the kabbalists believed that religious contemplation and ecstasy could bring their souls into direct communication with God.

The word *kabbalist* comes from the Hebrew word for "mysticism"—*kabbalah*, which literally means "tradition." Kabbalists assert that their mystical beliefs are based on centuries-old traditions.

Joseph Caro became a member of kabbalist circles that developed in the Balkans, then began to communicate with his *maggid*. Other mystics as well claimed to have heard the voice of Caro's *maggid*, which would, like a loving parent, encourage and praise him in his scholarly activities and chide him for personal failures. The *maggid* usually spoke late at night or early in the morning, after Caro had been reciting passages of the Mishnah, the compilation of Jewish law on which the Talmud is based.

Caro's response to the expulsions was not confined to the role of a mystic seeking to repent his own sins.

He also felt that as a scholar trained in the laws of the Talmud he had an obligation to work on behalf of the entire Jewish people. One of the greatest problems faced by Jewish refugees was encountering the widely different local religious practices of fellow Jews living in the Balkans and other such areas. Caro feared that these inconsistencies would ultimately destroy any sense of unity among the Jews. Instead of being a coherent religion based on the written Torah (the Bible) and the oral Torah (the Talmud), Judaism now appeared to be grounded in multiple Torahs, or versions of the law. As Caro himself put it, "As the days passed and we were poured from one vessel into another . . . troubles came upon us until . . . the Torah is now . . . like many laws."

The problem, Caro knew, was that over the centuries scholars in different parts of the Jewish world had written a variety of summaries of Jewish law. And sometimes the rulings in one summary contradicted those in another. To end the confusion and unify Jewish religious practice, Caro set out to write a major code of Jewish law. The task took him more than 20 years and resulted in a major work called the *Bet Yosef* (House of Joseph). In this book Caro dealt with each Jewish law separately. Beginning with the source of the law in the Talmud, he examined all the stages of each law's development and recorded all the opposing views about it. Finally, and most importantly, he stated conclusively how the law was to be carried out.

At first, Caro planned to write the *Bet Yosef* as a commentary on the *Mishneh Torah* (around 1178), the best-known summary of Jewish law, written by the 12th-century scholar Maimonides. In the end, however, he based his code on a later work, *Arba'ah Turim*, because, he said, the author of that code—Jacob ben Asher, who lived from about 1270 to 1340—had included opposing views of the different laws, something Maimonides had omitted.

In addition to this stated reason, Caro may have had two further reasons for basing his *Bet Yosef* on the later code. First, he wanted to make his code the only one needed by any Jew, regardless of national origin. Being of Spanish-Portuguese (Sephardic) descent himself, Caro knew that the Ashkenazic Jews—those of German or Polish descent—observed many rituals differently. Whereas Maimonides for the most part ignored the views of Ashkenazic scholars, Jacob ben Asher took their views into account.

Caro's second unstated reason for not basing his *Bet Yosef* on Maimonides' code arose from his desire to focus only on those Jewish laws relevant to his day. Maimonides had covered every single Jewish law, even those that could not be applied in current Jewish life, such as the laws about the duties of kings. By contrast, Jacob ben Asher included only those laws that Jews actually observed.

Scholars hoping that their work will become the most authoritative in its field are obviously ambitious people. Caro knew that to fulfill his hopes for uniting Jewish practice under "one law and one Torah," as he put it, he had to furnish a single, decisive ruling governing the observance of each law. But modesty was among the virtues recommended to him by his *maggid*. For this reason, Caro did not issue dogmatic rulings based on his authority alone. Instead he relied heavily on the opinions of Maimonides and two other renowned Jewish legal scholars. In general he accepted the majority ruling. On the occasions when he did otherwise, Caro stated modestly that if a community's established practice differed from his ruling, the community should feel free to ignore his recommendations.

Caro organized the *Shulhan Arukh* into four parts. This 1598 edition, published in Venice, is open to the title page of the second part, *Yoreh Deah* (Teacher of Knowledge), which concerns things forbidden and permitted, including all aspects of the dietary laws.

An Israeli soldier talks on a cellular phone in front of a shop near a synagogue named for Joseph Caro. The synagogue is tucked into a recess of a main shopping street in Safed, the hill town where Caro lived for the last 40 years of his life.

Caro began the *Bet Yosef* while living in the Balkans, but he finished it in Palestine, to which, guided by his *maggid*, he moved in 1535. Like many other Jewish scholars and kabbalists, he chose the hill town of Safed as his permanent home. There he was ordained as a rabbi by Rabbi Jacob Berab, a leading scholar of Jewish law. Seven years after arriving in Safed, Caro put the finishing touches on his great work, which was recognized as a masterly achievement and confirmed Caro as the major Jewish legal scholar of the age. But however much satisfaction he might have taken in the reception of his book, Caro knew that the very qualities that made it so impressive to scholars would also keep it from fulfilling his goal of providing a single guide to Jewish practice. While Jewish judges and scholars would certainly find the *Bet Yosef* a most important addition to their libraries, Caro understood that it was too detailed and comprehensive for the average Jew.

Therefore, in order to provide a handy guide for the majority of the Jewish people, Caro set out to condense his full opus. His intent was to enable students, scholars, and judges to find the single key ruling for any given legal matter without having to wade through many sources and opinions. To fill this need he produced the *Shulhan Arukh* (The Prepared Table). Caro divided this book into 30 sections so that by reading a section a day someone could review all the relevant Jewish laws in a single month. As Caro wrote in the introduction to this condensation, "I am confident that through Divine Grace, this work will fill the world with knowledge of the Lord and will be utilized by small as well as great scholars in addition to those who make legal decisions."

Published in 1565, the *Shulhan Arukh* did not automatically become the most widely accepted guide to

Jewish life and practice. Earlier codes had encountered the same problem, but for different reasons. All the earlier Jewish legal codes had been written before the invention of printing in the 15th century. These codes circulated slowly throughout the Jewish world in the form of hand-copied manuscripts, to which errors were often introduced during the tedious process of copying. By contrast, in uniform printed editions the *Shulhan Arukh* quickly reached a wide audience of Jews, both Sephardic and Ashkenazic, throughout the world.

Resistance to Caro's book arose from his tendency to follow the legal principles and customs of the Sephardic community to which he belonged. Even though he had taken pains to represent the Ashkenazic point of view as well, the Ashkenazic code he relied on dated from the 14th century. Caro's work therefore had not taken account of developments in Ashkenazic laws and customs over the ensuing two centuries. For this reason, the Ashkenazic Jews did not immediately embrace the *Shulhan Arukh* as a guide to their religious lives. (Although Sephardic and Ashkenazic Jews both accepted the Babylonian Talmud as the ultimate authority in belief and practice, they often followed different customs. For example, to this day Sephardic Jews eat rice on Passover, but Ashkenazic Jews do not, extending that holiday's ban on eating bread to rice as well.)

Among the Ashkenazic Jews who were disturbed by the gaps in Caro's *Shulhan Arukh* was a distinguished Polish rabbi, Moses Isserles (around 1520–72), who nonetheless recognized the greatness of Caro's achievement. Isserles had independently written his own commentary based on the same 14th-century code as Caro's. But where Caro's commentary had a distinctive Sephardic emphasis, Isserles's was Ashkenazic in flavor. By comparing his work with Caro's, Isserles prepared a summary of cases in which the rulings in the two commentaries differed. He published his summary, together with other clarifications of the *Shulhan Arukh,* in a work he wittily called *Mappah* (Tablecloth).

By in effect spreading a cloth of Ashkenazic design over a table prepared according to Sephardic custom, Isserles made it possible for the Ashkenazic Jews as well as their Sephardic cousins to accept Caro's *Shulhan Arukh.*

For example, nowhere in Caro's lengthy discussion of the obligation to study Torah does he mention the custom observed by Ashkenazic Jews of marking the completion of study of a section of the Talmud with a celebratory meal. So Isserles added the following comment: "Whenever a man completes a tractate of the Talmud it is a religious duty to rejoice and make a party, and such a party is called a 'religious feast.'"

From the 16th century until today, Caro's great work has remained the authority to which observant Jews turn when in doubt about matters of Jewish law and tradition. An observant Jew might turn to the *Shulhan Arukh* to answer questions ranging from "What special treatment is to be accorded a synagogue building?" to "How is respect shown the scholar and the aged?" to "How literally are the laws to recline and drink wine at the Passover seder to be taken?"

Jews became so dependent on the *Shulhan Arukh* that publishers foresaw the marketability of portable editions. The title page of a 1594 pocket-sized edition of the *Shulhan Arukh,* for example, boasts that the book's small size would enable people of all ages to benefit from its counsel "at all times and in every place."

Joseph Caro's legal works have remained so highly respected over the centuries that some modern scholars have disputed the idea that he could also be the author of the mystical diary published after his death. Recent research has proved conclusively, however, that Caro was at the same time a sober legal scholar and a mystic through whose mouth he claimed that a heavenly guide regularly spoke. The two aspects of Caro's personality do not seem to have conflicted. During the day he pursued his scholarly activities. At night—and especially on Friday night and early Saturday morning, the beginning of the Jewish Sabbath—Caro would often awaken and hear emerging from his own lips a voice that was not his own. This spirit did not reveal mysteries to him but did give him advice, criticism, and encouragement. Clearly, the ability to live two lives, so to speak, did not weaken Caro's health. When he died at the age of 87, he had long outlived one wife and several children, who were probably victims of epidemics that spared him. He went on to have at least two other wives and be survived by several children, one of whom was born only four or five years before Caro's death.

For observant Jews to this day, Joseph Caro remains the legal scholar whose guide to observance is consulted regularly. Caro also remains a model to contemporary Jews who combine sober everyday pursuits with mystical studies in their attempt to develop their connection to God in a variety of ways.

FURTHER READING

Pasachoff, Naomi, and Robert J. Littman. "Joseph Caro and the *Shulhan Arukh.*" In *Jewish History in 100 Nutshells.* Northvale, N.J.: Aronson, 1995.

Werblowsky, R. J. Zwi. *Joseph Karo: Lawyer and Mystic.* London: Oxford University Press, 1962.

LINKS IN THE CHAIN

Joseph Caro

BORN
1488
Probably Toledo, Spain

DIED
March 24, 1575
Safed, Palestine

EDUCATION
Studied as a boy with his father and uncle, both of whom were scholars of Jewish law; later studied under and was ordained as a rabbi by Rabbi Jacob Berab, the leading scholar of Jewish law until Caro succeeded him

ACCOMPLISHMENTS
Wrote the *Bet Yosef* (House of Joseph), the last great summary of Jewish law (1522–42), and a shorter version, the *Shulhan Arukh* (The Prepared Table; completed 1563, first printed 1565), which Orthodox Jews still regard as the guide for Jewish practice; also wrote the *Kesef Mishneh* (published 1574–75), an important commentary on part of Maimonides' legal code, the *Mishneh Torah*

Gracia Mendes Nasi

RESCUER OF HER PEOPLE

Most people have at one time or another tried to help out a friend in trouble. In 16th-century Europe, one Jewish woman pushed to its limit this human instinct to help others. By putting her own life and all her resources into this effort, Gracia Nasi helped form a Jewish tradition that has persisted to the present day.

The fact that Gracia Nasi began her career with a different name sheds light on the difficult times in which she lived and worked. Beatrice de Luna of Portugal became Gracia Nasi of Ferrara, Italy, and Istanbul, Turkey, because the practice of Judaism was banned in Spain and Portugal in the last decade of the 15th century. Jews who wished to remain in those countries (or their territories) were forced to convert to Catholicism, at least on the surface.

Some Jews underwent baptism willingly, whereas others were baptized by having water flung over them from a distance without their consent. Following their baptism, they were no longer known by their Jewish names. Instead, they had to use the names of the Christians who had sponsored their baptism. Despite these outward changes, many converts secretly continued to observe Judaism. Often, they chose to marry other converts. They struggled to pass on Jewish beliefs to their children and to instill in them the concept of loyalty to Judaism. Their Christian countrymen coined a new word—*Marrano*—to describe these converts. Although scholars are not certain where the name comes from, many think it derives from a Spanish word for "pig." Whatever its source, it was a name of contempt.

Around the year 1510, Beatrice de Luna was born somewhere in Portugal to a Marrano family with a distinguished background. In Spain several centuries before, members of the family had been Jewish community leaders. Like other Jews elsewhere at other times, the respect they commanded from Jews and non-Jews alike earned them the Hebrew title *nasi*, or prince. In the case of this particular Spanish-Jewish family, the title eventually became a last name.

The Nasis of Spain fled their home in 1492, when the Jews were expelled from Spain. They moved to Portugal, and then, a few years later, were ordered out of there as well. Some members of the Nasi family appear to have undergone forced conversion at this time. Quite likely de Luna was the Christian name of those who sponsored their baptism. The family called their new daughter Beatrice ("one who brings joy") when talking about her in the outside world. At home, however, they named her

This medal bears the likeness of the niece of Gracia Nasi, who was also named Gracia. The medal was cast in 1553 in Ferrara, where Doña Gracia lived for about two years, by the artist Pastorino de' Pastorini.

Gracia—Spanish and Portuguese for "charm" and "wit"—or "Hannah," the Hebrew name for the same traits. In fact, as the young girl grew into womanhood, it became clear that she would use her charm and wit to bring joy into many lives. Although no specifics are known about her upbringing, Gracia's future career suggests that her parents imbued her with a deep sense of loyalty to Jews and Judaism.

In 1528, when Gracia was only 18, she married a man from another branch of the same Spanish-Jewish family from which the Nasis had descended. Her husband, Semah Benveniste, along with his younger brother, Meir, had been among the Jews fleeing Spain for Portugal in 1492. The brothers had been baptized and their names changed in the outside world to Francisco and Diogo Mendes. By the time of Francisco's marriage to Beatrice, the Mendes brothers had become major figures in the commercial world. Their banking house in Lisbon, Portugal's seaport capital, had become so successful that in 1512 Francisco sent Diogo to Antwerp to open a branch there. (Antwerp, a seaport then part of the country of Flanders, is in present-day Belgium. At the time, Flanders, Spain, and Portugal all owed allegiance to the Holy Roman Emperor.) Thanks to Diogo Mendes's financial skills, the House of Mendes became significant in northern European economic life.

In 1536, after Gracia had been married for only eight years, her husband died, leaving her with a young daughter. And the year 1536 was disastrous for more than this most personal of reasons. In that year, the pope officially set up in Portugal a branch of the dreaded Inquisition. The Inquisition spearheaded the Catholic Church's campaign to root out heretics—baptized Catholics who persisted in opposing church beliefs. Marranos suspected of clinging to their Jewish roots were particularly at risk. The church kept suspected heretics from moving to non-Christian countries such as Turkey and other parts of the Ottoman Empire. But it was still possible for Marranos to leave Portugal for the Christian countries of northern Europe, where the Inquisition was not as vigorous. From there, many hoped to travel on to safety in Turkey. With something like this in mind, Gracia left Lisbon for Antwerp in 1536. She took her young daughter, two nephews, and her unmarried sister Brianda, who soon married Diogo Mendes, making him Gracia's brother-in-law twice over.

Over the next four years, until Diogo's death in late 1542 or early 1543, Gracia proved herself a worthy associate of her brother-in-law. She turned out to have excellent business instincts that helped increase the power and influence of the House of Mendes. She also became an equal partner in a risky sideline: helping other Marranos escape the long arm of the Inquisition. The extended Mendes family risked their own safety in Antwerp by continuing to practice Judaism in secret while attending Catholic mass in public. They would have been safer in the Ottoman domains but chose to stay because they believed Antwerp gave them the best opportunity to help endangered Marranos in flight. Agents of the House of Mendes aided fugitives in various ways: boarding ships to warn Marranos of possible dangers,

"With her golden arm and heavenly grasp, she raised most of those people from the depths of this and other infinite travail in which they were kept enthralled in Europe by poverty and sin; she brings them to safe lands and does not cease to guide them, and gathers them to the obedience and precepts of their God of old."

—from a description of Gracia Nasi's work in Samuel Usque's *Consolation for the Tribulations of Israel* (1553)

providing them with names of people to whom they could turn for help in cities along their route, and helping them transport their goods and valuables. Because of these activities, Diogo was arrested on one occasion and had to go into hiding on another.

After Diogo's death, the Holy Roman Emperor opened proceedings against him on charges of heresy. If the charges could be proved, the empire could confiscate all of Diogo's property, which was otherwise under Gracia's control. She used every means within her power, including the expenditure of large sums as bribes, to get the charges dropped. These legal difficulties ultimately convinced Gracia that she would have to find a more secure home base. Thus, in late 1544 she, her sister, and their two daughters moved under cover of night to Venice, Italy.

Nearly 30 years earlier, in 1516, all the Jews of Venice had been forced to live together in one area, which became the world's first ghetto. (The Jewish section of Venice took its name from the foundry—*ghetto* in Italian— that had once operated there, and the name was later applied to any section of a city where a minority group was forced to live.) If the Mendeses had moved to the ghetto, however, they would be admitting that they were in fact practicing Jews and would therefore come under surveillance. Gracia and her sister instead set up their household in the center of town, where they continued to live outwardly as Christians. From this new base, Gracia continued to oversee the

secret organization aiding the Marrano refugees.

Another threat now arose from a totally unanticipated quarter. Brianda, Diogo's widow, could not accept the idea that Gracia controlled all the wealth of the House of Mendes. So she suddenly denounced her sister as a Jew and claimed that Gracia planned to flee to Turkey with all her property. This accusation was indeed grounded in fact—for some time, Gracia had been sending property to Constantinople (now Istanbul), the capital of the Ottoman Empire.

Following her sister's accusation, the authorities in Venice arrested Gracia. Luckily, the Ottoman sultan knew of her case. Eager to have such a wealthy and influential businesswoman as one of his subjects, he intervened on Gracia's behalf. Following her release, she and Brianda were reconciled and moved yet again with their daughters. They did not go immediately to Istanbul but set up their household in Ferrara, in northern Italy, at the time an independent duchy. Ferrara's rulers, the dukes of the House of Este, observed the practice of giving refuge to persecuted Jews—especially those whose presence might benefit the duchy.

The sisters' move to Ferrara marked an important transition in their lives. The official document issued by the duke of Ferrara in 1550 welcoming them to his land promised them freedom of religion. This document was addressed to them as the wives not of the brothers Mendes, but of the brothers Benveniste, their original Jewish name. Delighted with the opportunity to live openly as Jews once again, the sisters chose also to return to their Jewish maiden name. Gracia Nasi happily discarded for once and all her Christian name, Beatrice de Luna. And Brianda began to use publicly her formerly private Jewish name for "queen": Reina in Spanish, Malkah in Hebrew.

Shortly after arriving in Ferrara, Gracia Nasi broadened her activities to help Marranos. As in the past, she continued to assist the refugees in finding personal safety and helped them keep their worldly goods. Now, in addition, she joined the effort to provide them with a Jewish education. Among the literary works produced at her expense was the Ferrara Bible, a translation of the Hebrew Bible into Spanish and Portuguese that appeared in 1553. One edition of this Bible, dedicated to the duke of Ferrara, was intended for Christian use. The second edition, intended for Jews, was dedicated to Gracia Nasi. Another work, *Consolation for the Tribulations of Israel* (1553), also dedicated to Gracia, contained an entire section about her work on behalf of the Portuguese Marranos. The author, Samuel Usque, compared Gracia to biblical heroines who had risked their lives to help their people. He also explained how she assisted the Marranos at every stage of their journey until, having reached safe haven, they could once again follow the "precepts of their God of old."

At about this time, Gracia's niece—also named Gracia, in her

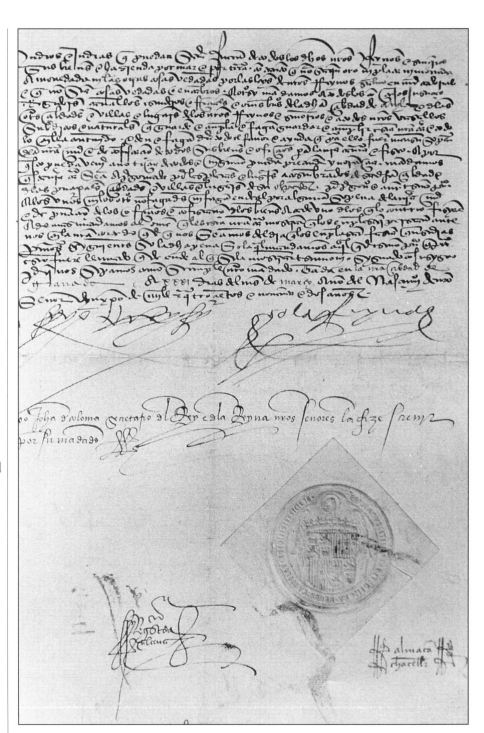

After Ferdinand and Isabella, the king and queen of Spain, issued this decree in 1492, calling for the conversion to Christianity or expulsion of their kingdom's Jews, Gracia Nasi's family and many other Jews fled Spain for nearby Portugal.

aunt's honor—sat for the artist Pastorino de' Pastorini (1508–72), who made a portrait medal of her that survives to this day. The name "Gracia Nasi" is engraved in Hebrew letters around its edge.

Ferrara turned out to be only a way station for Gracia Nasi, however. The situation for Jews had worsened in Italy and the arm of the Inquisition there had gained strength. Gracia and her daughter therefore left for Constantinople, where they arrived in the spring of 1553. Other members of the family soon joined them. Both Gracia and her nephew Joseph Nasi were to play important roles in the affairs of the Ottoman Empire for the rest of their lives. In return, the Ottoman sultan not only helped the Nasi family as individuals but also supported their efforts to help other Jews. From her new base, Gracia Nasi continued to assist Marrano refugees and provide financial support for institutions that served them and others, ranging from hospitals to synagogues to academies for Jewish learning. Ironically, her most memorable undertaking on behalf of persecuted Jews fell short, but its daring conception presents a vivid picture of Gracia Nasi's character and determination.

One of the branches of the House of Nasi, as the former House of Mendes was now known, operated from the seaport of Ancona, on Italy's Adriatic coast. Although Ancona had been under papal control for more than 20 years, a series of popes had welcomed Jewish merchants, including refugees from Portugal. They hoped to enrich the papacy by making the seaport a commercial center, expecting Marrano and Jewish merchants to help make their dream a reality. As a result, many Marranos left Portugal for Ancona, where they began to live openly as Jews. But in the spring of 1555 a new pope unsympathetic to the Jews came to power. That summer he sent a representative to Ancona to begin proceedings against the Portuguese heretics. Although a few Portuguese Jews were able to escape, the Inquisition arrested about 100 of them. The pope's first representative took bribes and freed some of the prisoners, but his successor was both unbribable and merciless. Prisoners who refused to renounce the Jewish faith were sentenced to death.

As soon as Gracia Nasi heard about the proceedings, she began to take action. Because some of the jailed merchants had connections to Turkish firms and others had property in Turkey, she was able to enlist the assistance of the sultan. He sent a representative to Ancona, demanding that all prisoners with any claim to Turkish protection be released immediately, and he threatened dire consequences if they were not. The pope indicated that he was willing to release Turkish subjects who could prove they had never been baptized, as well as property controlled by the House of Nasi, but he insisted that Marranos who had returned to their Jewish faith must die. In June 1556, 11 victims—including one of Gracia Nasi's agents—were burned in Ancona.

Gracia Nasi soon launched a campaign to punish the pope by

destroying Ancona's trade through a complete boycott of its port. The sultan himself placed an embargo on Ancona, prohibiting the movement of Ottoman merchant ships into or out of the port, and for a while it seemed the boycott scheme would work. Before long, however, members of the original Jewish community of Ancona, who had lived in the city long before the Portuguese Marranos arrived, begged that the scheme be dropped. If Ancona were ruined through Jewish action, they argued, the local population and the pope himself would take revenge on the Jews of Ancona. Although Gracia Nasi felt that the risk was worth taking, others disagreed, so the port began to thrive again and the pope remained hostile to the Jews of Ancona and other European cities. Gracia saw to it that no cargo controlled by the House of Nasi ever again passed through the port of Ancona, but she remained deeply disappointed that its Jews had failed to maintain a united front to combat persecution and punish their oppressors.

After the failure of the Ancona boycott in 1557, Gracia Nasi seems to have directed her hopes for the Jewish people toward Palestine. In 1554, the year after her arrival in Constantinople, she had gone to great lengths to fulfill the dying wish of her husband—then nearly 20 years deceased—that his remains be removed from a Christian cemetery in Lisbon and reburied in Palestine. He had hoped that this act might earn him God's forgiveness for having pretended to be a Christian. It must

have been extremely difficult for Gracia Nasi to have her husband's remains smuggled out of Portugal and reburied in the ancient Jewish cemetery on the Mount of Olives overlooking Jerusalem, but she succeeded in this daring exploit. She hoped herself to be buried next to her husband in that cemetery. In 1561, she and her nephew Joseph Nasi convinced the sultan to grant them a charter authorizing the Jews to resettle in Tiberias, in the Galilee region of northern Palestine. For the privilege of starting an independent Jewish settlement there they paid the sultan 1,000 ducats. A mansion was prepared in Tiberias for Gracia Nasi to live in, but she seems never to have succeeded in reaching Palestine.

The exact date and location of her death are unknown, but records show that in the summer of 1569, Jews around the world held memorial services in her honor.

FURTHER READING

Pasachoff, Naomi, and Robert J. Littman. "The Marranos." In *Jewish History in 100 Nutshells*. Northvale, N.J.: Aronson, 1995.

Roth, Cecil. *Doña Gracia of the House of Nasi*. Philadelphia: Jewish Publication Society, 1977.

Gracia Mendes Nasi

BORN

Around 1510
Portugal

DIED

Around 1569
Location uncertain

ACCOMPLISHMENTS

Used her personal wealth to help lead Marranos to safety; supported Jewish scholarship; established hospitals, synagogues, and academies for Jewish learning in the Ottoman Empire; renewed the Jewish settlement in Tiberias, Palestine

Isaac Luria

REPAIRING THE WORLD

I saac Luria was hardly the first Jewish mystic. Over the 16 centuries before his birth there had always been some Jews engaged in mysticism, the belief that the human soul can enter into direct union with God through the contemplation of divine things and the rapture to which such contemplation may lead. The Hebrew word for mysticism, *kabbalah*, actually means "tradition," since Jewish mystics, or kabbalists, claim that their approach to the mysteries of God and the universe is based on traditions handed down over the centuries. Although Luria lived only 38 years (from 1534 to 1572) and left behind no important writings, his reinterpretation of kabbalah reshaped Jewish mystical tradition. Lurianic kabbalah, as his discipline came to be known, also affected later Jewish thought and continues to be important in modern Hasidic, or ultra-Orthodox, Judaism.

Like many other important figures in Jewish history, Luria is often called by a name created by putting initials together. This name, Ha'Ari, is made up of the first letters of the Hebrew words meaning "the godly Rabbi Isaac." Indeed, during his lifetime Luria was known mainly for his saintly qualities. Ha'Ari is also a Hebrew word meaning "the lion." Though Luria's system of Kabbalah became widely known only after his death, from that time on his ideas have affected Jewish life as powerfully as a lion's roar penetrates the stillness of a jungle.

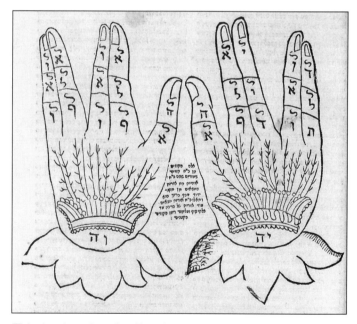

This drawing of a pair of hands, extended in a priestly blessing, appears in a popular kabbalistic work published 40 years after Isaac Luria's death. The Hebrew letters on the bottom of each hand spell one of the names of God.

About 20 years after Luria's death there appeared an anonymous biography called *Life of the Ari*, which remains the main source of information about his life. This book intermixes fact and legend, and it is not always clear where the boundary between them lies, but scholars accept certain items from it as true. It is known, for instance, that Luria's father, who came from German or Polish stock, moved from central Europe to Jerusalem and married a woman of Spanish-Jewish origin. During Luria's boyhood his father died and he and his mother left Jerusalem for the home of her wealthy brother in Egypt. Luria later married that uncle's daughter, his cousin.

In Egypt, Luria mastered traditional Jewish studies, but he also became attracted to Jewish mysticism and soon devoted himself to study of the kabbalah. He paid particular attention to the Zohar, the most sacred mystic text of the kabbalists, who rank this work with the Bible and the Talmud. Luria eventually began to study in seclusion, spending weekdays alone on an island in the Nile River that was owned by his uncle. He claimed that the prophet Elijah visited him there and explained secrets of the Torah to him. Luria would return to civilization once a week, to fulfill the talmudic law requiring a man to spend the Sabbath with his wife.

On one such visit in 1569 or 1570, Luria informed his wife that Elijah had ordered him to return to the land of Israel—not to his birthplace, Jerusalem, but rather to the northern town of Safed, in the region called Galilee. Safed was at that time a major center of Jewish learning where a large number of kabbalists lived. Luria explained that Elijah had urged him to waste no time in moving to Safed, because he would die within two years. In fact, an epidemic swept through Safed in 1572 and Luria was one of its victims.

Luria lived only briefly in Safed, but he had a powerful influence on its community of kabbalists. While studying there with Moses Cordovero, the greatest kabbalist of the time, Luria began to attract followers of his own. Writing did not come easily to him—he claimed that his thoughts overflowed to such an extent that it was hard to organize them. But his students and followers kept careful notes of his teachings. After his death his closest follower, Hayyim Vital, wrote a book that presented an imaginative account of Luria's life and also explained in detail Luria's system of kabbalah.

Lurianic kabbalah developed at a time when the Jews were struggling to make sense of the misfortune that had befallen them in Spain a few decades earlier. Although Jewish life had flourished in Spain for more than eight centuries, in late March of 1492 the Jews of that country were presented with a harsh choice: convert to Christianity or face expulsion. King Ferdinand and Queen Isabella—the same Christian monarchs who sent Christopher Columbus on his voyage to the Americas—issued the decree (which, interestingly enough, was not officially overturned until February 1990). Among the lands to which the Jewish refugees fled was Palestine. Many settled in Safed, because its location near the commercial centers of Syria to the north seemed promising for trade.

At first the newcomers were so stunned by their recent persecution and so engrossed in establishing homes and businesses that they had neither the energy nor the time to question the significance of what had befallen them. Then, as they became more settled, they began to ask why God permitted Jews to suffer to such an extent. Lurianic kabbalah helped make sense of Jewish suffering for the refugees and their children.

Luria's version of kabbalah was appealing in part because it addressed

"Now after this withdrawal...(which left an empty space or vacuum in the very center of the light...) there remained a place in which there could emerge the things to be emanated, to be created, to be formed and to be made."

—Luria, quoted in *Etz Hayyim* (date unknown) by Hayyim Vital (1542–1620), one of the greatest kabbalists

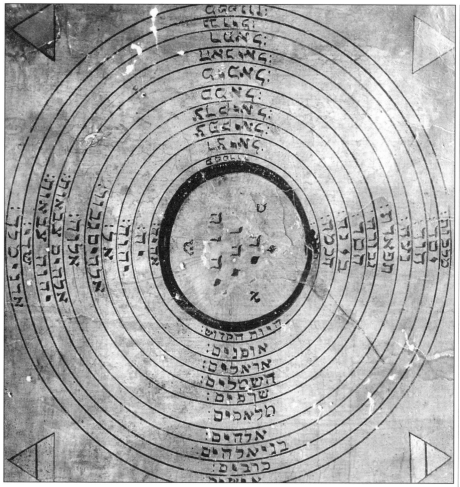

This wooden plaque depicts a kabbalistic view of the divine world. Although the history of kabbalah goes back to the first century C.E., Isaac Luria's influence transformed Jewish mysticism.

the very questions that vexed the Jews of his day: If God is good, why is there evil? Does the exile of the Jews from their homeland and their scattering throughout the world serve any purpose, or does it merely represent a punishment for their sins? Are Jews only victims, or do they have a more meaningful role to play in human history? Luria answered these questions by tracing the Jewish condition back to the birth of the universe. His description of what happened at that time may seem shocking at first. But, like other myths, it can help people make some sense of the world around them.

Luria took as his starting point an older mystical concept of creation that had gone largely unnoticed until he revived it. As his follower Hayyim Vital summarized Luria's belief, before the universe was created, divine light filled all space: "Know that . . . before any creatures were created a simple higher light filled everything. There was no empty space in the form of a vacuum but all was filled with that simple infinite light. This infinite light had nothing in it of beginning or end but was all one simple, equally distributed light." In order to provide empty space for the universe, God had to briefly withdraw some of the divine light. Expressed differently, God had to inhale deeply to make room for the universe to exist. God's withdrawal was actually the first act of creation, since if God had not contracted to create space, there could have been nothing but God, and thus there would have been no universe.

When God breathed out again, however, something unintended happened. The divine light that reentered the world was too intense. God had arranged for vessels to collect the light, but the light was so powerful that many of the vessels broke. This breaking of the vessels explains the existence of evil. When the vessels shattered, the broken pieces trapped some of the sparks of divine light. As a result of this cosmic accident, the universe as we know it is not the one God intended to create. Nothing in the universe is where it belongs. In other words, everything in the universe is in exile. Even part of God is in exile, since some sparks of the divine light are not where they belong. Before the universe can be what God intended, things must be put in their proper place. Everything must be repaired.

This idea that the world is in need of repair or improvement and that human beings have the task of performing that work is an old Jewish concept called *tikkun* that dates back to the rabbis of the Talmud. Isaac Luria gave a new dimension to this idea. According to him, *tikkun* involves freeing the sparks of divine light that became trapped when the vessels shattered. Only when all the light has been restored to its proper place will evil be eliminated from the world. And only when the process of *tikkun* is complete will God be made whole again.

Lurianic kabbalah reserves a special place for Jews in the process of *tikkun*. Because the Jews are scattered throughout the world, they can help liberate trapped divine sparks even at the world's remotest corners. In whatever location, whenever a Jew observes one of God's commandments the process of *tikkun* is advanced. Furthermore, according to Luria, each Jew has, without knowing it, been assigned a specific "repair" job, which no one else can accomplish. Each Jew brings the world a little closer to perfection by carrying out his or her own personal assignment. As a result, Jews cannot passively sit back and wait for the world to become a better place; they must actively participate in making it so. Because individual Jews do not know their specific tasks, all Jews must willingly perform a good deed whenever the opportunity presents itself, just in case the restoration of the world depends on the completion of that particular deed.

The particulars of Lurianic kabbalah may seem bizarre to some, but it is easy to see how the system comforted many troubled Jews. By describing exile as a condition affecting the universe and even God, it made the exile of the Jews from their homeland seem less of a punishment. By suggesting that the scattering of Jews throughout the earth actually helped speed up the process of cosmic repair, it helped restore a sense of self-worth and dignity to people who had felt like eternal victims. Even today, many Jews are heartened by Isaac Luria's assertion that each individual has a crucial role to play in repairing the world as we know it and transforming it into the world God intended.

FURTHER READING

Ariel, David. *The Mystic Quest: An Introduction to Jewish Mysticism.* Northvale, N.J.: Aronson, 1988.

Pasachoff, Naomi. "Isaac Luria." In *Great Jewish Thinkers: Their Lives and Work.* West Orange, N.J.: Behrman House, 1992.

————. "Isaac Luria and Tikkun." In *Basic Judaism for Young People: God.* West Orange, N.J.: Behrman House, 1987.

Pasachoff, Naomi, and Robert J. Littman. "Kabbalists at Safed." In *Jewish History in 100 Nutshells.* Northvale, N.J.: Aronson, 1995.

Scholem, Gershom. "Isaac Luria and His School." In *Major Trends in Jewish Mysticism.* New York: Schocken, 1961.

Isaac Luria

BORN
1534
Jerusalem

DIED
1572
Safed, Palestine

EDUCATION
In Egypt, first studied traditional rabbinic subjects and then the Zohar, the central work of kabbalah (Jewish mysticism), and other mystical works; continued Jewish mystical studies in Safed with Moses Cordovero, the greatest Kabbalist of the time

ACCOMPLISHMENTS
Developed Lurianic Kabbalah, a system of Jewish mysticism that explained the presence of evil and suffering in cosmic terms and affirmed the belief that Jews have a significant role to play in the world

The illustrations on this certificate, issued to members of B'nai B'rith, evoke the aims of this oldest and largest Jewish service organization. B'nai B'rith, or "sons of the covenant," was founded in 1843 in New York City, and other "lodges" were set up later in Europe and Palestine.

2 Shapers of Modern Judaism

What is most striking about the shaping of modern Jewish tradition, beginning in the 18th century, is that Judaism began to be divided into a variety of movements, which continue to flourish to this day. The first such offshoot to emerge in this period is the Hasidic movement, founded by Israel ben Eliezer, better known as the Baal Shem Tov. Sometimes called the ultra-Orthodox branch of Judaism, the Hasidic movement arose against the background of two historical events: the Chmielnicki massacres of 1648–49 in eastern Europe, which resulted in the deaths of tens of thousands of Jews, and the Shabbetai Zevi affair of 1665–66, in which many Jews were led to believe that the Messiah had come to redeem them. According to the Bible, the coming of the Messiah, God's anointed one, would signal "the end of days" and a restructuring of the world along peaceful lines.

Several other Jewish movements developed in the 19th and 20th centuries in response to increased opportunities for Jews to interact with non-Jews. As Jews intermingled more freely with Christians, they began to think about ways to reshape Judaism to improve the way it fit into the modern world. The movement we call Reform Judaism began in Germany, with Abraham Geiger comparing Judaism to a living organism that constantly grows and develops. In the United States, Isaac Mayer Wise was a pioneer of Reform Judaism and an advocate of new religious practices suited to the times. In England, Lily Montagu became a leader of what the British call Liberal Judaism, which sanctions the same sorts of breaks with the past as German and American Reform Judaism.

Gradually, as Reform Judaism became more popular, its adherents came to speak disdainfully of traditional Jews as "Orthodox," from the Greek words for correct belief. Also in Germany, a new movement among traditional Jews developed. This modern Orthodox or Neo-Orthodox movement, led by Samson Raphael Hirsch, stressed that God was the source of Jewish law, and that individual Jews were therefore not at liberty to decide which laws it was permissible to discard in modern times. Instead of trying to adapt Judaism to the times, argued Hirsch, Jews should focus on making the times conform with God's will.

A third movement, Conservative Judaism, arose to bridge the gap between Reform and modern Orthodox Judaism. As championed by Solomon Schechter in the United States, Conservative Judaism emphasized that Jewish law had to be responsive to the changing needs of every age but should not be lightly overturned.

Finally, the youngest and smallest movement in Judaism was developed in the 1920s in the United States by Mordecai Kaplan. His strain of what became known as Reconstructionist Judaism rejects all the supernatural claims associated with Judaism and emphasizes the fact that Judaism, like all other religions, is only part of a larger civilization.

Exposure to the Christian world also meant contact with new developments in science and new political beliefs. In the mid-1700s, Moses Mendelssohn absorbed the ideas of the European Enlightenment, according to which all human beings have the same natural rights. Mendelssohn argued that if Jews would learn the language and culture of their non-Jewish neighbors, they could overcome anti-Jewish prejudice and convince non-Jews to give them the rights they had previously been denied. Mendelssohn was the most prominent Jew to argue that Jews should be educated not exclusively in subjects particular to their religion but in secular subjects as well. At about the same time, Elijah ben Solomon Zalman, better known as the Gaon of Vilna, taught that secular sciences could be used to aid understanding of the Torah.

In the 1800s, Leopold Zunz became an advocate for the "Science of Judaism," a discipline that applied the same rigorous scholarly methods to Jewish studies as professors routinely used in studying the classical civilizations of Greece and Rome. In more recent times, Joseph Soloveitchik reshaped modern Orthodox Judaism for American Jews, arguing that new developments in science do not threaten traditional Judaism but rather enhance it.

Although new movements developed to help Judaism adapt to modern times, the average Jew living in that world became less knowledgeable about the religion itself. In order to strengthen the religious commitment of Jews living among non-Jews, new educational approaches had to be developed. In the United States, Rebecca Gratz established the Sunday school, designed to introduce Jewish children to the basic elements of their faith. And in Germany, Franz Rosenzweig realized that both children and adults needed Jewish education. He therefore introduced adult education to acquaint Jews with the central texts of their religious tradition.

In the modern period, Jewish tradition was shaped not only in response to religious and educational needs but also to humanitarian needs. It became customary for Jews in comfortable circumstances to answer the call of other, less prosperous Jews. The best-known Jew of the 19th century, England's Sir Moses Montefiore, demonstrated through his example that Jews fortunate enough to live lives of financial comfort and political security should feel responsible for easing the plight of other Jews.

Just as the expulsion from Spain in 1492 had a devastating effect on the Jews of the time, the modern era witnessed a catastrophe of even greater magnitude. The rise of Adolf Hitler in the 1930s in Germany led to anti-Jewish practices that culminated in the Holocaust, the systematic murder of 6 million Jews. Jewish thinkers are only now beginning to come to terms with what the Holocaust means for Jews' relationship with God and humanity. Two Jewish thinkers whose thought was not limited to analyzing the meaning of the Holocaust but who nonetheless shed light on it are Martin Buber and Abraham Joshua Heschel. Buber, famous for his philosophy of dialogue, argued that God sometimes is eclipsed, just as the moon sometimes blocks the sun's light from reaching the earth. Heschel spoke of the evil of indifference: it was, he said, people's silence, not God's lack of compassion, that permitted the Holocaust to take place. Although it seems unlikely that the meaning of the Holocaust for Jews will ever be fully resolved, these thinkers helped shape an ongoing tradition of attempting to make sense of this lowest of all points in Jewish history.

Israel ben Eliezer, the Baal Shem Tov

FOUNDER OF
HASIDISM

I n a number of cities in the United States, Israel, and elsewhere it is not unusual to see Jewish men dressed in black woolen coats, wearing long sidelocks and broad-brimmed black hats. To many observers, including many Jews, these individuals seem relics of 18th-century eastern Europe with little connection to contemporary life. Although a number of Jews feel that they have more in common with non-Jews than with these Hasidim, as the members of this community call themselves, the Hasidic movement has in fact played a significant role in shaping Jewish tradition and continues to do so. (In Israel today, the Hasidim are more often called *haredim*—"those who tremble in awe of God.")

The word *hasid* in Hebrew means "pious," or intensely religious. The contributions of Hasidism to Jewish tradition as a whole can be traced back to the personality and teachings of the movement's founder, who is usually called not by his name, Israel ben Eliezer, but by his title, the Baal

רבינו ישראל ב"ר אליעזר (בעש"ט)

לשנה טובה תכתבו

Israel ben Eliezer, known as the Baal Shem Tov or Besht. The second line of the Hebrew caption indicates that this portrait of the Besht was meant to be sent as a greeting for the Jewish New Year holiday.

Shem Tov. In typical Jewish practice, the Baal Shem Tov's title is often shortened to the name Besht, formed from its initial letters. The Besht practiced and preached a new way of living a life of intense Jewish devotion. In doing so, he introduced new kinds of community and leadership to the Jews of his area.

Israel ben Eliezer, born in a region that was then part of Poland, was neither the first nor the only Baal Shem. A Baal Shem—which means "master of the Name"—was a wonder worker of sorts who claimed to be able to cure ailments through secret knowledge of the names of God. Individuals using the Baal Shem title had operated among the Jews since at least the 12th century. In addition to using herbs and folk remedies, these wonder workers often made amulets, or good luck charms, from little slips of paper with different names for God written on them.

The word *tov* (Hebrew for "good") in the Besht's title was used to distinguish him from other wonder workers. Perhaps the description was meant to single him out as the "good Baal Shem" rather than an unscrupulous quack trying to make money by conning naive people. Or it may have indicated that he himself had a "good name" or reputation. Although many modern Jews (and some Jews of the Besht's time as well) might look askance at the idea of a Jewish medicine man, the fact remains that the Besht's personality and teachings enabled Judaism to recover from two serious blows.

Jews had lived in Poland since at least the 11th century, when they fled oppression elsewhere in Europe and were welcomed by Poland's kings, who hoped they would develop the country's economy. By the middle of the 17th century, there were several hundred thousand Jews in Poland. Not only were the country's Jews flourishing economically but they also excelled in Jewish scholarship.

However, in 1648 groups of peasants called Cossacks revolted against their Polish landlords, whom they blamed for charging excessively high rents. Since many Jews were employed by these landlords as agents, the Cossacks vented their rage on the Jews. The exact number of Jews massacred is unknown, but estimates range from 40,000 to 100,000. Entire Jewish communities in eastern Europe were wiped out as the Cossacks swept through them, killing and torturing, looting homes and synagogues, and defacing holy books. Many of the Jews who were not killed were taken captive and sold into slavery.

This catastrophe prepared the way for a crushing psychological blow that fell less than two decades later. According to Jewish tradition, a period of intense suffering will precede the coming of the Messiah, the figure whom the biblical prophets associated with peace for the entire world at "the end of days." So in the mid-1660s many Jews in eastern Europe and elsewhere were ready to believe the claims of a Turkish Jew named Shabbetai Zevi that he was the Messiah. Many went so far as to sell all their property to prepare for a return to Israel under his leadership. But Israel was then controlled by the Turkish sultan, who believed that Shabbetai Zevi's claims threatened his throne. Thus in 1666 the sultan offered the self-proclaimed Messiah a choice between death and conversion to Islam; Zevi chose to convert. His followers, many of whom felt that their entire system of belief had been destroyed, were devastated.

Israel ben Eliezer, the Baal Shem Tov

BORN

Around 1700
Podolia, Poland (now southwest Ukraine)

DIED

1760
Medzibozh, Podolia, Poland

ACCOMPLISHMENTS

Transformed Judaism into a joyous religion; inspired his followers to create the Hasidic movement

> *"The strength you were willing to lose through fasting, devote to Torah and to worship. Thereby will you ascend to a higher state."*
>
> —the Baal Shem Tov, quoted in *Kether Shem Tov* (1795), by Aaron of Opatow, a disciple who collected the statements of the Besht

A pall settled over the Jews of eastern Europe. Many assumed that their own sinfulness was responsible for the disasters they had suffered. In order to atone for these sins some began to deny themselves the basic necessities of life; others even punished themselves with whips. For many years, the Jewish common people and their leaders reeled under the impact of the Cossack massacres and the Shabbetai Zevi affair.

The Jewish communities of eastern Europe were still in crisis when the Baal Shem Tov appeared on the scene. His leadership and his comforting belief in the dignity of the common Jew helped resuscitate the weakened community. So forceful was his personality that he became the subject of legend even during his lifetime. As a result, it is not always possible to separate fact from fiction in describing his life. He left behind no writings except for a few letters, and later generations have had to rely on the sayings his followers jotted down and published after his death.

Historians believe that the Baal Shem Tov was probably born in about the year 1700 in the poorest region of southeastern Poland. His parents died when he was still a child, and he supported himself in a variety of ways: as an assistant teacher in an elementary school, a clay digger, and an innkeeper. According to his followers,

there was a period when he and his wife retreated into the Carpathian Mountains of central Europe. Then, on his 36th birthday, he emerged, ready to reveal his teachings to a world hungry for a message of hope.

At the core of the Baal Shem Tov's teachings is the belief that God is in everything, including sin and suffering, and "even in trifles." By sinning, a person suppresses God. By overcoming suffering, a person removes a covering that has hidden God's presence. Since the Baal Shem Tov taught that God is in everything, he maintained that one can worship not only through study and prayer but also through the simple daily activities of eating and drinking, conducting business, even tying one's shoelaces. One did not have to be a scholar to worship God properly.

The Baal Shem Tov taught that in performing any act at all one can hope to achieve a feeling of intense closeness to, and even oneness with, God. According to a saying recorded by his follower Jacob Joseph, the Baal Shem Tov claimed that "faith is the adhesion of the soul to God." A person should strive to adhere, or cling, to God not only through acts that are normally considered religious but also through all the aspects of life. All Jews—not just educated ones—can hope to achieve this oneness with God. Through teachings such as these the Baal Shem Tov raised the self-

These modern-day Hasidim from Israel observe the biblical prohibition, "You shall not round the corners of your heads" (Leviticus 19:27). According to the Talmud, this verse forbids men to remove "the growth of hair on the temple from the back of the ears to the forehead."

respect of the common Jew. In his view, any Jew can be a Hasid, or pious person.

The Baal Shem Tov condemned self-punishment as a form of religious behavior. He taught that a true Hasid approaches God with joy—even eating and drinking should be considered holy activities. Dancing and singing also can be expressions of the Hasid's love for God. (Because he emphasized the role of joyous behavior in religious observance, the Baal Shem Tov's critics dismissed him as a "merry-maker.")

According to the Baal Shem Tov, a community of Hasidim requires a special kind of leader. Every generation is granted a certain number of superior individuals with outstanding spiritual qualities and an ability to cling to God. Each of these spiritual leaders is called in Hebrew a Zaddik, which means "completely righteous one." The responsibility of the Zaddik was to become personally involved in the lives of the Hasidim. By functioning on their level, the Zaddik would help raise the Hasidim to a higher spiritual plane. For their part, by

following the Zaddik the Hasidim would move a step closer to achieving oneness with God.

The relationship between the Zaddik and his Hasidim, however, was as beneficial to the former as to the latter. The Baal Shem Tov taught that Hasidim can also inspire their Zaddik to live up to his full potential, as the following story shows. Once, as the holiest day of the Jewish calendar, Yom Kippur, drew to a close, the Baal Shem Tov scrutinized the heavens with a sinking heart. He was looking for the moon so that he could say the

Blessing of the New Moon, which he believed would help bring good fortune to the Jews. But clouds covered the moon, and try as he would to will the clouds to part and reveal the moon, the Baal Shem Tov was unable to affect weather. His Hasidim, unaware of the Baal Shem Tov's distress, began to dance joyfully around their Zaddik. At the height of their religious rapture, the Hasidim reached out for the Baal Shem Tov's hands and drew him into their circle. At that moment the clouds parted and the moon brilliantly illuminated the sky. Through their joy, the Hasidim were able to overcome their Zaddik's despair and participate as a community in his achievements on their behalf.

In its time, the Baal Shem Tov's concept of leadership aroused a great deal of opposition, as it continues to do today. Critics of Hasidism consider the hero worship of the Zaddik a form of idol worship.

When the Baal Shem Tov died in 1760, he had many followers, not only among the masses but also among the educated elite. There was as yet no Hasidic movement, however. It arose over the next dozen years, as one of his students sent representatives out through much of eastern Europe to spread the Baal Shem Tov's teachings. In this way the Hasidic movement took root. It continued to serve the Jews of eastern Europe for the next century and a half.

Large numbers of Hasidim died during World War II, but new centers of Hasidism have developed since then in the United States, such as in Brooklyn, New York, and in Israel, particularly Jerusalem. From these centers the teachings of the Baal Shem Tov continue to shape Jewish tradition in several ways, even for Jews who otherwise reject the ultra-Orthodox lifestyle and the leader-centered communities adopted by the Hasidim.

One way in which the Baal Shem Tov's beliefs have permeated Jewish tradition is through his emphasis on the joyful aspects of religion. Even Jews who claim no connection to Hasidic ideals have absorbed this aspect of Hasidism into their religious traditions at Jewish weddings and other celebrations and in synagogue services of Jews of eastern European origin. At Jewish weddings and bar mitzvah celebrations, for example, the bride and groom or bar mitzvah boy may be lifted into the air on chairs by joyful guests and carried around the room to the lively strains of musical accompaniment. In synagogue services, the congregation may be asked to join the cantor or rabbi in singing a joyful, wordless tune, another Hasidic tradition.

An emphasis on joy has not only transformed Jewish religious observance but also Judaism's culture. Hasidic melodies, dances, and stories have enriched the culture of all Jews. Jewish youth movements and summer camps with no other connection to Hasidism often incorporate such tunes, dances, and legends into their programs. In addition, tales about the lives of the Hasidic leaders teach a great deal about Jewish values to readers of all ages and backgrounds.

The Hasidic movement continues to play a role in shaping Jewish tradition because of its emphasis on what is known as outreach. Hasidim actively seek out Jews who might otherwise drift away from Judaism. One such target group includes those who grew up under communism. Because communist ideology required that the teaching of religion be suppressed, the Jews of the former Soviet Union and other communist nations had little opportunity to learn about their spiritual and cultural heritage. Wherever these Jews are living today, the Hasidic movement undertakes to educate them. In addition, Hasidism has appealed to many young Jews in the United States who did not feel that their spiritual needs were being met elsewhere in the Jewish community.

In seeking to incorporate individual Jewish souls into the broader Jewish community, the Hasidim are fulfilling another teaching of the Baal Shem Tov. Emphasizing the importance of each Jew, he taught, "The divine presence wails and says as long as a limb is attached to the body there is hope for its cure; but when it is severed, it cannot be restored; and every Jew is a limb of the divine presence."

FURTHER READING

Buber, Martin. *The Legend of the Baal-Shem*. New York: Harper, 1955.

Heschel, Abraham Joshua. *A Passion for Truth*. Philadelphia: Jewish Publication Society, 1973.

Newman, Louis I. "The Baal Shem Tov." In *Great Jewish Personalities in Ancient and Medieval Times*. Edited by Simon Noveck. Washington, D.C.: B'nai B'rith, 1959.

Pasachoff, Naomi. "Baal Shem Tov." In *Great Jewish Thinkers: Their Lives and Work*. West Orange, N.J.: Behrman House, 1992.

Pasachoff, Naomi, and Robert J. Littman. "The Development of Hasidism." In *Jewish History in 100 Nutshells*. Northvale, N.J.: Aronson, 1995.

Rosman, Murray Jay. *Founder of Hasidism: A Quest for the Historical Baal Shem Tov*. Berkeley: University of California Press, 1996.

Elijah ben Solomon Zalman, the Gaon of Vilna

UNDERSTANDING
TORAH IN ITS
TRUEST SENSE

S ome great leaders are late bloomers whose gifts become apparent only as they mature. The extraordinary abilities of other great leaders are apparent from the time they are children. Elijah ben Solomon fell into the second category. From his early childhood it was clear that this was no ordinary bright child. By the time he was 33, he was known as the Gaon, a term sometimes translated as "Excellency" that also means "genius." No official assembly of rabbis bestowed this title on him, but of their own accord scholars from near and far, including rabbis much older than Elijah, began to use it. From that time on, Elijah, the Gaon of Vilna, has symbolized the Jewish passion for intellectual excellence.

Elijah Gaon was born in 1720 in Selets, Lithuania, a small town not far from the city of Vilna, to which his family moved during his early years. As a young child, Elijah began to study with his father, Rabbi Solomon. His father, as well as everyone else who conversed with the boy, recognized immediately that Elijah was uniquely gifted. In 1727, when he was only seven years old, Elijah

צורת ארמו״ר גאון הגאונים וחסיד כאחד מראשונים רשכבה״ג נודע בשם
רבינו אליהו גאון וחסיד מ ווילנא נבג״ע זי״ע.
נולד־ביום ראשון דחג הפסח שנת,שלח לכם־אלי׳הו׳ועלה השמים ג׳דח׳ם׳ס׳שנת.עלות אלי׳הו׳

The inscription beneath this portrait of Elijah ben Solomon, also known as the Gaon of Vilna, attributes to him the additional title *Admor,* from the abbreviation for the Hebrew words meaning "our lord, teacher, and master."

The city that Eastern European Jews called Vilna and considered the "Jerusalem of Lithuania" is also known for its many old churches, like the one here. The Lithuanian name for Vilna is Vilnius.

was already considered a great scholar of the Talmud, the important collection of Jewish law and legend dating from the 5th century. At that tender age he was invited to speak on a talmudic topic before a large, distinguished congregation in Vilna's main synagogue. (At that time, Vilna was a major center of Jewish life.) Following his address the child answered the questions of the rabbi with great perceptiveness.

So apparent was the young boy's brilliance that, apart from a brief period during which he was tutored by famous rabbis, he was left to pursue his studies on his own. As a result, Elijah Gaon was able to follow up on interests and instincts that would not have been encouraged in the talmudic academies of the day. In those schools the teachers insisted that all the commentaries written on the Talmud over the centuries were correct. If one commentary contradicted another, scholars performed all sorts of mental tricks to show how the two commentaries

actually agreed with one another. Elijah, however, had only one goal in mind as he studied on his own: to find the true meaning of the original words of the Talmud.

In order to do so, Elijah Gaon broadened the concept of Torah. Traditionally, this concept has had more than one meaning for Jews. Sometimes it has indicated the first five books of the Hebrew Bible, the Pentateuch. Sometimes it means the scroll itself from which the words of those five books are read in synagogues. On other occasions it means all of Jewish studies. In the Gaon's time, other scholars had limited the meaning of Torah to Talmud studies exclusively, even ignoring Bible studies. To achieve his goal of uncovering the true meaning of every word and passage in the Talmud, the Gaon believed he had to acquire all sorts of knowledge.

One area the Gaon opened up for inquiry had been ignored for centuries. All Jewish law had long been based on

the Talmud, but scholars had generally ignored the rich literature from talmudic times that had not been included in the Talmud itself. The Gaon was one of the first scholars to look for solutions to problems in the Talmud by carefully studying those other texts, including another version of the Talmud that had been edited about a century earlier.

Sometimes he would discover that the simplest explanation for a confusing section of the Talmud lay in comparing it to a similar passage in the earlier version, called the Jerusalem Talmud because it recorded the discussions of rabbis in Palestine. (The later Talmud, which has always been the more authoritative version, is called the Babylonian Talmud, because it records the discussions of the rabbis in Babylonia.) Such a comparison might show, for example, that the confusion was due to human error dating to the time before books were printed. It sometimes happens, for instance, that a person taking notes will leave out a word or misspell something. In a similar way, the Gaon sometimes found that a garbled passage in the Babylonian Talmud was the result of a scribe's copying a passage incorrectly from the Jerusalem edition. Once the mistake had been made, other scribes faithfully copied out the erroneous word. Then, after printing was invented, the mistake continued to appear in the printed versions. If only the different commentators on such passages had been aware of this simple explanation, they could have saved themselves—and generations of later students—a great deal of unnecessary effort!

The Gaon of Vilna was also the only scholar of his day to pay much attention to the study of the Bible. After all, he reasoned, the source of every talmudic law was the Bible. In order to make sure that he understood the source books clearly, he paid a great deal of attention to the Bible's Hebrew grammar and vocabulary. The Vilna Gaon correctly sensed that mastering the language of the Hebrew Bible could shed light on discussions among the rabbis of the Talmud. These men were well versed in biblical Hebrew, even though they spoke Aramaic, a related language. By using his understanding of Hebrew, the Gaon of Vilna succeeded in clarifying talmudic passages that others had regarded as obscure.

The Gaon also included in his broad concept of Torah the Jewish mystical tradition, or Kabbalah. Other scholars studied the works of the Jewish mystics but tended to keep their Talmud studies separate from their studies in Kabbalah. The Vilna Gaon, however, was intent on showing that there were no real contradictions between the Kabbalah and the Talmud. Whatever evident disagreements there seemed to be, he claimed, arose from a failure to understand the true meaning of one source or the other. To clarify the texts of the Kabbalah, he applied the same methods he used in his talmudic studies.

In one famous case, a student asked him to explain what the Hebrew word *hesed*, which means kindness, had to do with the particular passage in the Zohar (the major text of the Kabbalah) in which it appeared. The Vilna Gaon knew the passage from memory and explained the problem to his student. When a scribe had copied the text long ago, he could not understand the passage. To indicate that some words must be missing, the scribe wrote in the margin the Hebrew word for "missing," or *hasar*. When the text was eventually printed, the printer made a mistake and substituted the similar Hebrew word *hesed* for the scribe's notation. According to one of his followers, the Gaon often succeeded in thus uncovering the true texts of other works of Kabbalah, by

bringing "them out of the darkness caused by copyists' errors."

More important for later Jewish tradition, however, is that the Vilna Gaon did not limit his broad conception of Torah to Jewish-related subjects. He insisted instead that to understand Torah in its fullest sense a Jew also had to have an understanding of such sciences as astronomy, geometry, algebra, and geography. According to one of his students, the Gaon used to say, "All knowledge is necessary for our holy Torah and is included in it. . . . To the degree that a person is lacking in knowledge and secular sciences he will lack a hundred-fold in the wisdom of the Torah." The Gaon believed that as long as Jewish scholars showed no interest in science, the nations of the world would have little respect for either Jews or Judaism. Gentile critics, he claimed, "like the roaring of many waters will raise their voice against us, saying, where is your wisdom? and the name of Heaven will be profaned."

The Vilna Gaon did not, however, master the new scientific discoveries of his day. He learned science and mathematics from Hebrew translations of treatises that had been written in the Middle Ages. As a result, he was unaware of the revolution in science that had been created by the theories of the British scientist Sir Isaac Newton (1642–1727), who discovered the laws of motion and gravitation.

Nor did the Gaon believe that Jews should study science for its own sake. The point of deepening one's scientific knowledge, he was convinced, was to enrich one's understanding of the Torah, to enable one to comprehend the details of specific laws and discussions in the Talmud. For that reason the Gaon did not look with favor on a new movement that was then developing in nearby Germany. The leaders of this movement, called the Jewish Enlightenment,

Elijah ben Solomon Zalman, the Gaon of Vilna

BORN

April 23, 1720
Selets, Lithuania

DIED

October 9, 1797
Vilna, Lithuania

EDUCATION

Mainly self-taught; studied Kabbalah, Talmud, biblical studies, and Hebrew grammar; to clarify various discussions in the Talmud he taught himself astronomy, geometry, algebra, and geography

ACCOMPLISHMENTS

Broadened the traditional concept of Torah to include both secular studies and Kabbalah; helped establish Vilna as a center for Talmudic scholarship

"Let not the teacher impose his yoke heavily on them [children], for instruction is only efficient when it is conveyed easily and agreeably. Give the children small presents of money and the like, to please them—this helps their studies."

—from a letter written by the Gaon of Vilna to his family in the mid-1700s

believed that Jews would be accepted by their non-Jewish neighbors only if they participated fully in modern culture. The Enlightenment leaders also thought that intense study of the Talmud should be limited only to those Jews who wanted to be rabbis. Others, they felt, should learn secular professions and trades. The Gaon did not share these goals and saw them as a threat to traditional Judaism. Despite his opposition to the Jewish Enlightenment, however, he did not actively seek to stamp it out.

As a scholar, the Vilna Gaon mainly occupied himself with solitary study and in giving regular lectures to a small group of other outstanding scholars. For the most part, he did not take an active role in community affairs. Despite his title he never had an official post in the Vilna Jewish community. He believed that he could best lead by letting his immense learning overflow to benefit other scholars, whose knowledge would in turn be passed on to those who came to study with them.

One Jewish movement of the day so worried the Gaon that he actively joined the attempt to eliminate it. This was the Hasidic movement, which had begun in neighboring Poland a few years earlier and reached Vilna by the early 1770s. The new movement threatened many of the ideals that the Vilna Gaon associated with authentic Jewish tradition. It focused on prayer rather than study and encouraged Jews to celebrate God joyfully, rather than to come close to God through intense intellectual effort. Worst of all, he felt, the Hasidic movement was based on a form of leadership that seemed to him totally alien to Judaism. The Hasidic leader, or Zaddik, was revered by his followers in a manner that seemed very much like idol worship to the Vilna Gaon. Until his death in 1797 he spared no effort to limit the spread of the Hasidic movement.

One story told about the Vilna Gaon emphasized how strongly he believed in an intellectual approach to Judaism. As the story goes, he was once asked if he would like to have an angel come and reveal to him all the mysteries of the Torah. The Gaon replied that he would not be at all pleased if that happened. He could best serve God, he rejoined, by working diligently on his own to uncover the Torah's secrets. The joy he felt each time his research helped him clarify one of those secrets was the reward of hard labor. Knowledge acquired without effort was of little value to him.

The contributions of those in the Vilna Gaon's closest circle demonstrate the immediate effect of his broadened concept of Torah. One of his followers translated the ancient Greek mathematician Euclid's *Geometry* and experimented in a laboratory set up by another of the Gaon's followers. One of the Gaon's brothers put together a short Aramaic dictionary; one of his sons wrote a Hebrew geography. Moreover, the effects of the Gaon's teachings and examples continue to our own day.

Although the Gaon of Vilna wrote no books himself, after his death, his students organized his marginal notes, their classroom notes, and his manuscripts, eventually publishing 40 volumes based on these sources. These convey the Gaon of Vilna's teaching that whoever studies Torah in its broad sense "communes with God—for God and the Torah are one." By emphasizing the value of intense scholarly effort and showing how Jewish studies are enriched by other knowledge, Elijah, the Gaon of Vilna, left a lasting mark on Jewish tradition.

FURTHER READING

Karp, Deborah. "Elijah, Gaon of Vilna." In *Heroes of Jewish Thought*. New York: Ktav, 1965.

Waxman, Meyer. "Vilna Gaon." In *Great Jewish Personalities in Ancient and Medieval Times*. Edited by Simon Noveck. Washington, D.C.: B'nai B'rith, 1959.

Moses Mendelssohn

BREAKING DOWN BARRIERS

At the time of Moses Mendelssohn's birth in 1729, there was very little interaction between Jews and non-Jews in towns like Dessau, Germany, where his parents lived, or anywhere else in Europe. The typical Jew's occupation, dress, speech, and education were very different from those of a typical non-Jew. Many types of jobs were forbidden to Jews, who were often forced to wear special garments (including a circular yellow badge for men and women and yellow pointed veil for women) that set them apart from the rest of the population. For the most part Jews took no part in the general European culture. Most spoke only Yiddish, a mixture of Hebrew and German that is written in Hebrew characters, or other blends of Hebrew and the local language. Since few Jews knew the language of those around them, they could not read the books presenting the new ideas then sweeping through Europe.

Even the standard Jewish education was very limited. It focused almost exclusively on the Talmud, the vast record of discussion among early rabbis, written in Aramaic and edited in the 5th century. Much of the rich Jewish cultural heritage, from poetry to philosophy, was not taught at all. The situation was somewhat different in big cities like Berlin, where many Jews spoke German and were permitted to engage in certain professions and businesses, but even the most privileged German-speaking Jews were still subject to prejudice.

Moses Mendelssohn helped break down the barriers that separated Jews from the world around them. His main weapon in this battle was education, which had helped him overcome numerous handicaps of his own during his early years. In addition to being a Jew in Germany, Mendelssohn was set apart by a habit of stammering and by a physical condition that left him hunchbacked. Like all Jewish boys, his first introduction to Jewish studies was the Hebrew Bible. Overcome by the beauty and power of its language, he continued to study biblical Hebrew on his own even after his formal Jewish education shifted its focus to talmudic studies. He also discovered some books by the great 12th-century philosopher Moses Maimonides, in which he was greatly impressed by the argument that Judaism is a religion based on reason.

When Mendelssohn was only 14 he left his parents' home to follow his rabbi and teacher David Fränkel to Berlin, 30 miles from Dessau. His mentor found him an attic room in the home of a wealthy Jew and gave the boy an occasional manuscript to copy so that he could eke out a living. Over the next seven years, Mendelssohn proceeded to educate himself, assisted by some young Jewish professionals who, impressed with the boy's eagerness and intelligence, helped him with his German and introduced him to other languages, mathematics, and philosophy. Books were expensive, especially for a boy living a hand-to-mouth existence, and the volumes he managed to acquire often did double duty. For example, he taught himself both Latin and philosophy from a Latin edition of a work by the 17th-century English philosopher John Locke. No matter what the subject, he was eager to master the contents of every book that came his way. A book written in German on Christian theology would have struck him as just as valuable as any other.

As word of the young man's accomplishments spread through Berlin's Jewish community, Mendelssohn was able to find a position as tutor to the children of a wealthy Jewish silk manufacturer. Now, with more disposable income at hand, he could buy more books and pursue his broad studies more systematically. His employer was so impressed by the young tutor that he soon took him into his business. After his employer's death, Mendelssohn, together with his benefactor's widow, took charge of the silk firm. He proved equally successful as a businessman, so that toward the end of his life the government commissioned him to write a report on the silk-manufacturing industry.

The turning point in Mendelssohn's life occurred 10 years after his arrival in Berlin when he was introduced to Gotthold Ephraim Lessing, a German playwright and critic. Lessing, like Mendelssohn, was 24 years old at the time. Friendships between Jews and non-Jews in Germany were extremely rare during this time, but Lessing, who was Christian, had since

The opening pages of Mendelssohn's Hebrew journal gives its name ("The Collector") and indicates that its contents were collected by the members of the Society for the Promotion of the Hebrew Language. The journal was published sporadically from 1783 until 1811, 25 years after Mendelssohn's death.

boyhood been unusually tolerant of other religions. In a Latin translation required for admission to a school to which Lessing applied when he was 12, he successfully translated a passage about the effect of Christianity on the ancient prejudice against the "barbarians," and then added his own comment: "Whatever we do, we achieve with the help of other people. Hence we are all 'neighbors.' For this reason we will not damn the Jews.... We will not condemn the Mohammedans, for among them, too, are good people. Hence, no one is a barbarian unless he be inhuman and cruel."

Lessing and Mendelssohn became partners in a literary magazine, and Lessing (without Mendelssohn's knowledge) also arranged for the publication of Mendelssohn's first book, a study of the 3rd Earl of

Shaftesbury, a noted 17th-century English philosopher. Having thus been launched into the literary world by his friend, Mendelssohn went on to earn a reputation as a philosopher in his own right. At the age of 38, this son of a poor Yiddish-speaking scribe from Dessau published a book in German on the immortality of the soul. The European intellectual community hailed him as the equal of the ancient Greek philosophers Plato and Socrates, and the book was translated into several languages.

Mendelssohn's fame opened doors for him, and he was soon mingling with the cream of German society, including King Frederick the Great of Prussia. But his new celebrity did not lead him to turn his back on his humble Jewish background. On the contrary, he used his position to combat anti-Jewish

> *"Let every man who does not disturb the public welfare, who obeys the law, who acts righteously toward his fellow men, be allowed to speak as he thinks, to pray to God after his own fashion or after the fashion of his fathers, and to seek his eternal salvation where he thinks he can find it."*
>
> —from *Jerusalem* (1783)

Moses Mendelssohn

BORN

1729
Dessau, Germany

DIED

1786
Berlin, Germany

EDUCATION

In Dessau, studied Talmud with Rabbi David Fränkel; in Berlin, taught himself modern and ancient languages, mathematics, and philosophy

ACCOMPLISHMENTS

Ushered in the Jewish Enlightenment by introducing the Jews of Europe to modern secular culture; wrote *Jerusalem* (1783), putting forth the first modern philosophy of Judaism; other works include *Phaedo, or On the Immortality of the Soul* (1764), a preface to the German translation of Manasseh ben Israel's *Vindication of the Jews* (1782), and *Morning Hours* (1785)

prejudice in Germany and to assist Jewish communities in distress. Furthermore, convinced that it was education that had made it possible for him to be accepted in German society, he determined to help other German Jews follow in his footsteps. To do so, he devised a three-part plan to transform Jewish education.

The first two parts of Mendelssohn's plan were rooted in his belief that speaking only Yiddish in their daily lives kept Jews from advancing in the modern world. Because he believed that they needed to speak, read, and write fluent German, he set about introducing German into the Jewish community. Mendelssohn was aware that over the course of each year Jews heard the first five books of the Hebrew Bible, the Pentateuch, read aloud in the synagogue. He thus concluded that a good German translation of the Pentateuch would be the perfect introduction to the new language. To make the transition even easier, Mendelssohn even set the German text in Hebrew letters. His translation, published between 1780 and 1783, served its purpose well. After working their way through Mendelssohn's work, many young German Jews found themselves familiar enough with German to read other literary pieces written in the language.

The second goal of Mendelssohn's educational plan focused on the use of Hebrew, which he believed could also be made a tool for entering the modern world. In Mendelssohn's day, Jews considered Hebrew too holy for everyday use and used it only for prayer and religious studies. To demonstrate that Hebrew could be used in the contemporary world, Mendelssohn and some colleagues wrote a Hebrew commentary to his German translation of the Pentateuch. Mendelssohn also began a journal in which topics of current interest were discussed in Hebrew. Today, of course, Hebrew has become very much a part of the modern world: it is the official language of the state of Israel, where it is used for everything from popular songs to government documents.

Mendelssohn's third goal for Jewish education was to broaden it considerably. Today there are many private Jewish schools in the United States that offer courses in English, science, math, and sports in addition to the traditional studies of the

Hebrew language and religious subjects. Before Mendelssohn's reforms few such schools existed, however. German Jews did not attend secular schools and studied just religion, privately. In 1781 he encouraged one of his younger colleagues to open a new Jewish school in Berlin. There students were exposed to a whole range of languages, including Hebrew and German, and a wide variety of courses, from bookkeeping to geography. Mendelssohn and his colleague argued that the traditional Jewish education, focused narrowly on the Talmud, was appropriate only for Jews planning to become rabbis. In their view, all other young Jews needed to be educated for occupations in the general community.

During the next century, Mendelssohn's efforts shaped the aims of the movement called the Jewish Enlightenment as it spread through the German-speaking world and into Russia. The goal of the Jewish Enlightenment was to bring the Jews of Europe into the modern world. Today this goal seems quite reasonable, but during the 18th century many Jewish authorities feared that Jews might turn their backs on Judaism if they were introduced to the language and culture of the outside world.

The suspicions with which these authorities viewed Mendelssohn and his activities were strengthened in 1783 when his book *Jerusalem* appeared. In this work he described Judaism and the laws of the Pentateuch in a new and sometimes shocking way. The first section of the book developed the argument that no religion has the right to use force to control what people believe. In the second part, Mendelssohn laid out a view of Judaism that made him famous in some circles and infamous in others. In it he claimed that God gave all people, not just the Jews, powers of

reasoning to establish proper codes of conduct. He asserted that what makes Judaism unique is the Pentateuch's specific set of laws, which Jews alone are obliged to follow. Even though all people are capable of using reason to establish religious truths, Jews must continue to observe the laws of the Pentateuch for three reasons: because they come from God, who alone can determine if they are no longer necessary; because observing the laws keeps the Jewish people united; and because those laws preserve a pure belief in God.

Needless to say, many Jews reacted badly to Mendelssohn's description of Judaism as merely a body of laws given by God in a supernatural act. They further rejected the conclusions that Mendelssohn's argument implied: that everything reasonable about Judaism could be found elsewhere, and that what made Judaism special was based on the supernatural.

However controversial Mendelssohn's philosophy of Judaism may have beem, the Jewish Enlightenment that he initiated brought many Jews into the modern world. His ideas about Jewish education have been adopted widely. And his insistence that Hebrew should be more than a language of prayer and religious scholarship helped lead to the rebirth of that language. Every Jew who participates in contemporary society while still maintaining a strong Jewish identity is in a sense walking in Mendelssohn's footsteps. In his book *Jerusalem* Mendelssohn offered profound advice to those who wished to live dignified lives as both Jews and secular citizens: "Adopt the mores and constitution of the country in which you find yourself, but be steadfast in upholding the religion of your fathers, too. Bear both burdens as well as you can." Many Jews have lived their lives according to these precepts.

FURTHER READING

Altmann, Alexander. *Moses Mendelssohn: A Biography and Study*. London: Routledge & K. Paul, 1973.

Arkush, Allan. *Moses Mendelssohn and the Enlightenment*. Albany: State University of New York Press, 1994.

Jospe, Alfred. "Moses Mendelssohn." In *Great Jewish Personalities in Modern Times*. Edited by Simon Noveck. Washington, D.C.: B'nai B'rith, 1960.

Mendelssohn, Moses. *Jerusalem and Other Jewish Writings*. Translated and edited by Alfred Jospe. New York: Schocken, 1969.

———. *Moses Mendelssohn: Selections from His Writings*. Translated and edited by Eva Jospe. New York: Viking, 1975.

Pasachoff, Naomi. "Moses Mendelssohn." In *Great Jewish Thinkers: Their Lives and Work*. West Orange, N.J.: Behrman House, 1992.

Pasachoff, Naomi, and Robert J. Littman. "Moses Mendelssohn and the Jewish Enlightenment." In *Jewish History in 100 Nutshells*. Northvale, N.J.: Aronson, 1995.

Rebecca Gratz

"SHE PRIZED HER RELIGION ABOVE ALL TERRESTRIAL OBJECTS"

For many years, Sir Walter Scott's novel *Ivanhoe* was required reading in many American schools. Some students had difficulty wading through Scott's sentimental prose. Most, however, came away with a vivid memory of the novel's heroine, Rebecca. This Jewish beauty nurses the wounded hero, a Saxon Crusader, who later rescues her from being burned as a witch. From the time of *Ivanhoe*'s publication, in 1819, it has generally been accepted that the Scottish author modeled his 12th-century character on an actual American Jew: Rebecca Gratz of 19th-century Philadelphia. These days fewer students are introduced to the fictionalized Rebecca Gratz through Scott's novel. However, attending Jewish Sunday schools or afternoon religious schools lets many participate in a tradition that the real Rebecca Gratz initiated.

About 17 years before Rebecca's birth in 1781, her father, Michael Gratz, arrived in Philadelphia, where his older brother had settled five years earlier. The brothers, born in Upper Silesia, a coal-rich region in Germany, had been sent to London for business training. There they

Rebecca Gratz, founder of the Hebrew Sunday School Society. Other members of the Gratz family founded Philadelphia's Gratz College, the first Jewish teacher-training institution in the United States.

"I am gratified at the evident improvement of a large class of children in religious knowledge, more particularly as I find it influencing their conduct and manners, and gaining consideration in the minds of their parents."

—from a letter to Maria G. Gratz (February 23, 1840)

became successful merchants, specializing in trade with North America. They also acquired substantial amounts of land around Louisville, Kentucky.

Michael Gratz married the daughter of another Jewish merchant in Pennsylvania. The couple had 12 children, two of whom died in childhood. In the years to come, their sons made significant contributions to the growth of the United States. One son, Jacob, for example, was twice elected to the Pennsylvania state legislature, while another, Benjamin, helped organize the Lexington and Ohio Railroad in 1830 and the Lexington branch of the Bank of Kentucky in 1835. But it was Rebecca, the seventh child, who had the greatest impact of any member of this outstanding family. Unlike some of her brothers, she received no university training. Her formal education was limited to grammar school, though she continued to read literature on her own. She lacked familiarity with Jewish texts, but her pioneering efforts with Jewish charities and education became the models for similar institutions throughout the country.

Members of the Gratz family were pillars of the first—and for many years only—Jewish congregation in Philadelphia, Congregation Mikveh Israel, founded during the early 1770s. The family moved just as comfortably in Christian circles as in Jewish ones, though. Among Rebecca's close gentile friends was the author Washington Irving (1783–1859). He was the link between Gratz and Sir Walter Scott. The two writers had met when the grieving Irving had traveled to England after the death of his 18-year-old fiancée. In the course of their conversations he spoke about his friend Rebecca Gratz. After *Ivanhoe* was published, Scott wrote to Irving, "How do you like your Rebecca? Does the Rebecca I have pictured compare well with the pattern given?"

Because the Gratzes intermingled with Christians so freely, it is perhaps not surprising that some members of that family married non-Jews. When Rebecca was in her early 20s, she succeeded in mending a rupture in the family that had been caused by intermarriage. Some years before, her mother's sister had married a Christian surgeon who was a good friend of George Washington. The news so unsettled the bride's father, Rebecca's grandfather Joseph Simon, that he refused to see his daughter again. In 1804, as Simon lay on his deathbed, Rebecca pleaded with him to forgive her aunt. Simon agreed and just a few days later died in the arms of his formerly banished daughter. Similarly, when Rebecca's youngest brother, Benjamin, married a Christian woman, Maria Gist, in 1819, Rebecca became her sister-in-law's devoted friend, even though she feared that Maria would try to convert other family members to Christianity. When it came to her own life, however, Rebecca Gratz chose to sacrifice her personal happiness to family unity. She fell in love with Samuel Ewing, a Christian lawyer, who courted her for a number of years. When it finally became clear to Ewing that Gratz would never marry him, he married another woman, and Gratz remained single.

By this time, 1810, Rebecca Gratz had enough community and family responsibilities to help numb the pain of her personal loss. In 1801 she had become the youngest founding member of Philadelphia's Female Association for the Relief of Women and Children in Reduced Circumstances, which assisted poor women and children. For many years she served as secretary of the association. After her mother died in 1808, she managed the Gratz family home for her father and her unmarried brothers and sister. Then, when her father died in 1811, her family responsibilities increased. When her sister Rachel died at the age of 40 in 1823,

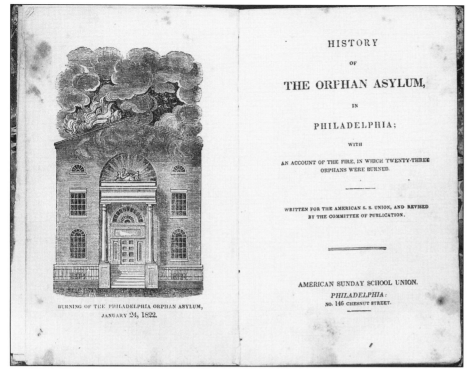

By the time of the Philadelphia Orphan Asylum fire in 1822 Rebecca Gratz had been the secretary of the institution for three years. She continued in that position until 1859.

Rebecca Gratz

BORN

March 4, 1781
Philadelphia, Pennsylvania

DIED

August 29, 1869
Philadelphia, Pennsylvania

EDUCATION

Attended grammar school; studied biblical history at home

ACCOMPLISHMENTS

Secretary of Philadelphia's Female Association for the Relief of Women and Children in Reduced Circumstances; charter member of the board of the Philadelphia Orphan Asylum and secretary of the orphanage (1819–59); founded the Female Hebrew Benevolent Society (1819), the first Jewish charitable organization in America not affiliated with a specific congregation; founded the Jewish Foster Home and Orphan Asylum (1855); established the first Hebrew Sunday School in the United States (1838)

Rebecca became a substitute mother to Rachel's nine children, the oldest of whom was only 16.

Her sister's offspring were neither the first nor the last motherless children for whom Gratz showed concern. She was a charter member of the board of the Philadelphia Orphan Asylum, founded in 1815, and served as the orphanage's secretary for 40 years.

In 1819, the same year she became secretary of the orphanage, the Jewish community of Philadelphia benefited from the experience she had gained in her 18-year association with the Female Association for the Relief of Women and Children. Until that year, the only Jewish charities in the United States had been branches of specific synagogues, each providing only for its own members. In founding the Female Hebrew Benevolent Society, Gratz established the first Jewish charity in the United States aimed at helping any needy member of the Jewish community, regardless of his or her synagogue association.

In 1855 the Jews of Philadelphia once again profited from Gratz's experience in general charity work. In the late 1840s thousands of Jews had begun to leave central Europe for the United States, and the nature of Philadelphia's Jewish community changed. Before that time, the majority of the city's Jews had become prosperous and well established. Many of these recent immigrants, by contrast, needed help to get started in their new country. Sometimes the adult newcomers did not live long enough to provide for their children. To help those children, Gratz established the Jewish Foster Home and Orphan Asylum. Eventually, this institution admitted Jewish orphans from a number of cities besides Philadelphia. Gratz's Jewish orphanage was only the third such institution in the United States.

As important as her charitable work was, Gratz is best remembered for her contribution to Jewish education in America. Although she did not formally found the Hebrew Sunday School Society until 1838, she had been preoccupied with the need to educate the Jewish children of Philadelphia for at least 20 years. For instance, in a letter to a friend in 1818, Gratz wrote of holding an afternoon class in her home. The session was attended by the children of members of the Congregation Mikveh Israel. The teacher, a young rabbi from Germany, had recently published a pamphlet called *Elements of the Jewish Faith,* which served as a textbook for the makeshift school. Although the experiment ended when the rabbi left for another city, Gratz remained committed to educating the city's Jewish children.

With the encouragement of Isaac Leeser, the spiritual leader of Mikveh Israel from 1829 to 1851, Gratz established and directed the first Jewish Sunday school in the United States. Such an initiative would have been almost unthinkable in Europe, where the teachers of Jewish children were all men. These men, known as *melamdim,* the Hebrew word for religious tutors, may not have been gifted educators, but they had all mastered the basics of Hebrew. This tradition did not in the least deter Gratz or the other women who helped found the school. It never occurred to them that their sex or lack of Jewish education disqualified them as teachers. Instead, they were convinced that they had both the right and the responsibility to transmit the Jewish tradition to the next generation. As director of the school from 1838 to 1864, Gratz showed how seriously she took her job by continuing to improve her knowledge of the Bible and Jewish history.

The Hebrew Sunday School was open to all Jewish children, not just those of members of Mikveh Israel. Gratz's school soon was serving 60 pupils. The faculty included some of Gratz's grown nieces. Each school session opened and closed with an assembly where Gratz personally presided. The opening assembly always began with a prayer she had composed herself, followed by a chapter from the Bible, which she read in English translation. At the closing assembly the children sang hymns in Hebrew and English. The curriculum included "Scripture Lessons," taught at first from an illustrated publication of the Christian Sunday School Union. One of Gratz's teachers recalled not only spending her summer vacation "pasting pieces of paper over answers unsuitable for Jewish children" but also "the fruitless efforts of those children to read through, over, or under the hidden lines."

Eventually, textbooks became available through the efforts of Congregation Mikveh Israel's spiritual leader, Isaac Leeser. In addition to his commitment to the congregation, Leeser founded the first Jewish Publication Society of America. Under its auspices he published the first American children's Hebrew primer and numerous textbooks for children, as well as the first English translation of the Hebrew Bible published in the United States.

Gratz arranged to hold yearly oral examinations of the Sunday school students. The most successful scholar in each class was handed a Bible by the beaming director. The two runners-up received other books Gratz had chosen carefully. But every student came away from the ordeal with a reward: an orange and a pretzel. Gratz was actively involved with the school until she retired in 1864, at the age of 83.

In October 1869, six weeks after Gratz's death, Isaac Leeser's successor as leader of the Congregation Mikveh Israel, the Reverend Sabato Morais, paid tribute to Gratz in a speech before the teachers and pupils of the Sunday school: "She devoted her best energies to service for the lowly and hapless, to improving the rising generation of her own brethren. The Sunday School, founded by Rebecca Gratz, became the mold for all others elsewhere." Perhaps referring to Gratz's sacrifice of her own emotional happiness many years earlier, Morais added, "She loved her people and prized her religion above all terrestrial objects; and she determined, doubtless when still young, that her conduct through life should reflect luster upon both." Morais called on the children to model their own lives on Gratz's.

Gratz's contributions to Philadelphia and the United States benefited more than just the generations lucky enough to know her personally. When a wave of Jewish immigrants entered the United States from eastern Europe in the late 1800s, their needs were met by institutions such as the National Council of Jewish Women, modeled after those created and sustained by Rebecca Gratz.

FURTHER READING

Karp, Abraham J. "The First Jewish Sunday School." In *Haven and Home: A History of the Jews in America.* New York: Schocken, 1985.

Osterweis, Rollin G. *Rebecca Gratz: A Study in Charm.* New York: Putnam, 1935.

Philipson, David, ed. *Letters of Rebecca Gratz.* Philadelphia: Jewish Publication Society, 1929.

Moses Montefiore

RELIEVING SUFFERING
AROUND THE WORLD

A tall, strikingly handsome Englishman, Sir Moses Montefiore was born in 1784 and lived for over 100 years. Though not a rabbi, a founder of a new religious movement, or a scholar, Montefiore gained renown among both Jews and gentiles, common people and heads of state.

Nowadays, the idea of a Jew being welcomed by the heads of foreign countries does not seem odd. Israel is a Jewish state, and its leaders regularly meet with their counterparts. But in Montefiore's time, even in more progressive countries like England, Jews were just beginning to gain rights long granted other inhabitants. There was no Jewish state, and few Jews had much influence beyond their own communities. Moses Montefiore was the first modern Jew whose prestige both in his home country and abroad led to improved conditions for other Jews. By using the good fortune that was his by birth and marriage to help advance the cause of Jews around the globe, Montefiore helped shape Jewish tradition.

An aged Sir Moses Montefiore sits in front of a portrait, possibly of his wife, Judith, who died 23 years before him, after 50 years of marriage. Sir Moses founded the Judith Lady Montefiore College in honor of his wife, who wrote the first Anglo-Jewish cookbook.

The Montefiore family originally came from Italy, where there is a town called Montefiore near the Adriatic seaport of Ancona. After a time they settled in Livorno, a city on the Ligurian Sea, in western Italy. In the early 18th century the family moved to London, where it soon became one of the leading Jewish families. Although Moses Montefiore was born during one of his parents' visits to Livorno, he was raised in England, where his education was scanty by today's standards. His family expected him to be a businessman, not a scholar. He was tutored in a variety of subjects, including elementary Hebrew, but was unable to attend an English university, whose doors were open only to members of the Church of England. After serving as apprentice to a firm of wholesale grocers and tea merchants, he became one of the 12 "Jew brokers" permitted by the British crown to conduct business in the London financial world.

As it turned out, Montefiore was not much of a businessman. But he was lucky enough to fall in love with the sister-in-law of Nathan Meyer Rothschild, the Jewish financial genius who founded one of the great English banking houses. The Rothschild connection enabled Montefiore to retire from business in 1824, financially independent if not notably wealthy.

Retirement from business did not mean withdrawal from the world for Montefiore, however—on the contrary. For the next six decades, until his death in 1885, Montefiore was actively involved in public life both in England and abroad as a spokesman for the Jewish people. In 1838 he became president of the Board of Deputies of British Jews, an institution created in 1760 that still functions as a representative organization of British Jewry. Except for a brief interval, Montefiore remained in that position until 1874. In 1837 he also became an important civil officer when he was elected sheriff of the City

Montefiore distributes charity during an 1839 visit to Safed, when the Palestinian hill town was still reeling from the effects of a violent earthquake two years earlier. After his retirement from business in 1824, Montefiore devoted his remaining years to charity.

of London. After Victoria became queen of England later that year, Montefiore became the first Jew to be knighted since 1701. As Sir Moses Montefiore he now had new social standing that was to benefit Jews around the world.

An opportunity to help a Jewish community in distress arose soon after Montefiore's knighthood. In February 1840, a Roman Catholic friar in Damascus (the capital of Syria, then part of the Ottoman Empire) disappeared without a trace, together with his Muslim servant. Other members of the friar's order blamed the Jews of Damascus by spreading a so-called blood libel. According to this oft-repeated accusation, Jews allegedly murder non-Jews in order to use their blood for Passover or other rituals. At the time, all Syrian Catholics were under the protection of the French consul. Hostile to Jews, the consul supported the baseless accusations. Together with the governor-general of Syria, the French consul conducted an investigation that was neither impartial nor humane. A Jewish barber was arrested and tortured until he "confessed" that seven Jews had committed the murder. Subsequently 63 Jewish children were seized in an attempt to

force their mothers to reveal where the friar's blood had been hidden.

As president of the Board of Deputies of British Jews, Montefiore volunteered to travel to Damascus to see if he could convince the Muslim authorities there to come to the aid of the imprisoned Jews. He was accompanied on this difficult journey by Adolphe Crémieux, a French Jewish statesman. The English government did whatever it could to smooth the path of the two Jewish delegates, who succeeded in their mission. Not only did they win the release of the accused Jews from prison, they also convinced the Ottoman sultan to issue a decree condemning blood libels.

Montefiore's Damascus mission was to leave its mark on Jewish tradition. The undertaking was the first in which privileged Jews succeeded in intervening on behalf of less fortunate Jews in another country. From that time on, it has become customary for Jews in all countries to use every means available to them, including the support of their own governments, to relieve other Jews in distress around the globe.

The Damascus mission proved to be only the first of Montefiore's diplomatic ventures on behalf of Jews in distress. He made a second major effort in 1846, when Czar Nicholas I of Russia proposed to divide Russian Jews into two main groups: a small minority whose occupations made them "useful" and a large majority of "exploiters and parasites" who would be dealt with severely. The "useless" Jews in the second group would be drafted in greater numbers into the czarist army and expelled from their villages. Backed once again by the British government, Montefiore traveled to Russia. He gained an audience with the minister in charge of Jewish affairs and even the czar himself. This time, however, his efforts were only partly rewarded. Although the czar's plan was not put into effect immediately (and was actually never fully carried out, because of the czar's death in 1855), the persecution of the Jews of Russia continued for the rest of Montefiore's life and beyond.

In 1846, shortly after Montefiore's return to England from his Russian mission, Queen Victoria raised him to the rank of baronet. She expressed the hope that this sign of royal favor would help Montefiore's attempts to improve the condition of Jews elsewhere.

In 1858, Montefiore traveled to Rome to see if he could use his influence in the so-called Mortara case. In June of that year, police agents serving the pope had seized the six-year-old son of the Mortara family, Jews living in Bologna. Taken to Rome, the boy was placed in an institution for converts to Catholicism. The authorities based their action on an event that had occurred five years earlier. At that time, the boy had been gravely ill. His Catholic nurse, fearing that he would die, had performed an informal baptism to save the child's soul. In the eyes of the church, he was therefore a Catholic. Unfortunately, Montefiore failed to secure the boy's release. The child grew up to be a professor of Catholic theology and a missionary. Fluent in six languages, he spread anti-Semitic ideas in all of them.

During the 1860s and 1870s, Montefiore made a variety of attempts to relieve Jewish suffering. For example, in 1863 he visited the North African country of Morocco, where the persecution of Jews was on the rise. The trouble stemmed from France's growing control over neighboring Algeria. Since the French invasion of Algeria in 1830, Moroccans had become increasingly alarmed about foreign influences. Even though Jews had lived in Morocco for centuries, some Moroccans began to suspect them of plotting to help Europeans gain a foothold in their country. To try to resolve the situation, Montefiore met with Morocco's ruler, who soon isssued a royal decree granting Jews equal rights with all other Moroccans.

In another incident, in 1866 the new ruler of Romania proposed granting equal rights to every inhabitant, regardless of religion. The thought that Jews might be included in this plan horrified a certain sector of the population, and a number of pogroms broke out. An anti-Jewish mob even threatened members of the legislature that had gathered to discuss granting rights to Jews. The lawmakers, intimidated, made the law they adopted extend only to Christians. After that, persecution of the Romanian Jews intensified. They were expelled from villages, then driven out of the country as vagabonds. The outbreak of a cholera epidemic in 1867 was also blamed on the Jews. When international protests over Romania's anti-Semitism led to the downfall of the government, the Jews were once again held responsible, and new anti-Jewish measures were proposed. In 1866–67, Montefiore and his French colleague Adolphe Crémieux visited Romania to see what they could do. Although the authorities promised them the persecution would stop, the intervention of the Jewish envoys only intensified the anger of the anti-Jewish forces, and new pogroms took place in 1868.

Moses Montefiore

BORN
October 24, 1784
Livorno, Italy

DIED
July 28, 1885
Near Ramsgate, Kent, England

EDUCATION
He was taught elementary Hebrew in London by his mother's brother; had private tutoring in a variety of subjects; received no higher education because Jews were barred from English universities at the time

ACCOMPLISHMENTS
One of 12 Jewish brokers in the City of London; sheriff of London (1837–38); knighted by Queen Victoria (1837); received baronetcy (1846) for his humanitarian efforts on behalf of Jews in distress; president of the Board of Deputies of British Jews (1838–74); met with heads of state to improve conditions for Jews of Damascus, Russia, and elsewhere; helped improve conditions for the Jewish settlement in Palestine

"Begin the hallowed task at once, and He who takes delight in Zion will establish the work of your hands."

—from *Diary of Sir Moses Montefiore* (1874)

A coin presented to Montefiore by his admirers on his 100th birthday. The countries whose names encircle the coin are places where Montefiore intervened on behalf of Jews.

The condition of the Jews of Persia (modern-day Iran) also aroused Montefiore's concern. In 1865, news of the persecution of the Jewish community in the western city of Hamadan reached England. Montefiore, now 81 years old, was about to depart for the Middle East when the British Foreign Office persuaded him not to go, warning that "the journey would be perilous even to a younger man and could be undertaken by him at the risk of his life." Eight years later, however, when the shah of Persia visited London, Montefiore seized the occasion to meet privately with him at Buckingham Palace. The shah issued promises of improved treatment for Persia's Jews but did not honor this pledge.

Montefiore also left his mark on Jewish tradition by devoting himself to the Jewish settlement in Palestine. As he wrote in his diary, he fully believed that one day there would once again be a true home for Jews in Palestine: "I do not expect that all Israelites will quit their abodes in those territories in which they feel happy," he wrote. "But Palestine must belong to the Jews, and Jerusalem is destined to be the seat of the Jewish Empire." In 1839, nearly 60 years before an organized Zionist movement developed to help bring about an internationally recognized Jewish land in Palestine, Montefiore began negotiations with the Egyptian ruler who controlled Palestine at the time. Montefiore hoped to gain an official charter for Jewish settlement in Palestine in exchange for a large loan to Egypt. However, the downfall of this ruler in 1841 doomed Montefiore's hopes.

Nonetheless, in seven trips spanning nearly a half century Montefiore transformed the quality of life of the Jews of Palestine. In fact, many of Montefiore's efforts in Palestine had lasting effects. His plan, as recorded in his diary, was to "begin in the first instance with the building of houses in Jerusalem." Montefiore's projects in that city included the central area of what is now the capital of the Jewish state. The windmill that still stands out somewhat oddly on the Jerusalem landscape testifies to Montefiore's attempts to industrialize the country. His efforts to improve living conditions, religious security, and education played a role in more than doubling the number of Jewish inhabitants over the period. In essence, world Jewry considered Montefiore their delegate to Jews in the ancient homeland as well those in other political hotspots. When the American Jewish philanthropist Judah Touro died in 1854, for example, he left instructions in his will for $60,000 to be used at the discretion of Montefiore—whom he had never even met—to relieve the poverty of the Jews of Palestine.

While Montefiore did not succeed in all his attempts to improve the lives of Jews in distress, without question he succeeded in transforming Jewish tradition. When today's Jews who are lucky enough to live in comfort and security feel responsible for less fortunate Jews elsewhere, they are acting in the tradition of Sir Moses Montefiore.

FURTHER READING

Loewe, Louis, ed. *Diaries of Sir Moses and Lady Montefiore.* 2 vols. Chicago: Belford-Clarke, 1890.

Pasachoff, Naomi, and Robert J. Littman. "Sir Moses Montefiore and 19th-Century Jewish History." In *Jewish History in 100 Nutshells.* Northvale, N.J.: Aronson, 1995.

Roth, Cecil. "Moses Montefiore." In *Great Jewish Personalities in Modern Times.* Washington, D.C.: B'nai B'rith, 1960.

Leopold Zunz

TRUE SCHOLARSHIP PRODUCES DEEDS

J ews today are able to express their commitment to Judaism in a variety of ways. For centuries some have expressed devotion in religious terms, through prayer or traditional study of the basic Jewish texts, the Bible and the Talmud. Others have taken part in community activities, such as raising money for Jewish causes at home and abroad. A growing number of modern Jews demonstrate their commitment to Judaism in a third way: by studying Jewish history and Jewish literature with the same sort of rigorous scholarship that scholars apply to other fields of study. These Jews may or may not be religious or involved in community activities. Their chosen form of commitment had its origin less than two centuries ago. The person most closely associated with this type of Jewish self-expression is Leopold Zunz, a 19th-century German whose careful, painstaking research into the Jewish past set a high standard on which generations of Jewish scholars have attempted to model their own work.

Leopold Zunz's research into the Jewish past sparked an interest in the study of Jewish history and literature that continues to this day.

Zunz served as editor of *The Periodical for the Science of Judaism* during its brief life, from 1822 to 1823. Among the articles appearing in the periodical was Zunz's groundbreaking biography of the medieval commentator Rashi.

Zunz was born into a world in which religious Jews studied and prayed but rarely questioned the source of their texts. They were devoted to their studies but did not know when and where these works were written or what had influenced the authors. These observant Jews gave no thought at all to the connections that might exist between the sacred writings they revered and works representing other cultures. Such concerns would never have suggested themselves, for example, to Zunz's first teacher, his father, who introduced the young Leopold to the five books of Moses, the Talmud, and Hebrew grammar.

Zunz's father suffered from a lung disease and died at the age of 43, when his son was only 8. Leopold's mother could not provide for him, and the following year, 1803, he was sent to a boarding school for poor Jewish boys in Wolfenbüttel, a town a long way from home. Leopold never saw his mother again.

Leopold's first years at the school were not happy. He later remembered his teachers as uninspiring educators and strict disciplinarians who nonetheless failed to keep the older boys from bullying the younger ones. Talmud was almost the only thing taught in the course of the long school day, which lasted until four o'clock in the winter and five o'clock in the summer. Instruction in the five books of Moses was limited to one morning a week. Only about an hour a day was set aside for arithmetic and for reading and writing in German. There was no physical education, and extracurricular activities consisted only of attending synagogue services or funerals and helping to bake matzoh, the unleavened bread that Jews eat instead of regular bread at Passover.

To make matters worse, the boys were fed and clothed poorly. Little attention was paid to personal hygiene, and the boys were led to the river for bathing only occasionally. When Leopold was 13, he wrote a Hebrew composition mocking the older students' bad habits and the teachers' self-righteousness and general lack of tolerance. Although his friends enjoyed the spoof, the teachers burned it as soon as they discovered it. But however much Leopold resented or mocked his rigorous talmudic education, it gave him the basis for a deep understanding of the world of the ancient rabbis. In later years, he was able to reveal the beauty of this part of the Jewish past to others.

In 1807, when Leopold turned 13, his attitude toward the school changed dramatically for the better. That year a new administrator, Samuel Meyer Ehrenberg, became the director of the school. Ehrenberg was a modern educator under whose direction the school's curriculum concentrated less on Talmud and was broadened to include not only German but also French, history, geography, math, and Latin. Ehrenberg also saw to it that the boys were clothed and fed properly. After Ehrenberg's death in 1853, Zunz prepared a loving, carefully researched biography of his former teacher, who had been like a father to Zunz for more than 40 years.

In 1809 Zunz became the first Jew admitted to the public high school in Wolfenbüttel. His favorite subjects there were algebra and optics. After he graduated in 1811, he supported himself for several years as an assistant teacher at Ehrenberg's school.

Zunz went to Berlin in October 1815 to enroll at the University of Berlin, and except for short absences he remained in that city until his death more than 70 years later. His professors of classics and biblical studies at the university deeply influenced him. He saw how detailed research could lead to a broad philosophy of history, and how ancient thought had survived and been applied over the ages. He began to think about making a similar analysis of the cultural influences of Judaism, even though Ehrenberg—who had wept when seeing Zunz off from Wolfenbüttel—lamented in his letters that Zunz was not applying himself to something more practical. Zunz completed his university career at the University of Halle, a city about 100 miles southwest of Berlin, where he wrote a dissertation on the 13th-century philosophical author Shem Tov Falaquera. He was awarded a doctorate for this work in January 1821.

In May 1818, while still a student at the University of Berlin, Zunz published his first work, *On Rabbinic Literature*. With this contribution Zunz began a new movement, which in Germany came to be known as the Science of Judaism. *On Rabbinic Literature* revealed the scope and beauty of the literature written by the ancient rabbis. It decisively refuted the claims of those who argued that Jewish culture had died at the end of the biblical period.

Moreover, Zunz's book outlined the aims of a new approach to Jewish research. In his view, Jewish works should no longer be read only to deepen faith or find out how better to observe Jewish law. Instead, they should be studied carefully with the tools of modern scholarship to shed light on the ways in which Jewish culture as a whole had contributed to general human advancement. Zunz proposed new types of research methods for scholarly Jewish studies. He said, for example, that researchers should consider looking for information about the Jewish past in sources that had thus far been ignored: inscriptions on tombstones, coins minted to commemorate historical events, questions sent to rabbis over the ages and the rabbis' responses, and the record books of Jewish communities.

In August 1819, Zunz and some of his Jewish friends at the University of Berlin were horrified when German students instigated anti-Jewish riots that spread throughout the land. As a response, the group of young men founded the Society for the Culture and Science of Judaism. The aim of this association was to promote the achievements of Jewish culture over the course of history. Zunz and his colleagues believed that by publicizing the contributions of Jewish civilization to modern culture, they could demonstrate that the Jewish past is just as worthy of study as any other great culture. From this it would follow that Jews deserve an equal place in modern society.

Although the society failed to achieve its grand aim, it did make a notable contribution to Judaism. During 1822–23, Zunz served as the editor of the group's journal, *The Periodical for the Science of Judaism*. Among the articles that appeared in the journal's single year of existence was Zunz's groundbreaking biography of Solomon ben Isaac, or Rashi (1040–1105), the great medieval commentator on the Bible and the Talmud. In the absence of any real biographical data about Rashi, Zunz collected and compared different manuscripts of Rashi's commentaries and used them to illuminate Rashi's personality and the times in which he lived.

When the Society for the Culture and Science of Judaism disbanded in 1824 after failing to gain much notice among either Jews or non-Jews, some of its founders converted to Christianity. They knew that as long as they remained Jews their talents would not earn them the positions in society that they deserved. Zunz considered but rejected this course, on the grounds that the Christian world might wish Jews to convert but thought poorly of those who did. Instead, he continued to pursue the society's mission for the

remaining 62 years of his life. He thus became the unofficial leader of a movement dedicated to analyzing Jewish culture in a scholarly and objective fashion.

The year 1824 was memorable in another way. At that time the government of Prussia, the German state whose capital was Berlin, officially limited Jewish religious freedom. Fearful that new religious ideas would lead to political revolution, the authorities forbade Jews to make changes in their religious affairs and services. The government was particularly opposed to Jewish sermons in the German language, claiming that they were imitations of Christian sermons. Zunz immediately began to do scholarly research into the history of the synagogue and the sermon to see whether he could uncover arguments to convince the government that its new policy was wrong. The result was his *History and Development of Jewish Sermons*, published in 1832.

In order to prepare his argument, Zunz did research in several private libraries. His careful studies revealed that Jewish sermons in German were hardly something new, since at many periods in Jewish history preachers had addressed their congregations in the local language. The "new" religious practices were thus not revolutionary but were part of the same normal development that synagogue worship had undergone continually through the course of Jewish history.

Zunz's research led him to make a broad political statement. In the introduction to his book he argued that mistreatment of the Jews was a result of the general public's ignorance of Jewish literature. If political leaders understood the Jewish heritage, he asserted, they would want to grant equality to the Jews. By the same token, when Jews understood their own history they would know how to reform their religious practices and prepare themselves for

> *"The neglect of Jewish science is connected with the civil disabilities of the Jews . . . many an ill-advised step of the legislature, and many a prejudice against Jewish antiquity were the immediate consequences of the abandoned condition in which Jewish literature and the science of Judaism have been plunged for the last century."*
>
> —from preface to *The History and Development of Jewish Sermons* (1832)

their new place in society. Zunz further stated that "the Jews in Europe . . . should be given freedom instead of being granted rights." Zunz concluded his book with the hope that Jews would participate in developing a united culture for all humanity.

Apart from its function as a political treatise, *The History and Development of Jewish Sermons* has been called the most important Jewish work of the 19th century. Its methods set high standards for further scholarly studies of Jewish topics. In a stunning way, Zunz showed how careful and objective research could illuminate the Jewish past. For example, like a detective who comes upon clues unexpectedly, Zunz bumped into many references to an as yet unknown rabbinic text as he read through a variety of medieval manuscripts. Even though this work was not finally discovered until three decades later, Zunz's research enabled him to suggest an order of contents for it. The accuracy of his findings has held up extremely well, and only details of his conclusions needed correction. Following the publication of Zunz's trailblazing book, researchers continued to make new discoveries about rabbinic literature by systematically organizing rabbinical writings, determining the dates of specific works, and publishing corrected and annotated editions.

Anti-Jewish decrees also prompted Zunz to write other books. In 1836, when the Prussian government prohibited Jews from adopting names considered to be Christian, Zunz responded with a volume entitled *On Jewish Names*. In this book he proved that Jews had always been called by "foreign" names and had intermingled with non-Jews throughout history.

Zunz's interest in politics was not limited to Jewish rights. He was born only a few years after the French Revolution of 1787, with its slogan of "Liberty, Equality, Fraternity." One of the earliest melodies he could recall was the *Marseillaise*, now the French national anthem, which became the rallying cry both of the leaders of the French Revolution and of the common people. Like many other Europeans who wanted to see a change in their repressive governments, Zunz participated in the revolutionary movement that swept Europe in 1848. Although the failure of the movement disappointed him and kept him out of politics for some time, Zunz participated in local politics in Berlin for a period beginning in 1859. He withdrew from political activity only when he became convinced that his democratic principles had no hope of being adopted.

The fortunes of politics never kept Zunz from pursuing his main goal of transforming Jewish studies into a respected field. To achieve that end he traveled to England in 1846 to study Hebrew manuscripts in the British Museum. In 1855 he made another trip abroad, to libraries in Oxford and Paris, and in 1856 he traveled to Hamburg to do additional research. In 1863 he delved into the Hebrew manuscripts of Italy. Though he was welcomed into the library of Parma, he was barred from the one at the Vatican because he was a Jew.

As a result of painstaking research, Zunz published three important works on synagogue literature between 1855 and 1867. His efforts in this area were the first to evaluate the poetry of the Jewish prayer book as part of Jewish intellectual history as well as an expression of devotion.

Zunz became the most widely respected Jewish researcher of his day. In 1864, on the occasion of his 70th birthday, the Zunz Foundation was established in Berlin with the goal of supporting his scholarly work and other similar projects. When Zunz turned 80, the foundation announced plans to publish his collected writings. Barely a week after that milestone, Zunz's wife of more than 40 years died, leaving him depressed and incapable of much new work. Nonetheless, his collected works were published in

Leopold Zunz

BORN

August 10, 1794
Detmold, Germany

DIED

March 18, 1886
Berlin, Germany

EDUCATION

Attended the University of Berlin (1815–19); earned a doctorate at the University of Halle (1821)

ACCOMPLISHMENTS

Outlined the Science of Judaism in *On Rabbinic Literature* (1818); edited the *Journal for the Science of Judaism* (1822–23) and in it published a life of Rashi, the first scholarly biography in Jewish literature; author of *The History and Development of Jewish Sermons* (1832), *The Names of the Jews* (1836), *On History and Literature* (1845), and works on synagogue poetry and ritual (1855–67)

three volumes in 1875 and 1876. In honor of Zunz's 90th birthday, the Zunz Foundation published a jubilee volume containing a wide variety of articles attesting to the new popularity of Jewish studies. Two years later, Zunz died after suffering a fall in his room.

Despite his many achievements, Zunz also suffered some disappointments, such as his failure to gain a professorship in Jewish history or Hebrew literature at a German university. He believed that Jewish studies would be taken seriously only if taught in a secular institution, and for that reason he thought poorly of the Berlin Academy for Jewish Studies, which opened its doors in 1872. He also tended to isolate himself, never taking on students and often finding fault with other scholars who modeled themselves on him and helped develop the field he founded. Nonetheless, he made a lasting impact on Judaism. One of Zunz's mottos was that "true scholarship produces deeds." This aphorism summarizes his belief that scholarly work could become the basis for a modern form of the Jewish religion. In fact, Zunz's way of reading Jewish texts helped some Jews who could no longer believe in traditional Judaism find a meaningful Jewish identity by studying and honoring the Jewish past. For such Jews, contributing to Jewish knowledge through careful research sometimes replaced faith itself.

Even though Leopold Zunz is hardly a household name, his promotion of the Science of Judaism is at least partly responsible for a new feature of the modern American university curriculum. Today, more than 400 colleges and universities in the United States and Canada offer courses in Jewish studies, in fields including the Bible, rabbinic texts, Jewish literature of all periods, Jewish history, archaeology, and so on. The existence of such programs is an acknowledgment that Jewish studies are widely considered a valuable part of a general education, just as Leopold Zunz always claimed.

FURTHER READING

Glatzer, Nahum N., ed. *Leopold and Adelheid Zunz: An Account in Letters, 1815–1885*. London: East and West Library, 1958.

Karp, Deborah. "Leopold Zunz." In *Heroes of Modern Jewish Thought*. New York: Ktav, 1966.

Schechter, Solomon. "Leopold Zunz." In *Studies in Judaism*. Third Series. Philadelphia: Jewish Publication Society, 1924.

Wallach, Luitpold. *Liberty and Letters: The Thoughts of Leopold Zunz*. London: East and West Library, 1959.

Samson Raphael Hirsch

"JUDAISM SEEKS TO LIFT US UP"

On a busy city street or a crowded subway car, it is easy to identify certain people as "ultra-Orthodox" Jews. In their old-fashioned dark clothing, they seem proud of their connection to an earlier century and their refusal to blend in with the world around them. But in the same setting, it is impossible to pick out the "modern Orthodox" Jews. Although these people are just as painstaking in their observance of Jewish law as the ultra-Orthodox, they dress like everyone else. When schools are letting out, the students from the modern Orthodox schools will be wearing the same styles as other schoolchildren. Only the knitted skullcaps or other head coverings on the boys' heads or an inspection of the girls' bookbags might give a clue to their religious affiliation. Along with the same history, English, science, and math textbooks that public school students use, one might also find Hebrew language texts and Hebrew Bibles with commentaries.

Believing that Judaism could be brought into the modern world without violating a single divine commandment, Rabbi Samson Raphael Hirsch broke with the past by adopting the garb of the Christian clergy for his modern Orthodox pulpit. Hirsch served the Orthodox community of Frankfurt for over 37 years.

That very observant Jews in the United States and other countries today look like other citizens, work at the same sorts of jobs, and fully participate in the modern world is in large part due to the work of Rabbi Samson Raphael Hirsch in Germany more than a century ago. While no champion of religious reform, Hirsch responded to the desire of many German Jews of his day to participate in the modern world.

Hirsch is considered the father of modern Orthodox Judaism. The word *orthodox*, from the Greek for "correct practice," was first applied contemptuously to traditional Judaism by 19th-century German Jews who were trying to reform the religion. These Reform Jews looked down on some of the "correct practices" other Jews were following. By the middle of the century, the term had come into common usage. When people began to call Hirsch the father of modern Orthodox Judaism, they did not mean that there was anything new about his devotion to Jewish law. What was new about Hirsch's orthodoxy was its affirmation of the modern world.

Hirsch made a careful distinction between God's commandments and the customs by which Jews observed those commandments. Though the commandments themselves were, he believed, not subject to change over time, customs were. Hirsch taught that even very old practices could be modified without damaging the essence of the commandments themselves. By showing traditional Jews that they could live comfortably within the modern world without giving up any of their means of expressing religious devotion, Hirsch enabled traditional Judaism to survive the attacks of the liberal Reform movement.

Hirsch was born into a scholarly family in 1808, but his businessman father was already a man of the modern world and saw to it that his son Samson had a strong education not only in Jewish but also in secular subjects. When he was about 10 years old, Samson witnessed a meeting at his parents' home in Hamburg, Germany, that left a deep impression on him. The city's first Reform synagogue had just opened and, to the horror of the observant Jews of Hamburg, its services seemed to mimic Christian church rituals—an organ provided musical accompaniment, and a choir of men and women sang together. Furthermore, the "New Religious Song Book" in use there had omitted every reference to the restoration of the Jewish people to their ancient homeland in Zion and to the coming of the Messiah and a peaceful future age. Young Samson sensed the helplessness of the adults around him who were trying to come up with an appropriate response to what they perceived as a threat to their historic faith.

Finally, the observant Jews of Hamburg invited Isaac Bernays, a scholar of Jewish texts who had also been trained in modern philosophy and literature at the University of Würzberg, to lead their community. They hoped that an orthodox spiritual leader with modern university training would be able to meet Reform leaders on their own ground. Bernays refused to take the title "rabbi," which he felt had been debased by the Reform movement. Instead, he preferred to be called "sage." Hirsch became one of the sage's students. Studying with Bernays convinced the young Hirsch to become a rabbi instead of a businessman like his father.

To become certified as a rabbi, Hirsch left Hamburg, at the age of 20, for the city of Mannheim, nearly 300 miles to the south. In those days, before the establishment of rabbinical seminaries, practicing rabbis granted rabbinical diplomas to their qualified students. There he received a rabbinical diploma from Rabbi Jacob Ettlinger, who, like Bernays, was a traditional

"Two revelations are given to us, Nature and the Torah. . . . The Torah, like nature, has God for its ultimate cause."

—from *Nineteen Letters on Judaism* (1836)

rabbi with secular university training. After his exposure to these two rabbis with university training, Hirsch became a university student himself. He spent the academic year 1829–30 at the University of Bonn, studying the languages, history, and philosophy of the ancient world. He also took a course in experimental physics, which had a profound effect on his religious thinking. Hirsch began to see a relationship between the laws of nature and the laws of the Torah, a link he would soon develop in his writings.

At Bonn, Hirsch became friends with Abraham Geiger, another Jewish student, who would later become his greatest opponent. Geiger, two years younger, was to become the central figure in early Reform Judaism, while Hirsch was destined to become the founder of modern Orthodox Judaism. Together the two students formed a debating society for young Jews at the university. The society met on Saturday afternoons in Geiger's room, where they practiced delivering sermons to each other.

At the time, several German states had laws regulating the life of Jewish communities. In these states government boards examined the rabbis before appointing them to their official positions. Hirsch was only 22 and had spent only a year at the university when he was appointed by the northwestern German state of Oldenburg to serve as rabbi to its Jewish population. During his 11 years in that position, Hirsch published his two most important works, *Nineteen Letters on Judaism* (1836) and *Horeb: Essays on Israel's "Duties" in the Diaspora (1837).*

Hirsch was less interested in making a name for himself than in convincing young Jews that they could remain true to traditional Judaism without being intellectually dishonest. As a result, he published his *Nineteen Letters* anonymously at first, although the identity of the author soon became

known. Written in elegant German, the book had a tremendous impact on Jews in Germany and elsewhere.

This work took the unusual form, for a theological text, of an exchange of letters between two fictional characters. The opening letter, from a young Jewish intellectual named Benjamin, expresses his dissatisfaction as a modern man with Judaism. He had once been religious but now describes Judaism as inconvenient and burdensome. Its laws, he writes, seem to cut modern Jews off from "everything which adorns and beautifies life." He says also that Jewish law makes it difficult for Jews to deal with non-Jews and to pursue professional careers. In the following 18 letters, a young rabbi named Naphtali responds to Benjamin's concerns and in doing so makes the case for traditional Judaism.

Among Hirsch's ideas, presented by Naphtali, is an assertion that the laws of the Torah, like those of nature, come from God. A scientist trying to understand how nature works cannot simply discard a law of nature if it contradicts a scientific theory. Similarly, a Jew cannot ignore a law of the Torah simply because no explanation can be found for it or because it seems inconvenient. "In the Torah, as in Nature, no fact may be denied, even though the reason for it and its connection with other facts or phenomena may not be comprehended."

Naphtali further explains to Benjamin that Jews have a specific role to play in the world, to teach the rest of humanity that God is the source of blessing. Naphtali extols emancipation, the lifting of restrictions against Jews and the granting of equal citizenship rights to them. But he emphasizes that the goal of emancipation should not blind Jews to their real mission. "I bless emancipation," he says, because it enables all human beings to enjoy equal rights, but "I should grieve if Israel understood itself so little . . . that it

would welcome emancipation as . . . the highest goal of its historic mission."

In his *Nineteen Letters*, Hirsch also argues that Jews should not be fooled by the claims of Reform Judaism into lowering their religious standards: "Merely to seek greater ease and comfort in life through the destruction of the eternal code set up for all ages by the God of Eternity, is not and never can be Reform. Judaism seeks to lift us up to its height; how dare we attempt to drag it down to our level?"

Reform Judaism is not Hirsch's only target. He also criticizes the growing trend toward modern Jewish studies. This movement advocated that Jewish texts be read and studied not religiously but objectively, as documents shedding light on human civilization. In presenting his case to Benjamin, Naphtali urges that the Torah not be read to support various scholarly investigations but only as Torah, "that is, instruction and guidance in this Divine world." Unless Jewish study strengthens Jewish observance, he contends, it is worse than pointless; it is in fact destructive of Jewish life.

Hirsch's *Nineteen Letters* had a stunning effect on young Jews. The book was translated into several different languages, including English, and a number of Jewish students moved to Oldenburg to study personally with Hirsch.

Although *Horeb* appeared in print after the success of *Nineteen Letters*, Hirsch had actually written it first. He wrote *Nineteen Letters* at the request of his gentile publisher, who promised to publish the longer *Horeb* if Hirsch first wrote a shorter summary of his views and that book proved a financial success.

The title of the longer book is a Hebrew name for Mount Sinai, where, according to Jewish tradition, the laws of the Torah were revealed. In *Horeb*, Hirsch fully developed his comparison of the Torah's laws with those of nature. Just as the laws of nature are valid for all time, so are the laws of the

The interior of the second synagogue building of Hirsch's Frankfurt congregation, which was dedicated in 1907, nearly 20 years after Hirsch's death. The first synagogue, built in 1852–53, no longer sufficed for a congregation that by 1900 had grown to more than 10 times its original size.

Torah, which likewise have God as their source: "It is the same God Who laid down the law which Nature follows of necessity, Who pronounced the law which Israel is asked to follow of its own free will. And just as the laws of Nature are unchangeable—despite any opinion many may hold—so all speculations on the laws of the Torah can only be an enlightenment of our own minds, but never the cause of their validity."

Though Hirsch firmly believed that Jews are required to observe the Torah's laws whether or not they understand their meaning, he also believed it wrong to perform religious rituals mechanically. In order to combat that tendency among observant Jews, he developed a system for classifying the commandments and explaining them.

In both *Horeb* and *Nineteen Letters*, Hirsch argued that true reform meant raising the world up to the Torah's standards, not lowering the Torah to the level of the world. Only then, in his view, "when the times will conform with God, will Judaism also conform with the times."

The two masterpieces Hirsch wrote in Oldenburg spread his fame throughout the Jewish world. In 1841, when he published a pamphlet refuting the claims of an anonymous writer who had attacked the morals of the Bible, his work earned a response from the Grand Duke of Oldenburg. The duke sent a special messenger to Hirsch, congratulating him for coming to the defense of the Bible, which Christians and Jews alike held dear.

Later in 1841 Hirsch moved to the city of Emden, some 50 miles northwest of Oldenburg, where he served as rabbi for two communities in the province of Hanover. During his five years in that position he founded a Jewish secondary school for girls. He did not ignore the larger community of the province, however, and participated in literary and social activities with non-Jews. In this period he also published a work refuting the theories of radical Reform Judaism. When he was invited at the end of 1846 to become rabbi of a region in the Austrian Empire, Christians and Jews alike tried in vain to persuade him to stay in Emden. Instead he became imperial chief rabbi of Moravia (now part of the Czech Republic) and Austrian Silesia (now part of Poland).

Hirsch soon had an opportunity to demonstrate publicly his belief that Jews could benefit from emancipation without giving up a bit of their traditional religious observance. He participated in the revolution of March 1848, which forced Austrian emperor Ferdinand to grant his people constitutional rights and freedom of the press. Following the success of the revolution, Hirsch was unanimously elected chairman of the Committee for the Civil and Political Rights of the Jews in Moravia. In this capacity he worked for full legal and political equality. In doing so he made it clear to the Jews he represented that emancipation would be meaningful for them only if they remained Jewish. As he put it, "What would you have achieved if you became *free* Jews, and you ceased to be *Jews?*"

In 1849, Hirsch was elected to the Austrian parliament. He soon issued a memo to his fellow lawmakers describing the humiliations and restrictions crippling full Jewish participation in society. He argued especially strongly against the "family law," which allowed only the first-born son of each Jewish family to marry without applying for special permission. Mainly as a result of Hirsch's efforts, the Jews of Austria gained emancipation in March 1849.

Despite his successes as imperial chief rabbi, Hirsch's own time in Moravia was not personally satisfying. The most observant members of the Jewish community objected to his attempts to modernize Jewish custom. They were not pleased that he led services dressed like a Christian clergyman, wearing a black robe with white collar bands, and gave his sermons in German. They also objected to his insistence that a Jewish education should consist of more than Talmud study. On the other hand, the more reform-oriented members of the Jewish community were displeased that despite his university background, Hirsch insisted that Jews had no right to dispense with a single Jewish law.

In addition, Hirsch also observed with distress that his achievements with regard to Jewish emancipation were already being undone. In 1850, the Jews of the Austrian Empire were once again denied permission to serve as lawyers or as teachers in state schools. Three years later, Jews were once again forbidden to own land, and the marriage restrictions of the hated "family laws" were reinstated.

On July 31, 1851, Hirsch gave up his position as imperial chief rabbi for one that seemed to offer less prestige and power: the post of rabbi for a tiny Orthodox community in the German city of Frankfurt. In fact, Hirsch's career move was destined to change the future of traditional Judaism around the world. Before returning to Germany, Hirsch wrote an open letter to the Jews of Austria and Moravia, asking them to have faith that they would eventually achieve true emancipation. He also urged them to ignore both the Reform Jews who wished to give up traditional forms of observance to suit the times and those Orthodox who said that a Jew could not be true to the Torah and learn science at the same time.

Before Hirsch's arrival in Frankfurt, the Reform majority in the community had been working to undermine traditional observance in the city. They had forced a Bible study group to stop its weekly meetings and had seen to it that kosher food would no longer be provided to Jewish prisoners and hospital patients. While the Reform Jews of Frankfurt had an impressive synagogue, the Orthodox Jews met for services in the back room of a private home.

Although the 11 men who had invited Hirsch to Frankfurt hoped their new leader's first move would be to build an Orthodox synagogue, Hirsch instead insisted on building schools first. In his words, "There is no hurry for a synagogue. First we need a school to build up a new generation of knowledgeable and loyal Jews for whom Judaism is their life's purpose. . . . What would be the use of a magnificent house of prayer if we had no young men and women to worship in it?"

And so Hirsch went from door to door begging for donations to set up a primary school and two high schools, one for boys and a second for girls. His schools opened in 1853 with 84 pupils; by the time of his death 35 years later, more than 600 students were enrolled. Hirsch's curriculum—which included German, math, geography, and natural sciences—was based on a statement from the Talmud, "The study of Torah is excellent together with secular education," which became the motto of modern Orthodox education. For Hirsch, the ideal Jew combined secular knowledge with commitment to and observance of all the commandments. He argued that it was a religious obligation to teach Jewish children the secular subjects that form the basis of contemporary civilization.

Hirsch's schools had to compete with a school founded some years earlier by the Reform movement in Frankfurt. Nevertheless, he emphatically denied that he had included secular studies in his schools' curriculum just to meet the competition. When the most traditional Jews argued against including secular subjects, he insisted that nothing in Judaism justified keeping Jews ignorant of secular knowledge. In the past, Jews had excelled in science and piety alike, and only political repression had barred their way to such dual competence in recent times. While maintaining this position, he published a pamphlet entitled *Religion Allied with Progress* (1854), refuting arguments of Reform leaders that secular education made it impossible to follow traditional Judaism.

Even though Hirsch's influence in Frankfurt led to the building of an Orthodox synagogue in 1853 and the strengthening of traditional Judaism in general, he began to believe that the German system of establishing separate religious communities undermined religious freedom. In Germany, Jews did not belong to a particular congregation but rather to the religious community of their cities. Rabbis all had to accept the superior authority of the ruling

Jewish community council, and individual Jews had to make payments to the community council, even if it used their money to support religious practices to which they objected. Because of Hirsch's efforts, a law was passed in 1876 allowing Jews to leave the official community without abandoning Judaism. Orthodox Jews were now free to leave Reform-dominated communities and form Orthodox organizations of their own. Although most Orthodox Jews in Germany chose to stay within the old framework, a new framework of modern Orthodox congregations began to take shape.

In 1885, Hirsch established the Free Union for the Interests of Orthodox Judaism, with the goal of training teachers, representing Orthodox Jews before governmental bodies, and assisting small Jewish communities. Just as Hirsch's schools became the model for modern Orthodox educational institutions elsewhere, so his union became the model for other Orthodox organizations.

Hirsch's many activities as leader of the growing Orthodox Jewish community in Frankfurt did not keep him from scholarly writing. He translated and wrote commentaries on the five books of Moses (1867–78) and on the book of Psalms (1883). In 1884 he published a pamphlet defending the Talmud against claims that it undermined social justice and recommended unethical business practices. He wrote a commentary on the Hebrew prayer book that was published after his death. He also founded and edited a German-language journal devoted to spreading "the spirit of Judaism and of Jewish life in home, community and school." The essays Hirsch wrote for this journal were collected after his death and published in two volumes under the title *Judaism Eternal*.

Samson Raphael Hirsch died on the last day of 1888, but his legacy lives on throughout the world. When the anti-Semitic Nazi regime seized power in Germany less than 50 years later, German Jews began to leave the country. Wherever Orthodox German Jews settled—in North America, South America, England, Australia, South Africa, or Palestine—they brought with them the convictions of the founder of modern Orthodoxy. They spread the belief that it was possible for an observant Jew to live as a completely modern person. Although the term *Orthodox* had been used at first as a slur on traditional Jewish practice, Hirsch turned that word into a badge of honor for many Jews around the world, who believe to this day that a Jew can live as a modern citizen without giving up a single religious responsibility.

FURTHER READING

Grunfeld, I. *Three Generations: The Influence of Samson Raphael Hirsch on Jewish Life and Thought*. London: Jewish Post, 1958.

Jelenko, Edward W. "Samson Raphael Hirsch." In *Great Jewish Personalities in Modern Times*. Edited by Simon Noveck. Washington, D.C.: B'nai B'rith, 1960.

Hirsch, Samson Raphael. *Judaism Eternal: Selected Essays from the Writings of Rabbi Samson Raphael Hirsch*. Translated and edited by I. Grunfeld. 2 vols. London: Soncino, 1956.

Karp, Deborah. "Samson Raphael Hirsch." In *Heroes of Modern Jewish Thought*. New York: Ktav, 1966.

Liberles, Robert. "Champion of Orthodoxy: The Emergence of Samson Raphael Hirsch as Religious Leader." *AJS Review: The Journal of the Association for Jewish Studies* 6 (1981): 43–60.

Schwarzschild, Steven. "Samson Raphael Hirsch—The Man and His Thought." *Conservative Judaism* (Winter 1959): 26–45.

Samson Raphael Hirsch

BORN

June 20, 1808
Hamburg, Germany

DIED

December 31, 1888
Frankfurt, Germany

EDUCATION

Studied classical languages, history, philosophy, and experimental physics at the University of Bonn (1829)

ACCOMPLISHMENTS

Author of *Nineteen Letters on Judaism* (1836), *Horeb: Essays on Israel's "Duties" in the Diaspora* (1837), German translations of and commentaries on the Pentateuch and the Book of Psalms (1867–78, 1883), and a commentary on the Hebrew prayer book (1895); participated in the struggle to obtain emancipation for the Jews of Austria and Moravia; founded schools where both secular and Jewish subjects were taught; founded the Free Union for the Interests of Orthodox Judaism (1885)

Abraham Geiger

BALANCING
INNOVATION AND
TRADITION

he synagogues in which most American Jews now worship share a number of common features. The service, for example, includes prayers in both Hebrew and English, and the rabbi's sermon is in English. In many congregations, women and men sit together, sometimes wearing prayer shawls and covering their heads; in others they do not. Today's Jews find nothing at all shocking about these characteristics of synagogue worship, which are part of the Jewish-American tradition. But when these features first began to make their appearance in Germany nearly two centuries ago, they were considered radical innovations.

Today most people know that there are different groups of Jews in the United States. Those who are strictest in their observance of Jewish law are Orthodox Jews. The group who believe that Jewish law has always been flexible and should respond to changes in contemporary life are

Abraham Geiger has been called the founding father of the Reform movement for his work in developing a scholarly justification for transforming traditional Jewish practices. Although neither the ideas nor the changes introduced by the movement originated with him, Geiger's theories provided direction and purpose to Reform Judaism.

"It is precisely to Judaism that all the great religious transformations . . . attach themselves. Christianity and Islam have issued forth from it, been nurtured by it, and it is within Judaism therefore that the new religious transformation must take place."

—from *Posthumous Writings* (1875-78), volume 5

Reform Jews. And those who take a middle position are Conservative Jews. Rabbis of each group are trained and ordained at different rabbinical seminaries. Before the early 19th century, however, there were no such distinctions among Jews. To be sure, Jews from different lands had their own traditions. Not all Jews were equally pious. But rabbis everywhere tended to have similar expectations for their congregations.

All this changed as a result of the influence of Abraham Geiger. Born in Frankfurt in 1810, Geiger was not the first Reform Jew. Nevertheless, he developed a scholarly justification for reforming Judaism that has continued to shape the religion to our day. Even though Reform Judaism no longer maintains all of Geiger's views, it still honors his idea of the relationship between change and tradition in Judaism.

Geiger grew up in a strictly traditional home. Six years before his birth, a new school for young Jews had opened in Frankfurt. In addition to having a broad range of Jewish courses, it also taught secular subjects. Geiger's parents did not send him to this school, fearing that such an education might undermine the quality of his religious observance. Instead he studied traditional religious works with his rabbi father, progressing from the

Hebrew Bible to the Mishnah (the 2nd-century classic of Jewish law), and the Talmud (the 5th-century collection of rabbinical commentaries). On the other hand, his parents did not prevent the young boy from learning about other things that interested him. Abraham was fascinated with mathematics and especially with German language and literature and the classical writings of ancient Greece and Rome.

Geiger's father died when Abraham was only 13. His half brother Solomon, who was 18 years older, took it upon himself to make sure that Abraham's Jewish education continued. But the boy also continued to study the classics of the non-Jewish ancient world. Soon he was able to compare his own Jewish heritage with the values transmitted by Greek and Roman writers. His thirst for knowledge was so strong that at the age of 19 he somehow convinced his family to allow him to attend a university, although very few Jews enrolled in them at that time. While studying first at Heidelberg and then at Bonn, he met other young Jews with diverse intellectual interests, including Samson Raphael Hirsch, who would become an ideological opponent of Geiger's. At that time, Geiger began to wonder why the universities had no faculty of Jewish theology. Over the years, he was to

Sally J. Priesand, the first American woman rabbi, holds a Torah scroll in a Reform religious service. In 1922 the Reform movement's Central Conference of American Rabbis determined that women "cannot justly be denied the privilege of ordination." Nonetheless, not until Priesand's ordination 50 years later, in 1972, did Hebrew Union College ordain its first female rabbi.

return again and again to this point: before non-Jews would accept Judaism as a significant contributor to civilization, the universities would have to offer a degree in Jewish studies.

As much as Geiger learned about a variety of subjects, he felt drawn toward a career as a rabbi. However, his wide learning convinced him that an unbiased, scientific study of Judaism's past was essential to the development of Judaism. While at Bonn, Geiger's studies of the Jewish past bore fruit. He won a prize for an essay describing the elements that Muhammad, the founder of Islam, had borrowed from Judaism. This piece, written in Latin and published in 1833, proved that he was a true scholar capable of meaningful research. Although he left Bonn without completing a degree, the professors at the University of Marburg were so impressed by his essay on Muhammad that they awarded him a doctorate. In Marburg, Geiger also became a rabbi when the community rabbi awarded him a rabbinical degree. At the time, because there were no rabbinical seminaries, older rabbis would award diplomas to deserving younger men.

Back in Frankfurt, the young Rabbi Geiger began to deliver sermons. Word of his effectiveness as a speaker spread and soon he was elected rabbi of a small, unsophisticated Jewish community in nearby Wiesbaden. Although the salary was modest, the position appealed to Geiger because it would leave him a good deal of time to continue his scholarly research. Since the early 19th century, groups of Jews in various German cities had been conducting services, without rabbinical leadership, in which they introduced reforms such as shortened worship, prayers in both German and Hebrew, and the mixed seating of men and women. Geiger had many thoughts himself about the need to reform Judaism, but he knew that his congrega-

tion in Wiesbaden was not the appropriate place for him to act fully on his inclinations. Nonetheless, he introduced a number of changes, omitting certain traditional poems he felt no longer spoke to the needs of the day, organizing a choir (to the horror of some members of the congregation), and preaching in German.

While still at Wiesbaden, the now-25-year-old Geiger began to publish a periodical in which he could discuss fully his ideas for reorganizing Judaism to meet the needs of the day. In this publication, *The Scientific Journal for Jewish Theology*, Geiger made it clear that by calling for reform he was not advocating the rejection of Judaism's past. Rather, he was proposing an investigation of that past. This would reveal just which elements of Judaism were truly vital to the future of Judaism and which were no longer relevant. "Salvation lies not in the violent and reckless excision of everything which has descended to us from the past," he wrote, "but in the careful search into its deeper meaning, and in the aim to continue to develop historically from that which has grown historically. . . . Much which is now believed and observed is not tradition . . . but is a product of a certain age, and therefore can be removed by time."

In 1838, Geiger left Wiesbaden for a new post in the city of Breslau (now Wroclaw, Poland). Unfortunately, he was not welcomed by Breslau's entire Jewish community. Breslau already had a rabbi, the strictly traditional Solomon A. Tiktin. However, a significant minority of Breslau's Jews wanted an additional rabbi with a good general education who would deliver sermons in German. Despite Rabbi Tiktin's opposition, Geiger was first invited to give a guest sermon, then elected to serve as assistant rabbi.

Tiktin raised a variety of loud— and false—objections to Geiger's appointment, alleging that Geiger's journal proved his contempt for Judaism, that his secular university degree disqualified him as a spiritual leader, and that he had been forced to leave Wiesbaden because he had fragrantly broken the laws of the Sabbath. Tiktin even convinced the government to check into Geiger's background, but the authorities found nothing unsavory. Still, Geiger's opponents would not give up. More than a year went by without a final decision on his appointment. During this time Geiger occupied himself with the publication of his journal and by translating into German a number of significant Hebrew texts.

When Geiger finally began his duties at Breslau in 1840, he found that they included a weekly Sabbath sermon in German—but no responsibility for making decisions on matters of Jewish law. He was also put in charge of religious instruction, but when he tried to require attendance at classes and have the school supported by a general tax on the entire Jewish community, his opponents blocked these measures.

Despite Orthodox opposition, Geiger became senior rabbi of Breslau in 1843, and he remained in that post for the next 20 years. During most of that period, he took comfort in the companionship of his wife, Emilie, who until her death in 1860 helped him cope with continuing opposition. The anti-Geiger faction was especially offended by claims in his essay "The Task of the Present" that Jews had every right to reorder prayers, introduce choral singing into their services, demand sermons with broad cultural insights, and insist that their children be taught that moral conduct was the most important value of Judaism. He also claimed that just as the rabbis of the Talmud had explained the Bible according to their particular understanding of religious

truth, modern-day rabbis had a responsibility to do so as well.

The dispute between Geiger and his Breslau opponents was partially resolved in 1846, three years after Tiktin's death. In that year the Jewish community of Breslau was officially split. The Orthodox community recognized Tiktin's son as their religious leader, and the advocates of reform recognized Geiger as theirs. Nevertheless, disputes between the two factions continued.

During Geiger's tumultuous years in Breslau, he experienced one particularly painful rejection. In addition to believing that the German universities should adopt Jewish studies, Geiger was also convinced that the German Jews themselves should establish an institute for advanced Judaic studies. Accordingly, in 1854 the Jewish Theological Seminary of Breslau—the first modern institution for training Jewish teachers and rabbis—was founded. Geiger had anticipated being chosen its dean, but his hopes went unfulfilled.

But Geiger did not let his personal disappointment distract him from his all-important research into Judaism's past. His studies confirmed his belief that each of the important Jewish texts, including the Bible itself, were written by human beings who were necessarily influenced by the times in which they lived. As a result, the texts were outdated in some ways, and none could be expected to provide answers to all the questions posed by modern Jews concerning belief and practice.

Geiger always stressed, however, that each of the texts remained valuable. All were sources of traditions that might still have meaning. He viewed each product of the Jewish past as part of the living body of Judaism. In 1861 he wrote, "the present can no more detach itself completely from the past without suffering damage than a single limb can be torn without harm

Abraham Geiger

BORN

May 24, 1810
Frankfurt, Germany

DIED

October 23, 1874
Berlin, Germany

EDUCATION

Studied classical and Oriental languages at the University of Heidelberg and philosophy and history at the University of Bonn; doctorate, University of Marburg

ACCOMPLISHMENTS

Provided a theory to justify the reform of Judaism; professor of divinity, Berlin Academy for Jewish Studies (1872–74); author of *the Original Text and the Translations of the Bible: Their Dependence on the Inner Development of Judaism* (1857), *Judaism and Its History* (1865), and many other works; founded the *Scientific Journal of Jewish Theology* (1835); published the *Jewish Journal of Life and Letters* (1862–74) to itself from the entire body of Judaism." Geiger argued that Judaism had been changing continuously from the beginning, and in order to flourish it had to go on evolving.

Geiger's historical research led him to two further conclusions, only the first of which is still maintained by the Reform movement today. First, he stated that the timeless aspect of Judaism was social justice. Just as the biblical prophets had taught, ritual acts are empty of meaning unless they are accompanied by moral and just behavior. Second, he concluded that Judaism was purely a religion, not a nationality. Stressing that he was a loyal German "of the Mosaic persuasion," he advocated eliminating all prayers that called for a return of the Jews to their ancient homeland. In 1854, he completed a prayer book that reflected this religious philosophy. (Interestingly enough, most of this prayer book was in Hebrew.)

When Geiger's wife died in 1860, he began to look for another position. Three years later he and his four children left for his native city of Frankfurt, where he served as rabbi for the next decade. After the years of turmoil in Breslau, Geiger felt immediately at home in Frankfurt's livelier intellectual community. He devoted more time to his *Jewish Journal of Life and Letters*, a new periodical he had begun to publish the year before. He prepared and delivered three series of lectures on Judaism and its history through the 16th century. In these lectures he stressed the need for Jews to give up the idea of a Jewish nationality. He also finished a work on the medieval Jewish poet Solomon ibn Gabirol.

As gratified as he was by the results of his research in Frankfurt, Geiger was eager to accept an offer that came for a position in Berlin, which had Germany's largest Jewish community. There he was accepted by the Orthodox, who were impressed with his scholarship. In Berlin, too,

Geiger succeeded in fulfilling a long-held dream when he was named a professor at the Academy for Jewish Studies, a research institute opened in 1872. For the remaining two years of his life, Geiger taught with enthusiasm while serving as the community's rabbi. He died in his sleep on October 23, 1874, three days before he was supposed to start a new semester of teaching and shortly after preaching the numerous sermons a rabbi gives during the Jewish High Holy Days each autumn.

Abraham Geiger shaped Jewish tradition by formulating a coherent theory to justify the reform of Judaism. As it happened, later Jewish scholars found errors in some of his conclusions. But Geiger's conviction that Judaism, like other living organisms, cannot survive without change continues to inspire the beliefs and practices of many Jews today.

FURTHER READING

Karp, Deborah. "Abraham Geiger." In *Heroes of Modern Jewish Thought*. New York: Ktav, 1966.

Meyer, Michael A. *Response to Modernity: A History of the Reform Movement in Judaism*. New York: Oxford University Press, 1988.

Plaut, W. Gunther. "The Great Controversy: Tiktin vs. Geiger." In *The Rise of Reform Judaism: A Sourcebook of Its European Origins*. New York: World Union for Progressive Judaism, 1969.

Wiener, Max. *Abraham Geiger and Liberal Judaism: The Challenge of the Nineteenth Century*. Cincinnati: Hebrew Union College Press, 1981.

Isaac Mayer Wise

"THE AMERICAN ISRAELITE"

In 1896, then-77-year-old Isaac Mayer Wise wrote, "Early in life there wakened within me an unutterable instinct to achieve something in the world, preferably in Judaism, and that not words but works." Although born in Europe, Wise sensed even as a young man that the future of Judaism lay in the United States. Over the course of his life, Wise tirelessly promoted his vision of American Judaism in newspaper articles, sermons, and books. But as he had foreseen, his great achievement came through works rather than words.

Wise was born in 1819 in a small town in Bohemia, then part of the Austrian Empire, where Jews did not enjoy full rights. According to one of his grandsons, Wise refused to talk much about the 27 years that preceded his arrival in the United States because the memories were so painful. In his *Reminiscences*, however, he described a turning point in his life that took place during his student years in Prague. One day, while browsing through a bookstore, he chanced

The union of congregations, school of higher education, and rabbinical association that Isaac Mayer Wise helped found established the institutional models of American Jewish life. Wise described himself as an "American born in the mountains of Bohemia."

upon a collection of American journals from the period just after the Revolutionary War. The democratic system of the United States, described in those journals, made a profound impression on the young Wise: "That literature made me a naturalized American in the interior of Bohemia."

Wise had a good background in both traditional Jewish studies and secular subjects, but he never earned a university degree. An 1837 government decree made a university degree a prerequisite for the rabbinate, so Wise never received a rabbinical diploma either. In 1843 he became a religious official in the town of Radnice, between Pilsen and Prague. For this position, he would have needed a certificate of competence from a board of rabbis. Wise probably served partly as a religious instructor and partly as a ritual slaughterer (who killed animals according to Jewish dietary laws so that their meat would be kosher—fit for Jews to eat). When he boarded a ship for the United States in the spring of 1846, along with his wife and young daughter, Wise listed his occupation as "instructor." We know that by the Jewish New Year that autumn he had a position as the first rabbi of Albany, New York. Thereafter he referred to himself as Rabbi Wise and sometimes used the title Doctor (of Divinity). What Wise lacked in official degrees, however, he more than made up for in energy, enthusiasm, and determination. His personality and abundant talents perfectly suited him to the rough-and-tumble life that awaited him in the New World.

When Wise arrived in the United States there were only about 50,000 Jews in the entire country, most of them recent immigrants from Germany. At most there was only a handful of rabbis in the country, all from Europe. Wise soon became convinced that Judaism would not survive in the United States unless it changed to meet the needs of the country's Jews. It seemed clear to him that adult Jews caught up in the need to make a living in the New World would no longer automatically observe the customs of their ancestors. As for the children, Wise feared they would soon drift away from Judaism altogether unless Jewish education and religious services were made meaningful to them.

Nearly from the outset Wise clearly saw himself as more than the rabbi of a single 130-member congregation in upstate New York. He took advantage of the Jewish press that already existed to communicate with Jews throughout the country. He had been in the United States barely more than two years when he published an article entitled "Call to Israelites" in *The Occident,* a Jewish monthly. In it Wise stated that American-trained teachers and rabbis were essential to ensure the survival of Judaism in the United States. He also advocated basic reform in synagogue practices as the only means to avoid a decline of religious observance. As he wrote, "If we do not unite ourselves betimes to devise a practicable system for the ministry and religious education at large,—if we do not take care that better educated men fill the pulpit and the schoolmaster's chair,—if we do not stimulate all the congregations to establish good schools, and to institute a reform in their Synagogues on modern Jewish principles,—the house of the Lord will be desolate, or nearly so, in less than ten years."

Not surprisingly, Wise used his own congregation in Albany as a laboratory to introduce the reforms he thought would make Judaism more appealing to American Jews. Taking his cue from the reforms that had first been introduced in German synagogues in the early 1800s, Wise set up a choir and an organ in his synagogue and began to deliver a weekly sermon in German. Many members of his congregation were pleased with these departures from tradition—but not all. Some thought Wise's services resembled church worship more than the synagogue practices familiar to them since childhood.

The friction between Wise and certain members of his congregation worsened in the summer of 1849. During a cholera epidemic that swept Albany, Wise's two-year-old daughter died. Although he was grief-stricken, he openly broke with Jewish tradition by refusing to observe two long-held mourning customs: tearing one's clothes and sitting barefoot on the floor. By taking this stance, he widened the rift between the traditional and liberal members of his congregation.

Matters came to a head in a remarkable way during Jewish New Year services in the fall of 1850, when the opposing factions actually came to blows in the synagogue and the police had to be called in. By the second day of the New Year holiday, Wise and his supporters had decided to form a breakaway congregation. When it was dedicated the following autumn, the new congregation became only the fourth in the United States based on Reform Jewish principles, which called for eliminating traditions that no longer seemed applicable in the modern world. For instance, Wise's new congregation became the first in America to establish seating by families, instead of segregating the women from the men. Wise's remaining years in Albany were characterized by harmony with his new congregation and his proud participation as a Jew in American democracy. For a week in January 1852, Wise served as provisional chaplain of the New York state legislature, in defiance of some Christian clergymen who did not want a Jew to have such a privilege. Eighteen years later, on May 21, 1870, Wise would become the first rabbi to deliver the opening prayer in the U.S. Senate.

For a man like Wise, who saw himself as a force to save American Judaism, a pulpit in Albany was not sufficient. Accordingly, in April 1854 he left to become rabbi of a congregation in Cincinnati, Ohio, where he served for the remaining 46 years of his life. Because of its strategic location on the Ohio River, Cincinnati became known as the Queen City of the West. Riverboats carried produce and goods between that city and the other settled parts of the United States. Under Wise's leadership, Cincinnati was also destined to play a major role in the growth of American Judaism.

Shortly after his arrival in Cincinnati, Wise founded a weekly Jewish newspaper, which he called *The Israelite*. As its editor and chief contributor, Wise was able to use this paper as a tool to Americanize Judaism. One area he focused on was education. Only an American seminary, he felt, could train rabbis to function effectively in America. And only American public schools could train Jewish children to lead fully American lives. In one early edition of the paper he issued a call to Cincinnati's Jews to establish "a college on the pattern of German universities, connected with a theological seminary, and a seminary for teachers, in order to promulgate . . . the interests of Judaism among our fellow citizens." In another edition he explained why he favored sending Jewish children to public schools and reserving religious education to afternoon synagogue schools: "Should our children be educated as Jews only . . . or should they be educated as Americans, as citizens of the same free country?" he asked. In an 1862 article he urged his readers to "be no Germans, no Polanders, no Englishmen, no Frenchmen; be Jews in the synagogue and Americans everywhere outside thereof. . . . Be Americanized in language, manners, habit, and appearances."

Wise also used *The Israelite* to make certain that the United States lived up to its ideals by protecting the rights of its Jewish citizens. For example, when the Cincinnati Board of Education permitted the reading of the Protestant Bible in the city's public schools, Wise argued in *The Israelite* that such behavior would lead to the suppression of other faiths. During the Civil War, when General Ulysses S. Grant issued an order expelling Jews from areas under his military command, *The Israelite* also took a firm stand, as it continued to do on a variety of issues over the years. In July 1874, after editing the paper for 20 years, Wise changed its name to *The American Israelite*, signaling his belief that Judaism was now completely at home in the United States.

In Cincinnati, Wise introduced a number of reforms that have since become standard practice not only in Reform congregations but also in the middle-of-the-road Conservative congregations. For example, in 1866, when his congregation moved to a splendid new building across from the city's Catholic cathedral, Wise proposed holding a brief service each Friday evening to usher in the Sabbath. Although his congregation rejected the idea initially, it was put into effect by two other congregations elsewhere, and in 1869 Wise's own congregation followed suit. Wise gave several reasons for this reform, including the inability of some businesspeople to attend traditional Saturday morning Sabbath services and the opportunity to introduce Judaism to non-Jews. Such Friday night services are now a standard part of American Judaism.

Shortly after arriving in Cincinnati, Wise published the most important of his many books, a prayer book in which modified forms of the traditional Hebrew prayers appeared along with their translation into

Wise edited *The Israelite,* one of the oldest Jewish journals in the United States, for close to half a century. To stimulate readership and promote fluency in English, the journal serialized novels of Jewish life.

English. Congregations all across America came to use this prayer book, called the *Minhag America* (The American Rite). By providing a form of worship widely used throughout the country, Wise's prayer book served as a unifying force. Today the reading of prayers in English is customary not only in Reform but also in Conservative congregations.

Wise's most important contributions to shaping and strengthening American Judaism are the three organizations that he began to call for from his earliest days in the country: a union of congregations, a college to train rabbis, and a regular conference of rabbis. Although these organizations came into being only after several false starts and they did not fulfill Wise's early hopes for unifying all American Jews, their significance cannot be overestimated.

In 1873, after Wise had failed more than once to bring about a lasting union of American congregations, the president of his congregation succeeded in doing so. The Union of American Hebrew Congregations (UAHC), originally intended to serve all American Jewry, grew into an association of U.S. and Canadian Reform congregations, affiliated with the World Union for Progressive Judaism, an organization founded in 1926 to unite the world's Reform congregations.

The first act of the UAHC was to set up Hebrew Union College (HUC), which formally opened in Cincinnati on October 3, 1875, with Wise as its first president. In *The American Israelite,* Wise described how highly he valued the presidency of the college, "where the finest opportunity is offered to contribute largely to the education of the young people of our country; to lay a solid foundation to the future greatness of American Judaism." Like its parent organization, HUC originally was intended to serve all American Jews, not merely the adherents of the Reform branch. The HUC curriculum included rigorous training in all the basic texts of Judaism, so that the rabbis ordained there would be able to lead any American congregation.

Things did not turn out as planned, however. In July 1883, HUC threw a celebration to honor the ordination of its first four students. The guests included representatives of traditional as well as Reform Judaism. According to Jewish law, ordination, like many other religious acts, is to be followed by a festive meal. Unfortunately, the caterer ignored the Jewish dietary laws, and the first course consisted of various kinds of shellfish, which are forbidden by Jewish law. The more traditional guests left the banquet and, when Wise failed to apologize for what had happened, broke away from the UAHC and

HUC. Before the end of the decade, Conservative Judaism had its own rabbinical seminary, and by the end of the 19th century Orthodox Judaism had a separate institution as well.

Hebrew Union College, now a Reform institution, went on to flourish. From its humble beginnings in the basement of a Cincinnati temple, with a tiny underpaid faculty, small student body, and virtually no library, it went on to ordain 60 rabbis during Wise's lifetime and to acquire a building that housed a faculty of nine and a growing library. Today HUC has satellite campuses in New York, Los Angeles, and Jerusalem, with a world-class faculty.

The third institution created by Wise's persistence, the Central Conference of American Rabbis (CCAR), was exclusively a Reform organization from the time of its founding in 1889. In his opening address to the CCAR's convention in July 1890, Wise explained the importance of a rabbinical organization: "If Judaism is to be properly respected, its bearers and expounders must first be, and this can be gained only by solid union." One of the first achievements of the CCAR was the preparation of a new prayer book, the *Union Prayer Book* of 1894, which replaced Wise's own *Minhag America.* Wise served as president of the CCAR until his death.

Wise, like other Reform Jews of his time, rejected the idea of a Jewish nationality. His point of view was reflected in one of the principles put forth at an assembly of Reform rabbis in Pittsburgh in 1885: "We consider ourselves no longer a nation, but a religious community, and, therefore, expect neither a return to Palestine, nor a sacrificial worship under the sons of Aaron [priests], nor the restoration of any of the laws concerning the Jewish state." Although today's Reform movement endorses and supports

Jewish statehood as embodied in the State of Israel, the movement continues to honor Wise for his lasting contributions.

On Saturday, March 24, 1900, Wise preached to his congregation during the weekly Sabbath morning service. After lunch with his family he gave his traditional Sabbath afternoon lecture to the students of HUC. At the end of the talk he suffered a stroke, which left him incapable of speech. Wise died two days later, a few days before his 81st birthday. On the day of his funeral many Cincinnati businesses closed, and the superintendent of the city's schools suspended classes so that students could attend the service.

In a lecture on Saturday, March 31, 1900, Wise's successor as president of HUC called Wise the American Johanan ben Zakkai. Jewish history remembers ben Zakkai, who died around 80 C.E., as the founder of a school that enabled Judaism to survive the Roman destruction of the temple in Jerusalem in 70 C.E. In a similar way, Wise enabled American Judaism to survive in the New World by founding a school and other institutions. The anniversary of Wise's death is still observed at HUC as Founder's Day. (One of Wise's sons, Jonah Bondi Wise, continued in his father's tradition by serving as rabbi of New York's Central Synagogue from 1925 until 1959.)

At the time of Wise's death, the nature of the Jewish community in the United States was changing rapidly. Many immigrants, fleeing the oppression of Jews in czarist Russia, poured into the United States. All three movements of American Judaism— Conservative, Orthodox, and Reform— were able to absorb the immigrants and help them adjust to American life in large part because all three had adopted the organizational setup created by Wise: a union of congregations, with national women's, men's, and youth groups; a school of higher education; and an association of rabbis.

When the Nazi Holocaust wiped out the Jewish communities of Europe, the American Jewish community was strong enough and sure enough of itself to become a world leader for Jewish interests. This came about in no small measure because of Isaac Mayer Wise's efforts to Americanize Judaism, to make it independent of Europe and responsive to the ways of the United States and the special needs of its own Jews.

FURTHER READING

Heller, James G. *Isaac M. Wise: His Life, Work and Thought*. New York: Union of American Hebrew Congregations, 1965.

Karp, Deborah. "Isaac Mayer Wise." In *Heroes of Modern Jewish Thought*. New York: Ktav, 1966.

Knox, Israel. "Isaac Mayer Wise." In *Great Jewish Personalities in Modern Times*. Edited by Simon Noveck. Washington, D.C.: B'nai B'rith, 1960.

———. *Rabbi in America: The Story of Isaac M. Wise*. Boston: Little, Brown, 1957.

Meyer, Michael A. *Response to Modernity: A History of the Reform Movement in Judaism*. New York: Oxford University Press, 1988.

Temkin, Sefton D. *Isaac Mayer Wise: Shaping American Judaism*. Oxford: Oxford University Press for the Littman Library, 1992.

Isaac Mayer Wise

BORN

March 29, 1819
Steingrub, Bohemia,
Austrian Empire

DIED

March 26, 1900
Cincinnati, Ohio

EDUCATION

Attended the University of Prague (1841–43) and possibly the University of Vienna; received a rabbinic certificate of competence in Prague (1843)

ACCOMPLISHMENTS

First rabbi of Albany, N.Y. (1846–54); founded fourth Reform congregation in the United States (1850); rabbi in Cincinnati, Ohio (1854–1900); author of *History of the Israelitish Nation* (Vol. 1, 1854), *History of the Hebrews' Second Commonwealth* (1880), and numerous other works, including 11 English and 16 German novels and hundreds of poems; published a weekly, *The Israelite* (1854–1900), one of the oldest Jewish journals in the United States; published *Minhag America—The Daily Prayers for American Israelites* (1857); helped establish the Union of American Hebrew Congregations (1873); ordained more than 60 rabbis as president of Hebrew Union College (1875–1900); president of the Central Conference of American Rabbis (1889–1900)

Solomon Schechter

"A WHOLE UNKNOWN JEWISH WORLD REVEALS ITSELF TO US"

The institutions of American Jewish life are so well established that it is hard to imagine that things were not always so. Although Jews have lived in America since the middle of the 17th century, a substantial Jewish community began to form only in the late 1840s, when many German Jews—disappointed with political developments or the economic opportunities at home—crossed the Atlantic. Then, beginning in the 1880s, hundreds of thousands of Jews began pouring out of eastern Europe in response to growing oppression, swelling the number of immigrants to the United States. Not surprisingly, given the unsettled nature of the community, many aspects of Jewish-American life that are taken for granted today, such as synagogues headed by American-trained rabbis and religious schools run by American-trained Jewish educators—were then little more than dreams. No one even imagined the departments of Jewish studies now operating in major American universities, where Jewish professors contribute regularly to the growth of knowledge in fields of Jewish interest. In addition, whole areas of contemporary Jewish scholarship were then still unknown, and most serious scholarly studies of the Bible and the works of the early rabbis were done not by Jews but by Christians. Although no single individual deserves all the credit for transforming these conditions, it is impossible to overestimate the contributions of Solomon Schechter both to Jewish scholarship and to the shaping of American Judaism.

Schechter, one of six children, was born in Focsani, Romania, in 1847. His father was a ritual slaughterer, one who killed animals according to the Jewish dietary laws so that their meat would be kosher. (The name Schechter actually comes from the German word for "slaughterer.") Although the young Solomon quickly mastered the traditional religious subjects, he also was thirsty for other sources of knowledge. By the time he was a teenager, he was no longer satisfied with the limited library in his parents' home, which included only prayer books, the Bible, and the Talmud (the 5th–century encyclopedia of Jewish law and lore). At the age of 12 he tried to understand the anti-Semitism he saw around him in Romania by reading a Hebrew translation of a book on hostility toward Jews in ancient Alexandria by the 1st-century historian Josephus. In a weekly Hebrew newspaper he learned about Abraham Lincoln, who became one of his heroes. Also on his own he studied the difficult work of the 12th-century Jewish philosopher Maimonides.

Solomon Schechter pores over piles of documents he managed to bring back to the library at Cambridge University from an old storehouse of ancient books and documents in Cairo. Schechter succeeded in retrieving the documents, after many others had failed, through the sheer force of his personality.

His limited exposure to works like these convinced the young Schechter that he could not satisfy his intellectual needs in Focsani. Worrying that his parents would not allow him to leave home at such a young age, he borrowed money from a friend and ran away to a nearby town to study in the traditional Jewish academy there. His parents found him and brought him back, but when he returned to the academy on his own a second time they decided to let him study there. After spending one unhappy teenage year at a rabbinical school in Lemberg, then part of Austria, he returned home, where he studied on his own for the next several years. During that time he was married briefly and miserably. The match, arranged for him by his parents, was so unsatisfactory that Schechter remained single until he was over 40.

In his early 20s, Schechter left home permanently. He went to study in Vienna, then a vibrant center for Jewish and secular studies. At the University of Vienna he attended lectures in philosophy and Romanian language and grammar. His main studies, however, were at the Jewish House of Study, where the faculty presented traditional Jewish subjects in a more modern way than most rabbis of the day. There he received a rabbinical diploma and became convinced that it was necessary to apply the same rigorous methods of historical inquiry to Jewish texts that scholars were already applying to other classical documents. For example, he proposed to compare all the old editions of a text to see how they differed and to devise a standard edition. Under the influence of one of his teachers in Vienna he also developed an idea that would remain central to his thought: that the course of Jewish life over history has been determined by the Jewish community as a whole. In other words, Jewish law is authoritative not because an orga-

nized legislature or judiciary says it is but only as long as it is firmly rooted in the practice of the Jewish people. Schechter called this concept "catholic Israel," a name that sometimes confuses English-speaking Jews today. For Schechter's purposes, the word *catholic* simply meant "all-inclusive" and had nothing to do with Roman Catholicism.

In 1879, Schechter left Vienna for Berlin, where he enrolled at both the University of Berlin and the Academy for Jewish Studies. At the academy he met a student from England whose friendship would prove a turning point in his life. Claude Goldsmid Montefiore was from a prominent family of English Jews (his great-uncle was the well-known Jewish philanthropist Sir Moses Montefiore). In 1882, Montefiore was ready to return to England, but he wanted to be able to continue his Jewish studies there. Although England's libraries had many important and ancient Jewish books and manuscripts, Montefiore was convinced that no Jew in his native country was competent to teach them. At the suggestion of the rabbi of Berlin, he invited Schechter to return to England as his tutor, and Schechter agreed.

Luckily for Jewish scholarship and the future of American Judaism, Schechter's responsibilities as a tutor left him plenty of time for other activities. In London's British Museum he was delighted to find that the collection of rare Jewish documents lived up to its reputation. He spent hours in the museum's library and began publishing scholarly articles on his discoveries. His work in the museum not only established Schechter as the most important scholar of Judaism in England but also led to his second marriage. While working there he often met Mathilde Roth, a well-educated woman who had come to England from Germany to teach German literature and study English literature. The two

Solomon Schechter, center, at a meeting of Jewish scholars overseeing a new English translation of the Hebrew Bible. The meeting took place at the Jewish Theological Seminary of America, where Schechter served as president for the last 13 years of his life.

were married in 1887 (in a former home of the English novelist Charles Dickens) and eventually became the parents of three children.

In 1890, Schechter was asked to take up a position at Cambridge University. In that ancient university town Schechter made his greatest contributions to Jewish scholarship and found the most significant personal satisfactions of his life. He thrived on his professional interactions with Christian scholars and was able to spend most of his time doing research. In May 1896, he received a visit from two Scottish sisters that opened up areas of Jewish history that had been buried for centuries. These two women had returned from a trip to the Middle East with some parchment fragments bought in Egypt. They asked Schechter to evaluate them. On one fragment he found some Hebrew verses from the book of Ecclesiasticus, which Roman Catholics (but neither Protestants nor Jews) consider part of the Bible. The book,

written in Hebrew in Palestine around 180 B.C.E., had survived over the centuries only in an ancient Greek translation. No one had ever thought it possible to recover the original Hebrew.

Excited by this discovery, Schechter published his findings in July 1896. Then, a few months later, he traveled to Egypt on behalf of the Cambridge University library. Scholars had known for more than a century that in the ancient city of Cairo there was a *genizah*—the Hebrew word for a storehouse for old books, religious objects, and documents too worn to permit regular use. Schechter's mission was to bring back from that *genizah*, which other scholars had not succeeded in entering, as much of the material buried there as possible. By force of personality, Schechter succeeded where others had failed. With the help of the chief rabbi of Cairo he gained access to the windowless, doorless, unventilated *genizah*, which could be entered only by crawling through a hole in the wall of the

1,000-year-old Ben Ezra synagogue. Over a period of six weeks he fought through centuries of dust to pore over the treasures of the *genizah*. In the end he was permitted to send back to the library at Cambridge about 100,000 pages from it.

Over the next six years, Schechter devoted himself to sorting and cataloging his *genizah* findings and publishing his results. As he sorted his documents into unromantic grocery cartons he was aware of the significance of his task to Jewish scholarship. To a leader of the Jewish community in the United States, Schechter wrote, "I am finding daily valuable treasures. A whole unknown Jewish world reveals itself to us." Schechter's research restored most of the Hebrew text of Ecclesiasticus and recovered many hitherto unknown religious poems and numerous historical documents that led to a new understanding of Jewish history. In particular, the contents of the *genizah* provided a wealth of knowledge about the Jews of Palestine and Egypt during the Middle Ages, a subject about which historians had previously known almost nothing. Schechter himself edited many documents relating to the life of the great Jewish thinker Saadia Gaon (882–942), who is usually considered the founder of Jewish philosophy. Realizing how vast a world he had uncovered, Schechter lamented the lack of trained Jewish scholars to interpret his findings. A hundred years after his initial discovery, the work of cataloging and analyzing the contents of the *genizah* continues. Among the researchers today are many highly trained Jewish scholars, a fact that would make Schechter proud.

Meanwhile, during the years when Schechter was completing his education and making his name as a scholar, the growing Jewish community in the United States was struggling to develop the institutions that would enable it to flourish. The first school to train American rabbis, Hebrew Union College (HUC), was formed in 1875, but its founders' hopes for unifying the Jewish community were dashed in 1883 when a rift occurred between the Orthodox and Reform Jews.

In 1885 a number of rabbis met in Pittsburgh to define the principles of the Reform movement. They formulated the so-called Pittsburgh Platform, which stated that only Judaism's moral laws were binding in modern times and called for such radical measures as abolishing the Jewish dietary laws. In response, Conservative Jews decided that the United States needed a traditional alternative to the Reform-dominated Hebrew Union College.

As a result, in 1887 a new rabbinical school, which was destined to become the central institution of Conservative Judaism, opened its doors in New York City. Called the Jewish Theological Seminary of America (JTS), it faced many struggles in its early existence. The JTS graduated only 17 rabbis during its first 13 years, and funding for the school

was uncertain. One of its founders believed that what the JTS mainly lacked was a dynamic leader, a scholar with a forceful personality. Schechter seemed the ideal candidate, if only he could be convinced to give up his scholarly routine in Cambridge. Ten years passed before Schechter could finally be persuaded to leave England for the United States. He made the decision for two key reasons: to raise his children in a thriving Jewish community, which was not possible in Cambridge, and to have a chance to shape both Jewish scholarship and observance in the United States, where he believed the future of Judaism lay.

In April 1902, Schechter took up his duties as president of the Jewish Theological Seminary of America. Over the next 13 years, until his death in 1915, Schechter worked tirelessly on behalf of the JTS, the Conservative movement, and the American Jewish community in general. By selecting a faculty of outstanding Jewish scholars from around the world he transformed the seminary into a major center of Jewish research and provided outstanding teachers and exemplars for its rabbis in training. In 1909, about halfway into his presidency, Schechter also broadened the mission of the seminary by founding its Teachers Institute. He dreamed of a system of Conservative day schools in the United States and hoped that the graduates of the seminary's Teachers Institute would eventually serve in such institutions. (Today such a day school system, named for Schechter, is in place.)

Although administration rather than scholarship now took up more and more of his time, Schechter remained a scholar to the core, and under his direction the seminary's library grew into one of the finest collections of Judaica in the world. (About 20,000 of the manuscripts and books from the *genizah*, for example, are now at JTS.) Some years after his death, the library extended its activities and opened its Museum of Jewish Ceremonial Objects. As that small museum grew, it eventually required a more spacious home

LINKS IN THE CHAIN

Solomon Schechter

BORN

December 7, 1847
Focsani, Romania

DIED

November 19, 1915
New York, New York

EDUCATION

Rabbinical diploma, Jewish House of Study in Vienna (1879); attended University of Vienna (1879), Berlin's Academy for Jewish Studies (1879–82), and the University of Berlin (1879–92)

ACCOMPLISHMENTS

Published scholarly editions of important rabbinical works; university lecturer, then reader in Talmudics at Cambridge University (1890–1902); chair of Hebrew at University College, London (1897–1902); president, Jewish Theological Seminary of America (1902–15); author of popular books, including *Studies in Judaism* (three volumes, 1896–1924), *Some Aspects of Rabbinic Theology* (1909), and *Seminary Addresses and Other Papers* (1915)

"There is no other Jewish religion but that taught by the Torah and confirmed by history and tradition, and sunk into the conscience of Catholic Israel."

—from inaugural address at Jewish Theological Seminary (1902)

in a former private mansion on New York's Fifth Avenue. There it continues to flourish as the Jewish Museum, one of the outstanding cultural sites along New York's Museum Mile.

Schechter's deeply felt beliefs helped the once-floundering Conservative movement establish its own identity. By insisting that Judaism could be modern without cutting itself off from tradition, Schechter defined a middle-of-the-road position for the Conservative movement. Under his guidance, Conservative Judaism identified itself as more open to justifiable change than the Orthodox movement but much more respectful of the authority of Jewish law than the Reform movement, which never claimed to accept the authority of Jewish law.

Because of Schechter's convictions, the Conservative movement's principles included support for Zionism, another fledgling movement, which called for a Jewish state in the ancient homeland of Palestine.

According to Schechter, "Every land and every age have contributed to [tradition], and our age has no right to withdraw itself from that sacred organism." As a result of the approach to Jewish law and tradition favored by Schechter, Conservative Judaism over the course of the 20th century has been able to justify striking changes. Most dramatically, during the 1970s and 1980s the movement's Committee on Jewish Law and Standards carefully weighed Jewish law on the role of women in Jewish life. As a result of its

deliberations, the committee first declared that Conservative congregations may count women as part of the *minyan*, the religious quorum needed for public prayer. Next, a minority of six committee members ruled that women should be allowed to serve as witnesses in Jewish legal matters. (Conservative congregations are free to follow a minority position held by more than three committee members.) Then a commission formed to examine the issue of ordaining women concluded that "there is no cogent argument" based on Jewish law "for denying a sincere, committed woman the opportunity to study for and achieve the office of rabbi." In 1984 the Jewish Theological Seminary of America voted to admit women to its rabbinical school. By contrast, the religious status of Orthodox Jewish women has not changed at all, despite vigorous and ongoing efforts toward that end by Orthodox feminists.

From the Jewish Theological Seminary of America's base in New York City, Schechter hoped to extend his religious and educational program throughout North America. In 1913, therefore, he founded the United Synagogue of America, which he believed would be his most important legacy to the continent's Jews. Today the United Synagogue is an association of more than 800 Conservative synagogues in the United States and Canada. The United Synagogue has provided Jews with prayer books that respond to changes in contemporary

life. It has led attempts to coordinate a Jewish response to various social issues. Schechter also hoped that the United Synagogue would play a major role in guiding the education of young Jews. Its first efforts on behalf of Jewish education in North America were directed at afternoon religious schools run by congregations throughout the continent, providing them with standards and suggestions for plans of study. If Schechter were still alive, he would doubtless take great pride in the Solomon Schechter Day School Association. For more than 30 years this organization has honored Schechter's ideals by coordinating the activities of the all-day Conservative Jewish schools in the United States and Canada.

FURTHER READING

Bentwich, Norman. *Solomon Schechter: A Biography*. Philadelphia: Jewish Publication Society, 1938.

———. "Solomon Schechter." In *Great Jewish Personalities in Modern Times*. Edited by Simon Noveck. Washington, D.C.: B'nai B'rith, 1960.

Ginzberg, Louis. "Solomon Schechter." In *Students, Scholars, and Saints*. New York: Meridian, 1958.

Mandelbaum, Bernard. *The Wisdom of Solomon Schechter*. New York: Burning Bush, 1963.

Marx, Alexander. "Solomon Schechter." In *Essays in Jewish Biography*. Philadelphia: Jewish Publication Society, 1948.

Lily Montagu

THE SPIRIT OF MODERNITY

The feeling that there must be more to Judaism than the rituals she saw being mechanically observed around her led one teenage girl, Lily Montagu, to grow up to be an important religious organizer and leader. Montagu was born into a distinguished family of Anglo-Jews, as the Jews of England are often called. Her father, Samuel (1832–1911), was a self-made millionaire who eventually became a member of the British Parliament. His political beliefs, which favored free education for all, legal aid to the poor, and other liberal measures, went hand in hand with his philanthropic efforts in support of both Jewish and secular causes.

As a Jew, Samuel Montagu was staunchly Orthodox in both faith and practice. He not only believed that the laws of the Torah and the later laws of the rabbis were transmitted by God to Moses, but he scrupulously carried out traditional rituals and observances. In addition, unlike certain other wealthy, prominent Jews in England and elsewhere, he was an early supporter of those seeking to establish Jewish settlements in Palestine. The British government officially recognized his achievements by making him a baronet in 1904 and naming him the first Baron Swaythling in 1907, thus entitling him to a seat in the House of Lords.

Lily Montagu's lineage on her mother's side of the family was equally distinguished. Ellen Montagu's father, Louis Cohen, was a wealthy banker and stockbroker, a long-time member of the British stock exchange, a philanthropist, and an amateur botanist.

Although Montagu would break with the Orthodox practices with which she was raised, she nevertheless modeled herself personally on her parents. She tried to emulate her father's ability to live both his private and public lives according to what he perceived to be basic Jewish values. Like him, she determined to make Judaism the focus of her life. "The accomplishment of his work, his form of entertainment, his personal sacrifices, expressed his faith," she said in 1950.

Montagu's parents raised all 10 of their children to be observant Jews, but their attitude toward religious education was typical of the day. They saw that their four sons received a solid background so that they, as males, could participate in prayer and study. The six daughters, who were expected to sit in the women's section of the Orthodox synagogue, where their presence would not distract the men, were less well trained. It appears that Lily's religious education consisted of being tutored in the Bible,

Lily Montagu delivers a sermon at the Reform Temple in Berlin in 1928, becoming the first woman in Germany to preach from a Jewish pulpit. Montagu sought to ensure that Liberal Judaism practiced absolute equality of men and women.

especially the prophetic books and the Psalms. She never attempted to compensate for this lack of religious scholarship, because for her religion would not be a matter of intellectual knowledge.

By the time Lily Montagu was a teenager, she began to feel that something was missing in the religious life of her family. As she later described it, Judaism seemed merely an "external fact" of life. Attending synagogue services and observing holidays seemed to tie her to her roots but had no effect on her innermost being. She became particularly upset during one particular Passover. At the seder, the ceremonial meal at which Jews recount the story of the Exodus from Egypt, her father solemnly read from the Haggadah, the special book for the holiday observance. Instead of

involving themselves in the reading, her brothers joked and sang in a way that struck her as completely inappropriate. When she explained her feelings to her oldest brother, he mocked her concern for piety.

Similarly, one Yom Kippur—the Day of Atonement, which marks the holiest time of the Jewish calendar, when Jews fast and pray to earn God's forgiveness—Montagu was distressed to see the seemingly pious Jews in the synagogue throw down their prayer shawls at the end of the fast and rush home to eat. Could prayer affect them so little, she wondered?

These stirrings of religious dissatisfaction came to a head after Montagu's formal education ended when she was only 15. For the next two years, she continued to be tutored at home and was allowed to follow a reading list of

her own choosing. The contemporary writers whose works she eagerly absorbed strengthened her conviction that something was wrong with the Judaism she saw being practiced around her. Her favorite authors—Thomas Carlyle, George Eliot, Robert Browning—all described true religion as a deeply personal force with a humanitarian outlook. These authors seemed to believe what Montagu felt intuitively: that religion was not a matter of observing rituals but of recognizing and answering God's call to service.

The contrast between her ideal of religion and the Judaism she knew was so distressing to Montagu that she actually experienced a breakdown. It is not known how long she remained in the grip of her illness, but within two years she was fully recovered. She had found a way to reconcile Judaism with what she now understood to be "true" religion, even if the Orthodox Judaism practiced in her parents' home could never satisfy her. Her recovery was aided in part by reading, partly by the encouragement of others.

The author whose works had the most beneficial influence on Montagu was Claude Goldsmid Montefiore (1858–1938), who was later to play a decisive role in her personal life. Montefiore, who also came from a distinguished Anglo-Jewish family, was a theologian and scholar whose books and essays convinced Montagu that Judaism could be a living faith, not merely an "external fact." Montefiore insisted that Judaism could develop from one age to the next. He contrasted Judaism's ethical laws, which he considered timeless and essential, with its rituals, which he thought nonessential. He called his outlook Liberal, as opposed to Orthodox, Judaism. By rejecting the idea that God literally transmitted the Torah and the later rabbinical rulings, Montefiore's Liberal Judaism allowed each Jew the freedom to observe only those laws that appeared personally meaningful. Montefiore also stressed the importance of maintaining a personal relationship with God and understanding the connection between a belief in God and one's daily behavior. According to Montefiore, God had chosen the Jews to fulfill a particular mission: to spread the idea of God's oneness throughout the world. Furthermore, asserted Montefiore, God's oneness meant that God is the God of all peoples. For that reason, he said, Jewish texts are not the only source of truth.

A few years after Montefiore's works had contributed to Lily Montagu's recovery, she met him at a party held by her aunt and uncle. Montefiore at the time was a widower, and there is reason to believe that Montagu fell in love with him; in any case, he remarried shortly thereafter and she never became romantically involved with anyone. But Montefiore continued to play a pivotal role in the unfolding of Montagu's career and her contribution to Jewish tradition.

Another factor in Montagu's recovery was her tutor, Simeon Singer, an Orthodox rabbi and close friend of her father. In guiding Montagu's studies of the Bible, Singer stressed the prophets' belief in the need to help the less fortunate. He encouraged Montagu to involve herself in helping others and asked her to begin special religious services for children at his synagogue. He thus gave his student the opportunity to develop herself personally while also awakening others to prayer. Montagu's services inspired both the children of the congregation and a number of the adults who also happened to attend. She then began to think about offering services aimed at an adult audience.

The opportunity to do so developed when a cousin introduced her to a social worker who ran Sabbath classes for young Jewish working women. At the social worker's suggestion, Montagu and her cousin began holding Sunday afternoon meetings for the class. Montagu soon decided that a more organized educational, social, and religious structure would be of greater benefit to the young working women and would enable her to more effectively share the things she valued most highly: education, friendship, and a belief in God. The result was the West Central Jewish Girls' Club, which Montagu founded in 1893 at the age of 20 with the financial backing of family and friends.

The West Central Jewish Girls' Club was unique because it was based on religious spirit. Montagu realized that most of its members were not religiously observant, but she tried energetically to awaken within each member an awareness of God. She organized special Sabbath and holiday services that she hoped would appeal to the members, and concluded evening club meetings with a brief religious service.

Having revitalized her own connection with Judaism and begun to awaken spiritual awareness in Jewish children and young working women, Lily Montagu began to think about a much larger, more diverse group of Jews in need of spiritual awakening. She later described her motives by contrasting her attitude with that of her father, who dismissed irreligious Anglo-Jews as "dead leaves which would drop off." He believed that the Orthodox would succeed in transmitting Judaism to the next generation and that the others simply did not matter. But as Lily put it, she herself "began to worry about the so-called dead leaves."

Although her own family was Orthodox, Lily Montagu was aware that there had been a Reform Jewish movement in England since 1840. The participants in Anglo-Jewish Reform

"Judaism does not consist in keeping observances, though observances have an important place nevertheless in Jewish life. They will be put in their right place when we find the way of life which is Judaism."

—from "What Is Judaism?" (open letter to the West Central Jewish Girls' Club, January 1942)

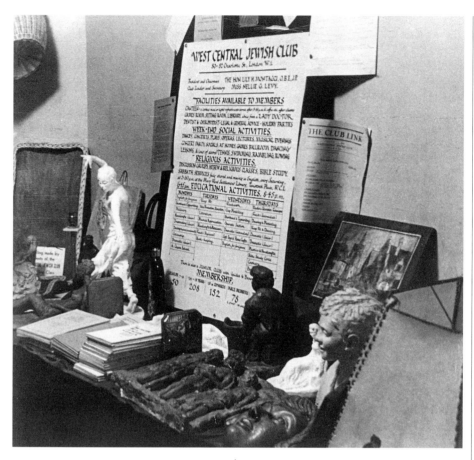

The West Central Jewish Girls' Club, founded by Lily Montagu, developed into London's West Central Liberal Synagogue. Montagu served as its unofficial spiritual leader from 1913 until 1944, when she was inducted as a "lay minister."

had modernized the service in numerous ways. As far as Montagu could tell, however, their motives were not spiritual. They seemed to her more interested in keeping the services short than in the ability of the prayers to touch them on an emotional basis. Still, the existence of a Reform movement indicated to her that other Anglo-Jews were interested in change; they simply had not gone about it in what she thought was the right way.

In June 1898, Montagu attended a conference on Jewish religious education. There she met some teachers who complained that their students seemed spiritually dead. They felt that the prevailing methods of teaching—emphasizing memorization of prayers in a foreign language—were at least partly to blame. While the conference confirmed Montagu in her belief that the future of Judaism in England was in jeopardy, it also brought her into contact with others who shared her dissatisfaction with the current state of affairs.

Some months later she wrote an article, "The Spiritual Possibilities of Judaism Today," which appeared in the January 1899 issue of the *Jewish Quarterly Review*, a journal coedited by Claude Montefiore. Her intention in the article was to call attention to the spiritual malaise among Anglo-Jewry. To keep young Jews involved in their ancestral faith, a new form of Judaism was needed, she argued. Her solution was to combine the best of the old with the spirit of modernity. Montagu thus proposed a new organization, not exclusively Liberal but designed to unite all Anglo-Jews, whether Orthodox, Reform, or those dissatisfied with both alternatives, in a common goal: the strengthening of Anglo-Jewish religious life.

The Jewish Religious Union (JRU) that was formed as a result of Montagu's efforts held its first meeting in February 1902. By that time, Montagu had convinced Claude Montefiore to be the JRU's official leader, a post he filled until his death in 1938. But it was Montagu herself who was the driving spirit behind the organization, who initiated its activities and kept up with its daily affairs.

In October 1902, the JRU held its first religious services, which were mainly in English, accompanied by instrumental music. The services were held not in a synagogue but in a rented hall at the Hotel Great Central in West London. The change of venue came about because the chief rabbi of England objected to the use of a synagogue for the JRU's purposes. Though he claimed to admire the motives of the organization and appreciated the founders' intention not to form a new Liberal Jewish movement, he warned that the services were not Jewish enough and that the organization's existence would further fragment Anglo-Jewry.

Within a year of the JRU's founding, Samuel Montagu, the chief rabbi, and other Orthodox leaders began pressuring those Orthodox rabbis who had joined the JRU to resign from it. Soon it became clear to Lily Montagu that "we could not work on a system of compromise and achieve anything worthwhile," and in 1909 the JRU became a specifically Liberal Jewish movement. In November of that year, the group changed its name to the Jewish Religious Union for the Advancement of Liberal Judaism. This expanded title reflected a greater mission. The group acquired a building to serve as a synagogue and hired a Reform rabbi from the United States. In 1910 the Jewish Religious Union established London's Liberal Jewish Synagogue.

From 1909 until his death two years later, Samuel Montagu barely spoke to his daughter Lily. After his death, she had a vision in which she saw him handing her a document. She interpreted her vision as a sign that her father now accepted the validity of her work, even though his will specifically forbade the use of his money to promote Liberal Judaism. This vision enabled her to continue her advancement of Liberal Judaism. In 1913 a branch of the Liberal Jewish Synagogue called the West Central section was founded. Since no rabbi was available to lead the West Central section, Montagu agreed to serve as unofficial spiritual leader. As such, she led the weekly Sabbath afternoon services, gave sermons, and prepared candidates for conversion to Judaism. She also assisted at weddings and funerals, under the guidance of the rabbi of the Liberal Jewish Synagogue, who was brought in on those occasions. In 1928, the West Central section became a fully independent Liberal synagogue on its own. As the West Central Liberal Synagogue, it continues to this day to have weekly Saturday afternoon services. In 1944, Montagu's years of service were recognized when she and others were inducted as "lay ministers" in a special service at the original Liberal Jewish Synagogue, where she had also been preaching since 1918.

Montagu's interest in advancing the goals of Liberal Judaism went beyond national boundaries. In 1925, the JRU accepted her suggestion that an international body of Liberal Jewish organizations be formed. As she wrote some years later, "This Union exists to make Judaism a strong, vital influence in the lives of our progressive congregations throughout the world." The following year, representatives of Reform and other Liberal congregations in England, France, Germany, India, and the United States met in London. There they decided to name the new organization the World Union for Progressive Judaism. Claude Montefiore was elected president, Lily Montagu, honorary secretary. Her responsibility for managing the World Union's daily affairs included organizing the first International World Union Conference, which took place in Berlin in 1928. At this conference, Montagu became the first woman to preach from a Jewish pulpit in Germany, when she spoke on "Personal Religion" at Berlin's Reform Congregation. The World Union continues to hold international conferences to strengthen the ties among the world's Reform and Liberal congregations.

For more than 30 years, the offices for both the JRU and the World Union were headquartered in Montagu's home. From 1938 to 1961 she was president of the JRU, a position to which she was unanimously elected following Montefiore's death. In 1954, at the age of 81, she became president of the World Union as well. But later that year the Union decided to move its headquarters to the United States, and Montagu announced that she would not seek

Lily Montagu

BORN

December 22, 1873
London, England

DIED

January 22, 1963
London, England

EDUCATION

Attended Doreck College until age 15, followed by two years of private tutoring

ACCOMPLISHMENTS

Founded London's West Central Jewish Girls' Club (1893), Jewish Religious Union (1898), and World Union for Progressive Judaism (1926); formally inducted as a Liberal Jewish "lay minister" in 1944 after more than 30 years' service as a spiritual leader; wrote 11 books, including *Prayers, Psalms, and Hymns for the Jewish Child* (with Theodore Davis, 1901), *The Faith of a Jewish Woman* (1943), and *God Revealed* (1953), and numerous articles and sermons reelection to the presidency. She was nonetheless made honorary life president.

Throughout her long life, Lily Montagu based all her activities on a few underlying principles. She believed that God assigns each person a specific task to perform and that a Jew's task is to bear witness to the reality of God. She taught that human beings are born unfinished but that "in partnership with God" each one may "grow in spiritual stature." Though she believed that Jewish laws "were not framed and directed by God," she urged Jews to observe those traditions that helped them feel inner holiness. Like Montefiore, she believed that God's oneness implied that all human beings were members of the same family. She insisted that serving others is the essence of true religion but that organized religion was necessary to keep people spiritually nourished.

As befitted one who believed that work enabled each individual to serve God, others, and self, Lily Montagu continued to work until the very end of her long life. After spending some time in her home library on the afternoon of Friday, January 18, 1963, she collapsed while mounting the stairs. After lingering in a coma she died on January 22, just a month after celebrating her 89th birthday. Before the end she had completed some notes for a sermon she was planning for that Saturday. Called "Seeking and Finding," it would have touched upon themes Montagu had been stressing since the 1890s— listening for God's call, praying, making religion permeate all aspects of life. She was also planning to discuss some issues relating to the politics of the day, notably communism. Her final heading was "Effort of Prayer."

Today, fewer than 10 percent of English Jews identify themselves as Liberal. But Lily Montagu nonetheless made several lasting contributions to Jewish tradition. Liberal Judaism in England is a thriving, albeit small movement that continues to honor the memory of its founding mother. The World Union for Progressive Judaism, a second offspring of Montagu's efforts, also endures. In addition, Montagu serves as a model for Jewish women seeking leadership functions in social service, religious organizations, and synagogues. Finally, Lily Montagu left her mark by calling for a Judaism that combines personal commitment with organized religion. As she said in her Berlin sermon of August 1928, "If we want personal religion I would urge in all sincerity that we do not cut ourselves adrift from organized religion; if we do, we lose the best nourishment we can obtain."

FURTHER READING

Meyer, Michael A. *Response to Modernity: A History of the Reform Movement in Judaism*. New York: Oxford University Press, 1988.

Umansky, Ellen. *Lily Montagu and the Advancement of Liberal Judaism: From Vision to Vocation*. New York: Edwin Mellen, 1983.

Umansky, Ellen, ed. *Lily Montagu: Sermons, Addresses, Letters, and Prayers*. New York: Edwin Mellen, 1985.

Martin Buber

SEEKING DIALOGUE

Martin Buber once said, "In a genuine dialogue each of the partners, even when he stands in opposition to the other, heeds, affirms and confirms his opponent as an existing other. Only so is it possible for conflict, though not to be eliminated from the world, yet to be subject to human arbitration, and so led to the point where it is overcome." Although Buber's philosophy of dialogue is not specifically Jewish in concept, it led him into Jewish studies and leadership. As a scholar and as a leader he made a lasting mark on Jewish tradition.

It may be that Buber's passionate belief in the importance of dialogue resulted from his childhood experience of what can happen when people fail to communicate with one another. His parents' marriage fell apart when Martin was only three years old. His mother left home, breaking up the family.

From that time until he was 14, Buber was raised by his father's parents in the Ukrainian city of Lemberg (now called Lvov). His grandfather, a wealthy banker, was also a scholar whose library of rabbinic literature is still of value to researchers in that field. He used his wealth to finance his scholarship. Despite his active business life he devoted himself to editing Midrashim, a type of rabbinic literature that explains and amplifies the Bible, often through maxims and stories. Solomon Buber taught his grandson Hebrew, but young Martin was more interested in secular German poetry than in Jewish learning.

Martin's interest in secular studies was broadened in grammar school, and as a teenager Buber rebelled against his religious roots. At the age of 14 he stopped wearing *tefillin*, the leather cubes containing biblical verses that observant Jewish men strap to the left arm and the forehead during weekday morning prayers.

Buber attended universities in Austria, Germany, and Switzerland, where he studied philosophy and art. In 1898, while still a student, he joined the Zionist movement, which aimed to establish a Jewish homeland in the land of Palestine. Through Zionism Buber found his way back to Judaism. Over the next quarter century Buber briefly edited a Zionist publication; founded a Jewish publishing company; took up the study of Hasidism (an ultra-Orthodox Jewish sect that emphasized prayer, zeal, and joy); founded a committee that worked throughout World War I to advance the interests of the Jews in eastern European countries occupied by Germany; and edited a journal, *The Jew*, which was read widely by German Jewish intellectuals. In 1925 Buber became a lecturer in Jewish religion and ethics at the University of Frankfurt, where he was appointed professor of religion five years later.

Martin Buber at a Jerusalem bookshop in March 1946. The most difficult part of Buber's 1938 move from Germany to Palestine was packing his library of 20,000 volumes under the supervision of a Gestapo official.

Buber presented his philosophy of dialogue fully in 1923 in his most famous book, called *Ich und Du* in German. The book was translated into English in 1937—and given the unfortunate title *I and Thou*. Though the translation is technically correct, to English speakers the word *thou* can seem stiff, antiquated, and formal. However, because German speakers use the word *du* when speaking to those with whom they have a very close relationship, Buber's intent is clearly to establish a sense of intimacy.

The title of the book notwithstanding, English speakers, like German ones, were deeply impressed by the philosophy expressed in *I and Thou*. According to Buber, people may have one of two types of relationships with each other and with the world around them. To deal effectively in the world, people need to engage in "I–It" relationships, which enable them to observe, study, or use

something else. But to be fully human, Buber taught, human beings must also engage in "I–Thou" relationships. These relationships involve true "encounters" or "meetings" on a deep, unrestrained level.

For Buber, a genuine I–Thou relationship is a form of dialogue. He took pains to emphasize that the dialogue of such a relationship is different from that in a conversation. Indeed, real dialogue need not involve words at all. What a dialogue requires is for both participants to see things from the other's point of view without in any way diminishing their own personalities. Without this shared understanding, there can be only monologue and an I-It relationship.

Just as people can have an I–It relationship with other human beings, they are also able to have an I–Thou relationship with nature, art, or literature.

What is required of the observer is to let go completely and be open to the effect of the encounter. Buber once spoke of God's commandment to each human being: "Thou shalt not withhold yourself."

For Buber, the commandment to become personally involved extends not only to other people and things but also to God. It would be a mistake for those seeking an I–Thou relationship with God to begin by trying to analyze the nature of God; such attempts turn God into an It. Buber taught that it was not necessary to know anything about God in order to talk to Him. While Buber did not presume that there was a foolproof technique for having an encounter with God, he suggested three possible approaches for doing so. One is through establishing I–Thou relationships with people, nature, and things. Rather than retreating from the world in search of a mystical relationship with the divine, one can find God by forming I–Thou relationships with God's creation. In Buber's philosophy, God is "the Eternal Thou in whom all other I–Thou relationships intersect."

A second approach to an I–Thou relationship with God is to participate in the ongoing process of creation. Like the Hasidim, the ultra-Orthodox Jewish followers of the Baal Shem Tov, Buber believed that all things are potentially holy and that each person has a specific contribution to make in hallowing God's creation. He asserted that it is not necessary to make a conscious effort to find God—it is possible to encounter God simply by living life to the fullest. In fact, Buber's conviction that God is everywhere led him to reject many aspects of formal religions. He believed instead that such religions may actually exclude God by setting aside only certain times, places, and acts through which worshipers are supposed to encounter the divine.

Buber's third route to an I–Thou relationship with God is more concrete than the other two. He recommended

> *"You need God in order to be, and God needs you—for that is the meaning of your life. . . . The world is not divine play, it is divine fate. That there are world, man, the human person, you and I, has divine meaning."*
>
> —from *I and Thou* (1923)

reading the Bible as if it were addressed to each of us individually. For example, if Jews would allow themselves not only to hear God's voice as their ancestors did long ago but also to act on the scriptural words instructing the Israelites to be a holy people, they would enter into a dialogue with God.

Buber cautioned that just as there are rocky periods in even the best I–Thou relationship with another person, there may be times when God seems unavailable. He used the phrase "the eclipse of God" to describe such occasions. During a solar eclipse the sun is still in the sky but its light, blocked by the moon, is prevented from reaching earth. Just as we do not despair of ever seeing the sun again during such an eclipse, we should remain confident that God's seeming absence from our lives is only temporary.

Buber's belief that each person can enter into dialogue with God led him to reject having fixed rules for religious behavior. As a proponent of dialogue he believed that Jews should observe only those religious laws that they feel God has addressed to them personally. Because of this stance, Buber has been called a religious anarchist. In political theory, an anarchist is one who rejects all forms of government as improperly interfering with individual freedom. However, although Buber's philosophy of dialogue placed him in conflict with some aspects of Judaism, it also led him into a life of deep involvement with Jewish studies and spiritual leadership.

Buber's impressive translation of the Hebrew Bible into German is grounded in his belief that the Bible is a record of the dialogue between God and the Jewish people over the course of history. For Buber, the Bible should be considered neither a literal truth nor living literature but, instead, proof that "our life is a dialogue between the above and the below." Buber and his close friend and colleague Franz Rosenzweig were convinced that everyone could enter into dialogue with the Bible by assuming its words are addressed to each individual. The first volumes of the collaborative Hebrew-to-German translation appeared in 1925. Rosenzweig died four years later, but Buber eventually completed the translation on his own in 1961.

The aim of the translation was to retain the spoken quality of the Bible. For that reason Buber and Rosenzweig did not try to make their German translation smooth where the Hebrew original was rough, or to clarify obscure passages in the original. Buber was aware of the awesome responsibility of daring to convey the meaning of God's words to others. He spoke of the "fear and trembling" he felt when attempting to translate or interpret a biblical text, because of the "inescapable tension between the word of God and the words of man."

Whatever fear and trembling these translators experienced, Buber and Rosenzweig made certain choices in their translation that give their Bible a specific point of view. For example, where many translators describe the

Buber poses with some of his students at the Hebrew University in Jerusalem in 1940. Buber taught at the university for many years. Along with the president of the university and others, Buber formed a union that advocated the establishment in Palestine of a binational state of Jews and Arabs.

Israelites as a "holy" people, Buber and Rosenzweig call them a "hallowing" people, ones who make things holy. This idea that individuals have a responsibility to make things holy is rooted in Hasidic concepts that originated with the Baal Shem Tov and are central to Buber's thought.

Buber's commitment to dialogue also led him to introduce Hasidic themes into Western culture. Buber was especially impressed by the Hasidic teaching that each person has his or her own specific capabilities. According to him, before we can have successful I–Thou relationships we must develop an understanding of our own uniqueness. Among other Hasidic ideas he admired is its insistence that mechanical performance of ritual is meaningless and that one must pray and fulfill religious requirements with personal commitment. Buber believed, however, that the theories of Hasidism were less important than how the Hasidic leaders led their lives. For this reason he translated from Yiddish numerous stories about these charismatic figures told by their followers.

Buber's beliefs led him to assume an influential role in the Jewish community, both in Germany and in Palestine. From 1933 on, when the Nazis came to power in Germany, until his departure for Palestine in 1938, Buber served as spiritual leader of German Jewry. As director of Jewish adult education throughout Germany, he put his belief in I–Thou relationships into practice. To keep people from despairing in the face of Nazi anti-Semitism, he set up communities of teachers and students who lived and worked together. These communities helped to strengthen the Jewish identity of the participants and prepare them for resettlement in Palestine. According to a German-Jewish colleague who later joined Buber on the faculty of the Hebrew University in Jerusalem, "Anyone who did not see Buber then has not seen true civic courage."

Ironically, Buber needed civic courage not only to confront the Nazis but also to oppose the many Jews who were distressed by certain political positions he felt obliged to adopt. For example, after the defeat of Nazism Buber believed that dialogue could heal the rift between Jews everywhere and non-Jews in Germany. He also argued that only dialogue would make it possible for Jews and Arabs to share the land of Israel in peace. When Buber agreed to accept two German peace prizes only a few years after the liberation of the Nazi death camps, many Jews vilified him, but he remained true to his convictions. During a visit to Germany in 1953, he told an audience, "Let us dare, despite all, to trust!"

Buber donated the money from both German awards to an organization to promote dialogue between Arabs and Israelis. The philosopher, whose chosen task in Nazi Germany had been to heighten the Jews' sense of their specifically Jewish identity, believed that his task in the ancient homeland was to remind Jews of their common humanity with the Arabs who lived there too. Even at the age of 20, when he first joined the Zionist movement to establish a Jewish homeland in Palestine, Buber had urged a meeting of minds with the Arab population of the region. Then, after his resettlement in Jerusalem, Buber helped found a movement supporting the establishment of a state run equally by Jewish settlers and Arab inhabitants. When Israel became an independent nation in 1948, Buber relinquished his dream of a binational state but not of the peaceful coexistence of Arabs and Jews. Understandably, this commitment made him unpopular with some Jews.

Martin Buber died in 1965, but his influence has lived on. In the late 1960s, Hebrew University in Jerusalem, where Buber taught social philosophy until his retirement in 1951, opened the Martin Buber Institute for Adult Education, aimed at promoting dialogue between Israelis and Palestinians. Undoubtedly, Buber would have taken profound satisfaction in the historic handshake between Prime Minister Yitzhak Rabin and Palestine Liberation Organization Chairman Yasir Arafat on the White House lawn in September 1993.

FURTHER READING

Buber, Martin. *Hasidism and Modern Man*. Atlantic Highlands, N.J.: Humanities Press International, 1988.

————. *I and Thou*. Translated by Walter Kaufman and S. G. Smith. New York: Macmillan, 1978.

————. *Tales of the Hasidim*. 2 vols. New York: Schocken, 1987.

Friedman, Maurice. *Martin Buber's Life and Work*. 3 vols. Detroit: Wayne State University Press, 1988.

Schmidt, Gilya Gerda. *Martin Buber's Formative Years: From German Culture to Jewish Renewal, 1897–1909*. Tuscaloosa: University of Alabama Press, 1995.

Martin Buber

BORN

February 8, 1878
Vienna, Austria

DIED

June 13, 1965
Jerusalem, Israel

EDUCATION

Attended the universities of Leipzig, Zurich, and Berlin; Ph.D., University of Vienna (1904)

ACCOMPLISHMENTS

Developed a philosophy of dialogue, expressed in *Ich und Du* (I and Thou) (1923); translated the Hebrew Bible into German (1925–61); brought Hasidic thought to a wide audience (1906–60); served as spiritual leader of German Jewry (1933–38); strove to repair relations between Germans and Jews and between Israelis and Arabs; wrote *Paths in Utopia* (1949), *Two Types of Faith* (1951), *Eclipse of God* (1952), *The Legend of the Baal-Shem* (1955), *Tales of the Hasidim* (two volumes, 1947–48), and *Hasidism and the Way of Man* (two volumes, 1958–60)

Mordecai Menahem Kaplan

RECONSTRUCTING JEWISH LIFE

Most of those who have made major contributions to Jewish tradition have been endowed with deep conviction and great self-confidence. This does not mean, however, that they were never afflicted with doubts about their abilities or even about the very nature of Judaism. Mordecai Kaplan, who was born in 1881 and lived to be more than 100, was so disturbed by certain aspects of his faith that he almost abandoned his career as a rabbi. Only halfway through his long life did he publicly express a new way of thinking about Judaism that enabled him to practice his religion with a clear conscience. His plan for reconstructing Judaism would have a major impact on the way many contemporary American Jews carry out Jewish traditions.

Kaplan was born near Vilna (today, Vilnius), the capital of Lithuania. As a young boy he moved with his family to the United States. His father—a rabbi and a scholar—had been offered a position in New York City. The elder Kaplan, who was very open-minded, welcomed into his home not only people who shared his traditional attitudes but also religious skeptics. Among them was a controversial Jewish biblical scholar whose detailed research into the text of the Torah, the first five books of the Hebrew Bible, led him to conclude that the Torah had clearly been written by human beings. Despite the claims of ancient Jewish tradition, this scholar asserted that God had not given the Torah to the Jews at Mount Sinai. Kaplan's father did not keep his son from listening to and reading the arguments of this scholar, who was barred from many other traditional homes.

As Kaplan continued his education in college and graduate school, he read widely in the social sciences. What he read confirmed for him the suspicions that had been planted by the skeptical biblical scholar. Kaplan found that he too could not believe in a God who, according to tradition, had singled out the Jewish people and handed them the Torah. As he learned more about the origin, development, and organization of human society, and about the social customs and beliefs of different groups of people, he became more and more convinced that all religions develop in a similar way. It was no longer possible for him to believe that any one religion was the only true faith. Instead, he now saw Judaism, like all other religions, as part of a larger culture. For this reason, Kaplan asserted that Judaism is more than a system of beliefs contained in religious texts. Rather, he affirmed, it is a religious civilization that includes language, literature, and even arts and crafts. By the time he described

A boy celebrates his bar mitzvah—the ceremony that marks his entrance into religious adulthood—at the pulpit of Mordechai Kaplan's Society for the Advancement of Judaism in New York. The SAJ was the first congregation in the United States to celebrate a bat mitzvah—a bar mitzvah for girls. Kaplan's daughter was the celebrant.

these conclusions in his first and best-known book, *Judaism as a Civilization: Toward the Reconstruction of American-Jewish Life* (1934), Kaplan was already in his 50s and had been a practicing rabbi for more than 30 years.

Kaplan's long experience as a rabbi convinced him that many modern American Jews shared his inability to accept the supernatural claims of Judaism. Like him, they could not believe in a supernatural God, in a Torah that had been handed down by God, or in a people of Israel who had been singled out from all other nations by God. To let others with these

concerns continue as practicing Jews without feeling like hypocrites, Kaplan called in his book for a "reconstruction" of Judaism: "Judaism, or that which unites the successive generations of Jews and all Jews of each generation, is more than a Religion. It is an evolving Religious civilization, and as such consists of Peoplehood, Culture and Religion. . . . Only deliberate reconstruction of our Jewish social structure, Jewish way of Life, and Jewish Religion, with a view to the realities and needs of our day, can prevent Judaism from being fossilized, or save it from disintegration."

According to Kaplan, not God but Israel—both the Jewish people themselves and the land of their origin—needed to be the primary focus of a reconstructed Judaism. However, the traditional Jewish claim of being God's chosen people offended Kaplan on at least two grounds: first, God is not a person who makes choices, and second, neither Jews nor any other people can claim to be better than those of any other group. At the time *Judaism as a Civilization* appeared, the state of Israel had not yet been formed; however, for nearly 40 years many Jews had been actively involved in the

Zionist movement, working to create a Jewish national home in Palestine. Kaplan's concept of a reconstructed Israel included a new emphasis on Zionism. Nevertheless, he objected to the position taken by many Zionists of the day who insisted that Jewish life in any country other than Palestine was pointless. Instead, Kaplan called for a reconstructed Jewish civilization that had its spiritual center in Zion—a poetic Hebrew name for the whole of the land of Israel—but still understood the importance of Jewish life elsewhere. Kaplan warned that Jews should not substitute Zionism for Judaism. In his view, the moral and religious teachings of Judaism were essential to Zionism. Without them, he feared, a Jewish state could end up as just another nation. In addition, believing that every civilization links its land and its language intimately, Kaplan also called for intense Hebrew language education for all American Jews, children and adults alike.

Even though Kaplan rejected the idea that God had revealed the Torah to the Jewish people, he still believed that God, the Torah, and the Jewish people were meaningfully linked. In Kaplan's reconstructed belief in the Torah, the Jewish people can reveal God to the rest of the world by living their lives according to the Torah's teachings. Kaplan also argued that Jews should reexamine their reasons for observing the Torah's commandments. Individuals should observe the commandments not because they fear punishment but because observance strengthens their ties to the Jewish people. Believing that the Torah's laws were man-made, not handed down by God, Kaplan insisted accordingly that modern Jews should feel free to change those laws to meet the needs of the moment. He urged Jews to find ways to make traditional laws meaningful for themselves. For example, some Jews might find that observing dietary

Rabbi Kaplan, second from right, participates in the Torah service at the Society for the Advancement of Judaism. While traditional teaching held that the Torah was revealed by God to the Jews, Kaplan offered the radical notion that the Jews reveal God through the Torah.

laws against eating the meat of certain animals made them more sensitive to the value of all forms of life. He also urged Jews to create new rituals to help strengthen their Jewish identity, such as the naming of baby girls in the synagogue.

The most controversial aspect of Kaplan's program was his concept of God. Kaplan defined God in a variety of ways, all having to do with forces that enable individuals to live worthwhile lives and fulfill their ideals. For example, he called God "the Power that makes for self-fulfillment" and "the Power that makes for salvation." In another famous passage, Kaplan described "the fact that the cosmos possesses the resources and man the abilities . . . to enable him to fulfill his destiny as a human being, or to achieve salvation" as "the Godhood of the cosmos." Many Jews found Kaplan's concept of God unsatisfying, though, because it seemed to ignore the

existence of evil in the world. However, Kaplan never expected his blueprint for the reconstruction of Judaism to serve as a fixed code. He merely offered suggestions for Jews who shared his concerns about the supernatural elements of Judaism. He felt that all Jews retained the right and the responsibility to work out the details of their personal Jewish identity for themselves.

In his reconstruction of the concept of God, Kaplan was led also to rethink the meaning of prayer. He was disturbed by the idea that in the process of praying, Jews might pay lip service to beliefs they did not hold or even express words they found offensive. Convinced, therefore, that new Jewish prayers were needed to reflect modern beliefs and needs, Kaplan and a few colleagues boldly published a new prayer book, with the unassuming title *Sabbath Prayer Book*, in 1945. When it appeared, a leading group of traditionalist rabbis was so horrified that some ran a match down the spine of the new prayer book in an act symbolizing burning. Kaplan's efforts nevertheless led to the variety of Jewish prayer books currently available in the United States, published by the Reform and the Conservative movements, as well as by the Reconstructionist movement.

In *Judaism as a Civilization,* Kaplan also expressed his belief that the existing synagogues were inadequate to meet the expanded cultural needs of reconstructed American Judaism. To fill these needs, which included recreation in addition to worship and study, Kaplan called for a new type of institution: a Jewish Center, sometimes referred to as "a *shul* [Yiddish for "synagogue"] with a pool and a school." Kaplan helped plan the first such American Jewish Center in New York City and served from 1916 to 1922 as its rabbi. These centers remain a fixture of American Jewish life.

Mordecai Kaplan's contributions as a practicing teacher and rabbi were at least as important as those he made through his writings. He had begun his career as an Orthodox rabbi, despite doubts about certain aspects of Judaism that had plagued him since boyhood. But when he lost his belief in a God who had transmitted a celestial Torah to a chosen people, he began to feel like an impostor. In addition, some of the wealthy businessmen in his New York City congregation began to object to his sermons championing the rights of workers. For a while Kaplan even considered abandoning the rabbinate and going into business himself.

If it were not for a phone call he received in 1909, Kaplan's life might well have taken a completely different route. The call came from Solomon Schechter, the president of the Jewish Theological Seminary of America, offering Kaplan the chance to become head of the seminary's new Teachers Institute. Shortly thereafter he also accepted a professorship at the

seminary's rabbinical school. Over the next four decades, in those two roles, Kaplan introduced numerous future Jewish educators and rabbis to his ideas about Israel, the Torah, and God. He especially sought to convince rabbinical candidates that Torah study should reflect contemporary concerns.

As a rabbi, Kaplan also played a significant role in altering the course of Jewish life in the United States. Fifty years before American Jewish women began to demand equal rights in Judaism, Kaplan began taking positive steps in that direction. In *Judaism as a Civilization* he had noted, "The Jewish woman became aware that she was accorded a more dignified status outside Jewish life. This explains why many talented Jewish women not only began to lose interest in Jewish life, but actually turned against it. . . . If we do not want our talented women to follow their example, we must find in Judaism a place for their powers. This cannot come about unless all taint of inferiority will be removed from the status of Jewish women."

When Kaplan became the rabbi at the Jewish Center in 1916, he took steps to advance women's rights there by designing a seating plan for the sanctuary that did not demean women. Traditionally, not only were women seated apart from men—so as not to distract the men from the serious business of prayer—but were relegated to a separate section either at the back of the main floor, with a curtain or grille separating the sexes, or in the balcony. The traditional seating had led many women to feel like second-class citizens and often made it difficult for them to see and hear clearly what was going on in the service. Although men and women still did not sit together in the Jewish Center, the women now sat in smaller sections on either side of the large central area, with an unobstructed view.

In 1922, Kaplan left the Jewish Center to set up the Society for the Advancement of Judaism, the first

Mordecai Menahem Kaplan

BORN

June 11, 1881
Svencionys, Lithuania

DIED

November 8, 1983
New York, New York

EDUCATION

B.A., College of the City of New York (1900); M.A., Columbia University (1902); ordained as a rabbi at the Jewish Theological Seminary of America (1902)

ACCOMPLISHMENTS

Principal, Teachers Institute of the Jewish Theological Seminary of America (1909–31); Dean, Teachers Institute (1931–46); Professor of Homiletics and Midrash, Jewish Theological Seminary (1910–47); Professor of Philosophics of Religion, Jewish Theological Seminary (1947–63); organized the first Jewish Center in the United States (1916); established the Society for the Advancement of Judaism (1922); founded the Reconstructionist movement; wrote *Judaism as a Civilization: Toward the Reconstruction of American-Jewish Life* (1934), *The Meaning of God in Modern Jewish Religion* (1937), *Questions Jews Ask* (1956), *Judaism without Supernaturalism* (1958), *The Religion of Ethical Nationhood* (1970), and other books; coedited the Reconstructionist *Sabbath Prayer Book* (1945) and other prayer books

> *"Judaism, or that which has united the successive generations of Jews into one people, is not only a religion; it is a dynamic religious civilization."*
>
> —from *Questions Jews Ask* (1956)

Reconstructionist congregation, also in New York. There, equality for women in Judaism was one of the foundations of the program. The next year Kaplan and his congregation became the first to open up to young women a practice that had been exclusively male for centuries. Traditionally, congregations have marked every Jewish boy's entry into religious adulthood with a bar mitzvah ceremony at the age of 13. To mark the occasion, the boy recites blessings over the Torah, reads a portion of the Torah, and recites a passage from the biblical prophets associated with it. Kaplan's daughter Judith was the first young woman in the United States to enter religious maturity with an official bat mitzvah ceremony. Today, at many congregations throughout the United States, bat mitzvah ceremonies for girls are as routine as bar mitzvahs for boys.

When Kaplan published *Judaism as a Civilization*, he had no intention of creating a new movement. Rather, he hoped that there would be a place for a reconstructed Judaism within the already existing Jewish movements of America. For years he ignored the pleas of colleagues to establish a separate institution to train Reconstructionist rabbis. But, in 1968, at the age of 82, he took part in dedicating a new Reconstructionist Rabbinical College. Reconstructionism thus became a separate movement, like the Orthodox, Conservative, and Reform movements already established in the United States. Although the college has trained many rabbis in the years since, most have found jobs in Conservative or Reform synagogues. Only a small number of American Jews specifically call themselves Reconstructionists.

All the same, Mordecai Kaplan's reconstructionist ideas have permeated American Jewish tradition. Many of his ideas, which seemed revolutionary when he introduced them, have now become fixtures of American Judaism.

For example, the idea that Judaism is a civilization with a rich culture in addition to its set of religious beliefs is now widely accepted. And most contemporary Jews believe that a good Jewish education should introduce the student not only to ancient religious texts but also to modern Hebrew language and literature, Jewish history, and Israeli culture. The idea that Jewish institutions must respond to women's needs can also be traced to Kaplan. Most fundamentally, his insistence that Jews should never carry out observances or mouth prayers that make them feel intellectually dishonest continues to help many Americans define their Jewish identity.

FURTHER READING

Cohen, Jack. "Mordecai M. Kaplan." In *The "Other" New York Jewish Intellectuals.* Edited by Carole S. Kessner. New York: New York University Press, 1994.

Eisenstein, Ira. "Mordecai M. Kaplan." In *Great Jewish Thinkers of the 20th Century.* Edited by Simon Noveck. Clinton, Mass.: Colonial Press, 1963.

Goldsmith, Emanuel S., and Mel Scult, eds. *Dynamic Judaism: The Essential Writings of Mordecai M. Kaplan.* New York: Schocken/Reconstructionist Press, 1985.

Goldsmith, Emanuel S., Mel Scult, and Robert M. Seltzer, eds. *The American Judaism of Mordecai M. Kaplan.* New York: New York University Press, 1990.

Nadell, Pamela S. "Mordecai Menahem Kaplan." In *Conservative Judaism in American: A Biographical Dictionary and Sourcebook.* New York: Greenwood Press, 1988.

Pasachoff, Naomi. "Mordecai Kaplan." In *Great Jewish Thinkers: Their Lives and Work.* West Orange, N.J.: Behrman House, 1992.

Pasachoff, Naomi, and Robert J. Littman. "Mordecai Kaplan and Reconstructionist Judaism." In *Jewish History in 100 Nutshells.* Northvale, N.J.: Aronson, 1995.

Franz Rosenzweig

A NEW COMMITMENT TO JUDAISM

Among observant Jews, the idea of adult education goes back to ancient times. In Babylonian days Jewish men would flock from the countryside for yearly month-long seminars with learned rabbis. In the Orthodox community adult study groups of different types have continued to flourish over the centuries. Among less observant Jews, however, the idea of adult education is quite new. The widespread adoption of this recent tradition can be traced back to the influence of a German Jew named Franz Rosenzweig.

Rosenzweig's personal story is filled with drama. Rosenzweig, born in Kassel, Germany, in 1886, was a great-grandson of Samuel Meir Ehrenberg, a Jewish educator whose students included Leopold Zunz, the founder of the "Science of Judaism." Rosenzweig's parents, however, were well-to-do and thoroughly assimilated Jews, who felt themselves to be German to the core. Judaism had only peripheral importance in their lives. Rosenzweig's father combined a career as a dye manufacturer with a life of civic activity as a member of the Kassel city council. His mother was devoted to German literature and culture.

Franz Rosenzweig in 1917, three years before his marriage to Edith Hahn and his appointment as head of Frankfurt's Independent House of Jewish Study.

"All of us to whom Judaism, to whom being a Jew, has again become the pivot of our lives . . . we all know that in being Jews we must not give up anything, not renounce anything, but lead everything back to Judaism."

—from draft of address at the opening of Frankfurt's Independent House of Jewish Study (1920)

Although the family marked Franz's 13th birthday with a bar mitzvah, they celebrated few other religious events. Not until he was a university student did Rosenzweig know that traditional Jews welcomed in the Sabbath on Friday evenings with a whole range of observances. When he was 18, Rosenzweig revealed in a letter to a friend that God meant nothing more to him than a "weather maker."

To earn his doctorate in philosophy, Rosenzweig wrote a thesis on the influential German philosopher Georg Wilhelm Friedrich Hegel (1770–1831); some years later the thesis became the basis of one of his books. Rosenzweig began as a great admirer of Hegel, who argued that an understanding of any aspect of human culture requires first an understanding of its history: why it developed as it did. Eventually, however, Rosenzweig concluded there was something missing from the Hegelian system of thought. Hegel, he believed, overemphasized history at the expense of the individual human being's life, which Hegel considered irrelevant to the "whole." Rosenzweig ultimately found Hegel's philosophy inadequate because it ignored the suffering and spiritual longing of real people.

A number of Rosenzweig's Jewish acquaintances had become aware of a spiritual longing in their own lives. Having no Jewish background to speak of, they had concluded that conversion to Christianity might fill their needs. When a member of the Rosenzweig family—another great-grandson of Samuel Meir Ehrenberg—chose the path of conversion, Rosenzweig's parents were aghast. Franz nevertheless wrote to tell them that he had supported his cousin's decision. He added that there was no visible difference between the way Christians and assimilated Jews like the Rosenzweigs lived: "We are Christian in everything. We live in a Christian state,

attend Christian schools, read Christian books. . . ." If assimilated Jews felt spiritually unfulfilled, Rosenzweig believed, they had only two alternatives: to become involved in Zionism—the political movement to found a Jewish homeland in Palestine—or convert to Christianity.

One of Rosenzweig's university professors was a former Jew who had converted to Christianity. In daily discussions with this man, Rosenzweig became convinced that unless he could find some compelling reason to remain a Jew, he too would have to convert. By the end of the summer of 1913, he had made the decision to become a Christian.

Rosenzweig postponed his conversion until after the Jewish High Holy Days that autumn. On the first of these holy days—Rosh Hashanah, the Jewish New Year—Jews traditionally reflect on their behavior and examine their consciences. Rosenzweig decided to attend Rosh Hashanah services in his family's synagogue in Kassel. The services left him untouched, as they always had. While at home during the 10 days between Rosh Hashanah and the second High Holy Day—Yom Kippur, the Day of Repentance—he confided in his mother that he intended to convert following the Yom Kippur services. Horrified, his mother said, "In our synagogue there is no room for one who abandons his faith."

Feeling, as a result, that he had been driven from home as well as from the family synagogue, Rosenzweig left for Berlin to attend Yom Kippur services at a small, traditional synagogue. There he experienced a spiritual transformation. Although he never described just what happened to him, in some of his writings he expressed his feelings that during Yom Kippur prayers a Jew comes "as close to God" as one can. Having entered the synagogue with the intent to convert to Christianity, he emerged instead as a Jew who would spend the rest of his life studying, teaching, and practicing Judaism.

To deepen his knowledge of Judaism, Rosenzweig spent a year at Berlin's Academy for Jewish Studies, poring over Jewish religious texts. Then in 1914 World War I broke out and he entered military service. Even as a soldier he continued to study, however, concentrating on Hebrew and Aramaic, the languages of the Bible and the Talmud, respectively. Reflecting on his own life, he concluded that he would never have experienced such confusion had he received a strong Jewish education. As a result, in 1917 he wrote an open letter addressed to a professor at the Academy for Jewish Studies (the philosopher Hermann Cohen). The letter, which was published under the title *It Is Time*, marked the beginning of a lifelong commitment to reforming German Jewish education. In it he proposed that the great works of Judaism could have a real effect only on students who actually read them— reading only what others had to say about them was inadequate. He also suggested that Jewish high school students be taught by teacher-scholars, who would combine their teaching with scholarly research in a still-to-be-created Jewish academy.

During his military service, Rosenzweig also began his major philosophical work, *The Star of Redemption*. Written mostly in trenches, army barracks, and military hospitals, the book was finally published in 1921. By then, Rosenzweig had determined to devote the rest of his life to helping other confused assimilated Jews find a way back to Judaism. Accordingly, he declined an invitation to teach at a German university with the explanation that "the questions asked by human beings have become increasingly important to me."

The year 1920 saw many changes in Rosenzweig's life. He married a Jewish woman from Berlin and was appointed head of a new center for adult Jewish studies, the Independent House of Jewish Study in Frankfurt. This center was unique in several ways. Few of the teachers were rabbis. Instead, like the students, they represented many different professions. And again like the students, the teachers were also in search of ways to live an authentic Jewish life in the modern world. The classes were not lectures but rather discussions in which students and teachers together grappled with Jewish texts. The teachers were not interested in conveying a particular point of view but in having the students react personally to each text.

Unfortunately, Rosenzweig was able to direct the Independent House of Jewish Study for less than three years. Toward the end of 1921, he had noticed that he no longer had full control of his body. Shortly thereafter, a few months before the birth of his only child, doctors confirmed that he had ALS—amyotrophic lateral sclerosis, also known today as Lou Gehrig's disease—a rare and as yet incurable disease that leads to complete paralysis. His physicians predicted he would die within the year, and by the end of 1922 he was confined to his apartment.

Rosenzweig continued to live an astonishingly productive life for another seven years, however. When he could no longer write, he dictated his thoughts to his wife, who transcribed them. When he could no longer speak, the General Electric Company manufactured a special typewriter according to his requirements. When he could no longer use that typewriter, he relied on his wife's uncanny ability to discern his thoughts. With her help he was able to revise *The Star of Redemption*; translate

Franz Rosenzweig

BORN

December 25, 1886
Kassel, Germany

DIED

December 10, 1929
Frankfurt, Germany

EDUCATION

Briefly studied medicine at the universities of Göttingen, Munich, and Freiburg; studied modern history and philosophy at Berlin and Freiburg; Ph.D., 1912; attended Academy for Jewish Studies, Berlin (1913–14).

ACCOMPLISHMENTS

Author of *The Star of Redemption* (1921); director of Frankfurt's Independent House of Jewish Study (1920–22); collaborated with Martin Buber on a German translation of the Hebrew Bible (1925–29); wrote many important essays on Jewish education and life; translated and annotated the poems of Judah Halevi and write a commentary on a group of Hebrew poems by the great medieval philosopher-poet Judah Halevi (1075–1141); and collaborate with the philosopher Martin Buber (1878–1965) on a new translation of the Hebrew Bible into German. Neither these works nor the reviews of new musical recordings he wrote for a Kassel newspaper revealed how desperately ill their author was. Rosenzweig also kept up a correspondence with friends and colleagues. On the Sabbath and holidays, visitors regularly came to the Rosenzweig home, enabling the family to practice their religion as part of a Jewish community.

Rosenzweig, who finally died in 1929, two weeks short of his 43rd birthday, is more than just a heroic figure. Some 80 years ago, he posed a question that remains pertinent for many Jews today: How can assimilated Jews avoid feeling like part-time Jews in an otherwise Christian world? Rosenzweig's two responses—that they can do so through education and religious practice—have left their mark on Jewish tradition.

For Rosenzweig, the first key to becoming a truly Jewish human being is to study the major works of Judaism. Rosenzweig's Independent House of Jewish Study was the first school for adult Jewish education that encour-aged each participant to come to personal terms with every text. Today Jews from many professions participate in such study groups, sometimes in traditional settings like synagogues or other Jewish institutions, and sometimes in less conventional settings like law firms or hospitals.

Rosenzweig's second key principle was for Jews to incorporate as much Jewish practice into their daily lives as possible. Just as he believed that each Jew must draw independent conclusions from personally struggling with the essential texts of Judaism, he also believed that the individual had to decide which Jewish practices made his or her life more meaningful. Jews traditionally speak of religious laws as commandments. For himself, Rosenzweig felt he could practice only those Jewish rituals that seemed to be commandments personally addressed to him by God. He believed, however, that Jews should not be satisfied with performing only a limited number of Jewish rituals. Rather, they should continue to seek personal meaning even in those laws that at first seemed irrelevant to their lives. When someone once asked Rosenzweig if he observed a certain religious practice, his response was "Not yet."

Rosenzweig's life and teachings continue to inspire modern Jews to learn more about Judaism's rich past and find personal meaning in its many rituals. He advised Jews not to try to fit themselves into a mold labeled "Orthodox," "Reform," or "Zionist." Instead he encouraged each one to create his or her own personal Jewish identity. In introducing the idea of a Jewish House of Study, Rosenzweig wrote, "There is one recipe alone that can make a person Jewish and hence—because he is a Jew and destined to a Jewish life—a full human being: that recipe is to have no recipe." Franz Rosenzweig molded Jewish tradition by helping modern Jews find their own path toward a truly Jewish existence.

FURTHER READING

Fackenheim, Emil L., and Raphael Jospe. *Jewish Philosophy and the Academy.* Madison, N.J.: Fairleigh Dickinson University Press, 1996.

Glatzer, Nahum N. *Franz Rosenzweig: His Life and Thought.* New York: Schocken, 1953.

Mendes-Flohr, Paul, ed. *Philosophy of Franz Rosenzweig.* Hanover, N.H.: University Press of New England, 1988.

Pasachoff, Naomi. "Franz Rosenzweig." In *Great Jewish Thinkers: Their Lives and Work.* West Orange, N.J.: Behrman House, 1992.

Joseph Dov Soloveitchik

THE LONELY MAN OF FAITH

Joseph Dov Soloveitchik came from a distinguished line of scholars of the Talmud, the fifth-century teachings that cover all aspects of Jewish life. He grew up to be the unchallenged leader of the Orthodox movement in Judaism, and ordained more than 2,000 rabbis—more than any other American seminary teacher. But despite his lineage and his personal achievements, he remained a shy and modest man. He once said, "I have many pupils, I have many disciples, but I never impose my views on anyone." Soloveitchik also turned down the position of chief rabbi of Israel because he valued his independence of thought over prestige. "I was afraid to be an officer of the state," he said. "A rabbinate linked up with the state cannot be entirely free."

In order to understand the contribution of Joseph Dov Soloveitchik to Jewish tradition, an understanding of the Hebrew word *halakhah* is helpful. Jewish law, called *halakhah*, is what makes Judaism a distinctive religion. The word *halakhah* comes from the Hebrew verb "to walk." Traditional Jews believe that halakhah shows them the proper path along which to walk.

When most people wake up in the morning, they follow a certain routine, but they know it is a routine of their own making. By contrast, as Orthodox Jews proceed through their daily activities, they believe each step is guided by halakhah, a routine prescribed by God. For nearly half a century,

Rabbi Soloveitchik holds the attention of a group of students at New York's Yeshiva University, where he taught Talmud for more than 40 years. He also ordained more than 2,000 Orthodox rabbis at the university's rabbinical seminary.

"In my 'desolate, howling solitude' I experience a growing awareness that . . . this service to which I, a lonely and solitary individual, am committed is wanted and gracefully accepted by God."

—from *The Lonely Man of Faith* (1965)

whenever American Orthodox Jews had questions about halakhah, the authority they were most likely to consult was Rabbi Joseph Dov Soloveitchik. As a sign that he was their preeminent authority, they called him simply the Rav, an affectionate Hebrew name for rabbi or teacher. From the early 1940s until the mid-1980s, when illness led to his retirement, Soloveitchik shaped American Orthodox Judaism through his thought and his rulings on halakhah. The work of his many students ensures that his contribution to Orthodox Jewish tradition will continue.

Soloveitchik was born in 1903 in Pruzhany, in today's Belarus, and was raised in Khoslavitch, where his father, Moses, served as rabbi. Until he was in his early 20s, his studies focused on the Talmud. Private tutors gave him a firm footing in secular subjects as well. At the age of 22 he enrolled at the University of Berlin, where he studied physics, mathematics, and philosophy, and in 1931 he received a doctorate in philosophy. The following year—shortly before Adolf Hitler became chancellor of Germany and the destruction of the Jews of Europe began—Soloveitchik and his bride (who also held a doctorate in education) emigrated to the United States. Soon after his arrival he became Chief

Rabbi of Boston, where he continued to live even after accepting the post of professor of Talmud at New York City's Yeshiva University, the major institution of higher learning for Orthodox Jews in the United States.

Soloveitchik was a spellbinding speaker. His lectures, which lasted two to five hours, drew large crowds that included many who were not Orthodox. At Yeshiva University he delivered an annual public lecture on the occasion of his father's death. American Orthodox Jews flocked to these lectures, which they considered the major intellectual events of the year.

Although Soloveitchik often lectured from written manuscripts, he published very little. He claimed to suffer a "family malady," which had also prevented his grandfather, father, and uncle—all distinguished scholars—from publishing much in their own day. All were perfectionists who felt that no matter how clearly they had explained a tricky problem or how elegantly they had cast a certain phrase, the product was never quite good enough.

From the few essays and slim volumes that Soloveitchik did publish, and from the selections from his lectures adapted by his students, we learn that Soloveitchik built his thought around describing different

"ideal" types of individuals. The two best-known human types Soloveitchik described are "Halakhic Man"—a person who lives according to halakhah—and "the Lonely Man of Faith"—a person who adheres faithfully to Jewish practice in a technological society where religious faith "is given little credence as a repository of truth." In his essay "Halakhic Man," published as an article in a Hebrew journal in 1944 and as a book in English in 1983, Soloveitchik addressed the question of whether a halakhic way of life has anything to offer individuals in the modern world. People in contemporary society value spontaneity and personal style, while halakhah seems to demand conformity by governing the life of an Orthodox Jew in every aspect— from food to married life to business and ethical dealings. Soloveitchik insisted, however, that a Jew can live a halakhic life without giving up creativity and personal control. In fact, he argued, only when a person lives in accordance with halakhah does he no longer become a creature of habit. By living a halakhic life, the Jew enters into an intimate relationship with God.

Some 20 years after publishing his first major essay, Soloveitchik produced an essay called "The Lonely

Man of Faith." Having made his case for the relevance of halakhah in the modern world, Soloveitchik now focused on a more specific question: Does a technological society have any room in it for the religious person, or is such a person a useless oddity?

Soloveitchik asked, "What can a man of faith like myself, living by a doctrine which has no technical potential, by a law which cannot be tested in the laboratory . . . what can such a man say to a functional utilitarian society?" Soloveitchik took it upon himself to demonstrate that the man of faith still has a contribution to make to our technological society. Though most people make religion merely a "useful adjunct to life," and look for the social—not divine—content of religion, the man of faith can demonstrate that "there is more to religion than the pious gesture and the reassuring ceremonial." Likewise, in the area of ethics the man of faith can demonstrate that God underlies human ethical concerns. Most people's ethical positions "are not anchored in the absolute," according to Soloveitchik, making it easier for them to compromise their ethics. But the man of faith can "envelop ethics with Godliness and restrain man's rampaging nature."

Ultimately, Soloveitchik found no way out of loneliness for the man of faith. But by stressing that such people have a "historical mission" to bring the message of faith to the world, he made it clear that our technological society has not done away with the need for the contribution of the Lonely Man of Faith.

Soloveitchik did not merely write about the Lonely Man of Faith and Halakhic Man; he also lived their lives himself. When, in 1932, he became Chief Rabbi of the Orthodox Jewish community of greater Boston, anti-Jewish prejudice was a serious factor in American society. Radio sets across the country were tuned regularly to

viciously anti-Semitic broadcasts made by Father Charles Coughlin. (The Catholic Church finally barred Coughlin from broadcasting in 1942.) The mayor of Boston proudly proclaimed that his city was "the strongest Coughlin city in America." A Massachusetts senator openly spoke of Jews as "inferior." The response of many Jews in the Boston community was to keep a low profile, to avoid calling attention to themselves.

A few years after his arrival, Soloveitchik approached members of Boston's Jewish community to enlist their support. He wanted to found a school for Jewish children where they could learn to be "modern Orthodox" Jews. This school would teach not only traditional Judaism but also all the subjects in a standard secular curriculum. The Jewish community did not welcome the idea, however. They felt that American Jews should put their American identity above their Jewish ties and send their children to public schools. Despite a lack of support, Soloveitchik succeeded in founding the Maimonides School in 1937. The first Jewish day school in New England, it continues to thrive today in Brookline, Massachusetts.

Soloveitchik's decision to name the school for the 12th-century Jewish intellectual giant Moses Maimonides grew out of his lifelong interest in the work of the earlier scholar. Ever since he was a boy, Soloveitchik had been deeply interested in Maimonides' major halakhic work, the *Mishneh Torah*. And as a graduate student at the University of Berlin he had hoped to write his thesis on Maimonides and Plato, but no one in the philosophy department there had felt capable of supervising the project.

Fittingly, Soloveitchik's achievement in the 20th century has been compared to Maimonides' accomplishment eight centuries before. In his own time, Maimonides built intellec-

LINKS IN THE CHAIN

Joseph Dov Soloveitchik

BORN

February 27, 1903
Pruzhan, Poland (now Belarus)

DIED

April 8, 1993
Brookline, Massachusetts

EDUCATION

Ph.D. in philosophy, University of Berlin (1931)

ACCOMPLISHMENTS

Chief Rabbi of the Orthodox community of greater Boston (1932–93); founded the Maimonides School, Brookline, Mass., the first Jewish day school in New England (1937); Professor of Talmud, Rabbi Isaac Elchanan Theological Seminary, Yeshiva University, New York (1941–78); Leib Merkin Distinguished Professor of Talmud and Jewish Philosophy, Rabbi Isaac Elchanan Theological Seminary, Yeshiva University, New York, (1978–93); ordained more than 2,000 rabbis; chairman of the Halakhah Commission of the Rabbinical Council of America (1952); author of *Halakhic Man* (1944, Hebrew; 1983, English translation) and *The Lonely Man of Faith* (1965, Hebrew; 1992, English translation)

Students and faculty of the Maimonides School pose for a 1947 photograph, ten years after Soloveitchik founded this first Jewish day school in New England. Soloveitchik's daughter, Dr. Atara Twersky, continues to serve on the school committee of the Maimonides School.

tual bridges between the best of Greek and Arab philosophy and the halakhic tradition. Similarly, Soloveitchik demonstrated that students of halakhah in today's world do not have to shy away from contemporary currents of thought. Instead of shutting out views that seem to challenge halakhic tradition, both Maimonides and Soloveitchik encouraged Jews to deal with those challenges. Both men insisted that the outside world has valuable contributions to make to the halakhic way of life.

After founding the Maimonides School, Soloveitchik continued to take an active interest in its adminis-

tration, and one of his daughters, Atara, began a long teaching career there. His main professional commitments were in New York, however, and he commuted between New York and Boston in order to teach at Yeshiva University.

Unlike most Jews who live according to halakhah, Soloveitchik actually had the opportunity to reshape it. Making a halakhic ruling is no trivial act. Orthodox Jews believe that halakhah originated when God gave the Hebrews the Torah at Mount Sinai. For it to remain meaningful, though, halakhah must also stay in tune with current conditions. There-

fore, rabbis entrusted with interpreting halakhah must not only be brilliant but must also command the respect of their colleagues.

For years, controversies about interpreting points of halakhah were referred to Soloveitchik. In 1952 he became chairman of the Halakhah Commission of the Rabbinical Council of America, the main American Orthodox rabbinical organization. One type of halakhic literature, called "responsa," consists of opinions and rulings on matters of halakhah in response to specific questions. As a halakhic authority, Soloveitchik wrote a few such responsa. These documents show his belief that halakhah must always be based on traditional sources but may also from time to time reflect social fact.

One case in point arose when men were being drafted into the United States Army from 1948 through 1972 because of deep U.S. involvement in world affairs. The question was whether Yeshiva University, an Orthodox institution, could require the graduates of its rabbinical school to serve as military chaplains, as the Reform and Conservative rabbinical schools required of their graduates. If forcing rabbis to serve as military chaplains risked violating halakhah, then the Orthodox seminary would have to refuse to join forces with the other two main branches of American Judaism.

Halakhaic thinkers had identified two possible violations of halakhah. First, halakhah values human life above all else. Did it thus violate halakhah for a rabbinical school's authorities to participate in an action that might jeopardize the life of a colleague? And second, did it violate halakhah to place chaplains in situations that might someday require them to break the laws of the Sabbath or another Jewish holiday?

Soloveitchik answered no to both questions and declared that it would be permissible for Yeshiva to follow the policies of the other schools. In making his decision he relied both on traditional sources and on less objective factors.

In time-honored fashion, Soloveitchik found a precedent in a halakhic text from the Middle Ages. According to that document, if a Jew had to travel in order to fulfill a religious commandment, it was allowable to make the trip even though in the course of the voyage the traveler might have to desecrate the Sabbath to save a human life. Soloveitchik admitted, though, that he was not making his decision on historical grounds only. He also took into account the way non-Orthodox Jews and non-Jews would be likely to react if Yeshiva University refused to participate in the military's draft procedure. In other words, Soloveitchik had public relations in mind when he made his ruling. He feared the reputation of Orthodox Judaism would be tarnished if it did not contribute its share of rabbis to the military chaplaincy.

A similar consideration for "what people would say" led Soloveitchik to make another halakhic ruling permitting Orthodox rabbis and synagogues to participate in the same organizations as their non-Orthodox colleagues. He felt keenly that public reaction to the self-segregation of the Orthodox movement would be negative. Soloveitchik refused to disregard such subjective, but very real, factors in making halakhic rulings. Human beings have the capacity to make not only logical judgments but also value judgments, he believed, and it would be wrong to keep the latter out of the realm of halakhic decisions. Public opinion cannot be dismissed in making halakhic decisions.

Just as Soloveitchik approved of making united efforts involving Orthodox groups and less traditional Jews, his teachings were respected by Conservative and Reform Jews as much as by the Orthodox. The respect that all groups of Jews felt for the Rav is summed up in this comment by a Reform rabbi: "Rabbi Joseph Soloveitchik seems to me more and more obviously the teacher of the time. How paradoxical that this doggedly Orthodox, European-born Talmudist should speak more clearly to our needs than the most sophisticated modernists from all the great universities of the West. . . . If I am not mistaken, people will still be reading him in a thousand years."

FURTHER READING

Besdin, Abraham R. *Reflections of the Rav: Adapted from Lectures of Joseph B. Soloveitchik.* Hoboken, N.J.: Ktav, 1989.

Borowitz, Eugene. "A Theology of Modern Orthodoxy: Rabbi Joseph B. Soloveitchik." In *Choices in Modern Jewish Thought.* New York: Behrman House, 1983.

Lichtenstein, Aharon. "R. Joseph Soloveitchik." In *Great Jewish Thinkers of the 20th Century.* Edited by by Simon Noveck. Clinton, Mass.: Colonial Press, 1963.

Pasachoff, Naomi. "Joseph Soloveitchik's Lonely Man of Faith." In *Great Jewish Thinkers: Their Lives and Work.* West Orange, N.J.: Behrman House, 1992.

Abraham Joshua Heschel

RECOVERING "RADICAL AMAZEMENT"

I n the late 1960s, Marshall Meyer, a rabbi serving in Argentina, visited Abraham Joshua Heschel in New York. Argentina at that time was under repressive military rule, and Rabbi Meyer, a fearless opponent of the ruling regime, confided in Heschel his concern that the Argentine Jewish community might be made to suffer for his outspoken opposition. Heschel pondered the rabbi's dilemma for a moment and then said, "You endanger their souls more by being silent." Heschel was hardly the first Jew to be a social activist. But by linking his social involvement to a unique understanding of God and religion, Heschel gave a new religious meaning to social protest. He also reawakened a passion for the wonders of the universe in Jews and Christians alike.

Heschel was born in Warsaw, Poland, in 1907, into a family with distinguished Hasidic roots. On his father's side he was descended from Dov Baer of Mezhirech, a disciple of the Baal Shem Tov, the original founder of Hasidism. After the Baal Shem Tov's death, Dov Baer spread his teacher's reinterpretation of Judaism, which emphasized joyous worship. On his mother's side Heschel was descended from Levi Isaac of Berdichev, another disciple of Dov Baer.

Not surprisingly, Heschel's family made sure their son had a strong background in traditional Jewish studies. Somewhat less predictably, although they were concerned by his abandonment of Hasidic circles for the larger world, they did not forbid him from pursuing advanced secular studies at the University of Berlin. While earning his doctorate at the university, Heschel also studied at Berlin's Academy for Jewish Studies, where he later taught Talmud, the collection of law and legends edited in the 5th century that has remained one of the key texts of Judaism.

Heschel seems not to have considered his Talmud teaching in Berlin a real job. He later claimed that he owed what he considered his first employment to the German-Jewish philosopher Martin Buber. In 1937, on the eve of Buber's departure for Palestine from Nazi Germany, the philosopher chose Heschel to succeed him as director of the Central Office for Jewish Adult Education. That office had been created in 1933 after Jews were prohibited by the Nazis from attending German educational institutions. At the same time, Buber also hired Heschel to teach at the Frankfurt Independent House of Jewish Study.

Heschel's career in Germany, where he had been studying and teaching since the age of 20, soon came to an abrupt end. On October 27, 1938, the Nazis expelled some 18,000 Jews who had originally come from Poland, regardless of how long they had lived in Germany. The Jews were

Rabbi Heschel, second from right, marches together with the Reverend Martin Luther King, Jr., and other civil rights supporters in Selma, Alabama. King organized this 1965 march to help secure voting rights for black Americans.

rounded up against their will and transported under inhumane conditions to the Polish border. Heschel fared better than most after this uprooting. He taught for eight months at the Warsaw Institute of Jewish Studies, then received an offer to teach in the United States and left Warsaw only a few weeks before the Germans invaded Poland. Before beginning his position in the United States, Heschel spent some months in London, where he founded the Institute for Jewish Learning. In 1940 he arrived in the United States to join the faculty of the Hebrew Union College in Cincinnati, Ohio. After teaching there for five years, Heschel moved to New York City, where for the rest of his life he was professor of Jewish ethics and mysticism at the Jewish Theological Seminary of America.

Although Heschel was able to leave war-torn Europe behind him, his acquaintance with the Holocaust—the Nazis' systematic murder of millions of European Jews—affected him deeply. His mother and sisters were among the victims. Later he described himself as "a brand [a charred piece of wood] plucked from the fire on which my people was burned to death . . . and on which so much else was consumed."

Heschel was in his early 30s when he left Europe. Although he could read English, he could neither write nor speak it. Nonetheless, within a few years he was able to write, in graceful, poetic English, *The Earth Is the Lord's*, a book that has been called the epitaph for the victims of the Holocaust. In this work and elsewhere Heschel suggested that not God but human beings were to blame for the horrors of the Holocaust. If people had reacted in a timely fashion, the Holocaust would never have happened. He pointed out the difference between guilt and responsibility. Only those who committed actual crimes bear the guilt for the Holocaust. But responsibility for its horrors is shared by all those who did nothing to prevent them. Heschel also contrasted evil as such with what he described as the evil of indifference. In his view, those people who are aware of injustice but remain unmoved by it are guilty of the evil of indifference. Heschel claimed that this evil of indifference is worse than evil itself, because it silently justifies evil and allows evil acts to become the norm.

Addressing those who had lost their faith in a God of justice and compassion as a result of the Holocaust, Heschel insisted that by blurring the difference between good and evil people had actually banished God from the world. In other books Heschel undertook to show how God's presence fills the entire universe. He suggested that modern life, with its emphasis on scientific explanations for natural phenomena, may have deadened people's sensitivity to God's existence. "As civilization advances," he wrote, "the sense of wonder declines. . . . What we lack is not a will to believe but a will to wonder." If only people would look at the world once again with the eyes of children, he thought, they could recover "radical amazement": a sense of wonder and awe at the workings of the universe that science alone cannot explain.

Heschel claimed that once people allow themselves to react with wonder to the mysteries of the universe, they open themselves up to a relationship with God. An awareness of God should, he argued, make people aware that God demands something from each individual. In *God in Search of Man* Heschel wrote, "God is not a being . . . to be sought after, but a power that seeks, pursues, and calls upon" human beings. Heschel explained that God relies upon people, but not in the way understood by the ancient Phoenicians and

"This is one of the goals of the Jewish way of living: to experience commonplace deeds as spiritual adventures, to feel the hidden love and wisdom in all things."

—from *God in Search of Man* (1956)

Ammonites, who sacrificed their children as offerings to their god Moloch. God does not need such sacrifices. Instead, God wants to enlist people in a partnership "for the fulfillment of [God's] ends in the world."

Other religious thinkers have taught that faith in God can be consoling. Heschel, however, insisted that the essence of faith is to make demands of human beings. The God who pursues humanity is a God who feels the pain of the mistreated and the unfortunate and demands that other human beings come to their aid.

Heschel told a story about himself as a child that helps explain his response as an adult to God's call. He said that when he was a boy of seven, he and his teacher were reviewing the Bible's story of how at the last moment an angel from God prevented the patriarch Abraham from sacrificing his son Isaac. To the teacher's surprise, young Heschel burst into tears. The boy remained inconsolable, troubled by what would have happened if the angel had come a second too late. His teacher assured him that angels cannot come late. But from then on Heschel realized that while angels may always be on time, human beings can in fact arrive too late. For that reason, he urged people to act immediately when their consciences prodded them.

Heschel's participation in a variety of movements to transform society can best be understood in the light of his concept of God's demands on each individual. Among the social causes in which Heschel became involved were the interfaith movement, the movement to obtain civil rights for African Americans, the opposition to U.S. military action in Vietnam, and the movement to overcome anti-Semitism in the Communist countries of Eastern Europe.

In the interfaith movement, Heschel was a pioneer in improving the official position of the Catholic Church toward the Jews. In 1963 the Vatican, the central authority of the Catholic Church, issued a document dealing with the "Attitudes of the Catholics . . . toward the Jews." The document stated that "the Church expects in unshakable faith and with ardent desire . . . the union of the Jewish people with the Church." In September 1964 Heschel wrote a letter to the second Vatican Council, called by Pope John XXIII to foster unity throughout the Christian world. In it he objected to the language of the document: "Jews throughout the world will be dismayed by a call from the Vatican to abandon their faith in a generation which witnessed the massacre of six million Jews and the destruction of thousands of synagogues on a continent where the dominant religion was not Islam, Buddhism or Shintoism." He also expressed his personal readiness "to go to Auschwitz any time, if faced with the alternative of conversion or death." Heschel's intervention did not end with this letter. At the pope's request Heschel made a secret personal visit to the Vatican. The final document issued by the council on the Church's attitude toward the Jews reflects Heschel's concerns. The declaration, called *Nostra Aetate* (In our time), and promulgated on October 28, 1965, reads in part, "in her rejection of every persecution against any man, the Church, mindful of the patrimony she shares with the Jews and moved not by political reasons but by the Gospel's spiritual love, decries hatred, persecutions, displays of anti-semitism, directed against Jews at any time and by anyone."

Heschel acted as guardian not only of Jewish interests, however. Heschel's address at a 1963 National Conference on Religion and Race influenced many other clergymen to participate in the August 1963 march on Washington organized by the respected black civil rights leader Dr. Martin Luther King, Jr. The aim of the march was to convince the federal government to eliminate racial discrimination in public places. In his address Heschel spoke out forcefully against racism, claiming that "what begins as the inequality of some inevitably ends as inequality of all." He challenged other members of the clergy to join the fight against racism by saying, "Prayer and prejudice cannot dwell in the same heart. Worship without compassion is . . . an abomination." In 1965 Heschel not only participated in the protest march to secure voting rights for blacks in Selma, Alabama, but also walked at Dr. King's side.

Deeply opposed to American involvement in the war in Southeast Asia, Heschel served as national cochairman of a group called Clergy and Laity Concerned about Vietnam. He cautioned people of all religions that "to speak about God and remain silent on Vietnam is blasphemous." Heschel was also one of the first clergymen to call the public's attention to the plight of the Jews in what was then the Soviet Union. Claiming that the remaining Jews of Eastern Europe were only a remnant of the vibrant community that had been destroyed in the Holocaust, he urged that the world not watch their destruction, too, in silence and indifference. "We must cry in public," he said, "because they can only cry in secrecy." Heschel would surely be heartened to know that the children of many Russian Jewish immigrants are today learning about their Jewish heritage in U.S. schools named in his honor.

Heschel's social involvement made him a controversial figure in certain Jewish circles. His participation, and his call for participation of other rabbis, in the civil rights movement, for example, led to an increase of anti-Semitism in the South, as some southern Jews had predicted. His antiwar position on Vietnam led some Jewish leaders to worry that his outspokenness would result in a hardening of U.S. policy toward Israel. But Heschel felt that he had to speak out against injustice even if his activism occasionally had negative consequences in the short term.

Although Heschel as a young man chose to enter the secular world instead of living in the closely knit, exclusive Hasidic community of his ancestors, his Hasidic upbringing left a strong mark on his thought. He once claimed that the most essential teaching of Hasidism is "the capacity to be tremendously surprised." Building on this idea Heschel used his term "radical amazement" to describe the sense of astonishment people feel when they are open to manifestations of God's presence in the world. On another occasion he recalled a different Hasidic idea—the concept that a leader can be a "living Torah," or a living source of religious truths. According to Heschel, "It is the personality of the teacher that the pupils read; the text that they will never forget." Heschel personally answered the demands of God by trying to make the world more just. In this way he himself became a "living Torah." His influence extended to his daughter, Susannah, who, following in his footsteps, involved herself fully in the Jewish women's movement. It also extended far beyond his immediate family. The educational and religious policy of the Abraham Joshua Heschel School of New York pays homage to the life and thought of its namesake. The school includes among its aims "active participation in the endeavor of creating a more just and peaceful world" and educating its students "to share these values and join in that endeavor."

FURTHER READING

Friedman, Maurice. *Abraham Joshua Heschel and Elie Wiesel: You Are My Witnesses*. New York: Farrar, Straus & Giroux, 1987.

Merkle, John C. *The Genesis of Faith: The Depth Theology of Abraham Joshua Heschel*. New York: Macmillan, 1985.

Neusner, Jacob, and Noam Neusner, eds. *To Grow in Wisdom: An Anthology of Abraham Joshua Heschel*. Madison, Wis.: Madison Books, 1990.

Pasachoff, Naomi. "Abraham Joshua Heschel." In *Great Jewish Thinkers: Their Lives and Work*. West Orange, N.J.: Behrman House, 1992.

Abraham Joshua Heschel

BORN

1907
Warsaw, Poland

DIED

December 23, 1972
New York, New York

EDUCATION

Ph.D., University of Berlin (1937); attended Academy for Jewish Studies, Berlin

ACCOMPLISHMENTS

Professor of Jewish ethics and mysticism at Jewish Theological Seminary, New York (1945–72); wrote many books, including *The Earth Is the Lord's* (1950), *Man Is Not Alone: A Philosophy of Religion* (1951), *The Sabbath: Its Meaning to Modern Man* (1951), *Man's Quest for God: Studies in Prayer and Symbolism* (1954), *God in Search of Man: A Philosophy of Judaism* (1956), and *The Prophets* (published in German in 1936 and in English in 1962); leader in civil rights movement and efforts to end the war in Vietnam, to save Soviet Jewry, and to further Christian-Jewish dialogue

More than 150,000 Israelis gathered in Haifa in 1953 for a parade to celebrate the fifth anniversary of Israel's independence. Israel's national day, declared a public holiday by law in 1949, is preceded by a day of remembrance for those who have died in defense of the country's independence and security.

3 Shapers of the Jewish State

Zionism—the movement to develop a Jewish state—and the creation of the state of Israel have had a profound impact on Jewish tradition. Nonobservant Jews who felt that Judaism had little to offer in the modern world suddenly were presented by Zionism with a new way to express their connection to the Jewish people. Although Judaism traditionally has had three focal points—God, Torah, and Israel—the emergence of Zionism enabled many Jews to overlook the first two elements and concentrate solely on the last.

Accordingly, instead of praying to God or studying Jewish texts, many Jews became involved in the Zionist movement. By raising money for the Jewish state or trying to influence the governments of the United States and other supportive nations, these Jews felt they could remain Jewish without having to be religious. And many, though not all, religious Jews were equally attracted to Zionism. By developing the ancient Jewish homeland they could help make God's promise to their biblical forebears once again a reality. They could also fulfill religious commandments that could be observed only on that sanctified ground.

The modern Zionist movement developed in Europe toward the end of the 19th century, but it had its roots in the distant past. The Jewish prayer book is filled with prayers on behalf of Jerusalem, the capital city of the biblical Jewish kingdom and the site of the ancient temples. Every year during the seder, the festive meal at Passover, Jews say, "Next year in Jerusalem." The same refrain is uttered at the end of services on Yom Kippur, the most solemn day on the Jewish calendar. Whenever Jews chant the grace after meals, they also pray for Jerusalem's future by asking God to rebuild the holy city speedily during their lifetime. And at traditional Jewish weddings, seven blessings are recited over wine. The last three of them ask God to comfort Zion, the name of a hill in Jerusalem that is often extended to mean the whole city or the entire land of Israel; to bring happiness to the married couple; and to make joy complete by restoring Jerusalem.

Centuries before the emergence of the modern Zionist movement, individual Jews expressed Zionist beliefs. Judah Halevi (around 1075–1141) gave up a successful career in Spain in an attempt to reach Zion, which he believed to be the only place he could find true meaning in his life. His poems captured the longing for the land of Israel that many Jews felt but were unable to express for themselves. Centuries later, Doña Gracia Mendes Nasi (around 1510–69), secured access to Jerusalem from the Turkish sultan and set up a school for Jewish learning in the Palestinian city of Tiberias.

In the decades before the modern Zionist movement appeared, other Jews proposed ideas for resettling the biblical land of Israel, then controlled by the Ottoman Turkish Empire. Beginning in 1834, Yehudah Alkalai, the rabbi of Serbia, also part of the Turkish Empire at that time, began to publish his thoughts on the matter. Influenced by the Serbs' attempts to shake off Turkish rule and by the success of the Greeks in securing independence from the Turks, Alkalai outlined a plan to set up a national fund with the purpose of buying back land from the Turks. Few people, however, became aware of Alkalai's plans and there was therefore little reaction to them.

A second early Zionist thinker was the German Jew Moses Hess. Unlike Alkalai, Hess was not religious, but he was deeply inspired by the national spirit of other peoples. Impressed by the way the Italian states had banded together to form the nation of Italy, Hess wrote a Zionist book, *Rome and Jerusalem,* in 1862. Just as the Italians imagined that Rome could be the center of a new world of nations, Hess argued, so Jerusalem could become a world center from which Jewish values such as social justice could spread. Like Alkalai's, Hess's ideas reached only a limited audience.

The modern Zionist movement had its first real growth spurt in 1881. That year, a group of Russian radicals assassinated Czar Alexander II of Russia. Though the assassins were Christians, a wave of violent anti-Jewish pogroms spread through Russia in the wake of the killing, abetted by the government. When the Russian Jews realized that the government was behind the pogroms and that even educated people were taking part in them, many lost hope of ever being accepted as equal citizens in Russia. Most of those who then left their homeland emigrated to America, but a small minority formed a movement they called Love of Zion. These Jews began to set up small colonies in the land of Israel, supported by the wealthy French Jewish philanthropist Baron Edmond de Rothschild.

Among the Jews who lost hope in Russia after 1881 was a Polish-born physician named Leo Pinsker. In an anonymous pamphlet, *Auto-Emancipation,* he argued that the Jews could find release from laws limiting their freedom only by their own actions. In his pamphlet Pinsker contended that emigration to other countries was no solution to the problems Jews faced in Russia, since anti-Jewish policies would arise in other countries as well. Instead, he asserted, Jews must once again think of themselves as a nation, as in biblical times, and direct their energies to building a country of their own. Pinsker's views found no favor in the eyes of Orthodox Jews, who believed that Jews must think not about redeeming themselves but must wait instead for the arrival of the Messiah. Pinsker's argument was also rejected by those who continued to believe that as Jews adapted to modern times they would eventually be accepted as equals by non-Jews. Only those who already shared Pinsker's views welcomed his pamphlet. In 1893, Pinsker joined the Lovers of Zion.

The shapers of the Jewish state who are profiled in this section include people who developed theories about Zionism, others who developed institutions for the Jewish state, and still others whose political leadership enabled the Zionist dream to become a reality. The theorists include Theodor Herzl, the father of "political Zionism," who changed the course of modern Jewish history more than any other single individual; Ahad Ha'am, the father of "spiritual Zionism," who believed that the return of the Jews to their ancient homeland would restore Jewish spiritual dignity; Eliezer Ben-Yehuda, the father of modern Hebrew, who believed that a united people needed a common, modern language; and Yigael Yadin, an archaeologist who believed that every discovery confirming an ancient Jewish presence in Israel justified Jewish claims to the land.

Among the institution builders, Henrietta Szold left an indelible mark on the character of the Jewish state. She not only founded Hadassah, the Women's Zionist Organization of America, and oversaw the development of its medical center in Jerusalem, but also developed institutions for social work that continue to flourish in Israel today. Another outstanding institution builder was Berl Katznelson, who helped found both the political party that brought the Jewish state into existence and many social institutions that served the Jewish state in its formative years. For his contributions to shaping the Israel Defense Forces as the first chief of staff, Yigael Yadin can also be considered a member of this group.

The political leaders profiled here include Chaim Weizmann, who helped Zionism reach its first significant milestone, the Balfour Declaration; David Ben-Gurion, whose leadership brought about the declaration of the Jewish state and enabled the young country to establish roots in its early years; Golda Meir, who played several major roles in the Israeli cabinet before going on to serve as prime minister; Menachem Begin, who after many years as leader of the opposition to Israel's elected government made significant—if controversial—changes in the Jewish state during his terms as prime minister; and Yitzhak Rabin, whose efforts to secure peace with Israel's Arab neighbors cost him his life. The work of shaping the Jewish state continues, of course, but the impact of all the trailblazers continues to be felt.

Ahad Ha'am (Asher Ginzberg)

✡

SPIRITUAL ZIONISM

The word *Zionism* was first used in the 1890s to describe efforts to set up a Jewish state in Palestine. Even before the word entered the dictionary, however, one man had begun to ask probing questions about the meaning of a future Jewish state. This man, known by the pen name Ahad Ha'am (the Hebrew words for "one of the people"), recognized a difference between what most other people called "the problem of the Jews" and what he called "the problem of Judaism."

The problem of the Jews was the oppression they suffered in many of the countries where they lived. Perhaps having a Jewish state to provide a refuge for mistreated Jews would solve that problem. But the problem of Judaism was another matter entirely. Ahad Ha'am saw that in the modern world many Jews no longer found meaning in the traditional forms of the Jewish religion. He believed that a Jewish state could not solve this problem unless that state also became the center of a revived Jewish culture, rooted in a high standard of morality, in which all Jews everywhere could take pride.

When Ahad Ha'am was born in 1856, his parents named him Asher Ginzberg. But just as readers of American literature recognize the author Mark Twain by that pen name rather than by Samuel Langhorne Clemens, his name at birth, so students of Zionist history are more familiar with Asher Ginzberg's pen name than his given one.

Ahad Ha'am did not live a very happy life. His first dozen years were spent in the small town of Skvire, about 50 miles southeast of Kiev, in Ukraine. He later called his birthplace a "benighted spot." His parents were well-to-do Hasidim who belonged to one of the small sects of extremely pious Jews scattered throughout eastern Europe. The Ginzbergs, who were very strict parents, expected their son to become a Hasidic scholar. Accordingly, from the age of three he attended a Jewish primary school. His parents forbade his instructors there to teach him the Russian alphabet. As Ahad Ha'am later explained, "My mother's father had with his own ears heard one of the great [Hasidic rabbis] say that the sight of a foreign letter made the eyes unclean." Nonetheless, at the age of eight Ahad Ha'am taught himself to read Russian from the street signs of Skvire.

Ahad Ha'am's father did little to encourage his son's self-confidence. Once a week he tested the boy, who was a very gifted student, on his studies. No matter how well the boy answered, his father beat him. Ahad Ha'am never felt love for his father but was nonetheless quite attached to him, and his father's death in 1899 affected him greatly.

Ahad Ha'am, seated, poses for a photograph in 1910 in St. Petersburg, Russia, with his younger daughter, Rachel, and his son, Shlomo. Ahad Ha'am's relationship with his children was distant and troubled. He viewed Rachel's marriage in 1912 to a non-Jewish Russian writer as a "catastrophe."

In 1868, when Ahad Ha'am was 12, the Ginzberg family moved to Gopchitse, a country estate that his father had leased in central Ukraine. By managing this property his parents became quite rich. On this remote estate, seven hours by wagon from the nearest railway stop, private tutors taught Ahad Ha'am the Talmud, the Jewish library of law and lore that dates from the 5th century. And on his own he also began to study subjects other than those usually studied by Hasidic scholars. First he read the works of Maimonides and other great Jewish philosophers of the Middle Ages. Then he went on to books forbidden by his father—works written in modern Hebrew, dealing with

modern issues, by living Jewish authors. Once, during his teens, while passing through the central Ukrainian city of Zhitomir, west of Kiev, he stopped in a bookstore and bought a volume or two of the Minutes of the St. Petersburg Academy of Science. In order to improve his Russian he committed much of the material to memory. When he was 20 he began to study modern literature and philosophy in Russian and German.

Ahad Ha'am was both a dutiful and a rebellious son. Dutifully, he obeyed his parents' wishes when they betrothed him at the age of 14 to a young woman from a well-connected Hasidic family. He was only 17 when the arranged marriage took place. Though he resented his father's attempts to limit his quest for knowledge, he disobeyed only on the sly. Once his father found Ahad Ha'am with a copy of a book by a modern Jewish author of whose ideas Hasidic Jews disapproved. He warned his son never to bring such material into the house again. When a Russian book peddler passed by, Ahad Ha'am took the opportunity to buy another book he knew his father would find scandalous. After reading the book during the night he carefully burned it before the household awakened the next morning.

For some years Ahad Ha'am hoped to obtain a university education in Russia, Germany, or Austria. For one reason or another—including his failure to meet the entrance requirements and a lack of self-confidence—he eventually gave up that hope and remained a self-taught man. His wide reading led him away from a belief in God, but without making him feel any less Jewish. He insisted that it made no more sense to ask him why he remained Jewish than to ask him why he remained his father's son. For a Jew, he believed, being Jewish is simply a law of nature.

Ahad Ha'am's studies also led him to develop a new belief in what he called "the Jewish national spirit." Just as each human being has a unique personality, Ahad Ha'am believed that each nation has its own spirit. For him the Jewish national spirit was based on an ideal that the Hebrew prophets had preached to the ancient world: the pursuit of justice rather than power. It was this ideal, he believed, that had enabled the Jewish people to survive over the centuries.

All these ideas began to develop in Ahad Ha'am's mind as a result of the reading he did while still on the Gopchitse estate. He began to spread his ideas only after the Ginzberg family was forced to leave the estate in 1886, following a decree by the Russian czar forbidding Jews from leasing land or estates. At this point, Ahad Ha'am went into business with his father in Odessa. In that Ukrainian seaport city, where father and son opened a liquor distillery and an olive oil factory, Ahad Ha'am also found a thriving center of Jewish culture to which he would make an important contribution. Of all the places he lived in his life, he found the greatest happiness in Odessa.

Ahad Ha'am had lived in Odessa for only three years when he made his publishing debut with a controversial essay called "The Wrong Way." This essay aroused the passions of the Russian Jews known as the Lovers of Zion. These Jews had responded to the 1881 pogroms by beginning to set up small farming colonies in Palestine. In his essay Ahad Ha'am criticized both the Lovers of Zion and their sponsor, the wealthy French-Jewish banker Baron Edmond de Rothschild, for going about the task improperly. He argued that they were guilty of too much haste and too little advance preparation. In their eagerness to resettle Palestine, he said, the Lovers of Zion had failed to "prepare the hearts" of the settlers for the task of rebuilding the nation. Instead they encouraged unprepared Jews to make the move, giving them incomplete or even misleading information. Not surprisingly, many of these would-be settlers had returned from Palestine in disappointment. He also argued that by propping up the settlements with his money, Rothschild was actually doing a disservice to the settlers who remained in Palestine. Instead of having to work out their problems for themselves, they knew that Rothschild would bail them out. Lacking true commitment, these settlers, he asserted, could not help rebuild a national spiritual center in Palestine.

"The Wrong Way" was also the first Zionist essay to raise a thorny problem whose resolution was still being worked out more than a century

Ahad Ha'am, third from right, with other Zionists in Palestine, in 1922. In that year Ahad Ha'am, the founder of spiritual Zionism, moved to Palestine, where he lived until his death in early 1927.

later. Ahad Ha'am pointed out that Palestine was not an uninhabited land, as some Zionists liked to claim. In fact, it had a substantial Arab population, with whom the settlers had not yet learned how to interact.

Shortly before "The Wrong Way" appeared, Ahad Ha'am and a small group of like-minded Odessa Jews started an organization they called the Sons of Moses. The purpose of this semisecret group was to help educate Jews properly for the task of transforming Palestine into a spiritual center for all Jews. Among the group's practical achievements were the establishment of a Hebrew publishing house, the modernization of Hebrew education in Palestine, and the founding of the settlement Rehovot in the coastal plain west of Jerusalem. Ahad Ha'am remained a member of the group until it disbanded in 1898.

When he published "The Wrong Way," Ahad Ha'am had not yet made a trip to Palestine, but he soon remedied that situation. In 1891 and 1893 he made his first journeys to the

Middle East. Upon his return from each trip he wrote an article summarizing his reactions under the title "Truth from the Land of Israel." What he witnessed during his trips convinced him that the settlers were not properly trained for the task of building a national center. They relied too much on charity, treated the local Arabs with disrespect, and squabbled among themselves. Ahad Ha'am worried that if the situation did not improve, the settlers would simply create "'a problem of the Jews' in a country in which it has not hitherto existed—in our ancestral land."

Even before Ahad Ha'am's second trip to Palestine, in 1893, his family's business had begun to lose money. He began to think about supporting himself as the editor of a Hebrew journal. Therefore, part of the purpose of his 1893 trip—which lasted nine months and took him to England, France, and Germany as well as Palestine—was to try to raise money for such a journal. Two years later, the family business in Odessa finally

collapsed. Ahad Ha'am became the editor of a Hebrew monthly, which grew into an important source of Zionist and Hebrew writing. He called his journal *HaShiloah*, after a biblical river whose "waters . . . go softly" (Isaiah 8:6). Like the river, his journal would follow a clear and slow direction; it would not be shrill in tone or promote hasty schemes. The funding for *HaShiloah* came from a wealthy Jewish tea merchant from Moscow named Kalonymos Wissotzsky (whose product, Wissotzsky Tea, is still a popular Israeli brand).

Within a year of *HaShiloah*'s appearance, Theodor Herzl had launched his political Zionist movement, and the focus of Ahad Ha'am's criticism broadened. Herzl's groundbreaking book *The Jewish State* (1896) dismissed the small agricultural settlements of the Lovers of Zion as insignificant. Only large-scale diplomacy, Herzl argued, would succeed in bringing about a Jewish state. But just as Ahad Ha'am had seen the flaws in the policies of the Lovers of Zion, he soon identified the weaknesses in Herzl's new movement.

Most of Ahad Ha'am's own essays in *HaShiloah* drew his readers' attention to the flaws of political Zionism. For example, he disputed Herzl's claim that a Jewish state would eliminate anti-Semitism. Ahad Ha'am argued that anti-Semitism would persist as long as the Jewish people did. He also disagreed with Herzl's claim that anti-Semitism was the greatest threat to the Jewish people. In his own eyes, the weakened Jewish national spirit was the greatest problem that Jews faced. It could be overcome only by the creation of a cultural and spiritual center in Palestine. From there, he hoped, the biblical prophets' ideals of justice and righteousness would spread around the world. Ahad Ha'am believed that even after the creation of a Jewish homeland many Jews would choose to live

> *"The secret of our people's persistence is . . . that at a very early period the Prophets taught it to respect only the power of the spirit and not to worship material power. . . . As long as we remain faithful to this principle, our existence has a secure basis and we shall not lose our self-respect."*
>
> —from *The Jewish State and the Jewish Problem* (1896)

elsewhere. Even so, Jews everywhere would take pride in the model set for them in the national spiritual center.

Ahad Ha'am also worried that Herzl's political Zionism would result in a Jewish state that would cease to cherish the prophets' ideals and would place too much value on military power. He feared that the loss of basic Jewish values would destroy, not strengthen, the Jewish national spirit. Nonetheless, Ahad Ha'am believed that the Jews of Russia should defend themselves as necessary. Thus, when new waves of pogroms swept Russia in 1903 and 1905, Ahad Ha'am became involved in Jewish self-defense efforts. In a document calling for the use of arms in self-defense he wrote, "Only those who know how to protect their own honor are themselves honored in the eyes of others." He called for the establishment of an organization to coordinate Jewish armed resistance throughout the districts where Jews were permitted to live.

Although he was an effective essayist whose clear, precise style served as a model for others, Ahad Ha'am was not a success as an editor-in-chief. Under his management the financial fortunes of *HaShiloah* declined, and at the end of 1902 he gave up his position at the journal. (Under other editors, the journal continued to publish until 1927.) The publication's backer, Wissotzsky, offered Ahad Ha'am a position in his tea firm's Odessa branch. Unfortunately, the new work was not to Ahad Ha'am's liking. It was hard on his health, required much travel, and left him little time for his writing.

In Ahad Ha'am's remaining five years in Russia he witnessed the Odessa pogrom of October 1905, which left 500 Jews dead and more than 3,000 injured. Nonetheless, he took pride in the fact that the city's Jewish self-defense efforts bore fruit, claiming that for the first time in a pogrom more pogromists than Jews were killed.

Although Ahad Ha'am began to think of leaving Russia, he was not tempted by an offer in 1906 from Dropsie College, a newly established institution of Jewish learning in Philadelphia. He valued his independence a great deal, leaving him to fear that he could not live up to the expectations of the college's trustees without compromising his own beliefs.

His personal situation in Russia continued to worsen, however. Because of his known involvement in Jewish self-defense, he became a target for the authorities. In May 1907 a policeman beat him on an Odessa street after a Jew in a neighboring town allegedly shot at the police. Soon thereafter, the police began a general investigation of Ahad Ha'am's activi-

ties. By 1908, he decided he would have to leave Russia, and he accepted a job as London branch manager of Wissotzsky's tea firm.

Ahad Ha'am's 14 years in London were not happy ones. He was impressed by the civility of English culture but found no intellectual excitement in the Anglo-Jewish community. He never felt completely comfortable expressing himself in English. There were some moments of satisfaction for him, however, during his London years. He made his fifth trip to Palestine in the autumn of 1911. Following that trip he published a report noting with pleasure that the spiritual center he had long hoped for seemed to be developing. More important, while in England Ahad Ha'am participated in the first real political success of the Zionist movement. Chaim Weizmann, who was to become the first president of the state of Israel, regularly consulted with Ahad Ha'am while carrying out negotiations with the British. These negotiations resulted in the Balfour Declaration of November 1917. Signed by the British foreign secretary, Lord Arthur James Balfour, this document stated that the British government viewed "with favour the establishment . . . of a national home for the Jewish people, and will use their best endeavors to facilitate the achievement of this object." Because the British then wielded great power in the Middle East, their pledge of support was a major step forward.

In 1922, Ahad Ha'am moved to Palestine, where he spent the last years of his life. In recognition of his contributions to Zionism and Judaism, the Jewish settlers of Palestine presented him and his wife a house in Tel Aviv, the first Jewish city in Palestine. The street on which he lived was not only named for him but was even closed off to traffic during his afternoon nap time. Although he was too ill to work as much as he had hoped, he nevertheless edited an edition of his letters and became involved in plans for the soon-to-be-founded Hebrew University. When the university opened its doors in 1925, speeches given at the dedication reflected many of Ahad Ha'am's ideas about turning the homeland into a national cultural and spiritual center.

Though Ahad Ha'am could take satisfaction in knowing that his hopes for a cultural renewal in Palestine were being realized, he saw little progress being made in another area that concerned him deeply: Jewish–Arab relations. Shortly after arriving in Palestine, he read disturbing news in the daily Hebrew newspaper *HaAretz*: as an act of revenge for several Arab attacks against Jews, a group of young Jews had murdered an Arab boy. In a letter to the newspaper, Ahad Ha'am made his heartbreak public: "Is this the dream of the return to Zion which our people dreamt for thousands of years: that we should come to Zion and pollute its soil with the spilling of innocent blood?" Ahad Ha'am's hopes for a meeting of minds between Jewish and Arab inhabitants of the land have yet to be fully realized.

Ahad Ha'am remained a controversial figure throughout his life. His criticisms of many aspects of the Zionist movement did not always fall on willing ears. But when he died in 1927, his funeral was attended by Jews from all over Palestine. And in the decades since his death Jews continue to grapple with the fundamental issues that he raised: What does it mean to be Jewish in a world that has lost its belief? What is the proper relationship between morality and power? In the words of an American scholar of Jewish history, Ahad Ha'am is a Jewish writer whose "time has come."

FURTHER READING

Pasachoff, Naomi. "Ahad Ha'am." In *Great Jewish Thinkers: Their Lives and Work*. West Orange, N.J.: Behrman House, 1992.

Simon, Leon. *Ahad Ha'am—Asher Ginzberg: A Biography*. Philadelphia: Jewish Publication Society, 1960.

Zipperstein, Steven J. *Elusive Prophet: Ahad Ha'am and the Origins of Zionism*. Berkeley: University of California Press, 1993.

Ahad Ha'am (Asher Ginzberg)

BORN

August 18, 1856
Skvire, Ukraine

DIED

January 2, 1927
Tel Aviv, Palestine

EDUCATION

Studied Talmud and Hasidic texts with private tutors; studied Russian, German, French, English, Latin, philosophy, and science on his own

ACCOMPLISHMENTS

Developed "spiritual Zionism," based on the belief that a Jewish state must be built on the spiritual and cultural renewal of the Jewish people; became the conscience of the Jewish nationalist movement with such essays as "The Wrong Way" (1889), and "Truth from the Land of Israel" (1891, 1893); edited the monthly *HaShiloah*, the most important eastern European journal for Zionist thought and Hebrew literature (1896–1903); played a behind-the-scenes role in bringing about the Balfour Declaration by advising Chaim Weizmann; published a four-volume collection of essays, *At the Crossroads* (1922), and a six-volume collection of letters (1923–25)

Eliezer Ben-Yehuda

THE REVIVAL OF SPOKEN HEBREW

Today Hebrew is the official language of the modern state of Israel. There it is spoken on a daily basis by several million people, who sing Hebrew popular songs; read Hebrew newspapers, magazines, and books; and tune in to Hebrew-language radio and television. Hebrew is also taught to Jewish students in Jewish schools throughout the world. These students learn the language so they can read not only the prayer book and the Hebrew Bible but also modern Hebrew literature. In some secular universities in the United States, students can also study modern Hebrew just as they would German or French.

Only 100 years ago, the situation was very different. At that time Hebrew had not been spoken as an everyday language for about 18 centuries. Jews around the world still studied Hebrew so that they could pray and read the Bible. Scholars read it because it was the language of important Jewish texts from the distant past. But for everyday purposes, even the early Jewish inhabitants of Palestine were not normally speakers of Hebrew. Depending on where they came from and when they arrived in Palestine, they might speak Arabic, Ladino (a mixture of Spanish and Hebrew), French, Russian, or Yiddish (a blend of German, Slavic languages, and Hebrew). Yiddish, not Hebrew, was the language that most Jews shared.

Many people played a part in reviving Hebrew as a spoken language, and many conditions and events combined to restore it as the national language of the Jewish people. But one man in particular has long been thought of as the reviver of Hebrew. That person is Eliezer Ben-Yehuda.

Eliezer's name at birth was Perelman, not Ben-Yehuda. He was born in 1858 in a town in Lithuania, then part of the Russian Empire. His parents were Hasidic Jews, members of one of the ultra-Orthodox sects spread throughout eastern Europe. Eliezer's father died when the boy was only five. When he was 13, he was sent to the home of an uncle in another Lithuanian town so that he could study Talmud—the vast library of Jewish law and lore—at an academy there. The family was unaware that the head of the school was secretly a believer in the ideals of the Jewish Enlightenment. That movement, which had begun in Germany about 100 years earlier, advocated a complete rethinking of Jewish education. Enlightenment leaders believed that Jewish students, instead of focusing on Talmud and other Jewish texts, should learn the local language and stop using Yiddish as their main language, read modern writings in Hebrew, and be exposed to a whole variety of nonreligious subjects. When Eliezer's

Eliezer Ben-Yehuda pores over a pile of Hebrew texts. His devotion to the revival of Hebrew helped transform it into a living language that continues to develop today.

uncle learned that the head of the Talmudic academy was teaching his nephew Hebrew grammar, he quickly removed him from the school.

Hoping to keep Eliezer from harmful influences, his uncle sent him to another Talmudic academy near the Lithuanian capital of Vilna. There, however, Eliezer met another believer in Enlightenment ideals, whose friendship would change his life. This man, Samuel Naphtali Herz Jonas, had also been raised in a Hasidic home. Now, however, he was a writer for Hebrew journals. At Jonas's urging, Eliezer began to prepare for the entrance exams that would admit him to a Russian high school. To help the teenager succeed in his studies, Jonas had his older daughter, Deborah, tutor Eliezer in Russian. After preparing for a year, Eliezer entered the Russian high school in Dvinsk, from which he graduated in 1877.

At that time Russia was engaged in a war against Turkey. By the end of the conflict in 1878, Russia had helped the Serbs and Romanians take steps toward their goal of independence from the Ottoman Empire. Eliezer followed the war's progress with interest. He was aware that Palestine, the ancient Jewish homeland, was also controlled by the Ottoman Turks. Russia's success at diminishing Turkish power awoke within him the idea that the Jews, too, might be restored to their former home. At about the same time he read *Daniel Deronda,* the last novel of the British writer George Eliot. In this book the hero, inspired by the cause of Jewish nationalism, goes to live in Palestine. Eliezer later wrote that he had a vision of "the rebirth of Israel on its ancestral soil."

In 1879, at the age of 21, Eliezer Perelman first used the name Ben-Yehuda (Hebrew for "son of Judah"), signing it to an article he published in Vienna. Entitled "A Burning Question," Ben-Yehuda's article was the first work in print to call for a modern Jewish nation. In it he argued that the Jews should learn a lesson from the struggle of other European peoples for

This bookplate of Eliezer Ben-Yehuda's bears his initial and last name beneath his portrait. Ben-Yehuda became convinced as a young man in his native Lithuania that the creation of a Jewish state required the revival of a national language.

political freedom and national restoration. He called for Jews to establish a Jewish community in Palestine to serve as a spiritual center for Jews everywhere, and he urged that Hebrew be designated the community's language. A few years later, after the author had himself moved to Palestine (then still under Turkish rule), he adopted Ben-Yehuda as his legal name.

When Ben-Yehuda made his decision to live in Palestine, he realized that he would have to prepare himself for some sort of career. He decided to become a doctor and accordingly moved to Paris to attend medical school. His medical studies were soon interrupted, however, when he caught tuberculosis. He began to train instead for a career as a teacher in Palestine. In 1870 the first Jewish school in Palestine had been opened by a world Jewish organization based in Paris. This organization, the Alliance Israélite Universelle, also ran a teachers' college in Paris, in which Ben-Yehuda enrolled.

During his student days in Paris, Ben-Yehuda had three encounters that strengthened his belief in the Hebrew language as the key to Jewish national unity. First, a Jewish journalist told him that whenever he had come across Jews during his travels throughout Asia and Africa, he had been able to speak with them in Hebrew. Second, one of his lecturers at the teachers' college, a specialist in the languages of the ancient Near East, told him that Hebrew could be modernized by adding new words to it. Finally, while hospitalized for his tuberculosis, Ben-Yehuda met a scholar from Jerusalem who spoke with a beautiful Hebrew accent very different from the European-accented Hebrew Ben-Yehuda was familiar with. The ailing scholar also told Ben-Yehuda that although the different Jewish communities of Jerusalem spoke different languages, they could all communicate in Hebrew.

In 1881, as soon as his health permitted, Ben-Yehuda left for Palestine. By prearrangement, Deborah Jonas, his former Russian tutor, met him in Vienna, and the young couple soon became husband and wife. They made an agreement to speak only Hebrew with each other and with the children they planned to have. When a son was born to them the following year, they named him Ben-Zion, Hebrew for "son of Zion"—the poetic name for Jerusalem, where the Ben-Yehudas had settled. Ben-Zion was a late speaker. He did not utter his first sentence—in Hebrew—until he was four. When he did, he spoke to interrupt an argument between his parents. Ben-Yehuda had learned that Deborah had broken her pledge by singing a song to Ben-Zion in Russian, and he was angry. However, Ben-Zion's first words seemed to show his mastery of Hebrew had not been impaired.

When Deborah died in 1891, Ben-Yehuda asked her younger sister to move from Lithuania to Jerusalem to be his wife. The young woman agreed, and Ben-Yehuda gave her the Hebrew name Hemda, which means "bliss." From the time of her marriage to him in 1892 until her death in 1951, Hemda Ben-Yehuda was active in the revival of Hebrew language and literature.

Obviously, if Ben-Yehuda was to succeed in his goal of reviving the Hebrew language, it would take more than a single family of Hebrew speakers. He therefore took a variety of different but related steps to achieve his aim. He agreed to teach in the Alliance's school in Jerusalem only after he received permission to teach the Jewish subjects only in Hebrew, not French. The school thus became the first in which some subjects were taught exclusively in Hebrew.

Ben-Yehuda did not remain a classroom teacher for long, but over the years he continued to shape Hebrew education in Palestine. He helped inspire other teachers to teach not only Jewish subjects but also the entire curriculum in Hebrew. In addition, he made sure that professional journals for teachers and magazines for students were published in Hebrew.

Publishing soon became a major focus of Ben-Yehuda's own efforts. Soon after his arrival from Paris he began to write regularly for a Hebrew-language newspaper that had been published on and off in Jerusalem since 1863. After three years he left to begin his own newspaper, which became the first nonreligious Jewish paper in Palestine. Because of the journalistic changes he made to it, Ben-Yehuda is considered the father of modern Hebrew journalism. In order to cover a whole variety of secular news, Ben-Yehuda felt the need for a broader Hebrew vocabulary and thus began to coin new Hebrew words.

Although Ben-Yehuda was not the first to create new Hebrew words, he was the first to go about the task in a systematic way. Even around the house, he had felt limited by the lack of Hebrew words for simple, everyday items. As a result, among the 200 or so new Hebrew words he created were those for *towel* and *handkerchief*, *doll* and *bicycle*, *soldier* and *airplane*, *restaurant* and *movie*. In one article he described the frustration of "someone like myself, who speaks Hebrew at home with the children, about everything in life, [and] feels every moment a lack of words without which living speech cannot take place." Ben-Yehuda resolutely set out to fill the huge gaps in a language that had not kept pace with the changes in society over many centuries.

Appropriately enough, one of the new Hebrew words Ben-Yehuda created was the term for *dictionary*. The major accomplishment of his

career was in fact his 17-volume *Complete Dictionary of Ancient and Modern Hebrew* (1910–59). This enormous work contained all the words used during the different stages of the development of the Hebrew language. To prepare this dictionary, Ben-Yehuda copied out by hand some 500,000 quotations from all of Hebrew literature over the centuries. The first five volumes of the dictionary appeared during his lifetime. After his death, Hemda Ben-Yehuda continued the task.

Obviously, no one could revive a language singlehandedly. Recognizing this, in 1890 Ben-Yehuda became one of the founding members of the Hebrew Language Committee. Among the committee's goals were to establish a Hebrew vocabulary as well as rules for spelling, punctuation, and grammar. Years later, after the founding of the state of Israel, the new nation's parliament officially replaced the Hebrew Language Committee with the Academy of the Hebrew Language. At that time, the overall aim of restoring the ancient language to everyday use was unexpectedly aided by the work of archaeologists. Whenever archaeological digs uncovered ancient Hebrew inscriptions, the Jews of Palestine saw physical proof of their own connection to their ancestors and their language.

Not all Jews were eager, however, to restore Hebrew to everyday use. Opposition came from at least three quarters. First, many Orthodox Jews believed that Hebrew was a sacred language. They resented the idea that the ancient language of the Bible and the prayer book would also be used to describe drainage systems and farm machinery. Infuriated by Ben-Yehuda's activities, one Orthodox group actually got him arrested in 1894 and sentenced to a year in prison. They pointed out to the Turkish authorities a statement in Ben-Yehuda's newspaper that they claimed was a call for

Eliezer Ben-Yehuda

BORN

January 7, 1858
Luzhky, Lithuania

DIED

December 16, 1922
Jerusalem, Palestine

EDUCATION

Attended medical school in Paris and the teachers' seminary of the Alliance Israélite Universelle in Paris

ACCOMPLISHMENTS

Founded several Hebrew periodicals; cofounded the Hebrew Language Committee (predecessor of the Academy of the Hebrew Language) and presided over it until his death (1890–1922); wrote *Until When Was Hebrew Spoken?* (1919); invented more than 200 new Hebrew words; compiled *The Complete Dictionary of Ancient and Modern Hebrew* (17 volumes, 1910–59)

> *"The Hebrew language . . . did not die of exhaustion; it died together with the nation, and when the nation is revived, it will live again! . . . We cannot revive it with translations; we must make it the tongue of our children, on the soil on which it once blossomed and bore ripe fruit!"*

—from an 1880 letter to the publisher of *HaShahar*

Jews to revolt against the Turks. Protests from Jews around the world led to Ben-Yehuda's release, but the Turkish censors continued to keep a watchful eye on his newspaper.

Jewish philanthropies in Europe were a second source of opposition to Ben-Yehuda's efforts. These organizations feared that the spread of Hebrew would undermine their own influence in Palestine. For example, Baron Edmond de Rothschild, the French philanthropist who supported many Jewish agricultural settlements, objected to the introduction of Hebrew in schools where the language of instruction was French. The conflict between the European philanthropies and those who favored Hebrew came to a head in 1913. A German-Jewish philanthropic organization sponsoring a new technical institute in Haifa, the Technion, insisted that classes be taught in German. Jewish students and teachers throughout Palestine responded by going on strike in protest. This language conflict led to the formation of a national Hebrew school system.

Finally, Ben-Yehuda and his colleagues were opposed by those who preferred to keep Yiddish as the Jewish common language. These Yiddishists worried that the revival of Hebrew would be the undoing of Yiddish.

Despite opposition from all these quarters, Hebrew was firmly established in Palestine by the end of World War I in 1918, which brought about the downfall of the Ottoman Empire.

During the war, Great Britain took political and military control of the Middle East. In December 1917, Britain's General Edmund Henry Hynman Allenby declared martial law in Jerusalem. To inform the population of this turn of events, the British circulated sheets of paper printed on both sides in which the announcement was repeated in seven languages. On one side of the sheet, Hebrew was the first of four languages, and on the other side English was the first of three.

When Allenby's forces issued this announcement, Ben-Yehuda was not in Jerusalem to see it. At the outbreak of hostilities in 1914, the Turkish commander in Palestine, Jamal Pasha, had outlawed all forms of Jewish nationalism, and Ben-Yehuda had decided to continue his efforts in the United States. During his four years there he wrote a book, *Until When Was Hebrew Spoken?* This book was published in 1919, the year Ben-Yehuda returned to Palestine.

Ben-Yehuda died in Jerusalem three years later. In that same year, 1922, the British authorities recognized Hebrew, along with English and Arabic, as an official language of Palestine. When the state of Israel was born 26 years later, Hebrew became its official language. By that time it had also become the only language spoken by more than half the nation's Jewish inhabitants. Eliezer Ben-Yehuda's life work of reviving Hebrew as the Jewish national language had clearly not been in vain. Today the Academy of the Hebrew Language, the successor of Ben-Yehuda's Hebrew Language Committee, continues his work by updating Israel's official language with new words for such items as in-line skates and toaster ovens. That the process of updating the language has become so routine is a tribute to Ben-Yehuda's pioneering work.

FURTHER READING

Fellman, Jack. *The Revival of a Classical Tongue: Eliezer ben Yehuda and the Modern Hebrew Language*. The Hague: Mouton, 1973.

Harshav, Benjamin. "The Revival of the Hebrew Language." In *Language in Time of Revolution*. Berkeley: University of California Press, 1993.

Hertzberg, Arthur. "Eliezer Ben-Yehudah." In *The Zionist Idea: A Historical Analysis and Reader*. New York: Atheneum, 1959.

Pasachoff, Naomi. "Eliezer ben Yehuda: The Father of Modern Hebrew." In *Basic Judaism for Young People: Torah*. West Orange, N.J.: Behrman House, 1986.

Pasachoff, Naomi, and Robert J. Littman. "Eliezer Ben-Yehuda and the Emergence of Modern Hebrew." In *Jewish History in 100 Nutshells*. Northvale, N.J.: Aronson, 1995.

Sáenz-Badillos, Angel. "The revival of Hebrew." In *A History of the Hebrew Language*. Translated by John Elwolde. Cambridge: Cambridge University Press, 1992.

Theodor Herzl

"THE WORLD NEEDS THE JEWISH STATE"

I n one of the strange facts of history, the man who became the father of the modern Jewish state grew up with very little knowledge of, or affection for, Jews or Judaism. Theodor Herzl was born in 1860 in Budapest, Hungary, to a comfortable family that, like many Jews of the time and place, had assimilated into Europe's Christian society. Herzl's family observed few Jewish traditions. For instance, although as a boy he attended services at the Reform synagogue near his family's apartment, there is no record of his celebrating his 13th birthday with the traditional Jewish bar mitzvah ritual. In fact, his diary includes negative memories of his early Jewish education.

For years, Herzl knew nothing about the plans for Jewish resettlement in Palestine that were being organized by a group of Russian Jews. Beginning in 1881, a wave of pogroms—*pogrom* is the Russian word for "riot"—was directed against the Jews of Russia. When neither the government, the press, nor the educated classes spoke out on behalf of the Jewish victims, the Russian Jews reacted in several ways. Some became involved in revolutionary movements aimed at overthrowing the government. Large

Theodor Herzl was the driving force behind the creation of the movement that called for the establishment of a Jewish state.

> "To create a new State is neither ridiculous nor impossible. . . . The governments of all countries scourged by anti-Semitism will be keenly interested in obtaining sovereignty for us."
>
> —from *The Jewish State* (1896)

numbers of Russian Jews left for the United States and elsewhere. A tiny group of them also favored emigration but believed that the Jewish people could revitalize themselves best in their ancient homeland of Palestine. Calling themselves Lovers of Zion (Zion is a traditional name for the land of Israel), they began in 1882 to settle in Palestine on a small scale.

Although Theodor Herzl did not know about the activities of the Lovers of Zion, he was very much aware of anti-Semitism. Jews had been hated because of their religion throughout history, but as more of them began to assimilate into European society, a new form of anti-Jewish hatred emerged. This new attitude, which claimed to be scientific, was based on the notion that Judaism was more than a religion. According to this doctrine, Jews belonged to a race whose destructive traits were passed on from generation to generation, even if a Jew converted to Christianity. Therefore, assimilated Jews were the most dangerous, according to this theory, since their threat to society was not easily recognized. In 1879, a German journalist coined the term "anti-Semitism" to describe this new racial theory, in a pamphlet accusing the "Semitic race" of attempts to destroy "Germandom."

Even before the new word had had a chance to enter the world's dictionaries, Herzl had experienced anti-Semitism, during his high school days. To rescue him from the local school's poisonous atmosphere, his parents transferred him to a high school where the majority of the students were Jewish. However, Herzl's response to anti-Semitism was not what one might have expected from the future father of the Jewish state. Perhaps surprisingly, he accepted many of the negative stereotypes that the anti-Semites promoted. In his diary he spoke about what he saw as certain positive effects of anti-Semitism: it

would, he believed, make Jewish businessmen more ethical, for example.

At the same time, however, Herzl felt there must be some way to make Jews more acceptable to society at large. Some of his musings on this subject were unusual, to say the least. He thought about challenging the leading anti-Semites to a duel. If he were killed, he would leave a letter behind whose contents would convincingly rebut anti-Semitism. And if he were successful in slaying his opponents, his trial would not only lead to his acquittal but also to exposure of the weaknesses of the anti-Semitic position. For a while Herzl tried to convince himself that once Jews assimilated themselves completely, there would be no more anti-Semitism. To help speed up this process, he imagined leading all the Jews of Vienna (where his family had moved in 1878) to the St. Stephan Cathedral to undergo mass baptism.

Anti-Semitism continued to dog Herzl's footsteps as he entered a career in journalism. One newspaper offered him a position, but only on the condition that he adopt a less Jewish-sounding pen name. Although Herzl refused the newspaper's offer, he still clung to his belief that assimilation could overcome anti-Semitism.

In 1891, Herzl moved to Paris as the local correspondent for an important Viennese newspaper. There, to his horror, he discovered that even in France, the home of the French Revolution's ideals of liberty, equality, and fraternity, anti-Semitism was a fact of life. "French Anti-Semites," an article Herzl published in late summer 1892, concluded that anti-Semitism was being used everywhere to shift people's focus from society's real problems.

In January 1895, Herzl was among the few journalists present at a ceremony at which a Jew in the

Herzl addresses the Second Zionist Congress, held in Basel, Switzerland, in 1898. Women delegates, who were excluded from voting in the previous year's congress, were given the opportunity to vote. In his opening address, Herzl called on Zionists to strive to replace assimilationists as spokesmen of the Jewish people.

French army, Captain Alfred Dreyfus, was stripped of all his military honors before being exiled to Devil's Island in French Guiana. Several months earlier, Dreyfus had been arrested on charges of high treason. Eventually it became clear that Dreyfus had been framed by anti-Semites, but the spectacle of the Jewish officer's public humiliation had a profound effect on Herzl and led to lasting consequences for Jewish—and world—history. Herzl later claimed that the so-called Dreyfus Affair, which was destined to tear apart French society for years, also converted him to political Zionism, the belief that the "Jewish problem" could be solved only by establishing a

Jewish state recognized by the great world powers.

Herzl began his career as a statesman on behalf of political Zionism in a most undiplomatic way. Hoping to win the support of wealthy and influential Jews, he turned first to France's Baron Maurice de Hirsch, a financier who was already supporting Russian Jewish settlers in Argentina. Herzl's suggestion that his plan would finally give the baron the chance to do something worthwhile with his money did not win the baron over. Herzl was shown the door without having had the chance to go into the details of his plan. In a follow-up letter Herzl outlined his Zionist views in writing

for the first time, but the baron never responded.

Undiscouraged by this lack of response, Herzl decided to turn to the eminent family of Jewish bankers and philanthropists, the Rothschilds. He spent a week writing into his diary an "Address to the Rothschilds," arguing that the family could safeguard its fortune from scheming gentiles by supporting a plan for the creation of a Jewish state. Herzl's address never made it from his diary to the Rothschilds' desks, however, because a physician friend persuaded him not to send the letter and tried to convince him that he was suffering from a nervous breakdown.

Herzl refused to give up. Deciding to address a broader audience, he revised his diary entries. The result, his Zionist pamphlet *The Jewish State*, was published in England's *Jewish Chronicle* in January 1896. Publication in Vienna followed a month later. The pamphlet's most famous sentence proclaims, "We are a people—one people." According to Herzl, Jewish peoplehood could be traced to an unexpected source: anti-Semites. Not long before, as an assimilated western European Jew, Herzl himself had accepted anti-Semitic stereotypes of eastern European Jews, to whom he had felt superior. But now he claimed that all Jews were in the same boat. The assimilated Jews of western Europe and the unassimilated ones of eastern Europe could, he argued, escape anti-Semitism only by settling in a homeland of their own.

Herzl's new train of thought continued along previously unexplored paths. Not only Jews, he now asserted, but also the countries in which they lived were the victims of anti-Semitism. Proposing that anti-Semitism disturbed the peace, Herzl concluded that "the world needs the Jewish state; therefore it will arise." Herzl's argument thus cast anti-Semitism in a new light, transforming it from a question of Jewish suffering into an international issue of some importance.

Having become aware by this time of the activities of the Lovers of Zion, Herzl took pains to distinguish his political Zionism from their small-scale settlements. The Lovers of Zion were engaged in entering clandestinely into Palestine, violating the immigration policy of the Ottoman Empire, which controlled the country. In his revolutionary pamphlet Herzl insisted on establishing a Jewish state instead by diplomatic means, through meetings between heads of state and representatives of the newly acknowledged Jewish nation. Until that time, the idea of a

This Hebrew postcard commemorating the life of Theodor Herzl summarizes his beliefs in this quotation: "Zionism strives to create for the Jewish nation a safe refuge in the land of the forefathers."

Jewish country had been discussed only within small groups having no influence on the world stage. Herzl was now bent on demonstrating that anti-Semitism was an international political issue that could be solved only on the level of international diplomacy. Believing that Zionism would work to the advantage of the nations of the world, Herzl was convinced that heads of state would be eager to help Jews set up their own state.

However, Herzl's Zionist tract *The Jewish State* did not insist on a particular location for the Jewish nation. Herzl considered two potential locations: Palestine, "our unforgettable historic homeland," and Argentina, "one of the most fertile countries in this world, [which] extends over a vast area, is sparsely populated and has a temperate climate." Only later, when the Lovers of Zion joined Herzl, did he come to focus on Palestine as the prospective site of the Jewish state.

The Jewish State was ultimately published in 80 editions and 18 languages, but initially many Jews in England and western Europe remained

unconvinced by its arguments. They worried that attempts to implement Herzl's plan would call into question the patriotism of Jews in the various countries in which they lived. They also feared that political Zionism would endanger the further development of the small-scale Jewish settlements already established in Palestine.

Nevertheless, Herzl found a receptive audience for his views among eastern European students studying in the West. Although their relatives back home were not able to read Herzl's pamphlet because of strict censorship, the students sent home enthusiastic reports about the handsome, well-educated, assimilated Jew who was proposing to lead his people back to their ancient home.

Herzl immediately began to make political contacts. In April 1896, he met with an uncle of German kaiser William II, who became a supporter of Herzl's plan. A meeting between Herzl and the kaiser himself took place in 1898. Although this meeting and Herzl's other encounters with heads of state produced few concrete results, each one was in fact a triumph. For every time any head of state agreed to meet with Herzl, he in effect admitted that there was a Jewish nation, whose interests Herzl represented.

In June 1896, Herzl traveled to Constantinople, capital of the Ottoman Empire, to meet with government officials. Along the way his train stopped in Bulgaria, where hundreds of Jews thronged the station, hoping to glimpse their new leader. Aware now that his leadership was welcomed by masses of eastern European Jews, Herzl began to arrange a conference for those with similar views. The result, the First Zionist Congress, convened in Basel, Switzerland, at the end of August 1897. Although about 200 delegates from nearly 20 countries attended, Herzl's own newspaper—owned by assimilated Jews who opposed Zionism—refused to cover the event. (It chose instead to cover a convention of Jewish tailors in Oxford to discuss fashions for women cyclists!) But 26 newspapers did send correspondents to report on the proceedings of the congress.

Herzl's pre-Zionist literary career had included not only journalism but also playwriting. At the First Zionist Congress, his theatrical flair came to the fore. Anxious to promote an image of dignity and aware of the effect of costumes, Herzl insisted that all delegates wear black tie. Although he could not have scenery built to create an appropriate mood, he did the next best thing: he arranged for a banner to be hung in the hall. This large white-and-blue cloth, with a blue Star of David in the center, would eventually become the flag of the state of Israel.

The First Zionist Congress defined the goal of political Zionism: to establish "a home for the Jewish people in Palestine secured under public law." During its three-day session, the congress also established the World Zionist Organization, with Herzl as its president, and set up institutions that would serve the Zionist movement for the next 50 years.

Commenting on the First Zionist Congress in his diary, Herzl claimed, "In Basel I founded the Jewish State. If I said this out loud today I would be greeted by universal laughter. In five years perhaps, and certainly in fifty years, everyone will perceive it." Herzl came close to prophetic accuracy in his second estimate. On May 14, 1948, just over 50 years after the close of the First Zionist Congress (and less than two years after the 22nd Zionist Congress), the State of Israel was established.

The road to the establishment of the Jewish state was not an easy one, however. Ironically, Herzl's greatest diplomatic triumph nearly destroyed his Zionist movement. In the spring of 1903 a vicious pogrom in Kishinev, the capital of Moldova, impelled Herzl to meet with the Russian minister of the interior and with British government leaders. Although the Russian gave Herzl a vague written statement pledging his government's aid for the Zionist cause, the British offered to assist suffering Russian Jews immediately. Anxious to keep more Russian Jewish immigrants out of Britain itself, the British government proposed setting up a self-governing Jewish colony in British East Africa.

When Herzl reported this development to the Sixth Zionist Congress in August 1903, he was stunned by the reaction. Although he clearly indicated that the ultimate goal would still remain to establish a homeland in Palestine, many delegates were horrified by the East Africa plan. To them, the idea of setting up a Jewish national settlement anywhere other than Zion was as unthinkable as conversion to a different religion. They were infuriated that Herzl could even contemplate such a scheme.

Theodor Herzl

BORN

May 2, 1860
Budapest, Hungary

DIED

July 3, 1904
Edlach, Austria

EDUCATION

Doctorate in law (1884), University of Vienna

ACCOMPLISHMENTS

Paris correspondent of the leading Viennese newspaper, *Neue Freie Presse* (1891–95); author of several plays, including *The Ghetto* (1894); founded political Zionism by writing *The Jewish State* (1896), in which he described "the Jewish question" as a political problem; organized the first Zionist congresses; wrote a novel, *Altneuland* (1902), describing a utopian Jewish state

"Zionism has already brought about something remarkable, heretofore regarded as impossible: a close union between the ultramodern and the ultraconservative elements of Jewry. . . . A union of this kind is possible only on a national basis."

—from the address to the First Zionist Congress (August 29, 1897)

By now many ardent Zionists had, in fact, long concluded that Herzl's lack of a solid Jewish background undermined his leadership. He often seemed out of touch with the very Jews whose salvation he sought. Then, when Herzl's novel *Altneuland* (German for "old-new land") appeared in 1902, their worst fears were confirmed. To be sure, the book's motto, "If only you will it, it is no dream," was adopted by the entire Zionist movement, and the novel's vision of a technologically modern Jewish state thrilled Jews everywhere. Nonetheless, his critics noted the absence both of the Hebrew language and Jewish culture from Herzl's vision of the new Jewish state.

When the East Africa plan came to a vote at the Sixth Congress, the opponents walked out, a number of them in tears. Herzl spent much of the remaining meeting time trying to salvage the movement. To calm the waters, he quoted publicly a verse from Psalm 137, "If I forget thee, O Jerusalem, may my right hand wither." The bitter controversy unfortunately had fatal consequences for Herzl's health. He had long suffered from a heart ailment, which worsened in the months following the conference. He died on July 3, 1904, at the age of 44.

After his death, even Herzl's opponents recognized his contribution to transforming the identity of the Jewish people. Menahem Ussishkin, who led the resistance during the East Africa controversy, paid tribute to the father of political Zionism in these words: "Those who came before him carried the ideal in their hearts but only whispered about it in the synagogues. . . . Herzl brought us courage and taught us to place our demands before the whole non-Jewish world."

Theodor Herzl's burial was carried out according to the terms of his will: he was to be interred in Vienna alongside his father's grave until the Jewish people could transfer his remains to the Jewish national home. Finally, in August 1949, 45 years after his death and a year after the establishment of the Jewish state, Herzl was reburied on a Jerusalem mountain named in his honor.

FURTHER READING

Elon, Amos. *Herzl*. New York: Holt, Rinehart & Winston, 1975.

Pasachoff, Naomi. "Theodor Herzl." In *Great Jewish Thinkers: Their Lives and Work*. West Orange, N.J.: Behrman House, 1992.

Pawel, Ernst. *The Labyrinth of Exile: A Life of Theodor Herzl*. New York: Farrar, Straus & Giroux, 1989.

Henrietta Szold

REHABILITATING
A NATION

A Jewish woman born in Baltimore in 1860 unintentionally became a model for future generations. Unlike most women of her time, Henrietta Szold switched careers more than once and excelled in a variety of professional positions. She never sat down to plan the course of her life's work. A self-appraisal at the end of her years focused on just how miscellaneous that work—including teaching, publishing, medical administration, and social work—had been. From her hospital bed in Jerusalem in 1945 she wrote, "I have not lived one life, but several, each one bearing its own character and insignia." But while Szold herself may not have identified the organizing principle that guided her professional choices, it is clear how much her work in each different area helped strengthen Jewish life, first in the United States, then in Palestine.

Szold's European-born, German-speaking parents were important influences on her. From her father, the rabbi of a Baltimore synagogue, she inherited a passion for Jewish scholarship. Rabbi Benjamin Szold had no sons, and so he educated Henrietta, the oldest of his eight daughters, as he would have educated a son. From her mother, who survived the deaths of three of her babies, Szold learned not only how to endure loss gracefully but also how to run a household economically. From watching and helping her mother attend to small details, she learned the importance

Henrietta Szold (front row, left) at a 1915 meeting in the New York Office of the Federation of American Zionists. Three years later American Zionist groups were united in the Zionist Organization of America. Szold's first assignment for the ZOA was to direct educational and public relations work.

of careful organization. Unlike her mother, she would not spend her 20s and 30s raising children of her own. Instead, Szold's upbringing and training made it possible for her, during her 70s and 80s, to give new life to thousands of children fleeing from persecution in Europe and a chance for a better life to countless other children in the Jewish homeland.

Szold embarked on her first career in the United States. After graduating at the top of her class from her Baltimore high school, she became a teacher herself. Szold had dreamed about studying at a women's college, but college education for women was still very rare in the 1870s. Although her high school diploma was the last one she earned, Szold never stopped educating herself.

Szold's main teaching position over a period of nearly 15 years took her outside of the Jewish community. At the Misses Adams' School for girls, Szold taught the daughters of genteel Baltimore families a variety of subjects: German (the language of the Szold household), French (which her father had taught her, along with Hebrew), mathematics, and botany (a science the entire Szold family pursued as a hobby). During this phase of her life, she also taught children's classes at the religious school in her father's synagogue, as well as Bible and history courses for adults. While teaching, she continued her own education by attending public lectures at Baltimore's Johns Hopkins University, which had opened its doors in 1876 but did not yet accept women as students.

In the late 1880s, Szold's teaching career took a new turn, involving her for the first time in a specifically Jewish cause. For several years, following the Russian pogroms ("riots") of 1881, many Russian Jews had been leaving that country. Most came to the United States, and a sizable community of them settled in Baltimore. It was clear to Szold that education was the key to turning these frightened refugees into Americans. She accordingly became the driving force behind a night school for immigrants that opened in 1891. Until 1893 she not only taught there but also served as its superintendent. This school, one of the first of its kind, became a model for others. By the time the city of Baltimore took over the school in 1898, it had helped Americanize more than 5,000 immigrants, Christians as well as Jews. Decades later, at a New York reception in honor of Szold's 75th birthday, New York's Mayor Fiorello La Guardia summarized the significance of Szold's school: "If I, the child of poor immigrant parents, am today Mayor of New York, giving you the freedom of our city, it is because of you. Half a century ago you initiated that instrument of American democracy, the evening school for the immigrant."

Szold was always as ready to learn from her students as to teach them. Many of the Russian Jewish immigrants were devoted to the idea that the Jewish people could overcome persecution only by building a Jewish national homeland in the ancient land of Israel, then called Palestine. In 1897 a group of them founded the Zionist Association of Baltimore, of which Szold became a member. From then on, Zionism—the worldwide movement that eventually helped establish the state of Israel and continues to foster its development—became the passion of her life.

Szold's second career, publishing, began in a sense when she was only a child. At the age of 12, she began helping her father proofread the German sections of a new prayer book he was preparing for publication. Her adult career in publishing began 16 years later, in 1888, when she joined a group of American Jews who deplored the lack of an American

Jewish culture. To remedy this, Szold and her colleagues founded the Jewish Publication Society (JPS), which still flourishes today. The goal of the Society was to make books of Jewish interest available to American Jewish readers and to publish works on Jewish themes by contemporary writers and scholars. Szold's contributions to the JPS included editing, translating, and looking for authors. Among the books she edited was the *American Jewish Yearbook*, a reliable chronicle of worldwide events affecting Jews and a statistical and biographical Jewish data book, which was jointly published by the JPS and the American Jewish Committee; she also wrote some 15 articles for the *Jewish Encyclopedia*.

Szold's father died in 1902. After the traditional year of mourning she moved to New York City with her mother. From there she commuted to Philadelphia, the home of the JPS. In New York, the Szolds occupied an apartment across the street from the new Jewish Theological Seminary of America. This gave Szold the idea of acquiring formal scholarly training, which she felt she needed in order to fulfill her goal of editing her father's scholarly work (a task she never got around to). After promising that she would not seek to become a rabbi (a career closed to Conservative Jewish women until the 1980s), she was permitted to study at the seminary. There she took classes from Professor Louis Ginzberg, whose writings were being published by the JPS with Szold's assistance as researcher, editor, and translator.

Szold fell deeply in love with Ginzberg, who was more than a dozen years her junior. She and other members of the seminary community had sufficient cause to believe Ginzberg reciprocated her love. However, after Szold and Ginzberg had worked together for several years, he returned from a trip to Europe with the news that he had become engaged to a young German-Jewish woman, whom he shortly did marry. Szold was devastated. A journey to Europe and Palestine with her mother (financed in part by a gift from her colleagues at the JPS) in 1909–10 helped restore her mental equilibrium and also proved to be a turning point in Szold's life.

While in Palestine, Szold and her mother were powerfully affected by the country's beauty but equally dismayed by the disease, poor living conditions, and limited medical facilities they found there. Szold was convinced that Zionist women could do something concrete to counteract such conditions. On February 24, 1912, she presented her ideas to a group of 38 Jewish women in New York, a meeting that led to the founding of Hadassah, the Women's Zionist Organization of America. Hadassah, which means "myrtle" in Hebrew, was the Hebrew name of the Bible's Queen Esther, who risked her life to save her people.

From this modest beginning Hadassah grew to become the largest Zionist organization in the world. Its constitution states that it is "dedicated to the ideals of Judaism, Zionism, American democracy, healing, teaching, and medical research." The organization's motto, "the healing of the daughter of my people," came from the words of the biblical prophet Jeremiah. Even before the first anniversary of Szold's stirring address in New York, Hadassah had sent out a team of two trained nurses to Palestine. Today, Hadassah's medical organization operates the most advanced health facilities in the Middle East.

When Szold's mother contracted a lung disease, which proved fatal in 1916, a group of her admirers established a fund for Szold's use, enabling her to devote herself full-time to the Zionist movement. Freed from the need to earn a salary, she left her position at the JPS. Hadassah, by now

"Clearly, rehabilitating a nation is not a pastime. It is a task, a heavy task, a holy task."

—from a 1917 address to the fourth annual Hadassah convention

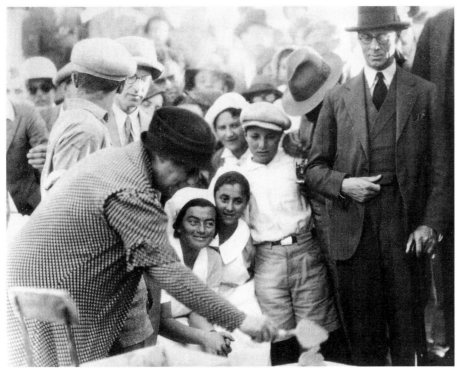

Szold lays the cornerstone of the Hadassah Medical Center in Jerusalem, built in 1934 next to the nine-year-old Hebrew University campus.

an organization of some 4,000 women, asked Szold to organize an American Zionist Medical Unit. She went on extended lecture tours to raise the hundreds of thousands of dollars needed and, by the early fall of 1918, 44 medical professionals (both male and female) and 400 tons of equipment and supplies arrived in Palestine.

The following year, the American Zionist Organization persuaded Szold to accept a two-year appointment as its representative to the Medical Unit in Palestine. She arrived there during the winter of 1920 only to learn that the director of the unit was planning to quit. As a result, Szold had to assume the directorship herself for a period. In her diary she wrote, "The whole of Palestine has been starved of medical aid. . . . In spite of all shortcomings, it is a great piece of work we are doing. But . . . why am *I* doing it?" It seemed absurd to her that a 60-year-old with no training in medical administration should be running hospitals, a nursing school, and clinics. Nevertheless, she made it her business to learn how to

manage this complicated set of facilities. On trips to the United States she gave fundraising speeches that not only bolstered Hadassah's membership rolls but also helped bring in much-needed funds without which the unit would have foundered.

In 1927, the World Zionist Organization appointed Szold a member of its three-person cabinet. Her responsibilities were education, health, and social welfare. Four years later she was invited to join the executive board of the Jewish National Council in Palestine, which cooperated with the world Zionist movement in making policy for the development of the Jewish settlement in Palestine. Szold was elected to its cabinet and asked to head a new department of social welfare. Once again, as she wrote in her diary, she felt that she was being led "beyond my depths." But just as she had mastered what was necessary to function as a medical administrator, she went about learning how to run a national social service department. By approaching social service

bureaus in New York, Berlin, and Vienna, she obtained information and acquired the various documents, such as questionnaires and registration cards, that modern social workers depended on. Lacking funds to acquire a library of books on social work, she relied on free pamphlets distributed by the Children's Bureau of the U.S. Department of Labor.

Szold's achievements as head of social work for the Jewish National Council included the introduction of family casework (the investigation and supervision of families in unfavorable circumstances, with a view to improving their conditions) and plans for a residential school to offer vocational training for boys who had difficulty coping with their lives. Hadassah later began its own extensive program for vocational education.

In 1933, Szold enjoyed a visit from her sister Bertha and planned to return with her to the United States for good. At that moment, however, came a plea that led her to make one of her most important contributions to the Jewish people, to the yet-to-be-born state of Israel, and to social welfare. Adolf Hitler, the anti-Semitic leader of Germany, had begun to put into effect a systematic attack on the Jews of that country. Hitler's book, *Mein Kampf* (1925), blamed all the world's problems on the Jews, and once he became chancellor of Germany in January 1933, Jews were dismissed from government jobs. Hitler's policy would soon develop into a careful plan to exterminate the Jews of Europe. Sensing that Hitler would not soon be overthrown, the wife of a Berlin rabbi devised a plan to save the young. Children would be trained in small groups to deal with life in Palestine and then resettled there. The rabbi's wife came to Palestine for Szold's help in overseeing the children's resettlement.

Thus began the branch of the Zionist movement known as Youth Aliyah. (Aliyah, which means "going up," is the Hebrew word used for the immigration of Jews to Israel.) Szold, in her 73rd year, became director of Youth Aliyah. About this new career turn Szold wrote, "My new job, the organization of the transfer of children from Germany to Palestine, is growing under my hands from day to day. It deals with children—it is not child's play. The responsibility is great."

Thanks largely to Szold's efforts, by the outbreak of World War II in 1939 more than 5,000 children were removed to Palestine from Germany, Austria, and other European countries. As long as her health held out, Szold personally met each boatload of children and escorted them to the settlements, where their arrival was eagerly awaited and celebrated. Szold's greatest challenge with Youth Aliyah came in the winter of 1943, when she greeted a trainload of 730 children who had wandered like hunted animals for more than three years to escape Hitler's armies. Unlike the children from intact homes who had arrived in the early years of Youth Aliyah, these new arrivals had been so affected by their experiences that some people believed they could never live normal lives or be incorporated into society. According to Szold, though, who was then 82, "It is for us who have been spared the extreme horrors of war to demonstrate that we are equal to the task of saving the remnants."

Youth Aliyah was not the only way Szold demonstrated her commitment to Jewish children. On her 80th birthday, she turned over all the cash gifts she had received to the Jewish National Council, with the goal of establishing a National Children's Bureau. After her death the bureau was named Mossad Szold, Hebrew for the Szold Foundation. For her 81st

birthday the national council assigned her the task of planning a fund for child and youth care. In drawing up the plans for the bureau and the fund, she followed two ancient teachings of the rabbis: "Nothing, not even the work of building the temple, may interfere with the studies of little schoolchildren," and "Only the breath of little schoolchildren maintains the world."

By the spring of 1944, Szold was ailing and confined to a hospital bed. She was too ill to celebrate her 84th birthday and died in February 1945, in the Hadassah hospital whose cornerstone she had laid in October 1934. Her death was mourned in Jewish communities throughout the world. At a memorial service for her held in New York City's Carnegie Hall, one of the mourners read aloud from the biblical Book of Job a passage including these words: "I searched out the cause of those whom I did not know. I dared reach out to the fangs of the wicked and pluck the victims from his grasp."

FURTHER READING

Fineman, I. *Woman of Valor: The Life of Henrietta Szold*. New York: Simon & Schuster, 1961.

Lowenthal, Marvin. *Henrietta Szold: Life and Letters*. New York: Viking, 1942.

Pool, Tamar de Sola. "Henrietta Szold." In *Great Jewish Personalities in Modern Times*. Edited by Simon Noveck. Washington, D.C.: B'nai B'rith, 1960.

Shargel, Baila Round. *Lost Love: The Untold Story of Henrietta Szold*. Philadelphia: Jewish Publication Society, 1997.

Zeitlin, Rose. *Henrietta Szold: Record of a Life*. New York: Dial, 1952.

LINKS IN THE CHAIN

Henrietta Szold

BORN
December 21, 1860
Baltimore, Maryland

DIED
February 13, 1945
Jerusalem, Palestine

EDUCATION
Graduated from Baltimore's Western Female High School (1877); studied Hebrew and Talmud at the Jewish Theological Seminary in New York

ACCOMPLISHMENTS
Cofounded one of the first night schools for immigrants in the United States (1891), superintendent (1891–93); cofounder, Jewish Publication Society of America (1888), and general editor, writer, and translator of Jewish classics for JPS (through 1916); helped compile the *Jewish Encyclopedia*; founded Hadassah, the Women's Zionist Organization of America (1912); organized the American Zionist Medical Unit for Palestine (1916–18); first woman elected to the World Zionist executive board (1927); director, Social Welfare Department of the Jewish National Council (1930–38); established a school to train social workers in Jerusalem; set up what became the Szold Foundation (1941); served as director of Youth Aliyah (1933–45), whose mission was to rescue young victims of Nazism and raise them in Palestine

Chaim Weizmann

"TO ZION! LET US GO!"

T he life of Chaim Weizmann, the first president of Israel, dramatizes how much sense it makes to pay attention both to academic subjects and to extracurricular activities. It was Chaim Weizmann's success in his chosen subject, chemistry, that enabled him to achieve an important milestone for his nonacademic passion, Zionism, the movement to establish an independent Jewish country. On the other hand, Weizmann was able to find refuge in his scientific work at times when his leadership of the Zionist movement was rejected.

Weizmann was born in 1874 in a small Jewish town called Motol, in the Russian Empire. He was the third of 15 children, 12 of whom would survive to adulthood. Nine of those 12 would eventually attend a university. Weizmann's father made a good living as a cutter and transporter of timber. The family grew its own fruit and vegetables and raised chickens and cows on its few acres of land. Weizmann's father was deeply religious but enough of a modern man to read widely in secular literature. On his bookshelves one could find Russian novels and science texts along with Zionist literature and the first Hebrew novels. (Since Hebrew was almost exclusively a language of prayer and Bible study for about 18 centuries, the first Hebrew novel was published only in 1853.)

When he was still a child attending the local Hebrew school, Weizmann was introduced to chemistry. The teacher, who officially taught biblical and Hebrew studies, also discussed political issues of the day. He justified the inclusion of the science in his classroom by the fact that the textbook for it was in Hebrew.

Several years earlier, when Weizmann was only four, the situation for Jews in Russia worsened. Russians carried out attacks on the country's Jews with the government's support, and the government issued laws placing new restrictions on Jews. Many Jews began to leave for the United States and elsewhere. Nearing the age of 11, Weizmann himself left home, but not for quite so far-off a destination. He was the first native of Motol to leave that Jewish village in order to pursue an education. Weizmann entered high school in nearby Pinsk, a center of Jewish life and Zionist activity. Zionism clearly appealed to him at this time. In a letter to one of his teachers back in Motol, he declared that only in the ancient homeland of Zion (then called Palestine) would the Jews achieve a better life: "In conclusion to Zion!—Jews—to Zion! let us go!"

In Pinsk, Weizmann lived first with friends of the family; his father paid for his room and board. Later he

Chaim Weizmann (left) smiles during a 1921 Zionist fund-raising tour to the United States. He was accompanied by the eminent scientist Albert Einstein (right), to stimulate American interest in Hebrew University.

some other boys from Motol were studying. But this time the daily workload of teaching duties and university studies proved to be too much for him. That summer he went home for some rest.

When he returned to Germany, it was to a technical university in Berlin, where he began research into how to make dyes. He also continued his Zionist activities in Berlin but made up his mind not to let either interest dominate the other. After two years in Berlin, where he gave private lessons to support himself, Weizmann returned to Russia for a year. Living in Pinsk, where his family had moved to benefit his father's business, Weizmann continued his chemical research by working in an oil-production factory owned by the family whose son he had tutored while in high school. He then returned to Berlin for another year, but in the summer of 1897 he moved to the University of Fribourg in Switzer-land, following his favorite professor, who had taken a position there. In January 1899, Weizmann received high honors for his thesis on dyes. Later that year he became an unsalaried university lecturer in chemistry at the University of Geneva.

Weizmann grew even more involved with Zionism in the late 1890s after Theodor Herzl began to lead the movement. Herzl believed in "political" Zionism, contending that Jews could earn respect as a nation only by securing a charter to Palestine from the Ottoman government, which controlled it at the time. By 1901, Weizmann and a number of other young Russian Jewish students in Germany had grown dissatisfied with Herzl's leadership. They believed that he made a lot of contacts but accom-plished little in advancing the goals of Zionism. They also objected to Herzl's failure to consult with others in the movement. Weizmann and his col-leagues therefore founded what they

moved into the home of one of the town's wealthiest Jews, where he earned his keep and expense money by tutoring his host's son. His major extracurricular activity was his in-volvement in Zionism: soliciting funds and raising people's awareness of the movement and its goals. Weizmann organized his time so well that he was able to carry on his schoolwork, Hebrew studies, tutoring, and Zionist activities while also learning French and German on his own. In Pinsk he

also developed what became a lifelong interest in chemistry.

At 18, Weizmann graduated from the high school in Pinsk. He now had to decide whether to try to attend university in Russia, which had a quota for Jewish students, or go to another country. In August 1892, he slipped across the border to Germany with no official papers. In Darmstadt he began to attend a technical univer-sity, earning his living by tutoring at a nearby Jewish boarding school where called the Democratic Fraction, hoping to encourage the pursuit of goals ignored by Herzl, such as the need for Hebrew education to prepare Jews to live in Palestine. At about the same time, Weizmann also began a project that would remain central to him for the rest of his life— a drive to establish a Jewish university in Palestine.

In 1903, new attacks against the Jews broke out in Russia. At the sixth Zionist Congress held that summer in Basel, Switzerland, Herzl reported that the British had offered the Jews a settlement in East Africa, to be under Jewish governance with British supervision. Herzl stressed that the East Africa project was not a replacement for a Jewish home in Palestine, merely a temporary refuge for Russian Jews fleeing persecution. Weizmann was among the opponents of the scheme. He went to London that fall both to promote the beliefs of his group, the Zionists of Zion, and to look for a new job. He succeeded in both ventures. By the end of 1903, the British had withdrawn their proposal. And in the spring of 1904 Weizmann had a new position—at the University of Manchester, a city that was home to a great dye industry.

Even though Weizmann had opposed the idea of a Jewish settlement in East Africa, he understood the underlying importance of the British offer. It implied that Great Britain considered the Jews a unified national group with whom political arrangements could be made. With this understanding in mind, Weizmann determined to make the most of his British contacts to advance the cause of Zionism. He began to teach himself English, in part by reading the English translation of the Bible (which he knew intimately in Hebrew), by attending English plays, and by memorizing his chemistry textbooks, which were in English. Although he never lost his Russian accent he soon became fluent in English—able to converse, lecture, and write letters, speeches, and articles in that language. He also continued his Zionist activities in Manchester.

In 1906, Weizmann had a meeting with Arthur James Balfour, then the leader of Britain's Conservative party, when Balfour was campaigning in Manchester. This meeting was to prove highly significant 11 years later. Weizmann was introduced to Balfour by Charles Dreyfus, a Manchester Zionist and member of the Manchester Conservative Association, who owned a local dye factory where Weizmann was doing some private research. In his memoirs, written more than 40 years later, Weizmann recalled that at the 1906 meeting Balfour asked him why the Jews had rejected the offer of East Africa. The young scientist responded by asking a question of his own. If Balfour were offered Paris, would he reject London? "Of course not," said Balfour, "but London is the capital of my country." Weizmann then replied that Jerusalem had been the capital of the Jews' country when London was still only a swamp.

Other significant milestones followed one another over the next five years. The year 1906 was memorable not only for the meeting with Balfour but also for Weizmann's marriage to Vera Khatzman, a Russian Jew he had met in Geneva, where she was attending medical school. The following year, just a few months after the birth of their first son, Benjamin, Weizmann made his first trip to Palestine, and in 1910 he became a British citizen.

By the summer of 1914, one of Weizmann's dreams began to become a reality. First a site was found on Mount Scopus in Jerusalem for the Hebrew University he had been working toward. Then, later that summer, World War I began. The war paved the way for a new connection between Weizmann and the British government. The War Office invited British scientists to inform them of any research with a possible military use. Weizmann was now working on a process that could aid the British munitions industry in making explosives. He left the University of Manchester and put his process to work in a large-scale industrial operation in London. Weizmann was thus able to make several important contributions to Britain's war effort, much to the satisfaction of David Lloyd George, who became minister of munitions in 1915.

Weizmann's important wartime contribution made British politicians more willing to listen to his arguments on behalf of the Zionist movement. His views were transformed into British policy after David Lloyd George became prime minister in December 1916, with Balfour as his foreign secretary. The British government transmitted a letter from Balfour to Lionel Walter Rothschild, 2nd Baron Rothschild, whom the government recognized as head of the Anglo-Jewish community. This letter, which came to be called the Balfour Declaration, was dated November 2, 1917. It stated that "His Majesty's Government view with favour the establishment in Palestine of a national home for the Jewish people."

The Balfour Declaration was a true milestone in Jewish history. With it, for the first time since the Romans had destroyed the Jews' Temple in Jerusalem in 70 C.E., a world power had publicly demonstrated its belief that the Jewish people were a nation. Yet from the outset it was clear that not all British public figures believed in the Balfour Declaration. The British had ousted the Turks from Palestine, but the British administration there made no attempt to publicize the Balfour Declaration. Few British officers in Palestine were even aware of it. And even after the League of Nations (the predecessor of the United Nations) gave Great Britain a mandate over Palestine to put "into effect the declaration originally made on

November 2, 1917," many British officers in Palestine worked hard to favor Arab interests over Zionist aspirations.

Thus, the initial elation over the Balfour Declaration was mixed with political disappointment. For Weizmann, however, there was only euphoria when in July 1918 twelve foundation stones of the Hebrew University were laid on Mount Scopus. As the sole speaker at the dedication ceremony, Weizmann predicted that the university would "mold itself into an integral part of our national structure which is in the process of erection."

Even at this early date, some Jews criticized Weizmann for not getting more than the Balfour Declaration out of the grateful British. For example, David Ben-Gurion, who would be the first prime minister of the Jewish state 30 years later, accused Weizmann of being too undemanding in his negotiations with the British. Weizmann, however, was not about to admit defeat. He soon began to make connections with American political leaders, hoping to win their support for the Zionist cause. These connections would also bear fruit.

By the time the League of Nations gave Great Britain its mandate over Palestine in July 1922, the British government had become aware that promoting Zionist interests would alienate not only the Arabs in that part of the world but also the non-Arab Muslims who populated much of the British Empire. Thus, during the following years, as Arabs in Palestine demonstrated in response to Zionist gains, the British government issued a series of official documents, called White Papers, on Palestine.

The final White Paper, issued in 1939, clearly showed how far Great Britain had retreated from its initial position in the Balfour Declaration. That White Paper stated that "His Majesty's Government now

Chaim Weizmann

BORN
November 27, 1874
Motol, Russia (now Belarus)

DIED
November 9, 1952
Rehovot, Israel

EDUCATION
Ph.D., University of Fribourg, Switzerland (1899)

ACCOMPLISHMENTS
Researcher and lecturer in chemistry at University of Manchester (1904–15); leader of Democratic Fraction opposition to Theodor Herzl (1901–1904); chemical adviser on acetone supplies to the British Ministry of Munitions (1915–18); a founder of Hebrew University in Jerusalem; spokesman for Zionist movement in negotiations leading up to Balfour Declaration (November 1917); president, World Zionist Organization (1920–31, 1935–46); founded what became the Weizmann Institute at Rehovot, Palestine (1934); helped form World War II Jewish Brigade Group in the British army; first president of Israel (1949–52)

declares . . . that it is not part of their policy that Palestine should become a Jewish state." It also limited Jewish immigration quite severely, a terrible hardship in view of the fact that Adolf Hitler had come to power in Germany in 1933. Hitler, whose hatred of Jews was unmatched, persecuted Jews under his control as no government leader had ever done before. As a result, the 1939 White Paper's strict immigration quotas amounted to a death sentence for the millions of European Jews who needed a refuge.

Many Zionists appeared to hold Weizmann personally to blame for the White Papers. In 1931, at the 17th Zionist Congress, held in Basel, Switzerland, many delegates hurled accusations at him, even though he had already resigned his leadership post in the World Zionist Organization, of which he had been president since 1920. One of the cruelest accusations made by his opponents was that he had "sat too long at English feasts." Weizmann did not let his disappointment overwhelm him, however. After an absence of 14 years, he returned to his scientific work in London.

In 1933, a friend's family tragedy opened up a new scientific possibility for Weizmann and led to a new cultural advance for Zionism. At that time, Daniel Sieff, the son of wealthy British Zionist Israel Sieff, committed suicide. While trying to console the heartbroken father, Weizmann suggested that Sieff build a scientific institute in Palestine in his son's honor, with Weizmann as its first director. Upon approval of the project, Weizmann chose the village of Rehovot, about 14 miles south of Tel Aviv, for the institute's home. On April 3, 1934, the Daniel Sieff Research Institute, later renamed the Weizmann Institute, was opened. Inscribed over the institute's gates was the motto "Work for this Country —Work for Science—Work for

Humanity." This credo summarized the three-part focus of Weizmann's own life's work. Soon the Weizmanns moved to their new home in Rehovot.

Although Weizmann officially held no Zionist office, he kept busy dealing with the problems caused for Europe's Jews by Hitler's rise to power. He met with government leaders and worked to raise funds. The Zionist movement was aware that now as never before it needed a leader who was known around the world. Accordingly, in 1935 Weizmann was returned to office as president of the World Zionist Organization.

When Britain declared war against Hitler's Germany in 1939, Weizmann once again offered his scientific abilities to the government. This time, though his research produced some benefits for the war effort, he did not achieve a major breakthrough to match his contribution during World War I. He also had little success in convincing the British government to lift the immigration quota for Palestine. "The slaughter of European Jews," he argued in vain, "can be redeemed only by establishing Palestine as a Jewish country."

Convinced that the United States was destined to play an important, perhaps decisive, role in the future of the Middle East, Weizmann began to spend much time in New York and Washington in the early 1940s. His outline for establishing a Jewish commonwealth in western Palestine, published in the influential American quarterly *Foreign Affairs*, became official Zionist policy in 1942.

In August 1944 Weizmann achieved a measure of success with the British government when British Prime Minister Winston Churchill agreed to his request to form a Jewish fighting force. But Weizmann's faith in British support for Zionism finally gave way. He would eventually turn in his British passport, signalling his rejection of his

On February 17, 1949, Israel's parliament—the Knesset—elected Chaim Weizmann (center, with upraised arm) the first president of the new nation. Weizmann, who had been provisional president since May 17, 1948, is sworn into office under the watchful eye of Theodor Herzl, whose portrait hangs on the wall.

British citizenship. Many Zionists still blamed him, though, for Britain's failure to liberalize its policy on Jewish settlement in Palestine. Finally, in 1946, Weizmann was voted out of office by the World Zionist Organization. Even so, he continued to argue the Zionist case before the United Nations and within the United States.

By the end of World War II, in 1945, Britain had decided to pull out of Palestine. In an address to the United Nations General Assembly in 1947, Weizmann movingly an-

nounced, "The Lord shall set His hands the second time to recover the remnants of His people, and he shall set up an ensign for the nations and shall assemble the outcasts of Israel and gather together the dispersed of Judah from the four corners of the earth." Britain's mandate in Palestine was officially scheduled to end on May 15, 1948. From New York, Weizmann urged his old opponent David Ben-Gurion to declare statehood, which Ben-Gurion did on May 14. Thanks in part to Weizmann's personal interven-

tion, President Harry Truman of the United States extended U.S. recognition to Israel. (The President acted without notifying the State Department officials speaking at the very moment on the floor of the United Nations against the establishment of the Jewish state.) As six Arab countries immediately launched armed attacks against the new state, Ben-Gurion telegraphed Weizmann, "Of all those living, no one contributed as much as you to [Israel's] creation. . . . Looking to the day when we shall be

"Our people is deathless, our land eternal. There are some things which cannot fail to come to pass, things without which the world cannot be imagined. The remnant shall work on, fight on, live on until the dawn of better days. Towards that dawn I greet you."

—from the farewell speech to 21st Zionist Congress (August 1939)

privileged to see you at the head of the State." Shortly thereafter, news arrived at the Weizmanns' hotel room in New York that he had been elected president of Israel. Among the many letters of congratulation Weizmann received was one from renowned scientist Albert Einstein, who wrote, "I read with real pleasure that Palestine Jewry has made you the head of their state and so made good, at least in part, their ungrateful attitude toward you."

Although thrilled to see his life's dream of a Jewish state realized, Weizmann was disappointed in his new role, which he held until his death in 1952: he was only a figure-head, with the power to make decisions reserved to the prime minister and cabinet. Furthermore, he felt slighted because he had not been asked to sign Israel's Declaration of Independence. Only posthumously, on November 2, 1967, on the 50th anniversary of the Balfour Declaration, was an attempt made to rectify this omission. On that occasion, Israel's president signed a scroll proclaiming Weizmann's key role in establishing the Jewish state. This scroll, alongside the Declaration of Independence, is now found in Israel's state archives.

In his eulogy at Weizmann's funeral, David Ben-Gurion summarized his colleague's important role in the shaping of Jewish tradition: "Chaim Weizmann . . . will take his place in the eternal history of the Jewish people alongside the great figures of the past— the Patriarchs and Kings, Judges, Prophets, and spiritual leaders who have woven the fabric of our national life for four thousand years."

FURTHER READING

Amdur, Richard. *Chaim Weizmann*. New York: Chelsea House, 1988.

Bentwich, Norman. "Chaim Weizmann." In *Great Jewish Personalities in Modern Times*. Edited by Simon Noveck. Washington, D.C.: B'nai B'rith, 1960.

Litvinoff, Barnet, ed. *The Essential Chaim Weizmann: The Man, the Statesman, the Scientist*. New York: Holmes and Meier, 1983.

Reinharz, Jehuda. *Chaim Weizmann: The Making of a Zionist Leader*. New York: Oxford University Press, 1985.

————. *Chaim Weizmann: The Making of a Statesman*. New York: Oxford University Press, 1993.

Rose, Norman. *Chaim Weizmann: A Biography*. New York: Viking, 1986.

Weizmann, Chaim. *Trial and Error: The Autobiography of Chaim Weizmann*. New York: Harper & Brothers, 1949.

David Ben-Gurion

FATHER OF THE NATION

Every nation has its heroes. In the United States, students learn to think of George Washington as the father of his country. He is honored both for his military skills during the American Revolution and for his political leadership as the first president of the United States. Another honored American historical figure is Thomas Jefferson, best remembered for drafting America's Declaration of Independence. Similarly, students in the state of Israel learn to honor as the father of their country a man who combined the roles of Washington and Jefferson. David Ben-Gurion not only guided Israel through its own war of independence and served as its first prime minister but also wrote and delivered its Declaration of Independence.

Unlike his American counterparts, Ben-Gurion is not known by a last name acquired at birth. When he was born in 1886, in the small Polish market town of Plonsk, he was named David Gruen. More than half of Plonsk's inhabitants were Jews whose everyday language was Yiddish, a mixture of German, Slavic languages, and Hebrew. Most of the town's Jews were traders or craftsmen, but David's father and grandfather were well-educated, well-off men who held well-regarded positions in the Jewish community. Both men were authorized to do legal work. Each believed fervently in the revival of the ancient Hebrew language as a modern tongue, and David began to learn Hebrew at the age of three while sitting on his grandfather's knee.

David's grandfather and parents played crucial roles in the development of his character and goals. Although David was a sickly child, his mother saw something extraordinary in his intelligence and instilled in him a deep self-confidence. A physician to whom she nervously took her son one day reassured her about David's health and predicted on the basis of the measurements of his skull that the child would grow up to be a great man. When his mother died, David was only 11 and the loss was a heavy one. After his father remarried, David never grew close to his stepmother, though his relationship with his father remained strong.

David's father instilled in him a love of Zion, the poetic Hebrew name for the land of Israel. Two years before David's birth in 1886, his father had joined the Lovers of Zion, a new movement dedicated to the development of Jewish settlements in the Jews' ancestral homeland, then known as Palestine. David would fall asleep listening to his father's tales about the land of their forefathers. He later wrote, "It is no exaggeration to say that at three I had dreams of coming to Palestine. And certainly from my

Ben-Gurion in 1918 in the uniform of the Jewish Legion, a group of Jewish volunteers who served in the British army toward the end of World War I. After returning to Palestine, Ben-Gurion formed a Zionist labor party together with another former member of the Jewish Legion, Berl Katznelson.

tenth year on, I never thought of spending my life anywhere else."

In 1897, the year David's mother died, Theodor Herzl founded the World Zionist Organization, whose aim was the establishment of a Jewish state. Three years later, David and two friends formed a youth group whose goals included Hebrew education for the Jews of Plonsk and emigration to Palestine. The group succeeded in teaching Hebrew to approximately 150 children in the town. In 1903, the idealistic young men looked beyond the educational needs of their home-town Jews and raised money to aid the victims of a savage pogrom ("riot" in Russian) against the Jews of Kishinev, the capital of present-day Moldova. David, then 17, and the two cofound-ers of the youth group were distressed to learn that Herzl's reaction to the Kishinev pogrom was to try to estab-lish, under British protection, a Jewish state in East Africa. The three young men believed fervently that the ancient land of Israel was the only appropriate spot for a Jewish state. They decided that the time had come to turn this belief into action. Between them they had just enough money to cover the cost of one passage to Palestine. They drew lots, and David won. He resolved to study engineering to prepare himself for a useful life in Palestine as soon as he was able to make the move.

At the age of 18, in 1904, David Gruen moved to Warsaw, the capital of Poland, then part of the Russian Empire. There he hoped to enter a Russian high school in preparation for engineering training. But Russian law strictly limited the number of Jews permitted to study in state schools, and by the time he applied, the quota had been filled. David next set his sights on entering a technical school for young Jews and began taking private lessons in Russian, physics, and math to enable him to pass its entrance

exams. Once again, though, admission was limited, this time to high school graduates, so David's educational dream evaporated. Disappointed, he turned to politics. While in Warsaw, he became an active member in Poalei Zion (Workers of Zion), a new Jewish workers' organization. At this time he became committed to the idea that Jewish workers would bring about a revival of the Jewish nation. In 1905, David returned to Plonsk, where he founded a local branch of Poalei Zion. As a labor organizer for Poalei Zion he organized the seamstresses of Plonsk into a union and led them in a success-ful strike. Because of his involvement with Poalei Zion, he was arrested twice. He concluded that it was time for him to depart for Palestine.

In September 1906, a month or so before his 20th birthday, David Gruen landed in the country of which he had been dreaming since he was a toddler. Immediately he was struck by the contrast between the paradise of his imagination and the ruined cities and barren, mosquito-infested country that lay before him. Even so, it was elation, not depression, that kept him from sleeping during his first night in Palestine. "I lay awake," he later wrote, "for who could sleep through the first night in the Land. The spirit of my childhood and my dreams had tri-umphed and I was joyous."

On his second day in Palestine, Gruen went to the Jewish agricultural colony of Petah Tikvah (the Gate of Hope), founded in 1878. There he found work in the orange groves, hauling manure to fertilize new trees. He later worked in other colonies where, like other Jewish pioneers in the land of Israel, he suffered from malaria, hunger, and poverty. How-ever, it was clear to many of his co-workers from the outset that David Gruen was cut out for quite different kinds of work. According to one story, he led a herd of oxen into the field one day but was so absorbed in a newspaper he was reading that he failed to notice that the oxen had wandered off.

Indeed, it was his involvement with a newspaper that was to transform David Gruen, the agricultural worker, into David Ben-Gurion, the political organizer. In 1910, at the age of 24, he moved to Jerusalem, where he became a member of the editorial board of the official paper of Poalei Zion. Like others on the paper's staff, he took a new name—which in Hebrew meant "son of a lion cub"— because, as he later wrote, this one "sounded like a name out of the Bible." For the remaining 63 years of his life, he was known only as David Ben-Gurion. After a year in Jerusalem, Ben-Gurion left Palestine to study law in Constantinople (today's Istanbul), the capital of the Ottoman Empire. Since the Ottoman Empire then controlled Palestine, Ben-Gurion was convinced that the Jews of Palestine needed leaders who spoke Turkish and were familiar with Turkish law. Then, when World War I broke out, in August 1914, Turkey soon joined the war on the side of Germany, against Britain and France. Because of his Zionist activities, the Turkish authorities expelled Ben-Gurion from the Otto- man Empire, together with his Poalei Zion colleague Yitzhak Ben-Zvi. (Ben- Zvi was later to become president of the state of Israel.)

The two Bens, as they came to be known, sailed together for the United States. On board ship, Ben-Gurion studied English and planned out the political activities he would pursue. The two traveled throughout the United States, trying to encourage young people to emigrate to Palestine. During this time they published two books that described the life of the pioneers in Palestine. While doing research at the New York Public Library, Ben-Gurion was assisted by Paula Monbaz, a nurse he met at the home of friends. In December 1917, Ben-Gurion and Monbaz were married at New York's City Hall. Immediately after the ceremony, the bridegroom rushed off to a Zionist meeting.

A month before Ben-Gurion's wedding, the British government had issued the Balfour Declaration. In this document, one of the most important in Zionist history, the British govern- ment expressed its sympathy for "the establishment in Palestine of a na- tional home for the Jewish people." With the appearance of the Balfour Declaration, Ben-Gurion came to feel strongly that Jewish soldiers should fight alongside the British to liberate Palestine from Ottoman rule. Thus, in the summer of 1918 David Ben-Gurion sailed for the Middle East with other members of the newly formed Jewish Legion. As it turned out, Turkey was defeated before Ben-Gurion's battalion could reach the front, and he never saw battle.

However, while serving in the Jewish Legion Ben-Gurion made an important contact that would help shape the course of his career. One of his comrades in arms was Berl Katznelson, another Zionist pioneer with similar views. Upon their return to Palestine in 1919, the two men assembled "a general conference of all the workers of the Land of Israel," which resolved to call their new labor organization Unity of Labor. A decade later, Unity of Labor joined with a second labor organization to found the Mapai labor party, which led the Zionist movement for nearly 50 years. Katznelson and Ben-Gurion hoped that a united workers' party would not only spearhead Zionist activity in Palestine but would also help shape the goals of the world Zionist move- ment. To those ends, in 1920 Katznelson and Ben-Gurion helped found the Histadrut, the General Federation of Hebrew Workers in Israel. While Katznelson preferred to

"The makers of the contemporary Jewish revolution have asserted: Resisting fate is not enough. We must master our fate; we must take our destiny into our own hands! This is the doctrine of the Jewish revolution.*"*

—from *The Imperatives of the Jewish Revolution* (1944)

work behind the scenes, Ben-Gurion soon assumed the leading position in the Histadrut. Its members, he believed, would reclaim Palestine for the Jews.

After the end of the war, the League of Nations gave Great Britain a mandate to govern Palestine. Under the terms of this mandate, Britain agreed to recognize "an appropriate Jewish agency . . . for the purpose of advising and cooperating with the administration of Palestine in such economic, social, and other matters as may affect the establishment of the Jewish National Home and the interests of the Jewish population in Palestine." Ben-Gurion became the leader of that agency. As head of both the Histadrut and the Jewish Agency, Ben-Gurion now found himself a major world Zionist leader. To prepare himself to guide a future Jewish state, he studied, on his own, political theory, the lives of great leaders, and the history of the Middle East and the Arab peoples.

During the 1920s, the Arab community of Palestine began increasingly to resent the stepped-up Zionist activity and the arrival of more and more Jewish settlers. Riots broke out periodically despite the Histadrut's organization in 1920 of a Jewish defense force called the Haganah.

In response to this unrest, the British appointed a series of investigative commissions. The findings and recommendations of each commission were summarized in policy statements called White Papers. With each White Paper, Britain withdrew a bit more from the pro-Zionist position of the Balfour Declaration. Finally, the White Paper of 1939 stated, "His Majesty's Government now declares unequivocally that it is not part of their policy that Palestine should become a Jewish state."

It had become increasingly clear to Great Britain that the oil supplies and many of the military installations on which the British Empire relied were in lands with large Arab or Muslim populations. (Although not all Arabs are Muslims, and the majority of the world's Muslims live not in the Middle East but in the Indian subcontinent and elsewhere in Asia and Africa, Muslims are members of a worldwide faith community and as such have always been concerned with the fate of Muslims in other parts of the world.) As Hitler's activities in Germany during the 1930s posed a growing threat of war, the British felt it imperative to retain Arab and Muslim loyalty. A rebellion of these inhabitants of the British Empire would severely compromise Britain's ability to wage a successful war against Hitler. The 1939 White Paper therefore proposed the creation in Palestine within 10 years of "an independent Palestine state" that would safeguard the interests of both Arabs and Jews. Accordingly, the influx of Jewish immigrants into Palestine was to be limited to a mere 75,000 over the next five years. Following that five-year period, no new immigration would be allowed without Arab approval.

In the meantime, the situation of the Jews in Nazi-occupied Europe had become desperate. The Nazis were determined to rid Europe of Jews, but no country was willing to admit large numbers of them as refugees. Ben-Gurion and other Zionist leaders understood that emigration to Palestine was the only hope for these Jews. When Germany invaded Poland in September 1939 and World War II began, Ben-Gurion immediately perceived the dilemma confronting the Zionist movement. On the one hand, Zionists had to try to save the lives of Europe's Jews, even if it meant violating the British policy. On the other hand, the Zionists shared the British determination to defeat the Nazis and therefore could do nothing to undermine the British war effort. Ben-Gurion summarized this problem in a sentence that guided the Jews of Palestine during the bitter war years: "We must help the British in the war against Hitler as if there were no White Paper, and we must resist the White Paper as if there were no war!"

From the outbreak of war, Ben-Gurion foresaw that the world upheaval could result in a Jewish state—if the proper advance work were done. Accordingly, he went to the United States in 1941 to obtain support for the establishment of a Jewish state in Palestine after the war. In May 1942, he helped organize the first national conference of American Zionists. Because the meeting was held at New York City's Biltmore Hotel, the resolution its delegates adopted became known as the Biltmore Program. The most important part of this program was its call for the postwar establishment in Palestine of "a Jewish Commonwealth as part of the structure of the new democratic world."

When Ben-Gurion returned to Palestine in 1942, he found that the British held firm to their White Paper's restrictions on immigration. Two Jewish terrorist groups, the Lehi and the Irgun, believed that terrorist activity could drive the British out of Palestine. Ben-Gurion, however, feared that terrorism might undermine Great Britain's war against Hitler. Therefore, when members of the Irgun and Lehi groups assassinated a British minister in Palestine in 1944, Ben-Gurion ordered the Haganah, the Jewish defense force, to hand the terrorists over to the British.

The war against Germany finally ended in May 1945, but not before the Nazis had exterminated 6 million Jews. When a Labour government was elected in England, Ben-Gurion expected that it might help further Zionist goals. His hopes were dashed,

however, when the new British government announced a continuation of support for the 1939 White Paper and its opposition to a Jewish state in Palestine. Ben-Gurion responded by ordering the Haganah to smuggle Jewish refugees into Palestine.

Britain soon decided that the costs of maintaining control over Palestine were too high. In 1947, the British government turned the entire Palestine question over to the newly formed United Nations. Members of the United Nations Special Committee on Palestine (UNSCOP) witnessed the plight of 4,500 survivors of Nazi death camps who arrived illegally in Palestine in the summer of 1947 aboard the ship *Exodus*. The sympathies of the UNSCOP observers were aroused when the British forced the newly arrived refugees onto British prison ships that would return them to Europe. When the prison ships returned the refugees to an internment camp in Germany, the world was aghast. Partly in response to the *Exodus* incident, UNSCOP recommended that Palestine be divided into two separate states, one Jewish, one Arab. Jews throughout Palestine celebrated when the United Nations General Assembly voted on November 29, 1947, for the partition of Palestine. Ben-Gurion, however, did not celebrate. As he later wrote, "I could not dance. I knew that we faced war and that in it we would lose the best of our youth."

Aside from his brief time in the Jewish Legion, Ben-Gurion had never had any military experience. Nonetheless, in 1946 he had asked the Jewish Agency to appoint him minister of defense for the Jewish community in Palestine. From that moment he began to prepare for the inevitable war with the Arabs. He studied books about military campaigns and worked with Haganah's commanders to develop strategy. The commanders thought he

David Ben-Gurion

BORN
October 16, 1886
Plonsk, Poland

DIED
December 1, 1973
Tel Aviv-Yafo, Israel

EDUCATION
Attended the University of Constantinople (1912–14)

ACCOMPLISHMENTS
Cofounded the Histadrut, the confederation of Jewish workers in Palestine (1920); headed Mapai, the Israeli Workers Party; author of the final draft of Israel's Declaration of Independence (May 14, 1948); defense minister of the Jewish Agency and the new state of Israel (1946–49); first prime minister of the state of Israel (1949–53)

was overestimating the Arab threat. They did not believe that Arab leaders around the Middle East would support the Arabs of Palestine, but Ben-Gurion's apprehensions proved accurate.

The British mandate over Palestine was not scheduled to end until May 14, 1948, but fighting with the Arabs began immediately after the vote for partition. In these months before the official establishment of the state of Israel, David Ben-Gurion made his first important military decision. He determined that Jerusalem was all-important and that any Arab attempt to cut the city off from western Palestine must be thwarted. His fears proved well-grounded. Arab attacks on Jewish convoys bringing supplies to Jerusalem left the city in a virtual state of siege. Although the Jewish forces undertook two operations to open the road to Jerusalem, each succeeded only long enough to permit some large convoys of vehicles bearing food and arms to reach the city. In both cases, Arab forces retook the strong points protecting the road to the city, and the siege of Jerusalem seemed unbreakable.

As troubling as the situation in Jerusalem was, Ben-Gurion found time to work on the document announcing the establishment of the state of Israel. A few days before the scheduled British departure from Palestine, the 13-member National Administration—soon to become the provisional government of the Jewish state—began to draft a Declaration of Independence. As head of the National Administration, Ben-Gurion had the opportunity to revise the first draft, which he considered too long, too flowery, and too detailed. He pointed out that the U.S. Declaration of Independence did not define the country's frontiers, for example, and he eliminated that passage from the draft. He also decided not to include any condemnation of the British mandate. On the afternoon of Friday, May 14,

1948, Ben-Gurion read Israel's Declaration of Independence aloud in Tel Aviv's Museum Hall.

Hours after Ben-Gurion proclaimed the new Jewish state, five Arab countries invaded Israel: Egypt, Syria, Transjordan, Iraq, and Lebanon. The Israelis would come to call the conflict their War of Independence. Because of Ben-Gurion's successes as a military leader, the war would leave Israel in possession of more territory than originally provided for in the United Nations partition plan. Understanding, as he would later write, "that if ever the people of the country saw Jerusalem fall, they would lose their faith," he came up with a plan to capture the vital route to Jerusalem, to ensure that relief convoys could pass through the Jerusalem hills. Ultimately, the siege of Jerusalem was broken only in June, when, under Haganah supervision, hundreds of elderly workers managed to convert an overlooked shepherds' path through the mountains into a road, thus re-establishing Jerusalem's link with the coast. Ben-Gurion also masterminded a plan that left Israel in control of the Negev Desert. By mid-1949, Israel had reached armistice agreements with each of the warring Arab states. In another crucial decision as defense minister, Ben-Gurion ordered the disbanding of the Lehi and Irgun forces. He understood that a country must have only a single army, and to that end he thwarted the Irgun's attempt to maintain its own arsenal.

David Ben-Gurion went on to serve two terms as Israel's prime minister, the first from 1949 through 1953. Among his significant accomplishments during those years was the introduction of the Law of Return, one of the earliest and most significant of the basic laws of the Jewish state, which declares that every Jew has the right to settle in Israel. In presenting the bill to Israel's parliament, the

Knesset, for first reading, Ben-Gurion said, "This law lays down not that the State accords the right of settlement to Jews abroad but that this right is inherent in every Jew by virtue of his being a Jew if it but be his will to take part in settling the land. This right preceded the state of Israel, it is that which built the state." The Knesset passed the Law of Return on July 5, 1950, the anniversary of the death of Theodor Herzl, founder of political Zionism. As a result of Ben-Gurion's commitment to the principle underlying the law, the Jewish population of Israel doubled during his first term.

In foreign policy, Ben-Gurion undertook a controversial alliance that strengthened the economy of the new country. In 1951–52, he convinced his doubtful fellow citizens that it was to Israel's advantage to accept payment of millions of dollars in cash and goods from the new West German government. Ben-Gurion made it clear that nothing could make up for the death of Germany's millions of Jewish victims during the war. But, he argued, "Let not the murderers of our people also be the beneficiaries of its property!" The German aid, he asserted, could help Israel attend to the pressing needs of the hundreds of thousands of Holocaust survivors who now made their homes in Israel.

In 1953, Ben-Gurion resigned from office. He had decided, as he wrote to a Tel Aviv resident, that "it is possible to help in building up the country not only by standing at the head of the government." He then joined a kibbutz, or communal settlement, in the heart of the Negev Desert. At Kibbutz Sdeh Boker, Hebrew for cattle-rancher's field, the 67-year-old Ben-Gurion began his career by hauling manure, the same task he had carried out at Petah Tikvah 47 years earlier. But soon the kibbutz found more appropriate jobs for the former prime minister, such as

Ben-Gurion, far left, addresses members of the United Nations Special Commission on Palestine (UNSCOP) in 1947. On November 29, 1947, the UN General Assembly approved the committee's recommendation that Palestine be partitioned into two independent states, one Jewish, one Arab, with Jerusalem under international control.

feeding the kibbutz's newborn lambs and overseeing its small weather station. Ben-Gurion's work still left him much time for reading and studying.

A political crisis soon cut short Ben-Gurion's time at the kibbutz, however. In 1954, General Gamal Abdel Nasser took control of Egypt after overthrowing King Farouk. Nasser began to launch attacks on Israel and went on to form a close relationship with the Communist bloc, the group of nations under the influence of the Soviet Union. In the face of the new threat, Ben-Gurion was persuaded to return to government, first as defense minister and then in 1955 as prime minister. He remained prime minister until 1963. During this period, he successfully led Israel on the

offensive against Nasser in the Sinai Campaign of October 29–November 5, 1956. Ben-Gurion was bedridden with the flu for the duration of this short war but Israel still wrested control from Egypt of the Sinai Peninsula and the Gaza Strip. Although Israel was forced by world pressure to withdraw from the occupied territory, Ben-Gurion was able to announce over the radio to the Israeli army and citizenry that "there is no power in the world that can reverse your great victory. . . . Israel after the Sinai Campaign will never again be the Israel [that existed] prior to this mighty operation."

A year to the day after the beginning of the Sinai Campaign, Ben-Gurion survived an assassination attempt. He generously wrote the parents of the mentally ill would-be

assassin, "I wish you and your son good luck. May you succeed in educating the rest of your children to do good deeds and to love Israel."

Having survived the attempt on his life, Ben-Gurion was able to oversee the trial of a Nazi official who had sent millions of Jews to death camps during World War II. In May 1960, Ben-Gurion announced that Israel had seized Adolf Eichmann, who had been living in Argentina under an assumed name. Ben-Gurion was anxious to put Eichmann on trial so that young Israelis and the world at large would be reminded of why a strong Jewish state was needed. "For the first time in Jewish history," he stated, "historical justice is being done by the sovereign Jewish people." Eichmann was convicted of war crimes and executed in Israel in May 1962.

After years of success, Ben-Gurion lost some support during his last years as prime minister. Older members of his Mapai party resented his handling of a government scandal and his seeming preference for younger leadership. As a result, Ben-Gurion resigned as prime minister in 1963 and formed his own party. He continued to hold a seat in Israel's parliament but became less influential on the political scene. On the eve of Israel's Six-Day War of June 1967, much of the public urged him to lead a government of national unity in response to Egypt's new military threats. But when Ben-Gurion made clear his opposition to military action against Egypt, the public became aware that the military leader of two earlier wars had lost his daring. After Israel's stunning victory in the war, in which it captured significant territory from Egypt, Syria, and Jordan, Ben-Gurion increasingly seemed a man of the past. Dissatisfied with, rather than elated by, the results of the Six-Day War, Ben-Gurion felt that Israel should withdraw from all the occupied territories except Jerusalem. He worried that the attempt to rule a million Arabs would undermine Israel's democracy. Over Ben-Gurion's objections, his opposition faction merged with the Mapai party and in 1970 he resigned from Israel's parliament and retired to the Kibbutz Sdeh Boker.

Despite David Ben-Gurion's political eclipse, on October 16, 1971, the entire nation celebrated his 85th birthday as a national holiday. On that festive occasion, the Israeli cabinet came to Sdeh Boker to honor the man now universally recognized as the Father of the Nation.

Ben-Gurion lived to see yet another military engagement, the Yom Kippur War of October 1973. Just days before the war's outbreak, however, he suffered a brain hemorrhage that left him paralyzed and incapable of speech. The nation was aware that as it struggled for survival in this unforeseen war, the man who had brought the nation into being was also battling for his life. On December 1, 1973, David Ben-Gurion died. He was buried alongside his wife, who had died five years earlier. Their graves overlook the wilderness through which the ancient Hebrews made their way in biblical times, in the Jewish people's first struggle to make a home in the land of Israel.

FURTHER READING

Avi-hai, Avraham. *Ben-Gurion, State-Builder: Principles and Pragmatism, 1948–1963*. New Brunswick, N.J.: Transaction, 1974.

Bar-Zohar, Michael. *Ben-Gurion: A Biography*. Translated by Peretz Kidron. New York: Adama, 1977.

Ben-Gurion, David. *Israel: A Personal History*. New York: Sabra, 1972.

Kurzman, Dan. *Ben-Gurion: Prophet of Fire*. New York: Simon & Schuster, 1983.

Teveth, Shabtai. *Ben-Gurion and the Palestinian Arabs: From Peace to War*. Oxford: Oxford University Press, 1985.

———. *Ben-Gurion: The Burning Ground, 1886–1948*. Boston: Houghton Mifflin, 1987.

Vail, John J. *David Ben-Gurion*. New York: Chelsea House, 1987.

Zweig, Ronald W., ed. *David Ben-Gurion: Politics and Leadership in Israel*. London: Frank Cass, 1991.

Berl Katznelson

THE MASTER BUILDER

Many visitors to Israel choose to spend their time not as traditional tourists, whiling away leisurely hours in museums and at archaeological sites, sleeping in world-class hotels, and eating in fine restaurants. Instead they choose to volunteer their labor to an Israeli kibbutz, or collective settlement. On these settlements, members traditionally neither earn wages nor own private property. The needs of the members are provided for by the settlement. From the time the first kibbutz was founded in 1909, the kibbutz movement has stressed the importance of personal labor while valuing all kinds of work equally, whether in the fields or in the kitchen. Though only a small percentage of the population of Israel at any given time has ever chosen to live on a kibbutz, the movement has nevertheless played an important role in the development of the Jewish state. Even before statehood, kibbutz members helped grow crops on lands previously considered impossible to cultivate. Kibbutz members became leaders in the army that fought Israel's War of Independence and that continues to defend the state of Israel. The collective settlements also helped to absorb new immigrants, including children who came to Israel on their own.

One of the first people to grasp the central role of the kibbutz in the Jewish homeland was Berl Katznelson. But his contribution to the Jewish state went far beyond his ideas about the nature of the kibbutz movement. He also helped shape many institutions that thrived for decades in Israel and played an important role in shaping the nation's culture and moral tone. He has often been called the master builder of the early Jewish state.

Katznelson was born in 1887 in the small Jewish town of Bobruisk in the Russian Empire, in what is now the nation of Belarus. Berl was the first child from the second marriage of his father, Moshe, whose first wife died after giving birth to one son. After Berl's birth, Moshe Katznelson and his wife had five more children, of whom one died in infancy. A successful timber merchant, Moshe was able to support his large family. His business, however, kept him on the road, so that he was able to return home only twice a year, for the Jewish holidays in the fall and the spring.

Despite the extended absences, Berl was deeply influenced by his father. Moshe was not only a businessman but also a scholar whose large library included Jewish religious works, novels and philosophical works by Russian writers, Yiddish literature, and the latest Hebrew journals. Since Berl

"What I want is to go to Erez Israel, to do something worthwhile, to light a little spark. I am drawn to the stubborn, hard-working few who have abandoned everything they had here to begin a new life and free themselves of Exile."

—from a 1908 letter to his brother Hayim

was a sickly child, his formal education began and ended with *heder*, or private Jewish elementary school, where he learned the basics of Hebrew, the Bible, and Jewish observance. In addition to being tutored privately in various religious and secular subjects, Berl continued his education on his own in his father's library.

Berl's father belonged to a group known as the Lovers of Zion, which reacted to the periodic pogroms ("riots") against the Jews of Russia in 1881 by looking toward the land of Israel, then called Palestine, as a new homeland for the Jewish people. Berl's exposure to Zionism—the movement supporting the development of a Jewish home in Palestine—deepened when one of his tutors introduced him to a Zionist group in nearby Bobruisk. The members of this group, though much older than Berl, helped him focus his Zionist beliefs. Later he met other young Zionists elsewhere in Russia who were interested primarily in labor issues. These Zionists argued that by having a country of their own, the Jews could become a "normal" people with masses of workers engaged in meaningful work. They believed that a Jewish homeland could be built only through the physical labor of the Jews themselves.

Another important childhood influence on Berl was his uncle Leib, who became his father's business partner. Leib was among the many Russians desiring a revolution to abolish the government of the czar, Russia's tyrannical ruler. Like other revolutionaries, Berl's uncle Leib believed that Russia could become a just society only if its workers were treated with dignity and the rights of all individuals were respected. Berl participated in lively political discussions with his father and uncle and read revolutionary literature. He was impressed by the writers' conviction that the working masses could be educated to understand the causes of their misery so that they would then join together, overthrow their oppressors, and create a just society.

Berl was only 12 when his father caught pneumonia during a business trip and died at the age of 37. The family was now left in the hands of his mother, who supported her children by opening a stall in the local market. There she sold rope, felt shoes, and gloves to the peasants who came from the surrounding areas. Berl soon left home and spent the next 10 years or so wandering through Russia and Ukraine in an attempt to broaden his education. At one point during these

wanderings, in 1904, he was in a small town when an anti-Jewish pogrom broke out; reacting decisively, he helped the local Jews collect weapons for self-defense.

Just before his 18th birthday, in January 1905, Katznelson was prepared to leave the Russian Empire for Zurich, Switzerland, where he hoped to enter the university. His plans were changed by a shattering event. On a day known ever after as Bloody Sunday, thousands of unarmed workers marched to the Winter Palace in St. Petersburg, petitioning the czar for reforms. Government troops opened fire on the marchers, killing and wounding hundreds. The slaughter touched off a wave of protest; for the rest of the year, Russia was convulsed by revolutionary upheavals. Katznelson decided to stay and further the revolutionary cause. He never attended a university.

Though the Revolution of 1905 failed to topple the czar, Katznelson continued working for the cause. He allied himself with a number of political parties, becoming disillusioned with each in turn. Then in 1907 he decided to become a worker himself, and for the next two years he attempted unsuccessfully to learn a trade. After first contemplating a move to the United States, to which two of his brothers had previously emigrated, Berl finally decided to move to Palestine. An award he received for putting together a catalog of Hebrew and Russian books in Bobruisk's Jewish library enabled him to pay for his passage. After recovering from a lengthy illness, he set sail for Palestine in 1909.

Katznelson was now 22 years old. For the next year he worked as a laborer in a number of Jewish colonies. At one colony he helped set up a club to improve the workers' cultural life: with dues contributed by the workers, the club purchased newspapers and occasionally brought in a lecturer. At this time, Katznelson began to form his own idea of the ideal Zionist agricultural labor settlement, whose members would perform all the work without relying on outside hired help. Katznelson's first significant labor activity in Palestine was his role in a workers' strike on a farm in the Galilee region. There he drew up a petition listing the workers' demands for improved living conditions. The strikers succeeded in having the farm's manager removed and replaced by one who brought about the desired reforms.

Katznelson later worked in Judea, the southern region of Palestine. In 1911 he was chosen to represent a group of workers at the Conference of Judean Workers. At this conference, Katznelson proposed that a health fund for workers be established from members' contributions. The delegates adopted his idea and went on to establish the forerunner of Israel's national health service. At the following year's conference, asked to deliver the opening address, Katznelson spoke about the need for Jewish settlements whose workers and families would be self-supporting by working their own farms. Within a few years, Katznelson had become the spokesman for the workers of the agricultural settlements.

During World War I, the British seized control of Palestine from the Ottoman Turks. Toward the end of the war, Katznelson joined the Jewish Legion, made up of Palestinian Jewish volunteers seeking to fight in the British army for the liberation of Palestine from Ottoman rule. Like many other Palestinian Jews who volunteered to serve in the legion, he was embarrassed that soldiers from the British Empire were shedding their blood on behalf of Palestine's Jews while the Jews themselves stood by as mere observers. In addition, Katznelson and other volunteers to the legion believed that fighting for Palestine would strengthen their claim to the land and also provide the practical experience they would later need to raise an effective army for a future Jewish state. Katznelson was not an outstanding soldier, but while training in Egypt with the Battalion he developed an important relationship with another Jewish soldier, David Ben-Gurion, who would become Israel's first prime minister.

After the war, Katznelson and Ben-Gurion established a workers' organization called Unity of Labor. This group was the forerunner of the Mapai labor party, which was the dominant force in Israeli society from its formation in 1929 until 1977. With the establishment of this new organization, the labor movement emerged as a significant force in Jewish Palestine. Although Katznelson shunned elective positions, he became the behind-the-scenes leader of the labor movement.

Katznelson played a major role in establishing some of the institutions that guided the Jewish state through its first half-century. In addition to his role in creating the labor party, in December 1920 he also helped establish the Histadrut, or General Federation of Jewish Workers in Palestine. For many years the Histadrut was not only the largest labor union and

Berl Katznelson

BORN

January 25, 1887
Bobruisk, Russia

DIED

August 15, 1944
Jerusalem, Palestine

EDUCATION

Privately tutored and otherwise self-taught

ACCOMPLISHMENTS

Cofounder of Unity of Labor, a Zionist labor party and forerunner of the Israeli Labor party that dominated Israeli politics until 1977; edited the labor daily *Davar* (1925–44); established and served as editor-in-chief of the Histadrut's publishing house, Am Oved biggest voluntary organization in Israel but also the largest Jewish labor organization in the world.

Katznelson also left an imprint on the kibbutz movement. He called attention to the rivalries among different types of kibbutzim, which included those committed to building a socialist society; those with less rigid political views; and those with a religious, rather than a political orientation. Aware that these different social visions sometimes led kibbutzim to put their own particular interests ahead of the overall welfare of the Jewish settlements in Palestine, Katznelson attempted to unite the entire kibbutz movement in the 1930s. Although he did not succeed in this attempt, his focus on the problems caused by ideological antagonism helped concentrate the attention of all kibbutzim on the common goal of serving the community as a whole.

Katznelson was highly effective in shaping the culture of Jewish Palestine. In 1925 he became the editor of the first daily newspaper of the entire Palestinian Jewish labor movement, *Davar*. The newspaper's name is a Hebrew word that usually means "speech" or "word" but can also suggest "vision" or "prophecy." Katznelson always retained his early belief that society could be changed by educating the masses. He was able to convince the novelist and short-story writer S. Y. Agnon, who, in 1966, would become the first Hebrew writer to win the Nobel Prize for Literature, to become a regular contributor to *Davar*.

Among that paper's important contributions was its opposition to developments in Soviet Russia. The Soviet Revolution of 1917 had finally overthrown the czar, but instead of bringing about a just society based on human dignity, it introduced its own forms of tyranny and terror. While other factions in the Palestinian labor movement continued to support the Soviet Union, Katznelson's *Davar* exposed and denounced its failure to live up to the goals of the revolution. In general, *Davar* shaped the outlook of the majority of Jewish Palestinians for two generations.

Katznelson's second major contribution to the culture of Jewish Palestine was a new publishing house, called Am Oved, Hebrew for "working nation." He conceived the idea for this publishing house during World War II. Realizing that he could do little to keep the Nazi regime from destroying European Jewry, Katznelson felt he could at least help educate the new Jewish society in Palestine. Thus, he published several series of books aimed at workers and their families: titles for adults, including modern Hebrew literature and political works translated from other languages; books for children and young adults, to teach them about Jewish history and the pioneering efforts of the Palestinian Jews; and others focusing on wartime problems. Like *Davar*, Am Oved affected the thinking of large numbers of Jews. In 1942–43, when there were only 450,000 Jews in Palestine, Am Oved sold nearly 150,000 books.

Finally, Katznelson did much to shape the moral tone of Jewish Palestine. Just as his newspaper, *Davar*, argued against Soviet terror, it also cautioned against acts of Jewish terror. During the 1920s and 1930s, for example, Palestinian Arabs periodically attacked Jewish settlers. *Davar* published articles warning against revenge. The newspaper printed articles headlined "Gleams of Light in the Darkness," describing the efforts of individual Arabs to protect Jews from rioters, sometimes at great personal risk. Katznelson firmly believed that a just nation could not participate in acts of savage retribution.

Katznelson also served as a model of personal morality for other Jewish Palestinians by exemplifying the need to come to the aid of Jews elsewhere. After the Nazis began to persecute the Jews of Europe, many of those Jews sought refuge in other countries, but few countries welcomed these Jewish refugees. At the same time, Great Britain began to reduce the numbers of Jews permitted to enter Palestine as legal immigrants. Katznelson became the unofficial head of the movement to smuggle Jews out of Europe and bring them into Palestine as illegal immigrants. At Zionist Congresses abroad and within the Jewish settlement in Palestine he urged others to contribute either funds or manpower to the movement, arguing, "From now on, not the pioneer but the refugee will lead us." Among those who rallied to Katznelson's call was Hungarian-born Hannah Szenes, who had immigrated to Palestine in 1939. At the end of 1942, concerned with the fate not only of her mother in Budapest but also of all of the Jews trapped in Europe, she joined a group of parachutists entering into Nazi-held territory to try to aid Jewish survivors. Arrested and tortured by the Hungarian police, she refused to inform on her colleagues and was executed by a firing squad in November 1944.

Katznelson also helped influence the moral tone of the Haganah, the forerunner of the Israeli army. The Haganah, established in 1920, responded to acts of Arab terror and also helped immigrants enter Jewish Palestine by eluding British officials. Katznelson, who abhorred terrorism of any kind, urged the Haganah to follow a policy of self-restraint in dealing both with Arab terrorists and with unsympathetic British personnel.

Despite his vital role in shaping the society that would become the state of Israel within four years of his death, Katznelson's personal life was unhappy. He and his life companion, Leah, were unable to have children. His childlessness seemed a mark of failure to him, and his relationship with Leah soured over the years. Katznelson also tended to focus on his failures, such as his inability to unite the kibbutz movement, rather than on his successes. He refused to live a comfortable life. Because he would not buy a car, he had to wait for offers of rides to return home from the many meetings he attended. And since he did not have a radio, he would stand under a neighbor's window to hear the news broadcasts. He never owned a wristwatch, and not until the 1930s did he and Leah own a clock—but only because his doctor gave him one, so that Katznelson could take his medications at the right times. Despite his doctor's best efforts, Katznelson's health declined over the years until he died of a brain hemorrhage in 1944, at the age of 57.

Although his name is not a household word, Berl Katznelson was one of the main architects of modern Israel. While other shapers of Jewish tradition have come to be known for one or two great achievements, Katznelson achieved a number of small successes that combined into a significant whole. His life's work shows how he lived up to an ideal he promulgated in an article published in a biweekly labor newspaper in 1911, to be "not merely interested in the Land of Israel, but dedicated . . . to a life of labor and liberation of the personality."

FURTHER READING

"Berl Katznelson." In *The Zionist Idea: A Historical Analysis and Reader*. Edited by Arthur Hertzberg. New York: Atheneum, 1959.

Katznelson, Berl. "On the Question of Languages." In *Language in Time of Revolution*. Edited by Benjamin Harshav. Berkeley: University of California Press, 1993.

Shapira, Anita. *Berl: The Biography of a Socialist Zionist*. Cambridge: Cambridge University Press, 1984.

Golda Meir

ISRAEL'S
UNCROWNED QUEEN

Although women have served as cabinet members in the United States government since 1933, the United States has yet to have a woman president. The state of Israel, however, had a woman in its first cabinet, the same woman who later served as prime minister for five years. Interestingly enough, this woman, Golda Meir, grew up and was educated in the United States.

Meir was born Golda Mabovitch in 1898 in Kiev, today the capital of Ukraine but then part of Russia. Her father, Moshe, was a skilled carpenter but was unable to make a good living because of Russian discrimination against Jews. For a while her mother, Bluma, who had seen five of her children die in infancy, helped support the family by nursing a child of well-to-do neighbors. One of Golda's earliest memories was the sight of her father boarding up the doors and windows of their home one night in 1902. In response to Golda's questions, he explained that a pogrom, a murderous attack against the Jews, was expected. None occurred in Kiev that night, but the following year in Kishinev, another Russian city, one of the worst pogroms in history erupted. Rather than protect the Jews of Kishinev from the violent mob, the police either stood by passively or disarmed the Jews who tried to defend themselves. Only five years old at the time, Golda joined the day-long fast organized by Jewish communities throughout Russia to protest the Kishinev pogrom.

Earlier in 1903, Golda's father had decided, like many other Russian Jews, to seek a better life in the United States. He traveled there alone, intending to send for his family after he was able to support them. The family now consisted of 14-year-old Sheyna, 5-year-old Golda, and a baby sister, Tzipke. The girls and their mother moved to the city of Pinsk, where they lived for several years with Bluma's father.

In Pinsk, Sheyna emerged as the primary influence on Golda. Instead of attending school, Golda remained at home, where Sheyna tutored her. More important, Sheyna's example had a powerful effect on Golda's future social and political ideals. Like many other young Russians in the early 20th century, Sheyna became involved in the movement to overthrow the tyrannical Russian czar, and she often held meetings at home. Although Golda was then only a little girl, she would sit in the back of the room, listening eagerly. Through her sister's friends she learned about efforts to improve the lot of working people. She also heard about the Zionist movement, which aimed to establish a Jewish homeland in the ancient land of Israel,

The girl who would grow up to be Golda Meir portrays the Statue of Liberty in a school pageant in Milwaukee. More than 60 years later, Meir explained to a group of American feminists why, after having found freedom from Russian anti-Semitism in America, she did not stay there: "I left to help build a nation of our own."

where the last independent Jewish government had been destroyed more than 1,800 years earlier. Although the Jews often called the land of Israel by its poetic name, Zion, the world at large knew it as Palestine.

As Sheyna became more and more deeply involved in revolutionary activity, her mother became increasingly concerned about the family's safety. She contacted her husband, urging him to send money for the family's passage. Finally, in 1906 the Mabovitches were reunited in Milwaukee, Wisconsin, where Moshe had settled.

In Milwaukee, at the age of eight, Golda began her formal education. She became a star pupil at the Fourth Street School, which decades later was renamed the Golda Meir School for Gifted and Talented Children. Although Golda soon adjusted to life in her new home, Sheyna was now unhappy. She missed her Russian comrades, in particular her boyfriend, Shamai. She refused to help her mother in the grocery store Bluma had opened. Instead, she left her parents' home and found a job in a factory. When Shamai came to join Sheyna in Milwaukee, the Mabovitches objected to the relationship and the couple left for Denver, Colorado. After Sheyna recovered from a bout of tuberculosis at the Jewish Hospital for Consumptives there, she and Shamai were married. Sheyna's parents severed their relationship with their rebellious daughter, but Golda kept up a correspondence with her older sister.

Meanwhile, Golda exhibited the deep sense of social responsibility she had absorbed from her sister. In those days, students in the Milwaukee public schools had to pay a fee for their textbooks, and Golda knew that the poorer children in her school could not afford to pay it. So, together with her best friend, Golda organized the American Young Sisters Society. At an evening event sponsored by the society, Golda's appeal to the audience proved so persuasive that enough money was donated to buy books for all the needy children in the school. These fundraising skills were to come in handy later in her life.

After Golda had been helping her mother in the store for six years, she had a serious falling out with her parents. She wanted to go on to high school, with the goal of becoming a teacher. At that time, high school attendance was not routine: children were required to attend school only until the age of 14, and parents who were not well off usually needed their children to begin earning money as soon as possible. Arguing that "Young women should seek husbands, not education," Golda's parents wanted her to get married and work full-time in their store. Nevertheless, over her parents' objections, Golda began attending North Division High School in the fall of 1912, earning spending money at a variety of part-time jobs. But when her parents began arranging a marriage for their 14-year-old daughter with a man more than twice her age, she ran away from home to Denver, where she moved in with Sheyna and Shamai. There she attended high school and helped out in Shamai's dry-cleaning shop.

Just as Sheyna's home in Pinsk had been a meeting place for young revolutionaries, her apartment in Denver also drew young Jewish activists. After listening to Sheyna's colleagues put forth a variety of ideas about how to improve the future of humanity in general and of the Jews in particular, Golda found herself drawn to the ideas of the Labor Zionists. They believed that by working the land of Israel with their own hands, Jews would prove to the world that they had a right to reestablish a Jewish home there. To help buy land for the Jewish settlers in Palestine, Golda began to raise money for the Jewish National Fund on the streets of Denver.

At one meeting in Sheyna's apartment, Golda met her future husband, Morris Meyerson, a self-educated man who was more interested in literature, music, and art than in reclaiming Zion. Despite the differences in their political views, the two became deeply attached to each other. Sheyna now found herself objecting to the amount of time Golda was spending with Meyerson instead of on her schoolwork. After the sisters argued inconclusively for a year, Golda moved out. In order to support herself, she had to drop out of school. Even though she spent her days working first in a laundry and then in a department store, she did not ignore her education. She asked Meyerson for a reading list, spent hours discussing poetry with him, and attended free lectures and concerts in his company.

Eventually, the Mabovitches learned of Golda's situation and convinced her to return to Milwaukee, even though doing so would mean leaving Meyerson behind. The Mabovitches agreed to let Golda attend high school, which she completed in less than two years, then go on for teacher training. By now, Golda's parents had also become involved in Zionism, and during World War I their home became a meeting place for volunteers to the Jewish Legion, the Jewish unit within the British army that hoped to liberate Palestine from the Ottoman Turks.

Now 17, Golda wanted to join the Jewish Legion herself but was disturbed to learn that they did not accept women. In theory her age also disqualified her from membership in Poalei Zion (the Workers of Zion), a branch of the Labor Zionist movement, which sought to combine Zionist and socialist ideals. (Socialism calls for the control of industries, land, and capital by the workers, the government, or the community as a whole.) Nonetheless, she succeeded in obtaining admission to that group. When Poalei Zion opened a part-time school at Milwaukee's Jewish Center, Golda began teaching Yiddish there several afternoons a week.

A turning point in Golda's life came with the issuance of the Balfour Declaration on November 2, 1917. In this document, Great Britain expressed its support for a Jewish homeland in Palestine. Golda felt the time had now come to put her beliefs into action. Although Meyerson did not share her Zionist dream, he dreaded the thought of losing her. The couple were married the following month, and in May 1921 they set sail for Palestine.

In the years between her marriage and her departure for Palestine, Golda set her sights on joining Kibbutz Merhavia (Hebrew for "God's wide space"). Only on a kibbutz, she was convinced, could she advance the Labor Zionist goal of reclaiming the land through productive labor. Like other kibbutzim, Merhavia was an agricultural community whose members owned nothing as individuals. The members of the kibbutz made all decisions together and shared equally in the work and the profits. In 1921, Merhavia had 40 members, 32 men and 8 women. At first, the members of the kibbutz were wary of accepting the Meyersons. The members did not feel ready to support any children the couple might have, and to some of

them Golda seemed like a spoiled American. But during a trial period, Golda soon impressed the members by working hard at a variety of jobs without complaint. She truly believed that each task—whether it was picking almonds, cooking for her comrades, or raising poultry—helped build the Jewish homeland. Within a year of the Meyersons' arrival, Golda was not only elected to the kibbutz's steering committee but also chosen as Merhavia's representative to the Histadrut, the main organization of Palestine's Jewish workers.

While Golda flourished at Merhavia, Morris declined. A very private person, he found the communal life of the kibbutz stifling. In addition, his health suffered because Merhavia was located in the Valley of Jezreel, which at the time was infested with malaria. Furthermore, he rejected the idea that the kibbutz as a whole should raise its members' children. After two and a half years, when the couple decided to start a family, Golda reluctantly agreed to leave Merhavia.

Eventually the Meyersons moved to Jerusalem, where the tables were turned: there, Morris was delighted with life in the ancient city, while Golda missed the communal atmosphere and shared sense of purpose she had enjoyed at Merhavia. They both found work with the Histadrut. Less than a year after their move, the Meyersons became the parents of a son, Menachem. When the baby was four months old, Golda left Morris and went back to Merhavia, taking Menachem with her. But she rejoined her husband after six months, determined to give the marriage a second chance. Then, in 1926, the Meyersons had a second child, Sarah. The family led a hand-to-mouth existence. When Menachem began nursery school, Golda took on the job of school laundress to cover the tuition. She later supplemented the family income

"My vision of our future? A Jewish state in which masses of Jews from all over the world will continue to settle and to build; an Israel bound in a collaborative effort with its neighbors on behalf of all the people of this region; an Israel that remains a flourishing democracy and a society resting firmly on social justice and equality."

—from My Life (1975)

by teaching English in a private school. Deep down, though, she knew that this was not the life she had sought in Palestine. In 1928, after much soul searching, she asked Morris to understand her decision to spend less time as a mother and more as an active builder of the Jewish homeland.

When news of Golda's decision spread, the Histadrut asked her to become secretary of its Women's Labor Council. In that capacity, she helped establish training farms to teach women pioneers how to till Palestine's rocky soil. She also set up day-care facilities to ease the lives of working mothers. Her work often required her to travel to the United States and England. She learned to accustom herself to feelings of guilt at leaving Menachem and Sarah behind. Once, in 1932, the Histadrut sent her to the United States for two years as national secretary of Pioneer Women, the sister organization to Palestine's Women's Labor Council. This time Golda took both children with her, leaving her husband behind.

Upon her return to Palestine, Golda was asked to take on a series of increasingly responsible jobs in the Histadrut. Her satisfaction with her growing role in the labor movement was offset, however, by the worsening situation of Europe's Jews. When Adolf Hitler came to power in Germany in 1933, he began to carry out his often-stated threats against the Jews. Then, as the rate of Jewish immigration from Germany to Palestine began to rise, Palestine's Arabs began to riot in protest. The British government, in control of Palestine since the end of World War I, resolved to clamp down on Jewish immigration. As a result, after World War II broke out in 1939 Golda found herself working both with the British and against them. She helped organize Jewish contributions to the British war effort but also joined Palestine's underground defense organization, the Haganah. As a member of that organization, she broke British law by helping to smuggle in Jewish refugees whom the British considered illegal immigrants.

In 1941, Golda and Morris Meyerson finally separated. In her memoirs, Golda later wrote, "What I do regret—and bitterly so—is that although Morris and I remained married to each other and loving each other until the day he died in my house in 1951 (when, symbolically enough, I was away), I was not able to make a success of our marriage after all."

After the war's conclusion, Golda Meyerson began to rise to positions of national responsibility. In 1946 she was asked to head the political department of the Jewish Agency, which then served as the interim government of the projected Jewish state. In that position, Meyerson volunteered to travel to the United States to raise funds for arms at the end of 1947, when it became clear that the Arabs would declare war on the Jewish state as soon as it was established. In contrast with the Arab armies, the Haganah was woefully unprepared for war. Among other things, it lacked artillery, armored vehicles, and aircraft. In her first speech to an American audience, Meyerson announced: "Every Jew in the country knows that within a few months a Jewish state in Palestine will be established. . . . You cannot decide whether we will fight or not. We will. . . . You can change only one thing—whether we shall be victorious. . . . Whether we live or not, this is a decision you have to make." When Meyerson returned to Palestine after two and a half months with $50 million in contributions, David Ben-Gurion, soon to be the prime minister of the new Jewish state, said, "Some-day when history will be written, it

Golda Meir, second from right, survives a vote of confidence during a stormy session of Israel's parliament in 1971. A little more than three years later, Meir resigned as prime minister in the aftermath of the Yom Kippur War of 1973, which took a heavy toll on Israel.

will be said that there was a Jewish woman who got the money which made the state possible."

As head of the Jewish Agency's political department, Meyerson was next asked to take on an assignment closer to home that entailed great personal risk. This job was to conduct secret talks with King Abdullah of Transjordan (now the major part of the Kingdom of Jordan), who was believed to be more open than other Arab rulers to peaceful coexistence with Palestine's Jews. Meyerson's second meeting with the king required her to travel by car to Amman, the king's capital, dressed as an Arab woman, and to pass through 10 Arab checkpoints in each direction.

Meyerson's efforts failed to prevent the king from yielding to Arab pressure and joining the war against Israel. Nevertheless, they proved without a doubt that Meyerson was ready to lay her life on the line to advance the interests of her nation.

On May 14, 1948, Golda Meyerson had the honor of signing the Declaration of Independence that signaled the birth of the state of Israel. As she later wrote, "All I recall about my actual signing of the proclamation is that I was crying openly, not able even to wipe the tears from my face." She soon was chosen the new state's first ambassador to the Soviet Union. Although she felt frustrated by her inability to establish firm ties between

the Soviet Union and Israel, she was heartened to discover that many Soviet Jews chose to identify themselves as Jews, despite the antireligious, anti-Jewish policies of their government. When thousands of Jews thronged the Great Synagogue in Moscow to join her and the Israeli delegation on the Jewish New Year in 1948, Meyerson was so overwhelmed that all she could say was, "Thank you for having remained Jews."

In January 1949, David Ben-Gurion, the first prime minister of Israel, asked Meyerson to serve in the new nation's first cabinet as labor minister. Israel's Law of Return soon opened the nation's doors to all Jews seeking to make their homes there,

Golda Meir addresses the Council of Europe in Strasbourg, France, a few days before the outbreak of the Yom Kippur War in October 1973. While in Europe, Meir learned that Arab troops were amassing on the Golan Heights.

and Meyerson's new position involved finding housing and jobs for these thousands of newcomers. Under her supervision, the labor ministry not only oversaw the construction of projects to house the immigrants but also trained 30,000 of them for jobs.

In 1956, Ben-Gurion asked Meyerson to change both her job and her name. If she were to accept the offer to serve as Israel's foreign minister, she would have to use a Hebrew last name. Out of respect for her deceased husband, she chose a Hebrew name, Meir (in Hebrew "to illuminate"), that sounded similar to Meyerson. From 1956 until her death 22 years later, the former Golda Meyerson became known throughout the world as Golda Meir.

As foreign minister, Meir faced one of her greatest challenges when hostile moves by Egypt led Israel to launch the Sinai Campaign of late October 1956. Although Israel won an astonishing victory in a matter of days, world opinion demanded that the Jewish state withdraw from the extensive territory it had conquered. Defending Israel before the United Nations, Meir declared, "We desire nothing more than peace, but we cannot equate peace merely with an apathetic readiness to be destroyed." In March 1957, when the political pressure became overwhelming, Meir announced to the world body that Israel would withdraw completely from Egyptian soil.

On the other hand, Meir's greatest satisfaction as foreign minister derived from Israel's relations with the nations of sub-Saharan Africa as they emerged from European colonial domination. Between 1958 and 1973, thousands of Africans received training in Israel in a variety of fields, including agriculture, public health, and education. At the same time, thousands of Israelis visited the developing African republics to share their expertise in those and other fields. In her memoirs Meir reflected, "I am prouder of Israel's International Cooperation Program and of the technical aid we gave to the people of Africa than I am of any other single project we have ever undertaken. For me, more than anything else, that program typifies the drive toward social justice, reconstruction and rehabilitation that is at the very heart of Labor Zionism—and Judaism."

In 1963, while serving as foreign minister, Meir learned that she had cancer of the lymphatic system. Resolved to continue working, she kept her health problems secret. Since in a small country there was no way to keep her frequent hospital visits from public knowledge, she told those who asked that she suffered from frequent dehydration. Still, recognizing that she could not ignore her physicians' advice, she cut back a little on her responsibilities. She resigned her cabinet position in the fall of 1965 but kept her seat in Israel's parliament and her membership on the executive board of Mapai, the labor party. In February 1966, the party asked her to become its secretary in order to help combat the dissension that was threatening party unity. While serving in this role, she nervously watched Israel's Arab enemies continue to threaten her country, then had the satisfaction of watching Israel achieve a stunning victory in the Six-Day War of June 1967.

In 1969, Israeli prime minister Levi Eshkol died suddenly of a heart attack. Unaware of Meir's own health problems, the party then turned to Meir to lead the country. Despite her continued regular treatments, Prime Minister Meir vigorously carried out the responsibilities of office but failed herself and the country in one crucial respect. As Israel's head of state, she was at the country's helm when Egypt and Syria attacked on October 6, 1973. Because the conflict broke out on the holiest day of the Jewish calendar, it became known as the Yom Kippur War. For some time, Prime Minister Meir had suspected that an all-out Arab attack could come at any moment. She allowed herself, however, to be dissuaded by her defense minister, other military advisers, and intelligence officers. When their advice proved wrong, the country found itself unprepared for war. As Meir wrote in her memoirs, "I should have listened to the warnings of my own heart and ordered a callup. . . . I shall never again be the person I was before the Yom Kippur War." Even though Israel prevailed once again, with the help of its American-made weapons and warplanes, the war took a heavy toll on the small nation: more than 2,500 Israelis, or 1 out of every 1,000 citizens, died in the fighting. In the war's aftermath, the public looked about for scapegoats. When not only the opposition but even members of her own party began to criticize her defense minister, Meir decided to step down. Accordingly, on April 10, 1974, she announced her resignation.

In the last years of her life, Meir completed her memoirs, which were published in English in 1975 under the title *My Life*. Her last years were marred by disappointment over the political direction the country was taking and by increasing physical pain. In 1977, for the first time since Israel had been founded, the voters failed to give the Mapai party a majority in the Knesset, Israel's parliament. Menachem Begin, who had been a thorn in the side of the labor movement for decades, became prime minister. Although Meir was pleased that Egyptian president Anwar Sadat offered a peace initiative and visited Israel on Begin's watch, she was deeply disturbed when critics accused her of passing up earlier opportunities to make peace. She spent her last

months planning to set the record straight in a press conference. To prepare for it, she sought classified documents, which Begin released to her only reluctantly.

This press conference never took place. On October 19, 1978, Golda Meir was admitted for the last time to Jerusalem's Hadassah Hospital, where she died on December 8. After her death, the public learned for the first time of the cancer that had been ravaging her for 15 years.

Meir's funeral was held in a driving rain on December 12, 1978. Although, in accordance with Meir's request, there were no eulogies, admirers around the world paid tribute to her dedication to the Jewish state. A French newspaper called her "Israel's uncrowned queen." In another tribute, an American newscaster said, "She lived a life under pressure that we in this country would find impossible to understand. She is the strongest woman to head a government in our time and for a very long time past."

FURTHER READING

Avallone, Michael. *A Woman Called Golda*. New York: Ivy Books, 1982.

Christman, Henry M., ed. *This Is Our Strength: Selected Papers of Golda Meir*. New York: Macmillan, 1962.

McAuley, Karen. *Golda Meir*. New York: Chelsea House, 1985.

Martin, Ralph P. *Golda: The Romantic Years*. New York: Ivy Books, 1990.

Meir, Golda. *My Life*. New York: Putnam, 1975.

Meir, Menahem. *My Mother Golda Meir: A Son's Evocation of Life with Golda Meir*. New York: William Morrow, 1983.

Slater, Robert. *Golda: The Uncrowned Queen of Israel*. Middle Village, N.Y.: Jonathan David, 1981.

Syrkin, Marie. *Golda Meir: Woman with a Cause*. New York: Putnam, 1963.

Golda Meir

BORN

May 3, 1898
Kiev, Russia

DIED

December 8, 1978
Jerusalem, Israel

EDUCATION

Attended Milwaukee Normal School for Teachers (1916)

ACCOMPLISHMENTS

Secretary, Histadrut's Women's Labor Council (1928–32) and member of its executive committee (1934–39); was a signatory of Israel's Declaration of Independence (1948); served as Israel's ambassador to the Soviet Union (1948), minister of labor (1949–56), and foreign minister (1956–65); secretary-general of the Mapai party (1966–67); helped merge Mapai with two opposition parties into the Israel Labor party (1967); prime minister of Israel (1969–74)

Menachem Begin

"JERUSALEM IS OURS"

In 1993, the Nobel Peace Prize was shared by three political leaders: Prime Minister Yitzhak Rabin and Foreign Minister Shimon Peres of Israel, and the president of the Palestine Liberation Organization, Yasir Arafat. Around the world, eyebrows were raised at the thought that Arafat, a terrorist with the blood of many innocent people on his hands, should be honored as a Nobel laureate. However, 1993 was not the first time the Nobel Peace Prize was bestowed upon a Middle Eastern leader with a terrorist past. Fifteen years earlier, in 1978, the prestigious prize had been shared by Egyptian president Anwar Sadat and Israeli prime minister Menachem Begin for their efforts in forging the first peace agreement between Israel and an Arab country. In that case it was the Israeli, not the Arab, who had the terrorist past.

Menachem Begin's contribution to the state of Israel was a combination of belligerency and peacemaking. He was from boyhood a different type of Zionist than David Ben-Gurion, Israel's first prime minister, and Chaim Weizmann, its first president, for example. He shared with these other Zionist leaders the basic Zionist belief that the Jewish people could find dignity only by creating a Jewish state in Palestine, the biblical land of Israel. He differed, however, in the means of reaching this goal and in the extent to which it should be pursued.

Ben-Gurion and Weizmann typified mainstream Zionism, and believed that by buying land in Palestine and working it with their own hands Jews could prove to the world their right to their own country. They also believed that by working gradually toward nationhood they would prove to the major powers of the world that the Zionist dream was a just cause deserving of international support. Mainstream Zionists were also willing to accept a partial fulfillment of their dream. When, in November 1947, the United Nations voted to partition Palestine into a Jewish state and an Arab state, mainline Zionists were swayed by the argument that half a loaf is better than none. They accepted the idea that the boundaries of the new Jewish state would not include all the territory that in ancient times had belonged to the Jewish people.

Menachem Begin, on the other hand, was a member of a breakaway Zionist faction called the Revisionists. This group believed in military solutions to political problems. Even the name of the Revisionist movement's youth organization, Betar, alludes to its conviction that only through armed conflict would Zionist goals prevail. Betar's name derives from two Hebrew words, Brit Trumpeldor, or Trumpeldor's Covenant. Joseph Trumpeldor (1880–1920),

Menachem Begin addresses a crowd in 1949 at New York's Yeshiva University. Like other Zionist Revisionists, Begin believed in the establishment of a Jewish state with a Jewish majority in the entire territory of Palestine, "on both sides of the Jordan."

who died defending the Jewish settlement Tel Hai against Arab attackers, became a symbol of the armed defense of Palestine. His last words are said to have been, "Never mind; it is good to die for our country."

From the Revisionist point of view, terrorist acts alone were capable of persuading the British, who controlled Palestine in the years between 1918 and 1948, to yield control of the land to the Jews. The Revisionists also held that every bit of land that had been occupied by the Jews in biblical times should be part of the modern Jewish state. In short, Begin believed that God had given the Jewish people the right to claim the entire land of Israel. But he also understood the value of peace. For this reason, both his Nobel laureate successors Rabin and Peres—in their willingness to give up some territory for the sake of peace—and their opponents—who claim that giving up an inch of Israel's land is a transgression of God's will—can claim to be working within the tradition of Begin.

Menachem Begin was born in 1913, 12 years before the official founding of the Revisionist movement. His home town was Brest-Litovsk, then part of the Russian Empire. A majority of the town's population was Jewish. Begin's father, Zev Dov, an early adherent of the Zionist movement, spoke Hebrew with his three children, an unusual practice at a time when most Jews spoke Yiddish. Later, when the Begin children entered the university and had to fill out official forms, they always wrote "Hebrew" as their native language. One of Begin's early memories was of his father returning home from a skirmish with a Polish sergeant, whom he hit with his cane for trying to cut off the beard of a rabbi with whom Zev Dov was walking. The rabbi and Zev Dov were both arrested and severely beaten, but Begin's father told his family how pleased he was to have had the chance to defend the honor of the Jewish people. Begin later wrote that he remembered "these two things from my childhood: Jews being persecuted and the courage of the Jews."

After attending an elementary school run in Hebrew by a religious Zionist party, Menachem went on to Brest-Litovsk's high school, where there were only three other Jewish students, and graduated with honors. While in high school, Menachem joined Betar, the youth arm of the Revisionists, whose members wore uniforms and participated in military drills. At 18 he left home to study law at the University of Warsaw. Since the family did not have enough money to support him during his studies, he worked his way through law school. Begin never practiced law, however. After serving as the leader of Betar in Czechoslovakia, he became the movement's chief organizer in Poland in the spring of 1939. That May, he and his bride, Aliza, herself a Betar member, were married in their organization uniforms.

In September 1939 Germany invaded Poland and World War II began. By the following month, the Soviet Union had taken over Lithuania. The Begins, along with other Betar leaders, had taken refuge in Vilna, the capital of Lithuania. Despite the fact that the Soviet Union had outlawed Zionist activity, Betar's leaders continued to perform military drills and made plans for emigrating to Palestine. In September 1940 the Soviet secret police arrested Begin. After he signed a confession admitting that he was the Betar chairman for Poland, Begin was sentenced to eight years in Soviet labor camps. Begin later described his prison experiences in his book *White Nights*. While her husband was a Soviet prisoner, Aliza Begin made her way to Palestine.

Begin's time in the Soviet camps was cut short when Germany attacked the Soviet Union in June 1941. At that time, the Soviet Union and Poland agreed that Polish prisoners should be set free so that they could participate in the fight against Germany. Begin proceeded to join the Polish army and was lucky enough to be in a unit sent to Palestine, where he was reunited with his wife. While still in Polish uniform he became an adviser to the Irgun, the underground military organization of the Revisionist party in Palestine. Soon the Revisionist leadership convinced the Polish general staff in Palestine to release all the party's members from the Polish army.

Begin then became the leader of the Irgun and devoted his energies to ousting the British from Palestine. Although Palestine's Jews had welcomed British administration over Palestine following World War I, they had become more and more disillusioned about it during the years between the two world wars. On the eve of World War II, when it was clear that Jews who could not escape from Europe would suffer a dreadful fate at the hands of Germany's anti-Semitic Nazi leadership, Great Britain refused to allow free Jewish immigration into Palestine. For Begin, this refusal deprived Great Britain of any moral basis for its control of Palestine. Since Great Britain was leading the fight against Nazi Germany, Begin made an agreement with David Ben-Gurion, the mainstream Zionist leader of Palestine's Jewish community, not to attack British military targets for the duration of the war.

This agreement broke down in November 1944, when two members of the Stern Gang, another underground Jewish militia, assassinated a British minister in Cairo, Egypt. In the wake of this event, Ben-Gurion decided to destroy the Irgun. For the next six months, until the end of World War II, Begin remained in hiding while the Haganah, the defense organization of the Palestinian Jews, sought to arrest him and hand him over to the British. Begin was determined, however, not to retaliate against Ben-Gurion. He foresaw that

the time would come, after the war's end, when the Irgun would join forces with the Haganah to fight against the British.

Despite Jewish hopes, at the end of the war Great Britain failed to agree to establish a Jewish state in Palestine. It also refused to allow the Jewish survivors of the Nazi Holocaust—the systematic slaughter of European Jews, which resulted in 6 million Jewish deaths—to emigrate to Palestine. And, as Begin had predicted, the Haganah then joined forces with the Irgun and the Stern Gang to undermine British rule in Palestine. For more than a year the partnership of these three groups functioned smoothly. Eventually, though, two Irgun-initiated operations in particular turned Ben-Gurion against Begin's militia. The first was on July 22, 1946, when the Irgun blew up the southern wing of Jerusalem's deluxe King David Hotel, where the headquarters of the British administration was located. Although the Irgun did transmit a warning of the imminent attack, the British failed to take it seriously. The explosion left 91 dead and 46 wounded. The following summer, in response to Britain's execution of several Irgun members, the Irgun kidnapped and hanged two British sergeants. The majority of Palestine's Jewish community, and in fact world opinion in general, was horrified by these acts. As a result, Begin and his movement were increasingly treated as social outcasts.

Nonetheless, the Irgun's activities played a decisive role in convincing the British that control of Palestine was not worth the consequences. Great Britain then turned over the question of Palestine's future to the United Nations. On November 29, 1947, the world body approved a plan to partition, or divide, Palestine into a Jewish state and an Arab state. While Ben-Gurion, as spokesman for Palestine's Jewish community,

accepted the partition plan, Begin detested it. As a Revisionist, he believed that control of both banks of the Jordan River belonged to the Jewish people by biblical right. For the rest of his career he would continue the struggle to extend the borders of the Jewish state.

In the months before the planned departure of British forces, scheduled for mid-May 1948, an undeclared war broke out between the Jewish inhabitants of Palestine and the Arabs. The Irgun and the Stern Gang, along with the Haganah, contributed to the defense of the Jewish community. But once again, two Irgun-initiated incidents further tarnished that organization's reputation. In the first operation, on April 9, 1948, the Irgun and the Stern Gang took part in a massacre of innocent civilians at Deir Yassin, an Arab village on the northwestern rim of Jerusalem.

The second operation took place a little more than a month after the declaration of the Jewish state and the outbreak of its War of Independence. In June 1948, the *Altalena*, a ship the Irgun had bought to bring in arms to help win the war, arrived in Palestine. Begin announced his intention to distribute most of the ship's arms to Irgun members serving in the Israeli Defense Forces. Ben-Gurion insisted instead that a nation could not have a private army within its official army. When Begin refused to turn over the munitions on the *Altalena* to the government, Ben-Gurion had the ship destroyed by artillery fire. Begin never forgave Ben-Gurion for his response to this incident, which ended the active life of the Irgun. In August 1948, Begin founded a political party, Herut (Hebrew for "freedom"), to carry on the struggle for Jewish control of both sides of the Jordan River. Herut went on to become the second-largest party in Israel, second only to Ben-Gurion's Mapai party. For nearly 30 years following the end of Israel's War of Independence in 1949, Begin was the leader of the opposition to Israel's elected government. As a member of the Knesset, Israel's parliament, Begin expressed his disgust with the territorial terms of the armistice agreements Israel had signed with the Arabs in order to bring about the end of Israel's War of Independence. For example, in May 1950 he challenged the government to explain "who gave you the right, in what election were you given the authority, to give up in the name of the people of Israel the legacy of our forefathers, the testament of generations, the command of history given at the cost of the blood of millions in the course of 120 generations?"

As opposition leader, Begin also questioned the Israeli government's willingness to come to terms with Germany. In January 1952, Ben-Gurion made known his intention to accept Germany's offer to provide money and equipment to Israel as reparations, or compensation, for the losses Jewish victims of the Nazis had suffered during World War II. Begin, whose parents and brother were among the victims of the Holocaust, led a demonstration against the reparations plan. Addressing a large crowd, he called all Germans murderers. He compared the German-made tear-gas grenades of the Israeli riot police to the poison gas the Nazis had used to kill Jews in death camps. Inflamed by his impassioned rhetoric, the crowd became violent, and hundreds of demonstrators and policemen were wounded. Despite Begin's opposition, however, the Knesset approved the reparations plan. Israel's parliament voted to suspend Begin from its membership for three months as punishment for what was characterized as unbecoming behavior.

Begin remained in the opposition until June 1967, when, on the eve of the Six-Day War (June 5–10), the

> *"These are not occupied territories. You've used this expression for ten years, but from May 1977, I hope you'll start using the word liberated territories. A Jew has every right to settle these liberated territories of the Jewish land. . . . You annex foreign land, not your own country."*
>
> —from an improvised press conference, West Bank (May 1977)

Israeli leadership decided to create a National Unity government. Begin then became minister without portfolio and remained in the newly formed government until August 1970. As a member of the cabinet, he played a role in bringing all of Jerusalem—previously divided into an Arab sector and a Jewish area—under Israeli control.

As the Six-Day War was raging, Begin heard in a late-night radio broadcast that the United Nations was on the verge of ordering a ceasefire in the conflict. He immediately picked up the phone and called Prime Minister Levi Eshkol, suggesting that Eshkol send troops into the Arab sector of Jerusalem before the United Nations ended the hostilities. As a result of the military operation that followed, the Israeli flag was soon flying over parts of the city that had been off-limits to Jews for nearly 20 years, including the area where the ancient temple had stood. Begin's dream of a united Jerusalem in Jewish hands had become a reality. Less than 18 years earlier, he had argued in front of the Knesset that "the foreign nations must know that Jerusalem is ours, it is all ours—the temple Mount, the Western Wall— and Jerusalem on both sides of the wall is ours, and Jerusalem is our capital, not only in theory but in practice."

Israel's victory in the Six-Day War also brought Begin's dream of Jewish control over the biblical land of Israel closer to reality. He was determined not to return to the Arabs any lands on the West Bank of the Jordan that were now in Jewish hands. When, three years later, Prime Minister Golda Meir accepted a United Nations resolution calling for Israel's withdrawal from territories taken in the Six-Day War, Begin resigned from the cabinet.

In September 1973, Begin's Herut party joined with several other ones to form a new party, Likud (Unity). Weeks later, on Yom Kippur—the most solemn day in the Jewish calendar—Egypt and Syria attacked Israel. Although Israel finally won what came to be called the Yom Kippur War, the country was shaken by its lack of preparedness for the war. As a result, dissatisfaction with the ruling Labor government grew, and four years later, in 1977, the Likud party won the national election. For the first time since the birth of Israel, the government was not in the hands of the Labor party. As the leader of Likud, Menachem Begin became prime minister of Israel.

Begin had long been identified with militant behavior. But Israel's first peace treaty with an Arab country was signed by Begin and Egyptian

Israeli prime minister Menachem Begin (left) participates in discussions with Egyptian president Anwar Sadat (right) and U.S. president Jimmy Carter at Camp David, the official retreat of the U.S. president. The resulting Camp David Accords led to the signing of an Israeli-Egyptian peace treaty in 1979.

president Anwar Sadat, in March 1979. During the previous year, both men had shared the Nobel Peace Prize in recognition of their groundbreaking work toward peace in the Middle East. In exchange for a formal end to the state of war between the two countries, Begin was willing to return to Egypt all of the Sinai Peninsula, which Israel had occupied since the Six-Day War. That meant giving up not only oilfields, airbases, and military installations but also some 20 Jewish settlements. The settlers of one Sinai community, Yamit, threatened to commit mass suicide rather than yield their town. But Begin insisted on the evacuation of Yamit and even had the settlement bulldozed to discourage its inhabitants from returning.

By giving back Jewish settlements in Sinai, Begin alienated some of his oldest supporters, but it was something he could do without compromising his Revisionist principles. Sinai had never been part of the biblical land of Israel. Begin felt otherwise, though, about the West Bank and Gaza Strip, the biblical regions of Judea and Samaria. In order to strengthen Israel's hold on these territories, Begin encouraged Israelis to build new settlements there. During his time as prime minister the number of Jewish settlements on the West Bank rose from 23 to 112, and in the Gaza Strip from one to five. The Jewish population in these areas grew from 3,000 to 40,000. Proud as Begin was of achieving a peace treaty with Egypt, that achievement was not, however, his ultimate goal. After the treaty was signed he was asked by a reporter how he wanted history to remember him. "I want to be remembered as the man who set the borders of Eretz Yisrael [the land of Israel] for all eternity."

Begin's Likud won another election, in June 1981. Shortly before the election, Begin ordered an attack on Iraq's nuclear reactor project. Fearing that if Iraq had the ability to produce nuclear bombs it would use them to destroy the Jewish state, Begin did what he believed necessary to prevent another Holocaust.

Begin hoped to use his second term to fulfill his dream of extending Israeli control to all the former biblical lands. He believed that by destroying the Palestine Liberation Organization (PLO)—then based in Beirut, Lebanon—he could end the movement to establish a Palestinian state in the West Bank and Gaza. To this end, he sent Israeli troops into neighboring Lebanon in 1982. Although Israel succeeded in driving the PLO out of Lebanon, the action actually strengthened the Palestinian cause and alienated many Israelis. Then, in September 1982, when the Israeli army did nothing to stop Christian Lebanese militiamen from massacring 750 men, women, and children in two Palestinian refugee camps, the world was horrified. How could Begin, who was constantly accusing the world of standing by while the Nazis destroyed the Jews of Europe, justify his army's inaction in the face of the massacres at Shatila and Sabra?

The Israeli people demanded the creation of a commission to determine whether their government was responsible for the massacre. The commission decided that the Christian Lebanese militia bore the direct responsibility but that Begin's "lack of involvement in the entire matter casts on him a certain degree of responsibility." Public opposition to the continuation of the war mounted and even spread to the army, as some soldiers preferred to go to jail than serve in what they considered an unjust war.

Less than two months after the massacres at Shatila and Sabra, Aliza Begin—the prime minister's wife of more than 43 years—died. Begin had already begun showing signs that he was tired of governing. Now he seemed to be tired of life. He stopped eating properly, often did not bother to shave, made few public appearances, and basically withdrew from leadership. On September 15, 1983, after

heading the government for six years and three months—longer than any other prime minister since David Ben-Gurion—Menachem Begin officially resigned as prime minister of Israel.

Although Begin lived another eight and a half years, he retreated completely from public life. In March 1992, he suffered a heart attack and a week later was dead. He left behind a mixed legacy as a man of peace and a man of war. He also left a country in which a growing sector of the population was arguing that Jews had no right to surrender even an inch of land that had once been part of their ancient biblical kingdom.

FURTHER READING

Amdur, Richard. *Menachem Begin*. New York: Chelsea House, 1988.

Feron, James. "Menachem Begin, Guerrilla Leader Who Became Peacemaker." *New York Times*, March 9, 1992.

Hurwitz, Harry L. *Begin: A Portrait.* Washington: B'nai B'rith International Commission on Continuing Jewish Education, 1994.

Peleg, Ilan. *Begin's Foreign Policy, 1977–1983: Israel's Move to the Right.* New York: Greenwood, 1987.

Perlmutter, Amos. *The Life and Times of Menachem Begin.* Garden City, N.Y.: Doubleday, 1987.

Schreiber, Mordecai. *Menachem Begin: His Life and Legacy.* New York: Shengold, 1990.

Silver, Eric. *Begin: The Haunted Prophet.* New York: Random House, 1984.

Sofer, Sasson. *Begin: An Anatomy of Leadership.* Oxford: Basil Blackwell, 1988.

Temko, Ned. *To Win or to Die: A Personal Portrait of Menachem Begin.* New York: William Morrow, 1987.

Menachem Begin

BORN
August 6, 1913
Brest-Litovsk, Poland (now Belarus)

DIED
March 9, 1992
Tel Aviv, Israel

EDUCATION
Law degree, University of Warsaw (1931–36)

ACCOMPLISHMENTS
Leader of the Polish branch of the Betar youth movement; commander of the Irgun Zvai Leumi (1943–48); leader of the Herut party and of the opposition in Israel's parliament (1948–67); minister without portfolio in Israel's National Unity government (1967–70); joint chairman of the Likud (Unity) coalition (1973–83); prime minister of Israel (1977–83); awarded Nobel Peace Prize jointly with Egypt's president Anwar Sadat (1978); signed peace treaty between Egypt and Israel (1979); wrote *The Revolt* (1948) and *White Nights* (1957)

Yigael Yadin

SOLDIER AND
SCHOLAR

ost ambitious people strive to leave their mark on the world by making contributions to one particular field of endeavor. Among the unusual things about Yigael Yadin was his ability to influence Israel directly—and the world indirectly—in two very different fields: military affairs and archaeology. The Israeli army is known throughout the world for its effectiveness thanks in part to Yadin's work as its first chief of staff. Tourists flock to Masada in southern Israel and to many other archaeological sites in the country thanks in part to his work as an archaeologist. Unfortunately, Yadin's life also demonstrates the so-called Peter Principle: that people tend to be promoted until they reach a level at which they prove incompetent.

Yadin was born Yigael Sukenik in 1917, to parents who had immigrated some years earlier from Lithuania to Palestine, as the region was then known. His parents, devoted Zionists, believed that the Jewish people could be redeemed from the demeaning experience of exile by rebuilding a Jewish national home in Palestine, the site of the ancient Jewish commonwealth. Their oldest son's Hebrew first name, Yigael, which means "he will be redeemed," reflects their beliefs. Yigael's mother was a kindergarten teacher. His father, Eleazar Sukenik, began life in Palestine as a high school math and geography teacher, but his real interest lay in archaeology. Eventually, he became a professor of archaeology at the Hebrew University in Jerusalem.

As a professional educator, Yigael's mother decided to send her children to a private school in Jerusalem, where children were taught to be self-reliant and self-confident. Instead of regular classes, the 200 pupils at the school engaged in projects that crossed the curriculum and developed different skills. Carpentry, for example, became a means to teach mathematics, art appreciation, and physical coordination. The school was set up as a small community, with a bank, store, and restaurant, and with boys and girls sharing equal responsibility for all aspects of every undertaking. Another important influence on young Yigael was his participation in the Organization of Hebrew Scouts. In his scouting group, from the age of 10 he became acquainted with various military arts. On hiking trips with the scouts he also became very familiar with the terrain of the country. Yigael's scout leader was a member of the Haganah, the underground army of the Jewish community in Palestine. In 1933, when Yigael was a high school student of 16, he was recruited into the Haganah. Tensions between the Jews and Arabs of Palestine were steadily mounting, and the Haganah was expanded to prepare for a possible war. The following year, Yigael graduated from Jerusalem's best high school, where he was known not as an outstanding student but rather as a witty young man who had a way with the girls. After graduation he tried his hand at a variety of jobs—as an agricultural worker in an orange grove, a map-maker for a surveying crew, and at a desk job in the Immigration Department. None of these positions suited him.

In 1935, Yigael chanced to accompany his father on an archaeological dig, which led the 18-year-old to conclude that his father's profession might be the right one for him as well. This was not the first time he had been at an excavation site with his father, however. In fact, his first such experience had been frightening rather than inviting. As a five-year-old, he had gone with his father to a dig outside Jerusalem that was run by an American archaeologist. While his father became involved in shop talk with his colleague, the child Yigael, alone in the ruins, was overcome with fear that his father had abandoned him.

Seven years later, in 1929, Yigael had a far more positive experience. He visited a site in the far north of Palestine, Beth Alpha, where his father had found the magnificent mosaic floor of an ancient synagogue. There Yigael witnessed the excitement of the current Jewish settlers of Beth Alpha, who now had tangible evidence that their settlement was located on the very spot where Jews had lived, worshiped, and died some 2,000 years before. Now, in the summer of 1935, Yigael announced his intention to register as a student of archaeology at the Hebrew University of Jerusalem, where his father was on the faculty. There Yigael began to study Islamic art. As part of his studies he was required to learn long passages of Arabic poetry. The task seemed tedious at the time, but what he learned from it would later prove useful in an unexpected way.

Yigael's university studies were soon interrupted, however, as the Haganah called on him to take on additional responsibilities in the face

of rising Arab violence. In the summer of 1937, a commission of the British government—which had been given a mandate to govern Palestine after World War I—recommended that the country be partitioned into a Jewish and an Arab state. When this recommendation set off new Arab demonstrations, the British decided to use young Jewish men to help keep public order. To this end they set up the Jewish Settlement Police. Yigael was chosen to command a unit of the new force. In addition, the Haganah assigned him the command of a platoon. As a Haganah commander, he came to know the area around Jerusalem intimately as he roved through it on his Haganah-issued motorcycle.

The Arab rebellion finally came to an end by the spring of 1939. Then a new challenge faced the Haganah. As the threat of war intensified in Europe, Great Britain's policy toward Palestine changed. In 1917, the British government had issued a document, the Balfour Declaration, expressing Britain's support for "the establishment in Palestine of a national home for the Jewish people." But now England was worried that the many Muslims in the British Empire might sabotage the wider British war effort if the government supported the Zionist cause. In May 1939, Great Britain issued a White Paper—an official government policy statement—severely limiting Jewish immigration into Palestine and otherwise favoring the Arabs of Palestine over the Jews. The Jewish community in Palestine then began to view the Haganah as a militia that would have to combat British rule as well as Arab violence. During this turbulent time, Yigael Sukenik steadily rose through the Haganah's ranks.

The British soon tightened their restrictions on the Haganah, breaking up training centers and arresting the organization's members. The members who were able to avoid arrest were

Yigael Yadin works at his desk. On the right sits the first of the volumes Yadin wrote about his archaeological excavations at Hazor, in Upper Galilee, which he led between 1955 and 1958.

forced to keep a low profile. As a result, in the fall of 1939, Yigael returned to his archaeological studies at the university. Though he was not the most brilliant student, he soon revealed a gift for taking miscellaneous facts and weaving them into a compelling story of how people lived in ancient times. The young Haganah commander became deeply interested in ancient warfare and made himself an expert on the weapons and tactics of long-vanished fighting forces.

The outbreak of World War II in September 1939 soon cut short Yigael Sukenik's studies again. At the war's outset, it was not at all clear that Great Britain would be victorious over Hitler's armies. When the German troops soon advanced across North Africa toward Palestine, its Jewish community realized that, more than ever, it would have to be prepared to defend itself. In the summer of 1940, Sukenik prepared to leave the university again when he was called back to the Haganah to train as a higher officer. He supplemented his official training by reading widely in the works of great military thinkers. Impressed by Sukenik's skills as a strategist, the Haganah's chief of staff chose him as his personal aide. For security reasons, each Haganah member was known by a code name. Sukenik's became *Yadin*, Hebrew for "he will judge."

By the time the war in Europe ended, in the spring of 1945, Sukenik had reached the highest ranks of the Haganah's leadership. Having devoted his free time to archaeological studies, he had been able to complete his master's thesis in March 1944 and immediately began work on his doctorate. Publishing under his own name, not his secret code name, he began to be known as an archaeological expert. In the fall of 1945, Sukenik resigned from the Haganah and returned yet again to the university.

Sukenik proceeded with his doctoral research into ancient weapons and military tactics used in the Middle East. In the fall of 1947, however, he was again called back from scholarly research into ancient warfare to practical involvement in the modern military world. By then the British had decided to wash their hands of all responsibility for Palestine and to evacuate their personnel from the country in mid-May 1948. David Ben-Gurion, the political leader of the Jewish community in Palestine and soon to be the first prime minister of the state of Israel, wanted Sukenik to serve as the Haganah's operations officer. Ben-Gurion fully expected war with the Arabs to break out as soon as the British officially left Palestine and the Jewish state was declared. As operations officer, Sukenik put his intimate knowledge of the country's terrain to good use. And he set up a foreign department to deal with a possible invasion by other Arab states, a domestic department to plan defense strategies for individual Jewish settlements, and a supervisory

department to coordinate overall strategy.

On May 14, 1948, Ben-Gurion declared Israel's statehood. Within hours, the countries of the Arab League—Egypt, Syria, Lebanon, Iraq, and Transjordan (now Jordan)—began their invasion of the newborn state. Twelve days later, the provisional government of Israel formally replaced the Haganah with the Israel Defense Forces, or IDF. Yigael Sukenik became chief of operations for the fledgling army. A month later, he was chosen acting chief of staff. On June 27, 1948, Ben-Gurion swore in the members of the IDF high command, insisting first that each one adopt a Hebrew last name. Since most chose their Haganah code names, Yigael Sukenik became Yigael Yadin. As acting chief of staff, Yadin not only planned and coordinated operations on each battle front but also functioned as the IDF press spokesman. The world news media thereafter carried reports of Israel's military successes as dramatically reported by the witty and charming Yadin.

After the cessation of hostilities, Yadin was chosen to represent the military in armistice talks with Egypt and in secret diplomatic discussions with Transjordan's King Abdullah. Yadin proved to be a capable diplomat. In one of the secret sessions with Abdullah, Yadin was able to use to advantage a passage of Arab poetry that he had painstakingly memorized in his early days at the university.

In November 1949, at the age of 32, Yigael Yadin became the first chief of staff of Israel's army. In this position he succeeded in establishing the reserve system. While on a diplomatic assignment in Switzerland, Yadin had been impressed with the Swiss army's civilian reserve units, which actually formed the nucleus of the army rather than merely assisting the career soldiers. By the fall of 1950, Yadin had successfully proved that the IDF's reserve units could be successfully mobilized on short notice for a military

emergency. That October he put into effect a nine-day surprise operation that called up 75,000 air, naval, and ground-force reservists to participate in extensive military exercises.

Yadin also hoped to use the army for the good of the nation in areas outside the military. Within the first three years of its existence Israel's Jewish population nearly doubled. The country had trouble absorbing the large wave of new immigrants, however. As winter 1950 approached, Yadin led an effort in which the army built permanent housing and schools, installed water and sanitation systems, and provided medical services to approximately 100 transit camps for immigrants.

By this time, Yadin had been married for about 10 years and had a family. He had kept up with archaeological developments and still longed to return to his studies. Thus, in November 1952, to the disappointment of Prime Minister Ben-Gurion, Yadin resigned from the military to resume his work on ancient warfare. He received a two-year research fellowship from the Hebrew University to study in England.

One of the things Yadin hoped to do while in England was to translate one of the Dead Sea Scrolls that his father had purchased from a Bethlehem antiquities dealer before Israel's War for Independence. The Dead Sea Scrolls, a collection of manuscripts dating from the 2nd century B.C.E. to the first century C.E., were accidentally discovered in March 1947, by a 15-year-old Bedouin boy, Muhammad adh-Dhib. Chasing a goat he was herding into a cave near the Dead Sea, Muhammad found a cache of manuscripts in pottery jars. It turned out that the scrolls included the earliest biblical manuscripts in existence. Others shed light on the origins, beliefs, and social organization of the Essenes, an ancient Jewish sect. Among the scrolls Yadin's father had begun to translate was one he named

"The War of the Sons of Light against the Sons of Darkness." Because this War Scroll, as it was nicknamed, contained detailed military language, Professor Sukenik decided its translation was best left to his son. After his father's death in February 1953, Yadin realized that translating the War Scroll would be a full-time job. He therefore received permission from the Hebrew University to submit the translation and a commentary on it as his doctoral dissertation instead of his proposed study of ancient warfare. Yadin received a doctorate for his work on the War Scroll in 1955.

Before the doctorate was awarded, however, Yadin made another significant addition to Dead Sea Scroll scholarship. In June 1954, Archbishop Samuel, spiritual head of the Syrian Orthodox archdiocese of the United States and Canada, placed an advertisement in the *Wall Street Journal* saying that four Dead Sea Scrolls were available for purchase. Yadin, who was on a tour of the United States at the time, was alerted to the advertisement. Aware that the archbishop would not sell to an Israeli, Yadin negotiated through a middleman. He raised the funds from various donors and purchased the scrolls for the Hebrew University. When the public learned of the clever way in which the scrolls had been obtained, Yadin became a celebrity.

Upon Yadin's return to Israel, he began a series of archaeological digs that increased his celebrity status. In 1955–58, he led a major dig at Hazor, near the Syrian border in Upper Galilee. The Hebrew Bible describes this city as one conquered by the biblical leader Joshua. Yadin's finds at Hazor led him to argue that the political and military achievements of the population of Israel were a modern extension of their biblical ancestors' conquest of the land. The Hazor dig helped turn archaeology into an Israeli national pastime, with schools organiz-

ing trips to sites and amateurs volunteering to participate in digs. In 1960, Yadin began to explore Megiddo, described in the Hebrew Bible as an administrative center of King Solomon. Yadin's discoveries there, including an impressive city gate, also helped Israelis celebrate their connection to a heroic Jewish past.

In 1960 Yadin played the leading role in a team expedition to search the caves of the Judean wilderness for artifacts from the revolt of the Jews against the Romans in 132–35 C.E., under the leadership of Simeon Ben-Koziba. Assisted by the IDF, Yadin discovered human bones, which he assumed to be the remains of rebels, as well as coins, textiles, and documents, including 15 letters signed "Simeon Ben-Koziba, Prince of Israel." Yadin's finds in the Judaean wilderness provided tangible evidence for the traditional stories recounted by the ancient rabbis concerning the rebellion against Rome. In May 1960, Yadin gave a lecture on the finds at the official residence of Israel's president. There he made a dramatic announcement once again connecting Israel's present with its past. "Your excellency," he said to President Ben-Zvi, "I am honored to be able to tell you that we have discovered 15 dispatches written or dictated by the *last* president of Israel 1,800 years ago."

The archaeological dig for which Yadin remains most famous took place in 1963–65 at Masada, a remote plateau on the western shore of the Dead Sea. According to the 1st-century historian Flavius Josephus, Masada was the scene of the last holdout of Jewish rebels in an earlier revolt against Roman rule (66–73 C.E.). Josephus related that the Jewish rebels at Masada ultimately committed suicide rather than be taken captive by the Romans. To underscore the importance of the Masada dig, Yadin attended a military ceremony there in summer 1963. After new recruits to the IDF's armored corps took

Yigael Yadin

BORN

March 21, 1917
Jerusalem, Palestine

DIED

June 28, 1984
Hadera, Israel

EDUCATION

M.A. (1945) and Ph.D. (1955) in archaeology, Hebrew University, Jerusalem

ACCOMPLISHMENTS

Chief of general staff of the Israel Defense Forces (1949–52); deputy prime minister (1977–81); leader of archaeological expeditions at Hazor (1955–58; 1968), the Judaean Wilderness Caves (1960–61), and Masada (1963–65); professor of archaeology at Hebrew University (1963–84) and head of its Institute of Archaeology (1970–84); Laureate of Israel Prize (1956) and the Rothschild Humanities Prize (1964); author of *The Message of the Scrolls* (1957, 1962), *Hazor* (3 volumes, 1958–62), *The Art of Warfare in Biblical Lands in the Light of Archaeological Discovery* (2 volumes, 1963), *Masada: Herod's Fortress and the Zealots' Last Stand* (1966), and other books their oath of allegiance, Yadin said, "When Napoleon stood among his troops next to the pyramids of Egypt, he declared that 'four thousand years of history look down upon you.' But what would he not have given to be able to say to his men: 'four thousand years of *your own* history look down upon you.' The echo of your oath this night will resound throughout the encampments of our foes. Its significance is not less powerful than all our armaments."

At Masada, Yadin found bones he believed to be those of rebels who had committed suicide. He also found pottery shards with names on them and surmised that these were cast as lots by the last surviving rebels. When Zalman Shazar, then president of Israel, visited the site, Yadin declared, "Masada was the symbol of our refusal to live as slaves." Masada soon became the most popular archaeological site in Israel, visited by more than half a million tourists annually.

Yadin's military career was to intrude twice more upon his archaeological pursuits. In the spring of 1967, the IDF began to worry about sudden Egyptian military action that had begun in Sinai. Prime Minister Levi Eshkol called Yadin back into active service as his special adviser on security affairs. On June 5, 1967, the Six-Day War began. In two days Israel was in control not only of all of Jerusalem but also of Bethlehem, which had been under Jordan's control since 1948.

Yadin took advantage of the military turn of events to score another coup for Israeli archaeology. For seven years he had known about a certain Dead Sea Scroll in the hands of a Bethlehem antiquities dealer but had been unable to secure it. Now, on June 8, 1967, he sent a small group of intelligence officers to Bethlehem, where they tracked down the dealer, who turned the scroll over to the officers. (Yadin later arranged payment to the dealer.) By the end of the next month, Yadin had left military service again and begun work on the new scroll. He soon came to believe that this document, which he named the Temple Scroll, was a lost book of the Bible that described, among other things, the layout, architecture, and sacred ceremonies of the First Temple in Jerusalem.

Yadin was called back to the war room one last time, during the Yom Kippur War of October 1973. The surprise Egyptian-Syrian attack on Israel on October 6, 1973, caught the IDF off guard. Although Israel went on to military triumph, capturing 325 square miles of Syrian and about 1,600 square miles of Egyptian territory, the public was outraged by the country's lack of preparedness, which resulted in a large number of Israeli casualties. Afterward, Yadin agreed to participate in a commission to investigate the conduct of the country's leadership prior to the war.

Yadin's wife, who had been his closest adviser, died in February 1976. Within months, Yadin decided to enter politics. From 1977 to 1981, he served as deputy prime minister in the government of Menachem Begin. Although Yadin had shone as a military leader and an archaeologist, his brief political career shed no luster on him. He had hoped to serve as a moderating influence on Prime Minister Begin, many of whose policies he disagreed with. Instead, Begin denied him any real power. While Yadin's friends advised him to resign, he clung to the belief that he might yet make a difference. After suffering a heart attack in 1979 and another in 1981, however, Yadin decided to close out his political career.

Over the next three years, Yadin continued his archaeological research. His commentary on the Temple Scroll, published in English in 1983, was greeted with high praise. His sudden death on June 28, 1984, was followed the next day by a state funeral.

Today, Yadin is best remembered as a shaper of Israel's armed forces and of its national identity, which is strongly tied to the ancient history of the Jewish people in the land of Israel. As Yitzhak Rabin (one of Yadin's contemporaries, who after winning a Nobel Peace Prize was felled by an assassin's bullet) noted, Yadin's political experience was "a tragic end to a magnificent career."

FURTHER READING

Miller, Shane. *Desert Fighter: The Story of General Yigael Yadin and the Dead Sea Scrolls.* New York: Hawthorn, 1967.

Shanks, Hershel, ed. *Understanding the Dead Sea Scrolls: A Reader from the Biblical Archaeology Review.* New York: Random House, 1992.

Silberman, Neil Asher. *A Prophet from amongst You: The Life of Yigael Yadin: Soldier, Scholar, and Mythmaker of Modern Israel.* Reading, Mass.: Addison-Wesley, 1993.

Yitzhak Rabin

"THE TIME FOR PEACE HAS COME"

On Saturday night, November 4, 1995, about 100,000 Israelis gathered at a giant rally for peace in Tel Aviv's Kings of Israel Square. Politicians and entertainers expressed their support for the "land for peace" policy of the Israeli government headed by Prime Minister Yitzhak Rabin. Two years earlier, Rabin had signed a historic agreement with the chairman of the Palestine Liberation Organization, Yasir Arafat, pledging Israel to withdraw from lands it had seized in the Six-Day War of 1967 and to clear the way for Palestinian self-government in those areas. The steps outlined in the agreement were being taken, one by one. Not all Israelis, however, supported the government's policy. Some believed that the lands being surrendered had been set aside by God for the biblical ancestors of the Jewish people. Although the dissidents had threatened to disrupt the peace rally, the event proceeded without incident.

Yitzhak Rabin (right), then chief of staff of the Israeli Defense Forces, makes a triumphant entry into the Old City of Jerusalem during the Six-Day War of 1967. The territory had been under Jordanian control since 1948.

"The time for peace has come. . . . We, who have come from a land where parents bury their children, we who have fought against you, the Palestinians—we say today in a loud and clear voice: Enough of blood and tears. Enough."

—from speech at signing of the Israeli–Palestinian agreement in Washington, D.C. (September 13, 1993)

The last person to speak was Prime Minister Rabin. He told his assembled supporters, "This gathering must broadcast to the Israeli public and the Jewish public throughout the world . . . that the people of Israel want peace and support peace. I always believed that most of the people want peace and are ready to take a risk for it." Just how great a personal risk Rabin was taking in the search for peace became clear only minutes later. As the prime minister was about to get into his car, he was shot to death by a 25-year-old Israeli law student intent on killing the peace process and preserving Israel's control over all the land in its possession.

Two days later, on Monday afternoon, November 6, 1995, Yitzhak Rabin and his peace policies were memorialized at a remarkable and historic funeral. Among the approximately 40 heads of state who attended were Jordan's King Hussein and Egypt's President Hosni Mubarak, both of whom delivered eulogies to the man whose nation had been their enemy in several wars. Also in attendance were a large delegation of Palestinians and even some heads of state from Arab countries that had not yet made peace with Israel.

The man whom so many dignitaries came to honor was the first Israeli prime minister to be born in Palestine, as that land was known before Israel declared its statehood in 1948. His Russian-born parents, Nehemia and Rosa Rabin, devoted themselves to the building of a national home for the Jewish people, a model that their first child, Yitzhak, would adopt as his own. Long before he became prime minister, Rabin was to play a significant role in many of the major events of his country's history.

Although Yitzhak Rabin was born in Jerusalem in 1922, his family soon moved to Tel Aviv, where his father was active in the Jewish labor

movement and his mother was a member of the city council. Because his parents were so busy with their political activities, young Yitzhak learned to be self-reliant and became accustomed to hiding his feelings. His mother could not even spare the time to help Yitzhak adjust to his first days at school. Nevertheless, he found his experience at the School for Workers' Children rewarding. He later praised the school for "placing education before instruction, inculcating values before imparting book learning. Responsibility, involvement, concern for the welfare of the school and its pupils were of cardinal importance."

Rabin planned to be an agronomist, a scientist specializing in soil management and the production of field crops. He expected to live on a kibbutz, one of the communal settlements that Jewish pioneers were developing throughout the land. To advance this goal he attended the Kadourie Agricultural School in Galilee, which trained young people planning to start new agricultural settlements. His studies there were interrupted when the British, who then controlled Palestine, closed the school in response to widespread Arab demonstrations that culminated in the general strike of 1936. Before Kadourie was closed, there were several Arab attacks on the school, and its students were trained in the use of arms. In the months during which the school remained closed, Rabin moved to a kibbutz on the Sea of Galilee, where he worked in agriculture and became an auxiliary policeman. Kadourie's doors were reopened in October 1939, a month after Nazi Germany invaded Poland, beginning World War II. Despite the distraction created by the war, Rabin finished school, graduating first in his class. The school's principal arranged for him to continue his studies at the University of California at Berkeley. But Rabin felt he could not leave his country or his friends during the war. He never completed his studies in agronomy.

After graduation, Rabin joined a group of young people at a kibbutz north of Haifa. He and his colleagues planned to get additional training, then establish a new kibbutz. Fate intervened before these plans could be carried out. While Rabin was having supper in the kibbutz dining hall one evening, he was approached by a local commander of the Haganah, the underground army of the Jewish community in Palestine. (Rabin's mother was also a member.) The commander, Moshe Dayan, only seven years older than Rabin, would himself go on to become a distinguished Israeli soldier and statesman. Dayan had just been released by British authorities after spending two years in prison for belonging to the Haganah. Now the German army and its allies were approaching Palestine through Africa and the Arab world had begun to declare its sympathies with Britain's enemies. The British administration realized the advantage of having a loyal Jewish fighting force. As a result, with British approval the Haganah decided to recruit new volunteers and create a permanent strike force. This new organization was named the Palmach, from the Hebrew words for "assault companies." Rabin readily agreed to join the Palmach and, as he recorded in his memoirs, he began to ask questions only afterward.

In this casual way began an extraordinary career that was to end so tragically more than 40 years later. During World War II, Rabin participated in the British invasion of Greater Syria. The youngest member of his Palmach unit, he was assigned the task of wriggling up telephone poles and cutting wires to prevent the enemy from calling up reinforcements. In this assignment Rabin used his Palmach training to advance Britain's

Rabin (right) confers with Chief of Staff Yigael Yadin (left), and another soldier during Israel's War of Independence in 1948. The young Rabin contributed to Israel's victory by commanding the brigade that broke the Arab siege of Jewish Jerusalem.

goals. However, as soon as the threat of an enemy invasion of Palestine passed, the British once again had reason to regret the existence of the Haganah and its Palmach units.

Before the outbreak of war, Britain had adopted a policy of strictly limiting Jewish immigration to Palestine, even in the face of Nazi threats to eradicate the Jews of Europe. Jewish immigrants who reached Palestine but did not fit under the quota were detained, placed in special camps, and often returned to Europe. A few months after the war ended, Rabin was deputy commander of a successful Palmach operation to release about 200 illegal Jewish immigrants from a British internment camp near Haifa. While preparing for a second operation, however, Rabin broke his leg. On Saturday, June 29, 1946, while Rabin was still hobbled by a cast, the British rounded up all the leaders of the Jewish settlement they could find, along with thousands of people they suspected of Palmach membership. Rabin was sent to a detention camp in Gaza. Not until November did the British release the detainees.

A year later, at the end of November 1947, the United Nations voted to partition Palestine into two states, one Jewish and the other Arab. Even before Israel officially became a sovereign nation, hostilities broke out. In this War of Independence, Rabin was named commander of the brigade that lifted the Arabs' siege of Jewish Jerusalem by opening a supply route to the city.

Newly promoted to the rank of colonel, Rabin was next sent to the southern front, where he broke Egypt's hold on the Negev Desert and led Israeli troops into Sinai for the first time. In the midst of the war, Rabin married Leah Schlossberg, a volunteer in his Palmach battalion. She remained her husband's confidante and closest companion for the rest of his life.

At the war's end, Rabin was part of the team that engaged in Israeli–Egyptian armistice talks. In his memoirs, Rabin told a personal story about his participation in those negotiations. During his years as a student and soldier he had never had to wear a tie. Now, however, it was required. Rabin's driver tried to show him how to tie a

"There is only one radical means of sanctifying human lives. The one radical solution is a real peace."

—from the Nobel Peace Prize acceptance speech in Oslo, Norway (December 10, 1994)

knot, but Rabin could simply not master the technique. To get around the problem, he decided to leave the tie permanently knotted—he could remove it by loosening the knot and slipping the tie over his head, and when he needed it again he had only to slip it back on and tighten it. Apparently ties remained a nuisance for Rabin for the rest of his life. About two weeks before his assassination, he attended a formal dinner in New York in honor of the United Nations' 50th anniversary. U.S. president Bill Clinton later recalled that Rabin showed up in a tuxedo but without the customary black bowtie. He managed to borrow one, which the president helped him with.

In 1948–49, the Palmach was disbanded and the Israel Defense Forces (IDF) were reorganized. Rabin joined the general staff of the IDF, and the military sent him for a year's study in England, where he graduated from the British Staff College at Camberley. When Rabin returned to Israel, he held a variety of high posts in the army, most involving the training of soldiers. Rabin was named chief of staff in 1964. Three years later it appeared inevitable that Israel would have to fight another war with its Arab neighbors. After mobilizing Israel's reserve forces in response to threatening actions taken by Egypt, Rabin sought encouragement from David Ben-Gurion, the founding father of the state of Israel and its first prime minister and defense minister. Ben-Gurion was then living in retirement on a kibbutz in the Negev. But instead of encouraging Rabin, Ben-Gurion's words demoralized him completely. The grand old man questioned the wisdom of calling up the reserves: "You, or whoever gave you permission to mobilize so many reservists, made a mistake. You have led the state into a grave situation. We must not go to war. We are isolated. You bear the responsibility."

Ben-Gurion's criticism affected Rabin so powerfully that he suffered a nervous breakdown. Rabin managed, nonetheless, to recover—the public was told he had nicotine poisoning from smoking too much—and carried out his responsibilities during the Six-Day War of June 1967. Israel's stunning military successes in that war included the unification of Jerusalem (half of which had been in Jordanian hands since the founding of the state) and the capture of huge territories formerly in Arab hands.

In his memoirs, Rabin reported that from the start he understood that the victory was in some ways a mixed blessing. Israel was now in control of an area three times its former size, and defending these gains with limited manpower would be a problem. More seriously, Israel now found itself ruling a million hostile Arabs in the West Bank and the Gaza Strip. "They were not citizens of the state," Rabin recalled, "but they were human beings and had to make a living, eat, receive services, and be permitted freedom of movement. All the while, however, we were conscious of the fact that they would be subject to the temptation to harm us." The seeds of Rabin's later peace initiatives were thus sown immediately after his most impressive achievements in war.

In recognition of the IDF's successes under Rabin during the Six-Day War, the Hebrew University in Jerusalem awarded him an honorary doctorate. In his acceptance speech, Rabin took the honor not in his own name but on behalf of the army. He recalled in his memoirs that he spoke "of a nation that desired peace but was capable of fighting valiantly when enemies forced it into war." In the speech, Rabin said that although young Israelis and in particular Israeli soldiers "do not tend to be sentimental . . . the strain of the battle, the anxiety which preceded it, and the sense of salvation and of direct confrontation with Jewish history itself cracked the shell of hardness and shyness and released wellsprings of emotion and stirrings of the spirit." He referred specifically to the joy all Israelis felt upon gaining access to Jerusalem, especially to the city's Western Wall, which dated back to the time of the Second Temple, destroyed by the Romans nearly 1,900 years earlier.

On January 1, 1968, Rabin resigned from the military and took up a new post as Israel's ambassador to the United States. Although he no longer wore a military uniform, Israel's defense needs remained paramount in his mind as he carried out his new responsibilities. Over the course of the next five years, Rabin was successful in negotiating U.S.–Israeli arms deals, as well as U.S. economic aid. During his years as ambassador he also became close to Henry A. Kissinger, national security adviser and later secretary of state under President Richard Nixon. Kissinger had such faith in Rabin's military instincts that he relied on him not only for intelligence about military activity in the Middle East but also for occasional advice on Vietnam, where the United States was involved in a war of its own.

Several times during Rabin's ambassadorship, he was asked to consider leaving that post for a role in the Israeli cabinet. But when he returned to Israel in March 1973 at the end of his term, no cabinet post had been set aside for him, and Rabin was uncertain about his future. As it turned out, the lack of a specific government role worked to his advantage. After the Yom Kippur War took Israel by surprise in October 1973, the government of Prime Minister Golda Meir fell. In 1974, at the age of 52, Rabin became Israel's fifth and youngest prime minister. Upon assuming office he said, "The time has come for

the sons of the founders of the state to take over their role."

Rabin's first term as premier was notable in a number of ways. He was the first Israeli prime minister to make an official state visit to West Germany, which many Jews still considered a haven for murderers of Jews. He held six secret meetings with Jordan's King Hussein in an unsuccessful attempt to start Israeli–Jordanian peace talks. He successfully completed a round of talks with Egypt about control of the Sinai Peninsula, offering what he called "a piece of land for a piece of peace."

In July 1975 Israel carried out a dramatic rescue of passengers on an Air France plane bound from Tel Aviv to Paris, after the plane was hijacked by terrorists and taken to Entebbe airport in Uganda. The success of the operation led Rabin to be hailed as a hero again.

Rabin's first term as prime minister ended, however, not in glory but in scandal. In 1977 an Israeli newspaper revealed that Rabin and his wife, Leah, had broken Israel's currency regulations by failing to close their bank accounts in the United States upon their return to Israel. Soon afterward, the currency laws in question were repealed. In the meantime, Rabin had resigned his office.

After Rabin's resignation, his Labor party lost a general election for the first time in Israeli history, and a new government was formed by the opposition Likud (Unity) party. Rabin's political career did not come to an end at this point, though. For seven years he served in Israel's parliament as a member of the Labor party. Then, in 1984, he was named minister of defense by a Labor–Likud coalition government. He was still in that position when, in December 1987, a Palestinian uprising broke out in the West Bank and Gaza, ushering in years of violence and bloodshed. Rabin

LINKS IN THE CHAIN

Yitzhak Rabin

BORN
March 1, 1922
Jerusalem, Palestine

DIED
November 4, 1995
Tel Aviv, Israel

EDUCATION
Graduated first in his class from the Kadourie Agricultural School in Galilee (1940); graduated from the British Staff College at Camberley, England (1953)

ACCOMPLISHMENTS
Deputy commander of the Palmach, a unit of the underground army, the Haganah; deputy chief of staff of the Israel Defense Forces (1961), chief of staff (1964–68); Israeli ambassador to the United States (1968–73); minister of labor (1973); prime minister (1974–77); minister of defense (1984–90); prime minister and minister of defense (1992–95); signed an agreement with the Palestine Liberation Organization initiating self-government for Palestinians and Israel's withdrawal from the Gaza Strip and West Bank (1993); signed a declaration marking the end of a 46-year state of war between Israel and Jordan (1994); shared the Nobel Peace Prize with Foreign Minister Shimon Peres of Israel and Yasir Arafat, chairman of the Palestine Liberation Organization (1994)

After the signing of the historic peace agreement between Israel and the Palestine Liberation Organization (PLO) on September 13, 1993, Yasir Arafat, chairman of the PLO, speaks with Prime Minister Rabin, as Shimon Peres, Israel's foreign minister, listens.

adopted a severe policy against the Palestinians, instructing Israeli soldiers to respond with "force, might, beatings," if they deemed it necessary. When the coalition government broke up in 1990, Rabin's term as defense minister ended. By that time, he had decided that Israel could not rule nearly 2 million captive Palestinians and still remain a democracy and a Jewish state. The idea of a negotiated peace began to develop in his mind.

In February 1992, Rabin again became head of the Labor party, and Labor's victory in the election that June returned Rabin to the post of prime minister. Within little more than a year, the world was surprised to learn that secret peace negotiations between the Palestinians and the Israelis had succeeded. Rabin, once hailed around the world as a tough military man, was transformed overnight into a dove of peace. On September 13, 1993, Prime Minister Rabin and his foreign minister and partner in peace Shimon Peres signed a historic accord with their old enemy Yasir Arafat, leader of the Palestine Liberation Organization. The

accord promised to the Palestinians much of the land that the Israel Defense Forces had captured under Chief of Staff Rabin in 1967. In the dramatic signing ceremony on the South Lawn of the White House, Rabin not only directly faced Arafat, the man Israelis blamed for acts of terrorism against them; he also visibly overcame his loathing and shook his foe's hand. He later said, "Of all the hands in the world, it was not the hand I wanted or even dreamed of touching."

In Rabin's speech at the White House ceremony, he explained his mixed feelings: "This signing of the Israeli–Palestinian declaration of principle here today—it's not so easy—either for myself as a soldier in Israel's war nor for the people of Israel. . . . It is certainly not easy for the families of the victims of the war's violence, terror, whose pain will never heal, for the many thousands who defended our lives and their own and have even sacrificed their lives for our own. For them this ceremony has come too late." Rabin stressed that Israel sought not revenge but peace.

A little more than a year later, on October 26, 1994, Rabin and King Hussein signed a peace treaty that ended 46 years of hostilities between Israel and Jordan. At the ceremony Rabin said, "It is not only our states that are making peace with each other today, not only our nations that are shaking hands in peace here." Addressing King Hussein directly, Rabin went on, "You and I, Your Majesty, are making peace here, our own peace, the peace of soldiers and the peace of friends."

Less than two months later, these historic moves toward peace in the Middle East were recognized by the awarding of the Nobel Peace Prize to Rabin, Peres, and Arafat. In his acceptance speech, Rabin regretted that "under my responsibility, young men and women who wanted to live, wanted to love, went to their deaths instead." He spoke of "the failure of national leaders to sanctify human life" and identified "a real peace" as the only guaranteed method "of sanctifying human lives."

Nevertheless, even as Rabin came closer and closer to achieving the peace he had been longing for, some of his own countrymen saw him as a traitor. Ironically enough, Rabin's memoirs, published in English in 1979, concluded with a passage about the dangers of peace. According to Rabin's final words in that book, "There is no doubt whatsoever in my mind that the risks of peace are preferable by far to the grim certainties that await every nation in war." Rabin was also aware that the path he had chosen placed his own life in jeopardy. Tragically, Israel's military hero, who had transformed himself into a healer, became a martyr before his dream could be completely fulfilled. In an interview two weeks before the assassination, Rabin stated that the peace process might be destroyed, but "only if terror will succeed." It remained to the Israelis and Arabs who survived Rabin to do their best to ensure that peace, not terror, should prove victorious in the Middle East.

FURTHER READING

Ben Artzi-Pelossof, Noa. *In the Name of Sorrow and Hope*. New York: Knopf, 1996.

Ben Meir, Dov B. *Yitzhak Rabin: 1922–1995*. Van Nuys: Syndicated International Trade, 1996.

Caspit, Ben. *Song of Peace: Remembering Yitzhak Rabin*. New York: Kensington Publishing Corporation, 1996.

Jerusalem Report Staff. *Shalom, Friend: The Life and Legacy of Yitzhak Rabin*. New York: Newmarket Press, 1996.

Kort, Michael G. *Yitzhak Rabin: Israel's Soldier Statesman*. Brookfield, Conn.: Millbrook Press, 1996.

Makovsky, David. *Making Peace with the PLO: The Rabin Government's Road to the Oslo Accord*. Boulder: Westview Press, 1995.

Peres, Shimon. *Battling for Peace: Memoirs*. London: Weidenfeld & Nicolson, 1995.

Rabin, Leah. *Rabin: Our Life, His Legacy*. New York: Putnam, 1997.

Rabin, Yitzhak, and Yoram Peri. *The Rabin Memoirs: An Expanded Edition with Recent Speeches, New Photographs, and an Afterword*. Berkeley: University of California Press, 1996.

Slater, Robert. *Rabin of Israel: Warrior for Peace*. New York: HarperCollins, 1996.

Glossary

Aramaic—the language of everyday speech in Palestine and much of the ancient Middle East from 300 B.C.E. to 650 C.E.

Ashkenazim—Jews of central and eastern Europe or their descendants.

Babylonian captivity—the period of the exile of the Jews in Babylonia (from about 586 B.C.E. to 538 B.C.E.).

Balfour Declaration—a statement issued by the British government on November 2, 1917, favoring the establishment in Palestine of a national home for the Jews while upholding the civil and religious rights of preexisting non-Jewish communities in Palestine.

Bar mitzvah, Bat mitzvah—literally, "man of obligation," "woman of obligation"; the stage at which a young person (usually a 13-year-old boy or a 12- or 13-year-old girl) becomes responsible for fulfilling the obligations of a Jewish adult; the ceremony that marks this milestone; a boy or girl who has reached this stage of Jewish life.

Circumcision—the removal of the foreskin of the penis; an operation performed on an eight-day-old boy as part of the ceremony confirming his membership in the Jewish people.

Conservative Judaism—generally considered middle-of-the-road Judaism, guided more by Jewish law than Reform Judaism but more liberal in interpretation of Jewish law than Orthodox Judaism.

Dead Sea Scrolls—a number of scrolls dating from about 100 B.C.E. to 135 C.E., containing partial texts of some of the books of the Hebrew Bible and some non-biblical scrolls, found in caves near the northwest coast of the Dead Sea beginning in 1947.

Diaspora—the scattering of Jews to countries outside of Israel after the Babylonian captivity; the group of such countries; the body of Jews living in countries outside Palestine or modern Israel.

Emancipation—from the Latin word meaning "to free from control"; in Jewish history, the abolition of laws limiting the full participation of Jews in society.

Exilarch—literally, "leader of the exiled"; one of a line of hereditary rulers of the Babylonian Jewish community from about the 2nd century C.E. to the beginning of the 11th century.

Gaon—literally, "majesty"; a title of honor for the directors of the Jewish academies at Sura and Pumbedita in Babylonia from the end of the 6th century C.E. to about the beginning of the 11th century; an eminent Jewish scholar noted for knowledge of the Talmud.

Hadassah—Women's Zionist Organization of America, founded in 1912 by Henrietta Szold.

Haganah—literally, "defense"; the "people's army" of the Jewish settlement in Palestine during the latter part of the British mandate and the forerunner of the Israel Defense Forces.

Halakhah—from the Hebrew word "to walk"; the entire body of Jewish law.

Hasidism—from the Hebrew word meaning "pious"; the principles and practices of the Hasidim, members of a sect founded in Poland in the 18th century by the Baal Shem Tov and characterized by its emphasis on mysticism, prayer, religious zeal, and joy.

Herut—literally, "freedom"; Israeli political party established by the Irgun to promote Revisionist ideals.

Histadrut—literally, "arrangement"; the General Federation of Labor in Israel, organized by the Jewish settlement in Palestine in 1920, to unite and organize the workers in Palestine.

Holocaust—the systematic mass slaughter of European Jews during World War II.

Irgun—literally, "organization"; secret Jewish military organization founded in Palestine in 1931 and absorbed into the Israel Defense Forces in 1948.

Jewish Brigade—separate Jewish fighting force formed in September 1944 as part of the British army.

Jewish Enlightenment—the movement begun in Germany under the leadership of Moses Mendelssohn (1729–86), aimed at bringing Jews and Judaism into the modern age by promoting secular education and encouraging adoption of the dress, customs, and language of the general population.

Jewish Legion—Jewish fighting units in the British army (1917–18).

Kabbalah—literally, "tradition"; Jewish mysticism.

Karaite—from the Hebrew word for "Scripture"; a member of a Jewish sect founded in the 8th century that viewed the Bible as the sole source of Jewish law and practice and therefore rejected the Talmud.

Kibbutz—Israeli collective agricultural settlement.

Knesset—Hebrew name of the parliament of the state of Israel.

Law of Return—law passed by the Knesset on July 5, 1950, declaring the right of every Jew to settle in Israel.

Likud—literally, "consolidation" or "unity"; political party formed in 1973 by the merger of Herut with several other parties.

Mapai—initials for Hebrew words meaning "party of the workers of the land of Israel"; founded in 1930 from the merger of two Jewish labor parties in Palestine; forerunner of the Israel Labor party.

Marrano—a Spanish or Portuguese Jew who was forcibly converted to Christianity, especially one who remained secretly faithful to Judaism.

Messiah—literally, "anointed one"; a savior who will reestablish the kingdom of Israel and bring a time of prosperity and peace for the entire world.

Mishnah—literally, "study" (by oral repetition) or "teaching"; basic code of Jewish law, compiled by Rabbi Judah Hanasi and his followers at Jabneh by 200 C.E.

Mount Sinai—the mountain, of uncertain identity, on which Moses received the Torah.

Orthodox Judaism—the form of Judaism that holds that the Torah is God-given and that its laws governing every aspect of Jewish life are eternal.

Palmach—Hebrew abbreviation for "assault companies"; permanent strike force of the Haganah (1941–48).

Pentateuch—from the Greek words for "five" and "vessel"; the first five books of the Hebrew Bible, also called the five books of Moses: Genesis, Exodus, Leviticus, Numbers, and Deuteronomy.

Poalei Zion—literally, "workers of Zion"; movement combining ideologies of Zionism and socialism.

Reconstructionist Judaism—the fourth movement in American Judaism, founded by Rabbi Mordecai Kaplan (1881–1983), advocating that Judaism is a religious civilization in need of constant adaptation to contemporary conditions.

Reform Judaism—also called Liberal or Progressive Judaism; the form of Judaism that regards the Torah as a divinely inspired human document containing many laws that may no longer be appropriate; the first modern challenge to Orthodoxy.

Revisionists—a Zionist party founded in 1925 by Vladimir Jabotinsky (1880–1940) that called for a more militant approach to achieving Zionist goals than those favored by mainstream Zionists.

Sanhedrin—the highest council of the ancient Jews.

Science of Judaism—a movement founded by young Jewish intellectuals in Germany during the 1810s and 1820s aimed at applying modern methods of research to the study of Jewish texts and Jewish history.

Sephardim—from the Hebrew word for "Spain"; Jews of Spain and Portugal or their descendants.

Shema—literally, "hear"; the first Hebrew word of the prayer that begins "Hear, O Israel, the Lord is our God, the Lord is One," and the name by which that prayer is known; considered the "watchword" of the Jewish people.

Synagogue—from the Greek word for "assembly" or "meeting"; a Jewish house of prayer.

Talmud—literally, "learning" or "instruction"; basic text of Judaism, completed by 500 C.E., containing the discussions of the rabbis of the academies in Babylonia (Babylonian Talmud), touching on all aspects of Jewish life; a less influential Talmud, called the Jerusalem Talmud and completed by 400 C.E., contains the discussions of the rabbis of the academies in Israel.

Tikkun—literally, "repair" or "improvement"; in Kabbalah, the process through which human beings can restore the world to its proper order.

Temple—either of the two central houses of worship of Judaism located in Jerusalem in biblical times: the First Temple was built by Solomon and destroyed by the Babylonians in 586 B.C.E.; the Second Temple was rebuilt beginning in 538 B.C.E. and destroyed by the Romans in 70 C.E.

Torah—literally, "guidance" or "instruction"; the whole of Jewish beliefs, practices, and writings; the Pentateuch, or five books of Moses; the scroll on which the Pentateuch is inscribed.

Unity of Labor—Zionist Socialist Labor party founded in Palestine in 1919 and incorporated into Mapai in 1930.

Yiddish—language written in Hebrew letters, with a vocabulary combining Hebrew, Slavic languages, and German, spoken mainly by Jews of eastern and central Europe and by Jewish emigrants from these areas and their descendants.

Zion—a hill in Jerusalem on which the Temple was built; Palestine as the Jewish homeland and symbol of Judaism.

Zionism—worldwide movement that resulted in the establishment and development of the Jewish state of Israel.

Chronology

586 B.C.E.
Babylonians destroy the First Temple and force many Jews into exile in Babylonia.

538 B.C.E.
Cyrus the Great of Persia issues edict permitting the Jewish exiles to return home.

515 B.C.E.
The Second Temple in Jerusalem is completed.

63 B.C.E.
Rome takes advantage of Jewish disunity in Israel, captures Jerusalem, and imposes heavy taxes.

6 C.E.
Rome assumes direct rule over Israel.

66–70
Jews revolt against Rome, leading to the destruction of Jerusalem and of the Second Temple.

70s
The Sanhedrin, the highest council of the ancient Jews, reassembles in Jabneh.

74
Masada, the last stronghold of the Jewish rebels, falls.

132–35
Jews revolt in Israel under Simeon bar Kochba.

135
Romans intensify their anti-Jewish persecutions in Palestine, leading to martyrdom of Rabbi Akiba and other scholars.

200
The Mishnah—the basic code of Jewish law—is edited under the direction of Judah Hanasi.

400
The editing of the Jerusalem Talmud is completed.

500
The editing of the Babylonian Talmud is completed.

740
Khazars living along the Volga River in western Russia begin to convert to Judaism.

760s
The Karaite sect breaks away from mainstream Judaism.

1146
Muslim Spain begins to persecute the Jewish minority.

1475
The first known Hebrew work, Rashi's commentary on the Pentateuch, is printed.

1492
The Jews are expelled from Spain.

1497
The Jews are expelled from Portugal.

1530s
The Spanish Inquisition gains power.

1560s
The Shulhan Arukh is published; Isaac Luria begins to teach his interpretation of Kabbalah.

1648–49
Cossack uprising leads to widespread massacres of Jews in Polish Ukraine.

1665–66
Shabbetai Zevi's claim that he is the Messiah attracts a large following of Jews around the world, but his conversion to Islam provokes a crisis of confidence and belief for his followers.

Mid- to late 1700s
Hasidic sect develops around the figure of Israel ben Eliezer, the Baal Shem Tov, provoking anti-Hasidic backlash by such leaders as Elijah, the Gaon of Vilna.

Mid-1700s
The Jewish Enlightenment spreads under the leadership of Moses Mendelssohn.

1838
The first Jewish Sunday School opens in the United States under the leadership of Rebecca Gratz.

Late 1840s
Many Jews immigrate to the United States from central Europe.

Mid-1800s
The Reform movement begins in Germany.

1845
The first American translation of the Hebrew Bible is published.

1870s
Reform rabbinical seminaries open in Berlin, Germany, and in Cincinnati, Ohio.

1879
The term *anti-Semitism* is first used.

1881
Efforts to transform Hebrew into a modern language begin with the arrival of Eliezer ben-Yehuda in Palestine.

1881–82
Many eastern European Jews immigrate to the United States and a small number immigrate to Palestine following a wave of pogroms in Russia.

1894
Captain Alfred Dreyfus of the French army is convicted of treason based on false evidence, leading to an explosion of anti-Semitism in France.

1897
The First Zionist Congress is held in Basel, Switzerland.

1902
Solomon Schechter becomes president of the Jewish Theological Seminary, the main institution of American Conservative Judaism.

1917
The British government issues the Balfour Declaration, stating that it views favorably and will work toward achieving the establishment of a Jewish homeland in Palestine.

1922
The League of Nations approves the British mandate in Palestine.

1925
Vladimir Jabotinsky founds the Revisionist movement in Zionism.

1926
The World Union for Progressive Judaism holds its first international conference.

1933
The Nazi party comes to power in Germany, setting in motion an anti-Jewish policy that will culminate in the Holocaust.

1947
The United Nations General Assembly votes in favor of the partition of Palestine into two separate states—one Jewish, the other Arab—with Jerusalem under international control.

1948
The State of Israel is founded.

1949
A cease-fire ends Israel's War of Independence.

1956
In response to several years of provocative Egyptian acts, Israel invades Egypt in the Sinai Campaign.

1967
Israel defeats Egypt, Jordan, Syria, and Iraq in the Six-Day War, which leaves Israel in control of the Sinai Peninsula, the Gaza Strip, the West Bank, East Jerusalem, and the Golan Heights.

1968
The Reconstructionist Rabbinical College opens in Philadelphia, making Reconstructionist Judaism into a separate Jewish American movement.

1973
The Yom Kippur War begins with a surprise attack on Israel by Egypt and Syria and ends with a cease-fire.

1979
Egyptian president Anwar Sadat and Israeli prime minister Menachem Begin sign a formal peace treaty in March.

1990
Spain signs an accord officially placing Judaism on a par with Roman Catholicism, effectively overturning the 1492 decree ordering expulsion or conversion of Spain's Jews.

1993
Israel and the Palestine Liberation Organization sign accords aimed at leading to Palestinian self-rule within the Israeli-occupied territories.

1994
Israel and Jordan sign a declaration marking the end of a 46-year state of war between the two countries.

1995
An Israeli gunman assassinates Prime Minister Yitzhak Rabin at a peace rally in Tel Aviv.

1996
Portugal offers atonement for the royal edict of 1496 that ordered expulsion or conversion for the Jews of Portugal.

Further Reading

Each of the major entries in *Links in the Chain* includes a list of further readings; refer to the index for page references to the individual figures profiled in this book.

The following reading list is intended as a supplement. Although the following books vary in level of difficulty, nearly all are written for a general audience. Books preceded by an asterisk (*) are especially appropriate for younger readers.

General Encyclopedias of Judaism

* Bridger, David, ed. *The New Jewish Encyclopedia.* New York: Behrman House, 1976.

Isaacson, Ben, and Deborah Wigoder. *The International Jewish Encyclopedia.* Englewood Cliffs, N.J.: Prentice Hall, 1973.

Roth, Cecil, and Geoffrey Wigoder, eds. in chief. 16 vols. *Encyclopaedia Judaica.* Jerusalem: Keter, 1972.

Wigoder, Geoffrey, ed. *The Encyclopedia of Judaism.* New York: Macmillan, 1989.

Jewish Religion

de Lange, Nicholas. *Judaism.* New York: Oxford University Press, 1987.

Einstein, Stephen J., and Lydia Kirkoff. *Every Person's Guide to Judaism.* New York: Union of American Hebrew Congregations, 1989.

* Gates, Fay C. *Judaism.* New York: Facts on File, 1991.

Jacobs, Louis. *The Jewish Religion: A Companion.* New York: Oxford University Press, 1995.

Katz, Steven T. *Jewish Ideas and Concepts.* New York: Schocken, 1977.

Kugel, James L. *On Being a Jew.* San Francisco: Harper & Row, 1990.

Neusner, Jacob. *The Way of Torah: An Introduction to Judaism.* 4th ed. Belmont, Calif.: Wadsworth, 1988.

* Pasachoff, Naomi. *Basic Judaism for Young People.* 3 vols. West Orange, N.J.: Behrman House, 1986, 1987.

Steinberg, Milton. *Basic Judaism.* New York: Harcourt, Brace, 1947.

Jewish History

Ben-Sasson, H. H., ed. *A History of the Jewish People.* Cambridge: Harvard University Press, 1976.

Eban, Abba. *Heritage: Civilzation and the Jews.* New York: Summit, 1984.

Gilbert, Martin, ed. *The Illustrated Atlas of Jewish History: 4,000 Years of Jewish History.* New York: Macmillan, 1990.

Johnson, Paul. *A History of the Jews.* New York: Harper & Row, 1987.

Pasachoff, Naomi, and Robert J. Littman. *Jewish History in 100 Nutshells.* Northvale, N.J.: Jason Aronson, 1995.

Sacher, Harry. *Israel: The Establishment of a State.* Westport: Hyperion Press, 1975.

Seltzer, Robert M. *Jewish People, Jewish Thought: The Jewish Experience in History.* New York: Macmillan, 1980.

Seltzer, Robert M., ed. *Judaism: A People and Its History.* New York: Macmillan, 1989.

*Shamir, Ilana, and Schlomo Sharit, eds. *The Young Reader's Encyclopedia of Jewish History.* New York: Viking, 1987.

Jewish Movements

Borowitz, Eugene, and Naomi Patz. *Explaining Reform Judaism.* New York: Behrman House, 1985.

Danzger, M. Herbert. *Returning to Tradition: The Contemporary Revival of Orthodox Judaism.* New Haven: Yale University Press, 1989.

Davis, Moshe. *The Emergence of Conservative Judaism: The Historical School in 19th Century America.* Philadelphia: Jewish Publication Society, 1963.

Hertzberg, Arthur, ed. *The Zionist Idea: A Historical Analysis and Reader.* New York: Macmillan, 1972.

Hundert, Gershon David, ed. *Essential Papers on Hasidism: Origins to Present.* New York: New York University Press, 1991.

Idel, Moshe. *Hasidism: Between Ecstasy and Magic.* Albany: State University of New York Press, 1995.

Laqueur, Walter. *A History of Zionism.* New York: Fine Communications, 1996.

Meyer, Michael A. *Response to Modernity: A History of the Reform Movement in Judaism.* New York: Oxford University Press, 1988.

Nadell, Pamela S. *Conservative Judaism in America: A Biographical Dictionary and Sourcebook*. New York: Greenwood Press, 1988.

Rabinowicz, Tzvi M., ed. *Encyclopedia of Hasidism*. Northvale, N.J.: Jason Aronson, 1996.

Raphael, Marc Lee. *Profiles in American Judaism: The Reform, Conservative, and Reconstructionist Traditions in Historical Perspective*. San Francisco: Harper & Row, 1984.

Silverstein, Alan. *Alternatives to Assimilation: The Response of Reform Judaism to American Culture, 1840–1930*. Hanover, N. H.: University Press of New England for Brandeis University Press, 1994.

Sklare, Marhsall. *Conservative Judaism: An American Religious Movement*. Glencoe, Ill.: Free Press, 1955.

Vital, David. *The Origins of Zionism*. New York: Oxford University Press, 1980.

———. *Zionism: The Crucial Phase*. New York: Oxford University Press, 1987.

———. *Zionism: The Formative Years*. New York: Oxford University Press, 1982.

Wheatcroft, Geoffrey. *The Controversy of Zionism: Jewish Nationalism, the Jewish State, and the Unresolved Jewish Dilemma*. Reading, Mass.: Addison-Wesley, 1996.

Jewish Thought

Blau, Joseph L. *The Story of Jewish Philosophy*. New York: Ktav, 1971.

Borowitz, Eugene. *Choices in Modern Jewish Thought: A Partisan Guide*. New York: Behrman House, 1983.

Cohen, Arthur A., and Paul Mendes-Flohr, eds. *Contemporary Jewish Religious Thought: Original Essays on Critical Concepts, Movements, and Beliefs*. New York: Macmillan, 1987.

Glatzer, Nahum N., ed. *Modern Jewish Thought: A Source Reader*. New York: Schocken, 1977.

Guttmann, Julius. *Philosophies of Judaism: A History of Jewish Philosophy from Biblical Times to Franz Rosenzweig*. New York: Schocken, 1973.

Jacobs, Louis. *Hasidic Thought*. New York: Behrman House, 1976.

———. *Jewish Ethics, Philosophy and Mysticism*. New York: Behrman House, 1969.

———. *Jewish Thought Today*. New York: Behrman House, 1970.

*Pasachoff, Naomi. *Great Jewish Thinkers: Their Lives and Work*. West Orange, N.J.: Behrman House, 1992.

Anthologies of Jewish Wisdom

Klagsbrun, Francine. *Voices of Wisdom: Jewish Ideals and Ethics for Everyday Living*. New York: Random House, 1980.

Montefiore, C. G., and H. Loewe. *A Rabbinic Anthology*. New York: Schocken, 1974.

Newman, Louis I. *Hasidic Anthology: Tales and Teachings of the Hasidim*. New York: Schocken, 1963.

*Petuchowski, Jakob J. *Our Masters Taught: Rabbinic Stories and Sayings*. New York: Crossroad, 1982.

Silverman, William B. *Rabbinic Wisdom and Jewish Values*. New York: Union of American Hebrew Congregations, 1971.

Telushkin, Joseph. *Jewish Wisdom: Ethical, Spiritual, and Historical Lessons from the Great Works and Thinkers*. New York: Morrow, 1994.

Index

References to main biographical entries are indicated by **bold** page numbers; references to illustrations are indicated by *italics*.

Acknowledgments

I owe a debt of gratitude both professionally and personally to a number of individuals who assisted me during the years in which this book developed. Scholars in the United States and in Israel whose expertise I called upon frequently and who generously provided advice include Professor Shaye Cohen, Brown University; Rabbi William Cutter, Hebrew Union College; Rabbi David Gordis, Hebrew College; Professor Paula Hyman, Yale University; Professor Milton Konvitz, Cornell University; Dr. Eran Nardi, Weizmann Institute; and Professor Jacob Neusner, University of South Florida. Others who assisted with specific queries include Bryan Diamond, Liberal Jewish Synagogue; Sam Hartstein, Yeshiva University; Milton Himmelfarb, American Jewish Committee; Julie Miller, Jewish Theological Seminary of America; and Dr. Diana Spielman, Leo Baeck Institute. I would also like to thank Gilbert Bettman of Cincinnati, Ohio, for reading a draft profile of Isaac Mayer Wise on behalf of Wise's descendants, and Eric Conrad, of London, England, who answered a few queries about his late relative Lily Montagu. Although in many cases these individuals steered me away from error, whatever inaccuracies or omissions remain in the book are my own.

At the Children's and Young Adult Books division of Oxford University Press, editorial director Nancy Toff and project editors Tara Deal and Paul McCarthy provided encouragement when it was needed and expert editorial advice in the many stages that a manuscript goes through en route to becoming a book.

As the first draft of the book neared completion I successfully weathered a health crisis. Family, friends, colleagues, and acquaintances too numerous to mention individually rallied to me and helped give me the strength I needed to make it through. I will never forget how each of you sustained me during the difficult months.

A special word of thanks to my parents and to my husband and daughters. Anna and Isaac Schwartz, my first and best teachers, gave me the gifts of a rigorous Jewish education, a joyous Jewish home environment, and a commitment to a life of meaningful work. My husband, Jay, and our daughters, Eloise and Deborah, do double duty as in-house editors and sources of emotional support. I cannot thank them enough for their assistance and encouragement in this, as in all of my undertakings.

Naomi Pasachoff, a research associate at Williams College, is the author of *Basic Judaism for Young People, Great Jewish Thinkers: Their Lives and Work, A Topical Bible*, and coauthor of *Jewish History in 100 Nutshells*. She has taught English composition and literature at Williams College, Rensselaer Polytechnic Institute, and Skidmore College. She holds an A.B. from Radcliffe College, Harvard University, an A.M. from Columbia University, and a Ph.D. from Brandeis University.

Picture Credits